DEVIANCE TODAY

DEVIANCE TODAY

Alex Thio
Emeritus Professor, Ohio University

Thomas Calhoun
Jackson State University

Addrain Conyers
Marist College

PEARSON

Boston Columbus Indianapolis New York San Francisco Upper Saddle River
Amsterdam Cape Town Dubai London Madrid Milan Munich Paris Montreal Toronto
Delhi Mexico City São Paulo Sydney Hong Kong Seoul Singapore Taipei Tokyo

Editorial Director: *Craig Campanella*
Editor in Chief: *Dickson Musslewhite*
Publisher: *Karen Hanson*
Editorial Assistant: *Joseph Jantas*
Editorial Project Manager: *Mayda Bosco*
Marketing Manager: *Kelly May*
Marketing Assistant: *Diana Griffin*
Production Manager: *Meghan DeMaio*
Creative Director: *Jayne Conte*
Cover Designer: *Suzanne Duda*
Cover Design: *alterfalter/Shutterstock, DelicatePhoto/Shutterstock, Charles Knox/Shutterstock, Mike Flippo/Shutterstock, Peter Kim/Shutterstock*
Editorial Production and Composition Service: *Chitra Sundarajan/PreMediaGlobal*
Printer/Binder/Cover Printer: *LSC Communications*

Library of Congress Cataloging-in-Publication Data

Thio, Alex.
Deviance today / Alex Thio, Thomas Calhoun, Addrain Conyers.
p. cm.
Includes bibliographical references.
ISBN-13: 978-0-205-18272-5 (alk. paper)
ISBN-10: 0-205-18272-0 (alk. paper)
1. Deviant behavior. I. Calhoun, Thomas C. II. Conyers, Addrain. III. Title.
HM811.T458 2013
301–dc23
2011045178

9 18

ISBN-10: 0-205-18272-0
ISBN-13: 978-0-205-18272-5

BRIEF CONTENTS

TABLE OF CONTENTS

PART FIVE Sexual Deviance 107

PART SIX Physical Manifestations of Deviance 135

PART SEVEN Elite Deviance 167

PART EIGHT Medical Deviance 197

PREFACE

Deviance Today is a contemporary collection of original articles in the field of deviant behavior. All of the articles reflect the current trend in the sociology of deviance. The diverse inclusion of criminal deviance (e.g., robbery, prostitution, and white-collar crime) and noncriminal deviance (e.g., obesity, pornography, and tattooing) provides a great insight into the contemporary world of present-day norm-violating behavior. Some of the noncriminal deviances, such as the proliferation of cyberdeviance, have only recently emerged on the scene; others, such as prescription drug use and paranormal beliefs, have been around for a long time but have only recently become the subject of research by sociologists.

On the theoretical front, there is a change in emphasis from the positivist perspective to the constructionist one. In research methodology, there is greater use of ethnography at the expense of the traditional use of surveys. All these contemporary trends are showcased in this reader.

As this reader's editors, we decided against taking a single theoretical approach when selecting articles. Instead, we present a great variety of articles that represent the full range of deviance sociology. We believe that students should be exposed to different theories of deviance as well as the different methodologies used to gather data.

This reader covers major theories in deviance sociology, from classic ones such as anomie/strain theory and labeling theory to modern ones such as feminist theories. In addition, this anthology encompasses a wide spectrum of deviant behaviors. There are articles about deviances, such as suicide, drug abuse, and obesity, that have long attracted sociological attention. There are also articles on deviances, such as terrorism, self mutilation, clergy misconduct, and cyber deviance, that in recent years have leapt into public and sociological consciousness. Analyses of these subjects rely on data from theory-informed research that runs the gamut from surveys to ethnographic studies. All these analyses are multidisciplinary, coming not only from sociologists but also from scholars and researchers in other fields. They all effectively reflect what the sociology of deviance is like today: diverse, wide ranging, and exciting.

This is a user-friendly reader, put together with students in mind. The articles are not only authoritative but also interesting. The articles were written by respected experts in their field of study. The articles were all solicited from sociologists and researchers. Most important, unique to this reader, most of these articles have been carefully written for clarity, conciseness, and forcefulness. Students will therefore find them easy and enjoyable to read while learning what deviance is all about.

Instructor's Manual and Test Bank (ISBN 0205182747): The Instructor's Manual and Test Bank has been prepared to assist teachers in their efforts to prepare lectures and evaluate student learning. For each chapter of the text, the Instructor's Manual offers different types of resources, including detailed chapter summaries and outlines, learning objectives, discussion questions, classroom activities and much more.

Also included in this manual is a test bank offering multiple-choice, true/false, fill-in-the-blank, and/or essay questions for each chapter. The Instructor's Manual and Test Bank is available to adopters at www.pearsonhighered.com.

MyTest (ISBN 0205182755): The Test Bank is also available online through Pearson's computerized testing system, MyTest. MyTest allows instructors to create their own personalized exams, to edit any of the existing test questions, and to add new questions. Other special features of this program include random generation of test questions, creation of alternative versions of the same test, scrambling question sequence, and test preview before printing. Search and sort features allow you to locate questions quickly and to arrange them in whatever order you prefer. The test bank can be accessed from anywhere with a free MyTest user account. There is no need to download a program or file to your computer.

PowerPoint Presentation (0205182763): Lecture PowerPoints are available for this text. The Lecture PowerPoint slides outline each chapter to help you convey sociological principles in a visual and exciting way. They are available to adopters at www.pearsonhighered.com.

MySearchLab®

Save TIME. Improve Results.

MySearchLab is a dynamic website that delivers proven results in helping individual students succeed. Its wealth of resources provides engaging experiences that personalize, stimulate, and measure learning for each student. Many accessibletools will encourage students to read their text, improve writing skills, and help them improve their grade in their course.

Features of MySearchLab

Writing

- Step by step tutorials present complete overviews of the research and writing process.

Research and citing sources

- Instructors and students receive access to the EBSCO ContentSelect database, census data from Social Explorer, Associated Press news feeds, and the Pearson bookshelf. Pearson SourceCheck helps students and instructors monitor originality and avoid plagiarism.

eText and more

- **Pearson eText**—An e-book version of **Deviance Today** is included in MySearchLab. Just like the printed text, students can highlight and add their own notes as they read their interactive text online.
- **Chapter quizzes and flashcards**—Chapter and key term reviews are available for each chapter online and offer immediate feedback.
- **Primary Source Documents**—A collection of documents, organized by chapter, are available on MySearchLab. The documents include head notes and critical thinking questions.
- **Gradebook**—Automated grading of quizzes helps both instructors and students monitor their results throughout the course.

INTRODUCTION

What is deviant behavior? Why ask what it is? Does not everybody know it has to do with weirdos and perverts? Not at all. There is, in fact, a great deal of disagreement among people about what they consider deviant. In a classic study, sociologist Jerry Simmons asked a sample of the general public who they thought was deviant. They mentioned 252 different kinds of people as deviants, including homosexuals, prostitutes, alcoholics, drug addicts, murderers, the mentally ill, communists, atheists, liars, Democrats, reckless drivers, "self-pitiers," the retired, career women, divorcées, Christians, suburbanites, movie stars, perpetual bridge players, prudes, pacifists, psychiatrists, priests, liberals, conservatives, junior executives, girls who wear makeup, smart-aleck students, and know-it-all professors. If you are surprised that some of these people are considered deviant, your surprise simply adds to the fact that a good deal of disagreement exists among the public about what deviant behavior is.

There is a similar lack of consensus among sociologists. We could say that the study of deviant behavior is probably the most "deviant" of all the subjects in sociology. Sociologists disagree more about the definition of deviant behavior than they do on any other subject.

Conflicting Definitions

Some sociologists simply say that deviance is a violation of any social rule, but others argue that deviance involves more than rule violation—it also has the quality of provoking disapproval, anger, or indignation. Some advocate a broader definition, arguing that a person can be a deviant without violating any rule or doing something that rubs others the wrong way. According to this argument, individuals who are afflicted with some unfortunate condition for which they cannot be held responsible are deviant. Examples include psychotics, paraplegics, the mentally challenged, and other people with physical or mental disabilities. These people are considered deviant because they are disvalued by society. In contrast, some sociologists contend that deviance does not have to be negative. To these sociologists, deviance can be positive, such as being a genius, reformer, creative artist, or glamorous celebrity. Other sociologists disagree, considering "positive deviance" to be an oxymoron—a contradiction in terms (Heckert and Heckert 2002).

All of these sociologists apparently assume that, whether it is a positive or a negative, disturbing, or disvalued behavior, deviance is real in and of itself. The logic behind this assumption is that if it is not real in the first place, it cannot be considered positive, negative, disturbing, or disvalued. Other sociologists disagree, arguing that deviance does not have to be real behavior for it to be labeled *deviant*. People can be falsely accused of being criminal, erroneously diagnosed as mentally ill, stereotyped as dangerous because of their skin color, and so on. Conversely, committing a deviant act does not necessarily make a person a deviant, especially when the act is kept secret. It is, therefore, the label *deviant*—a mental construction or image of an act as deviant, rather than the act itself—that makes an individual deviant.

Some sociologists go beyond the notion of labeling to define deviance by stressing the importance of power. They observe that relatively powerful people are capable of avoiding the fate suffered by the powerless—being falsely, erroneously, or unjustly labeled deviant. The key reason is that the powerful, either by themselves or through influencing public opinion, or both, hold more power for labeling others' behavior as deviant. Understandably, sociologists who hold this view define deviance as any act considered by the powerful at a given time and place to be a violation of some social rule.

From this welter of conflicting definitions, we can nonetheless discern the influence of two opposing perspectives: positivism and social constructionism. The positivist perspective is associated with the sciences, such as physics, chemistry, or biology. It influences how scientists see and study their subject. In contrast, the constructionist perspective has more to do with the humanities, such as art, language, or philosophy. This perspective affects how scholars in these fields see and study their subjects. These two perspectives can be found in sociology; some sociologists are more influenced by the positivist perspective and others by the constructionist. Positivist sociologists tend to define deviance in one way, whereas constructionist sociologists pursue another way. The two perspectives further influence the use of certain theories and methodologies for producing knowledge about deviant behavior. The conflicting definitions that we have discussed can be couched in terms of these two perspectives. The definitions that focus on deviance as rule-breaking behavior are essentially positivist, whereas those that center on labeling and power are constructionist. Let us delve more deeply into the meanings and implications of these two conflicting perspectives.

Conflicting Perspectives

The knowledge about deviance basically consists of answers to three questions: (1) What to study? (2) How to study it? (3) What does the result of the study mean? The first question deals with the subject of study, the second has to do with the method of study, and the third concerns the data-based theory about the subject. Positivism and constructionism provide conflicting answers to each question.

Subject: What to Study?

Positivism suggests that we study deviance or deviants. The reason deals with the positivist's absolutist definition of deviance. According to this definition, deviance is absolutely or intrinsically real in that it possesses some qualities that distinguish it from conventionality. Similarly, deviants are thought to have certain attributes that make them different from conventional individuals. By contrast, social constructionism suggests that we study law enforcers and other such people who are influenced by society to construct an image of certain others as deviants and then label them as such, or how the process of such labeling takes place and affects the labeled. This is because the constructionist assumes the relativist stance in defining deviance as a socially constructed label imposed on some behavior. Such a definition can be said to be relativist by implying that the deviancy of a behavior is relative to—dependent on—the socially constructed negative reaction to the behavior.

Absolutism: Deviance as Absolutely Real. Around the turn of the twentieth century, criminologists believed that criminals possessed certain biological traits that were absent in noncriminals. Those biological traits included defective genes, bumps on the head, a long lower jaw, a scanty beard, an unattractive face, and a tough body build. Because all these traits are inherited, people were believed to be criminals simply because they were born criminals. If they were born criminals, they would always be criminals. As the saying goes, "If you've had it, you've had it." No matter where they might go—they could go anywhere in the world—they would still be criminals.

Then the criminologists shifted their attention from biological to psychological traits.

Criminals were thought to have certain mental characteristics that noncriminals did not have. More specifically, criminals were believed to be feeble-minded, psychotic, neurotic, psychopathic, or otherwise mentally disturbed. Like biological traits, these mental characteristics were seen as inherent in individual criminals. Also, like biological traits, mental characteristics would stay with the criminals, no matter where they went. Again, because of these psychological traits, criminals would always remain criminals.

Today's positivist sociologists, however, have largely abandoned the use of biological and psychological traits to differentiate criminals from noncriminals. They recognize the important role of social factors in determining a person's status as a criminal. Such status does not remain the same across time and space; instead, it changes in different periods and with different societies. A polygamist may be a criminal in Western society but a law-abider in Muslim countries. A person who sees things invisible to others may be a psychotic in Western society but may become a spiritual leader among some South Pacific tribes. Nevertheless, positivist sociologists still largely regard deviance as intrinsically real. Countering the relativist notion of deviance as basically a social construction in the form of a label imposed on an act, positivist Travis Hirschi (1973) argues:

> The person may not have committed a "deviant" act, but he did (in many cases) do something. And it is just possible that what he did was a result of things that had happened to him in the past; it is also possible that the past in some inscrutable way remains with him and that if he were left alone he would do it again.

Moreover, countering the relativist notion of mental illness as a label imputed to some people's behavior, positivist Gwynn Nettler (1974) explicitly voices his absolutist stance: "Some people are more crazy than others; we can tell the difference; and calling lunacy a name does not cause it." These positivist sociologists seem to say that just as a rose by any other name would smell as sweet, so deviance by any other label is just as real.

Relativism: Deviance as a Label. Social constructionists hold the relativist view that deviant behavior by itself does not have any intrinsic characteristics unless it is thought to have those characteristics. The so-called intrinsically deviant characteristics do not come from the behavior itself; they originate instead from some people's minds. To put it simply, an act appears deviant only because some people think it so. As Howard Becker (1963) says, "Deviant behavior is behavior that people so label." Based on this definition, no deviant label means no deviant behavior. The existence of deviance depends on the label. Deviance, then, is a mental construct (an idea, thought, or image) expressed in the form of a label.

Because they effectively consider deviance unreal, constructionists understandably stay away from studying it. They are more interested in the questions of whether and why a given act is defined by society as deviant. This leads to studying people who label others as deviant—such as the police and other law-enforcing agents. If constructionists study so-called deviants, they do so by focusing on the nature of labeling and its consequences.

In studying law-enforcing agents, constructionists have found a huge lack of consensus on whether a certain person should be treated as a criminal. The police often disagree among themselves about whether a suspect should be arrested, and judges often disagree about whether those arrested should be convicted or acquitted. In addition, because laws vary from one state to another, the same type of behavior may be defined as criminal in one state but not in another. Prostitution, for example, is legal in Nevada but not in other states. There is, then, a relativity principle in deviant behavior; behavior gets defined as deviant relative to a given norm, standard of behavior, or the way people react to it. If it is not related to the norm or to the reaction of other people, a given behavior is in itself meaningless—it is impossible to say whether it is deviant or conforming. Constructionists strongly emphasize this relativistic view, according to which, deviance, like beauty, is in the eye of the beholder.

Method: How to Study It?

Positivism suggests that we use objective methods, such as survey, experiment, or detached observation. The subject is treated like an object, forced, for example, to answer the same questions as presented to everybody else with the same value-free, emotionless demeanor. This is because positivists define deviance as a largely objective fact, namely, a publicly observable, outward aspect of human behavior. By contrast, social constructionism suggests that we study individuals with more subjective methods, such as ethnography, participant observation, or open-ended, in-depth interviews. With these methods, subjects are treated as unique, whole persons and are encouraged to freely express their feelings in any way they want. This is because constructionists define deviance as a mostly personal experience—a hidden, inner aspect of human behavior.

Objectivism: Deviance as an Objective Fact. By focusing on the outward aspect of deviance, positivists assume that sociologists can be as objective in studying deviance as natural scientists can be in studying physical phenomena. The trick is to treat deviants as if they are objects, like those studied by natural scientists. Nonetheless, positivist sociologists cannot help being aware of the basic difference between their subject, human beings, and that of natural scientists, plants, animals, and inanimate objects. As human beings themselves, positivist sociologists must have certain feelings about their subject. However, they try to control their personal biases by forcing themselves not to pass moral judgment on deviant behavior or share the deviant person's feelings. Instead, they try to concentrate on the subject matter as it outwardly appears. Further, these sociologists have tried hard to follow the scientific rule that all their ideas about deviant behavior should be subject to public scrutiny. This means that other sociologists should be able to check out the ideas to see whether they are supported by facts.

Such a drive to achieve scientific objectivity has produced substantial knowledge about deviant behavior. No longer popular today are value-loaded and subjective notions such as maladjustment, moral failing, debauchery, demoralization, sickness, pathology, and abnormality. Replacing these outdated notions are value-free and objective concepts such as innovation, retreatism, ritualism, rebellion, culture conflict, subcultural behavior, white-collar crime, norm violation, learned behavior, and reinforced behavior.

To demonstrate the objective reality of these concepts, positivist sociologists have used official reports and statistics, clinical reports, surveys of self-reported behavior, and surveys of victimization. Positivists recognize the unfortunate fact that the sample of deviants in the studies—especially in official statistics—does not accurately represent the entire population of deviants. Nevertheless, positivists believe that the quality of information obtained by these methods can be improved and refined. In the meantime, they consider the data, though inadequate, useful for revealing at least some aspect of the totality of deviant behavior.

Subjectivism: Deviance as a Personal Experience. To social constructionists, the supposedly deviant behavior is a personal experience and the supposedly deviant person is a conscious, feeling, thinking, and reflective subject. Constructionists insist that there is a world of difference between humans (as active subjects) and nonhuman beings and things (as passive objects). Humans feel and reflect, but animals, plants, things, and the others do not. It is proper and useful for natural scientists to assume and then study nature as an object, because this study can produce objective knowledge for controlling the natural world. It may also be useful for social scientists to assume and then study humans as objects, because it may produce objective knowledge for controlling humans. However, this violates the constructionist's humanist values and sensibilities.

Constructionists are opposed to the control of humans; instead, they advocate the protection and expansion of human worth, dignity, and freedom. One result of this humanist ideology is the observation that so-called objective knowledge about human behavior is inevitably superficial whenever it is used to control people. In order for the former white racist government in South Africa to control blacks, for example, it needed only the superficial knowledge that blacks were identifiable and separable from whites. However, to achieve the humanist goal of protecting and expanding blacks' human worth, dignity, and freedom, a deeper understanding of blacks is needed. This understanding requires appreciating and empathizing with them, experiencing what they experience as blacks, and seeing blacks' lives and the world around them from their perspective. We must look at the black experience from the inside as a participant rather than from the outside as a spectator. In a word, we must adopt the internal, subjective view instead of the external, objective one.

The same principle, according to constructionists, should hold for understanding deviants and their deviant behavior. Constructionists contrast this subjective approach with the positivists' objective one. To constructionists, positivists treat deviance as if it were an immoral, unpleasant, or repulsive phenomenon that should be controlled, corrected, or eliminated. In consequence, positivists have used the objective approach by staying aloof from deviants, studying the external aspects of their deviant behavior and relying on a set of preconceived ideas to guide their study. The result is a collection of surface facts about deviants, such as their poverty, lack of schooling, poor self-image, and low aspirations. All this may be used to control and eliminate deviance, but it does not tell us, in Howard Becker's (1963) words, "what a deviant does in his daily round of activity, and what he thinks about himself, society, and his activities." To understand the life of a deviant, constructionists believe, we need to use the relatively subjective approach, which requires our appreciation for and empathy with the deviant. The aim of this subjective approach, according to David Matza (1969), "is to comprehend and to illuminate the subject's view and to interpret the world as it appears to him."

As a result of their subjective and empathetic approach, constructionists often present an image of deviants as basically the same as conventional people. People who are deaf, for example, are the same as those who hear in being able to communicate and live a normal life. They should, therefore, be respected rather than pitied. This implies that so-called deviant behavior, because it is like so-called conventional behavior, should not be controlled, cured, or eradicated by society.

Theory: What Does It Mean?

Positivism suggests that we use etiological, causal, or explanatory theories to make sense of what research has found out about deviant behavior, because positivists favor the determinist view that deviance is determined by forces beyond the individual's control. By contrast, constructionism suggests that we go for largely noncausal, descriptive, or analytical theories. Such theories provide detailed analyses of the subjective, experiential world of deviance. Constructionists feel at home with these analyses because they regard most deviance as a voluntary act, an expression of free will.

Determinism: Deviance as "Determined" Behavior. Overly enthusiastic about the prospect of turning their discipline into a science, early sociologists argued that, like animals, plants, and material objects that natural scientists study, humans do not have any free will. The reason is that acknowledgment of free will would contradict the scientific principle of determinism. If a killer is thought to will, cause, or determine a murderous act, then it does not make sense to say that the murderous act is caused by things such as the individual's physical characteristics, mental condition, family background, or some social experience. Therefore, in defending their scientific principle of determinism, the early sociologists maintained their denial of free will. However, today's positivist sociologists assume that humans do possess free will. Still, this assumption, they argue, does not undermine the scientific principle of determinism. No matter how much a person exercises free will by making choices and decisions, the choices and decisions do not simply happen but are determined by some causes. If a woman chooses to kill her husband rather than continue to live with him, she certainly has free will or freedom of choice so long as nobody forces her to do what she does. However, some factor may determine the woman's choice of one alternative over another, or the way she exercises her free will. One such factor, as research has suggested, may be a long history of abuse at the hands of her husband. Thus, according to today's positivists, there is no inconsistency between freedom and causality.

Although they allow for human freedom of choice, positivists do not use it to explain why people behave in a certain way. They will not, for example, explain why the woman kills by saying "because she chooses to kill." This is no explanation at all, because the idea of choice can also be used to explain why another woman does not kill her husband—by saying "because she chooses not to." According to positivists, killing and not killing (or, more generally, deviant and conventional behavior), being two contrary phenomena, cannot be explained by the same thing, such as choice. The idea of choice simply cannot explain the difference between deviance and conventionality; it cannot explain why one man chooses to kill when another chooses not to kill. Therefore, although positivists do believe in human choice, they will not attribute deviance to human choice. They will instead explain deviance by using such concepts as wife abuse, broken homes, unhappy homes, lower-class background, economic deprivation, social disorganization, rapid social change, differential association, differential reinforcement, and lack of social control. Any one of these causes of deviance can be used to illustrate what positivists consider a real explanation of deviance, because, for example, wife abuse is more likely to cause a woman to kill her husband than not. Etiological theories essentially point out factors like those as the causes of deviance.

Voluntarism: Deviance as a Voluntary Act. To social constructionists, the supposedly deviant behavior is a voluntary act or an expression of human volition, will, or choice. Constructionists take this stance because they are disturbed by what they claim to be the dehumanizing implication of the positivist view of deviant behavior. The positivist view is said to imply that a human being is like "a robot, a senseless and purposeless machine reacting to every fortuitous change in the external and internal environment." Constructionists emphasize that human beings, because they possess free will and choice-making ability, determine or cause their own behavior.

To support this voluntarist assumption, constructionists tend to analyze how social control agencies define some people as deviant and carry out the sanctions against them. Such analyses often accent, as Edwin Lemert (1972) has observed, "the arbitrariness of official action, stereotyped decision-making in bureaucratic contexts, bias in the administration of law, and the general preemptive nature of society's controls over deviants." All this conveys the strong impression that control agents, being in positions of power, exercise their free will by actively, intentionally, and purposefully controlling the deviants.

Constructionists also analyze people who have been labeled deviant. The deviants are not presented as if they are robots, passively and senselessly developing a poor self-image as conventional society expects. Instead, they are described as actively seeking positive meanings in their deviant activities. In Jack Katz's (1988) analysis, murderers see themselves as morally superior to their victims. The killing is said to give the murderers the self-righteous feeling of defending their dignity and respectability because their victims have unjustly humiliated them by taunting or insulting them. Katz also portrays robbers as feeling themselves morally superior to their victims—regarding their victims as fools or suckers who deserve to be robbed. If robbers want to hold up somebody on the street, they first ask a potential victim for the time, for directions, for a cigarette light, or for change. Each of these requests is intended to determine whether the person is a fool. The request for the time, for example, gives the robber the opportunity to know whether the prospective victim has an expensive watch. Complying with the request, then, is taken to establish the person as a fool and hence the right victim.

Summary and Conclusion

Each of the positivist and social constructionist perspectives consists of three related assumptions, and each assumption suggests a strategy for contributing to the sociology of deviance. For the positivist perspective, the first is the absolutist assumption that deviant behavior is absolutely real. This suggests that we study deviance or deviants. Second is the objectivist assumption that deviant behavior is an objective, publicly observable fact. This suggests that we use objective research methods, such as survey, experiment, or detached observation. Third is the determinist assumption that deviance is determined or caused by certain social forces. This suggests that we use causal theories to make sense of research data. With the social constructionist perspective, the first assumption is that deviant behavior is basically a label, mental construct, or social construction. This suggests that we study law enforcers and other labelers, the process of labeling, and the consequences of labeling. The second assumption is that the supposedly deviant behavior is a personal experience. This suggests that we use less objective research methods, such as ethnography, participant observation, or open-ended, in-depth interviews. The third assumption is that the so-called deviance is a voluntary, self-willed act. This suggests that we develop noncausal, descriptive theories. (See Table I.1 for a quick review.)

The diverse definitions, theories, methodologies, and data we have discussed reflect many different aspects of deviant behavior. Although they appear to conflict, they actually complement one another. They may be compared with the different views of a house. From the front, the house has a door, windows, and a chimney on top. From the back, it has a door and a chimney on top but fewer windows. From the side, it has no doors, but it has windows and a chimney on top. From the top, it has no doors or windows, but a chimney in the middle. It is the same house, but it looks different, depending on one's position. Taking in the different views on the house ensures a fuller knowledge of what the house actually looks like. Similarly, knowing the different views on deviant behavior ensures a fuller understanding of deviance. This reader is intended to make that possible.

TABLE I.1
A summary of two perspectives

Positivist Perspective	Constructionist Perspective
Absolutism Deviance is absolutely, intrinsically real; hence, deviance or deviants are the subject of study.	*Relativism* Deviance is a label, a social construction; hence, labelers, labeling, and the impacts of labeling are the subject of study.
Objectivism Deviance is an objective, observable fact; hence, objective research methods are used.	*Subjectivism* Deviance is a personal experience; hence, subjective research methods are used.
Determinism Deviance is a determined behavior, a product of causation; hence, casual, explanatory theory is developed.	*Voluntarism* Deviance is a voluntary act, an expression of free will; hence, noncausal, descriptive theory is developed.

References

Becker, Howard S. 1963. *Outsiders: Studies in the Sociology of Deviance.* New York: Free Press.

Heckert, Alex and Druann Maria Heckert. 2002. "A New Typology of Deviance: Integrating Normative and Reactivist Definitions of Deviance." *Deviant Behavior* 23:449–79.

Hirschi, Travis. 1973. "Procedural Rules and the Study of Deviant Behavior." *Social Problems* 21:166–71.

Katz, Jack. 1988. Seductions of Crime: Moral and Sensual Attractions in Doing Evil. New York: Basic Books.

Lemert, Edwin M. 1972. *Human Deviance, Social Problems, and Social Control,* 2nd ed. Englewood Cliffs, NJ: Prentice Hall.

Matza, David. 1969. *Becoming Deviant.* Englewood Cliffs, NJ: Prentice Hall.

Nettler, Gwynn. 1974. "On Telling Who's Crazy." *American Sociological Review* 39:893–94.

DEVIANCE TODAY

PART ONE

Positivist Theories

Imagine an 11-year-old girl attempting to smuggle items into a maximum-security prison filled with male ex-offenders. Do you think it would be successful? Well, this almost happened when an 11-year-old, with her 25-year-old sister, tried to smuggle 74 cell phones and a .38-caliber revolver to her brother incarcerated for illegal gun possession. The 11-year-old actually made it past the first security check point but was more thoroughly inspected at the second point due to the odd shapes noticed underneath her clothing. The pistol was taped to her back. The sisters were taken into custody for questioning after their unsuccessful attempt. Unfortunately, it is not uncommon for children to be used to smuggle items into a prison.[1]

As a society, our major concern is what lays ahead for this young girl. Many might predict a life of crime, which follows her older brother and sister. Positivist theorists believe one's behavior is heavily influenced by their social environment and/or biological and psychological traits. This little girl, at a young age, has already been involved in criminal activities. Her social environment has put her in a position to more likely follow the path of a criminal. However, positivist theorists also argue if one can be conditioned to practice criminal behavior, then there is also possibility for reform and rehabilitation. Timothy Brezina and Miranda Baumann discuss the everyday pressures life can bring, which can result in strain and anomie. They discuss many positivist theorists including, but not limited to Durkheim, Merton, Cohen, and Agnew. These theorists speak on how one's social situation can lead to a life of crime. Part One is concluded with Robert Agnew's article, "Control Theories." Control theories examine how inner and external controls vary from person to person. This abundance or lack of control can prevent or lead someone to become involved in deviant behavior.

Note

1. Tyler, Elizabeth. 2011 "The Littlest Smuggler: Girl Tries to Bring 74 Phones into Colombian Prison." *Time*, February 9. Retrieved May 12, 2011. (http://newsfeed.time.com/2011/02/09/the-littlest-smuggler-girl-tries-to-bring-74-phones-into-colombian-prison/).

ARTICLE 1

Timothy Brezina
Georgia State University

Miranda Baumann
Georgia State University

Strain and Anomie Theories

Jacob spent hours each day studying for his criminology exam, but no matter how hard he tried, he just couldn't get the answers right. A lot was riding on this exam—he had already failed his first exam and needed an A to keep his scholarship. When exam day came, he still didn't feel prepared. One of the smartest kids in class always sat right next to him. Jacob knew that he shouldn't cheat, but he just couldn't afford to get a bad grade. So, during the exam, Jacob copied answers from his classmate's paper.

Mark wanted it all. He wanted the brand new car that was being advertised. He wanted the nice clothes and jewelry that his favorite music idols wore. Everywhere he looked, the message was clear: success equals nice things and lots of money. Mark wanted it, but he didn't know how to get it. He came from a poor neighborhood and, although his mother worked very hard, it seemed she earned only enough to scrape by. She encouraged Mark to get a good education, but he never got fantastic grades in school. Not sure what else to do, Mark started selling drugs for quick cash. Before long, he too had the car, the clothes, and the jewelry.

These vignettes (or stories) may sound familiar. College students often feel pressure to succeed academically. Moreover, countless movies and popular songs emphasize the importance of material success. These vignettes also help to illustrate strain and anomie theories of crime and deviance. Strain and anomie theories are concerned with the internal and external pressures that drive individuals to crime and deviance. To explain offending behavior, contemporary strain theorists typically focus on the stressors (e.g., inability to achieve desired goals) that lead some people to engage in crime, delinquency, or drug use. Following a similar tradition, contemporary anomie theorists describe how certain cultural values and goals, such as the American cultural emphasis on material success, can weaken society's ability to restrain undesirable behavior, leading to high rates of crime and deviance.

These distinctions can be confusing for students new to strain and anomie theories. In this article, we introduce the reader to the concepts of strain and anomie by tracing the historic development of these concepts to their common origin. We then show how the strain and anomie traditions in criminology developed over time. We conclude by discussing the current status of strain and anomie theories in contemporary criminology.

Before proceeding, it is important to note that strain and anomie theories are rich and evolving theories within criminology. Over time, criminologists have developed many different versions of strain and anomie theories—more than we could hope to cover in this short article. In the following sections, we describe the dominant versions, focusing on the key concepts and ideas that are common to strain and anomie theories in general. We hope this brief introduction will enhance your appreciation of the strain/anomie tradition and will spur your interest in learning more (for further reading, we recommend the book and article titles highlighted in the following discussion).

To understand the development of strain and anomie theories, it is necessary to explore the pioneering work of the French sociologist Emile Durkheim. Durkheim's treatment of "anomie" inspired the development of the strain/anomie tradition in criminology and provides the starting point for our discussion.

Emile Durkheim

Emile Durkheim came to prominence during a time of social upheaval in late nineteenth-century France. Not only had France endured a bloody revolution less than a century before; the nation was rapidly industrializing. It was against this backdrop of social change that Durkheim developed the concept of anomie.

According to Durkheim, stable institutions are the backbone of social order. Society's moral institutions, such as family and religion, play a central role as these institutions provide guidance and direct the energies of individuals into collective pursuits that provide meaning and fulfillment. These institutions also help to keep the selfish and potentially destructive tendencies of individuals in check. The norms and expectations surrounding family life, for example, direct the energies of the individual toward the care of one's kin. Likewise, religion directs individual energies toward collective worship and community solidarity.

In Durkheim's view, the wants, needs, and desires of individuals are essentially limitless and thus insatiable. Left to their own devices, individuals can always imagine the possibility of having "more" for themselves—a condition that lends itself to a "longing for infinity," perpetual dissatisfaction, and the potential for various destructive behaviors (Durkheim [1897] 1951). For this reason, moral institutions are essential—they make society possible by providing moral direction, by regulating the wants of individuals, and by curbing the expression of selfish or egoistic desires. In essence, society's moral institutions keep a lid on the egoistic desires that would otherwise erupt among individuals.

When these institutions become weak or ineffective, society is at risk of degenerating into a state of normlessness or *anomie.* When institutionalized norms or expectations lose their force and no longer have the power to guide behavior, individuals are free to pursue their egoistic desires, their potentially destructive tendencies are no longer restrained, and rates of various deviant behaviors—including crime and suicide—tend to rise. For Durkheim, a key challenge faced by modern societies is that of maintaining strong regulating institutions and avoiding widespread anomie.

Classical Strain Theory

In a now classic article titled "Social Structure and Anomie," a young sociologist by the name of Robert K. Merton (1938) expanded upon Durkheim's anomie framework and applied it directly to the problems of crime and deviance. This single piece was among the most influential contributions to criminology and provided the foundation for all future versions of strain and anomie theories.

MERTON'S "SOCIAL STRUCTURE AND ANOMIE"

Merton agreed that people are prone to insatiable desires, but rather than locating such desires in human nature, he viewed them as a product of culture and socialization. In the United States, for example, the cultural ethos of the "American Dream" encourages all individuals to strive for personal success, with a special focus on the accumulation of monetary wealth. At the same time, the means by which people accumulate wealth are not so emphasized. This cultural exaggeration of the success goal, combined with relatively little concern for the means of goal attainment, contributes to an "ends over means" mentality and the common occurrence of fraud, corruption, and crime. The American Dream, then, encourages individuals to focus on egoistic pursuits and desires—the very types of pursuits and desires that Durkheim viewed as a threat to the social order.

Moreover, the culturally prescribed goal of monetary success is universal in nature—*all* Americans are encouraged to get ahead. Americans are expected to "pull themselves up by their own bootstraps" and continually strive to achieve economic success regardless of their position within society. Yet, as Merton recognized, pervasive inequalities in American society create serious barriers to success for some groups and individuals; that is, existing opportunities for achieving success are unequally distributed within society. When large segments of the population have internalized the American Dream ethos but lack the legal or legitimate means to attain monetary wealth, this is said to create *strain* in the social structure. In essence, a gap or *disjunction* occurs between the culturally prescribed success goal and the legitimate means of goal attainment.

Particularly among disadvantaged groups, strain is said to contribute to anomie, thereby increasing the likelihood of deviant behavior. When people accept the goal of monetary success but lack the legal ability to attain this goal, they may lose faith in the value of hard work or playing by the rules. In other words, the norms surrounding the culturally approved means of goal attainment may lose their force and fail to regulate behavior, resulting in a state of normlessness or anomie. *Innovation* is one possible response to this condition: people may give up on the legitimate means of goal attainment and pursue monetary success through innovative but illegal means, such as drug dealing, theft, or prostitution.

Of course, not all individuals react to strain or anomie with crime. While the experience of strain increases the likelihood of crime and deviance ("innovation"), Merton recognized that other adaptations were possible. In fact, *conformity* is a much more common adaptation and occurs when strained individuals remain committed to culturally prescribed success goals as well as the legitimate means of attaining these goals. Many people, for example, may realize that they do not currently have the means to attain monetary success, but they conform to society's rules nonetheless and, perhaps, maintain the dream of getting rich in the future (by playing the lottery, for instance). *Retreatism*, the least common adaptation, occurs when individuals reject both the goals and the means as unachievable or ineffectual and cease to function within the social context. Substance abuse and suicide are considered retreatist responses to strain. *Ritualism* occurs when individuals consider the goals unattainable but still conform—they may lower their aspirations and come to accept their low status. *Rebellion* refers to the substitution of new goals and means following the rejection of those endorsed by society, as illustrated by those who push for radical social or political change, such as the equal distribution of wealth.

You may have noticed that Merton's account contrasts sharply with pathological explanations of deviance that trace the causes of offending behavior to some defect in the individual's biological or psychological makeup. In fact, Merton developed his sociological account of deviance partly in reaction to the pathological explanations that were popular in his day, arguing that crime and deviance more often represent "the normal reaction, by normal persons, to abnormal conditions" (Merton 1938:672, note 2). In doing so, Merton was not commenting on the ethical desirability of deviant behavior; rather, he was arguing that crime and deviance represent predictable responses to strain, even in otherwise normal and healthy populations. Abnormality, according to this view, is not a prerequisite for offending behavior to occur.

Several interesting implications follow from Merton's theoretical framework. First, if Merton is correct, then the roots of the crime problem can be traced, in part, to the contradictory configuration of cultural and structural arrangements that characterize American society, namely, a cultural exaggeration of monetary success goals in a society plagued by high levels of inequality. This fact may help to explain why crime is such a challenging social problem to address, and why attempts to reduce crime by changing the attitudes and behaviors of individual offenders have met with limited success.

Second, while pathological explanations of deviance tend to highlight the unusual or abnormal motivations of offenders, Merton's account suggests that conformists and offenders often share common motivations. In Merton's framework, both conformists and offenders are motivated by and committed to the conventional success goal of monetary wealth. McCarthy and Hagan's (2001) study of successful drug dealers provides a useful illustration. They find that the most successful drug dealers are intelligent, are willing to take risks, are willing to network with others to expand their markets, and possess a strong desire for monetary success—the same characteristics that are usually attributed to legitimate business entrepreneurs. From the perspective of Merton's strain theory, the key difference between these groups lies in the means they have selected to achieve the same goal. The entrepreneur achieves monetary success through institutional means, while the drug dealer succeeds through criminal activity.

Despite the enormous influence of Merton's strain theory, Merton left a number of questions unanswered. For example, how would strain theory explain acts of crime and deviance that are not oriented toward culturally prescribed success goals? After all, many acts of juvenile delinquency—acts such as vandalism, joyriding, and fistfights—seem relatively pointless. Further, why do some strained groups and individuals resort to innovation, while others respond to strain with conformity, retreatism, or rebellion? These and other questions were addressed by subsequent strain theorists.

COHEN'S "DELINQUENT BOYS"

Merton's explanation of crime and deviance emphasized the functional or utilitarian nature of criminal adaptations. In contrast, Albert Cohen (1955) observed that most juvenile delinquency was nonutilitarian in nature, not being specifically directed toward the achievement of conventional success goals. To make strain theory more applicable to juvenile delinquency, Cohen expanded and revised the theory.

Cohen agreed with Merton that delinquency was a response to strain created by goal blockage (the inability to achieve valued goals), especially among lower-class youth. To Cohen, the emphasis that schools place on middle-class values and achievements leaves many lower-class juveniles at a distinct disadvantage. These youths often enter school without the knowledge or skills necessary to "measure up" to middle-class expectations and are subsequently defined as problems by school officials and middle-class peers. Furthermore, once labeled problem children, these youths are effectively denied legitimate pathways to middle-class status and success. Cohen theorized that this inability to live up to the middle-class "measuring rod" creates *status frustration* among lower-class youths.

Cohen believed that the nonutilitarian nature of juvenile delinquency was related to the way in which status-frustrated youths come together and collectively respond to strain. Similar to Merton's adaptation of rebellion, Cohen argued that similarly rejected youths engage in *reaction formation* by rebelling against middle-class expectations in favor of an alternative status system. This alternative system is the antithesis of middle-class status and glorifies goals that these youths *can* achieve, such as toughness and fighting prowess. This collective response to strain results in the formation of a delinquent subculture, which is characterized by a number of deviant activities designed to flaunt disregard for middle-class values.

CLOWARD AND OHLIN'S "DELINQUENCY AND OPPORTUNITY"

Cloward and Ohlin (1960) were also interested in the impact of strain on the formation and function of juvenile gangs. Like Cohen, Cloward and Ohlin believed that lower-class individuals who experience problems of adjustment are likely to congregate, blame their inability to achieve middle-class goals on conventional society, and form justifications for criminal behavior. Yet, while Cohen highlighted the rebellious nature of juvenile delinquency, Cloward and Ohlin observed that the type of delinquency that strained youth pursue varies across neighborhoods and depends on the criminal opportunities available to them. Some strained youths have greater access than others to the *illegitimate means* of goal attainment, such as exposure to more experienced criminals (criminal "role models") or access to illegal markets.

Differential access to illegitimate means, in turn, contributes to the emergence of different types of subcultural adaptations to strain. *Criminal subcultures* tend to form when commitment to conventional goals is strong and illegitimate means of goal attainment are highly accessible. Members of this subculture are actively instructed by successful criminals and have easy access to a host of potential victims. In contrast, *conflict subcultures* lack the social cohesion necessary to foster effective criminal learning. When social disorganization is high, conflict subcultures specializing in violent behavior are common. When there is a failure of both legitimate *and* illegitimate means, *retreatist subcultures* sometimes emerge. Drug use is said to be common among retreatist subcultures.

Although the classic strain theories of Merton, Cohen, and Cloward and Ohlin were influential throughout much of the twentieth century and helped to inspire antipoverty efforts, they began to fall out of favor by the 1970s. By this time, strain theories had been criticized for their failure to adequately explain why only *some* strained individuals resort to crime or delinquency, for their failure to explain crime and delinquency committed by middle-class individuals, for their neglect of goals other than monetary success or middle-class status, and for their lack of empirical support. For example, the experience of strain or goal-blockage—as measured by the individual's perceived inability to attain valued goals, such as a good job or college education—did not prove to be a strong correlate of crime or delinquency.

Contemporary Strain and Anomie Theories

During the 1990s, strain and anomie theories experienced an impressive revival. This revival was due largely to the publication of two influential works: Agnew's (1992) "Foundation for a General Strain Theory of Crime and Delinquency" and Messner and Rosenfeld's (1994) "Crime and the American Dream." Following the tradition of the classic strain theorists, especially Cohen and Cloward and Ohlin, Agnew focused on the social-psychological links between goal-blockage and crime, revised and expanded the concept of strain, and attempted to address the criticisms described earlier. Messner and Rosenfeld returned more closely to the idea of anomie as formulated by Merton and further explored the larger cultural and structural forces that give rise to high crime rates. (Some criminologists have argued that Merton actually developed two related theories of crime, one that focused on strain/goal-blockage and another that highlighted the cultural and structural conditions that foster normlessness or anomie; see Featherstone and Deflem 2003.)

AGNEW'S GENERAL STRAIN THEORY

Robert Agnew (1992) recognized that classic strain theory was limited in its ability to explain crime and delinquency. In particular, the classic strain theories of Merton, Cohen, and Cloward and Ohlin focused quite narrowly on the goals of monetary success and middle-class status and failed to consider the importance of other goals—goals that, when blocked, may also generate strain or frustration. To address this issue, Agnew expands the range of goals that are said to be important. For example, the goals that are often important to young males include the desire for respect and masculine status (e.g., the desire to be treated "like a man"), the desire for autonomy or independence from others, and the desire for excitement. Further, these more immediate goals are often more important to young males than future economic status. Agnew therefore defines goal-blockage in more general terms and identifies the *failure to achieve positively valued goals* as a major source of strain.

In addition, Agnew's General Strain Theory (GST) highlights two additional types of strain: *the loss of positively valued stimuli* and *the presentation of noxious or negatively valued stimuli.* The loss of positively valued stimuli encompasses a wide range of situations, including the theft of valued property or the loss of a loved one. Similarly, the presence of negative stimuli can include a host of aversive experiences, such as child abuse, failing grades, negative relationships with teachers, and criminal victimization (Agnew 1992, 2006). It should be noted that these types of strain are not limited to lower-class members of the population; they can be experienced by middle- or upper-class individuals as well.

Further, GST helps to explain how and why the experience of strain increases the likelihood of crime and delinquency. All three types of strain are important because they often generate strong negative emotions, such as anger, depression, or despair. These negative emotions, in turn, are said to create pressures for "corrective action" with crime, delinquency, or drug use being one possible response. Anger is likely to occur when individuals blame others for their experience of strain and is said to be especially conducive to crime and delinquency. Anger, for example, reduces one's tolerance for injury or insult, lowers inhibitions, energizes the individual to action, and creates desires for retaliation and revenge (Agnew 1992).

Individuals may choose to cope with strain in legal or conventional ways. For example, strained individuals may try to convince themselves that a valued but unattainable goal is not really important after all. Or, following the experience of being unjustly or unfairly treated, they may use relaxation techniques to calm themselves down. To explain why only *some* strained individuals resort to crime or delinquency, GST points to a number of conditions that influence the likelihood of a criminal/delinquent response to strain. According to GST, a criminal response to strain is most likely when individuals endure repeated strains of a severe nature, when conventional coping strategies are unavailable or have proven ineffective, and when the strained individual is predisposed to crime (e.g., when the individual lacks self-control, associates with delinquent peers, or has a past history of criminal or delinquent behavior; for a discussion of additional factors that shape the likelihood of a criminal response, see Agnew 2006).

Empirical tests of GST typically find that the theory has some potential to explain crime and delinquency. For example, tests of GST regularly show that various strains increase the likelihood of criminal and delinquent behavior, including parental rejection, harsh or erratic discipline, child abuse, negative experiences in school, homelessness, chronic unemployment, criminal victimization, and residence in economically deprived communities. Some (but not all) studies indicate that the impact of these strains on crime and delinquency is due, in part, to the fact these strains are associated with negative emotions. Further, certain studies indicate that criminal/delinquent responses to strain are most likely among individuals who are impulsive, are chronically angry, lack conventional social support, or associate with delinquent peers;

however, results in this area are mixed (for a review of the evidence, see Agnew 2006).

Although additional research is needed, the positive findings that have been produced to date are important because they suggest that GST has merit and may have potential to inform effective crime control policies and interventions. The major crime control strategies that follow from GST include efforts or interventions that are designed to: (1) reduce or alleviate the strains that are conducive to crime or delinquency, (2) equip individuals with the tools and skills that will allow them to avoid such strains, and (3) reduce that likelihood that individuals will cope with strain in a criminal or delinquent manner (for a detailed discussion of such strategies, see Agnew 2006).

MESSNER AND ROSENFELD'S INSTITUTIONAL-ANOMIE THEORY

While contemporary strain theorists have focused primarily on the role of social-psychological processes in the etiology of crime, contemporary anomie theorists call attention to the larger, macro forces that are said to contribute to high crime rates. Like Merton, Messner and Rosenfeld (1994) highlight the criminogenic consequences of the American value system, with its exaggerated emphasis on personal monetary success. Their Institutional-Anomie Theory (IAT), however, represents a significant extension and elaboration of Merton's (1938) anomie framework.

While recognizing the positive aspects of the American Dream, especially its potential to foster high levels of motivation and innovation, Messner and Rosenfeld (1994) highlight a "dark side" to this cultural ethos. In particular, the American Dream ethos is said to define success in excessively narrow and materialistic terms. Individual achievement and monetary success are glorified, more so than the means that individuals use to achieve success. As a result, individuals face strong pressures to succeed at any cost and may be tempted to pursue success by the "technically most efficient means, that is, by any means necessary" (Messner and Rosenfeld 1994:8). Simultaneously, nonutilitarian pursuits (e.g., social or educational contributions to one's community) are implicitly devalued.

According to IAT, the criminogenic effects of the American Dream depend, in part, on the extent to which the economy dominates the institutional landscape, that is, the extent to which social life is organized around the pursuit of personal economic gain. When the economy dominates, and when noneconomic roles associated with family, school, and the larger community are consistently devalued, the norms that encourage socially constructive goals and pursuits (e.g., playing by the rules, playing fair, investing time and energy to help others) lose their perceived importance and become difficult to enforce, resulting in a condition of anomie. At the individual level, this anomic condition is reflected in extreme competition, individualism, and an "anything goes" mentality.

The criminogenic effects of the American Dream are also exacerbated by high levels of economic inequality. When economic differences in society become extreme, large segments of the population are positioned at the bottom rungs of the economic ladder and, by the standards of the American Dream, are relegated to the role of "failure." The desire to avoid this fate intensifies the pressure to succeed at any cost. As a result, normative means of goal attainment lose their restraining force, anomie prevails, and high rates of crime are the result.

In short, IAT draws attention to the institutional balance of power that exists within society, especially the extent to which the economy dominates and thus weakens noneconomic institutions (i.e., family, school, and community—those institutions that help to restrain antisocial behavior and that encourage socially acceptable means of goal attainment). The crime control recommendations that follow from IAT include policies that are designed to strengthen these noneconomic institutions. Messner and

Rosenfeld (1994) also entertain the possibility of a cultural transformation—one that would provide alternative definitions of success and encourage commitment to community, responsibility, and public altruism.

To date, IAT has received mixed support in the research literature, although further testing of the theory is clearly needed. To help illustrate IAT and how it may help to explain crime rates across communities, we highlight a recent test of the theory conducted by Baumer and Gustafson (2007). The authors of this study examined a large number of communities across the United States, including metropolitan areas and rural counties. Consistent with IAT, they observe a significant relationship between commitment to monetary success and instrumental crime rates (robberies, burglaries, larcenies, and auto thefts) in certain communities. Instrumental crime rates tend to be relatively high in communities where people express both a strong commitment to monetary success (agreeing that, "next to health, money is the most important thing") and a weak commitment to the legitimate means of obtaining success (agreeing that "there are no right or wrong ways to make money, only hard and easy ways"). Further, this particular value configuration tends to have the strongest impact on instrumental crime in communities that suffer from extensive economic inequality—where many residents occupy positions of low economic standing.

Baumer and Gustafson (2007) also find evidence to support IAT's assertion that noneconomic institutions help to restrain crime. Specifically, in communities characterized by strong family ties and above-average levels of welfare assistance for the poor, an emphasis on monetary success does not contribute to a high rate of instrumental crime. These findings lend support to some of the policy recommendations proposed by Messner and Rosenfeld, namely, policies designed to strengthen families and those that shield people from the market forces of poverty and unemployment.

Conclusion

Strain and anomie theories continue to inspire and guide the research of criminologists. After experiencing a strong revival in the 1990s, much research is now being conducted to evaluate the latest versions of these theories. Agnew's GST and Messner and Rosenfeld's IAT, in particular, have shown early promise and tests of these theories indicate that they have some potential to explain crime and delinquency at both the micro and macro levels of analysis (these contemporary strain and anomie theories will likely evolve and will themselves be revised and refined as new evidence comes to light). Although strain and anomie theories are not likely to replace control and social learning theories, they appear to provide an important supplement to these other theories and help to provide a more complete account of the forces that contribute to crime and deviance.

Discussion Questions

1. What mode of adaptation do you most commonly use? Why?
2. Do you feel the American Dream leads to strain? How?

References

Agnew, Robert. 1992. "Foundation for a General Strain Theory of Crime and Delinquency." *Criminology* 30:47–87.

____. 2006. *Pressured into Crime: An Overview of General Strain Theory.* Los Angeles, CA: Roxbury.

Baumer, Eric P. and Regan Gustafson. 2007. "Social Organization and Instrumental Crime: Assessing the Empirical Validity of Classic and Contemporary Anomie Theories." *Criminology* 45:617–63.

Cloward, Richard A. and Lloyd E. Ohlin. 1960. *Delinquency and Opportunity.* New York: Free Press.

Cohen, Albert. 1955. *Delinquent Boys.* New York: Free Press.

Durkheim, Emile. 1897[1951]. *Suicide: A Study in Sociology.* Translated by J. A. Spaulding and G. Simpson. New York: Free Press.

Featherstone, Richard and Mathieu Deflem. 2003. "Anomie and Strain: Contexts and Consequences of Merton's Two Theories." *Sociological Inquiry* 73:471–89.

McCarthy, Bill and John Hagan. 2001. "Capital, Competence, and Criminal Success." *Social Forces* 79:1035–59.

Merton, Robert K. 1938. "Social Structure and Anomie." *American Sociological Review* 3:672–82.

Messner, Steven F. and Richard Rosenfeld. 1994. *Crime and the American Dream.* Belmont, CA: Wadsworth.

ARTICLE 2

Robert Agnew
Emory University

Control Theories of Deviance

Most theories assume that it is necessary to explain why people engage in deviance. For example, they assume that it is necessary to explain why some people cheat on exams or shoplift from stores. Control theories, by contrast, assume that deviance requires no special explanation. We all have unfulfilled needs and desires, and deviant acts are often the easiest way to satisfy them. For example, it is much easier to get good grades by cheating than by studying. And it is much easier to get the things we want by stealing than by working and saving. So everyone has a strong incentive to engage in deviance. What requires explanation is why most people conform.

This may seem like a rather strange argument. We tend to take conformity for granted, believing that it is necessary to explain acts such as theft and aggression. Consider, however, the behavior of very young children. When these children want something, such as the toy of another child, they often grab it from the child. And when something upsets them, they often hit others, including their parents. Tremblay (2006) has conducted research on the behavior of infants and young children, and he found that it is quite common for them to physically attack others (assault); take things from others (theft), sometimes using force (robbery); destroy the property of others (vandalism); and—when they are able to talk—lie to others. Tremblay (2006:6), for example, states that as soon as infants "are in sufficient control of their muscles they use physical aggression to express their anger and obtain what they desire." These deviant behaviors usually do not strike us as odd: the infants and young children are simply trying to satisfy their needs and desires in the most expedient manner. Control theorists ask why most older children and adults do not do the same. That is, why do they conform?

Control theorists state that *people conform because of the controls or restraints to which they are subject.* Parents, for example, spend much effort trying to control the deviant behavior of their young children. Among other things, they monitor the behavior of their children, sanction their children when the children misbehave, and try to teach their children that acts such as hitting and stealing are wrong. Others, such as teachers, neighbors, and the police, also spend much effort trying to control deviant behavior. According to control theory, the control exercised by these people explains why most out-of-control infants and children eventually turn into adults who generally conform.

There are several major versions of control theory (e.g., Shaw and McKay 1942; Nye 1958; Matza 1964; Hirschi 1969; Kornhauser 1978; Gottfredson and Hirschi 1990; Patterson, Reid, and Dishion 1992; Sampson and Laub 1993; Sampson 2011). Each describes the types of control to which people are subject. Most were developed by criminologists, and so argue that criminal behavior is more likely when control is low. Control theory, however, is relevant to a broad range of deviant acts. People low in control are free to pursue their needs and desires in the most expedient manner. This unrestrained pursuit of needs and desires may result in a wide range of deviant acts, including excessive drinking, reckless driving, risky sexual behavior, and suicide attempts. And control theory has been successfully applied to the explanation of these and other deviant acts (e.g., Jones and Quisenberry 2004; Maimon, Browning, and Brooks-Gunn 2010). There are, however, certain types of deviance that the theory has trouble explaining, such as those types of mental illness with a strong biological basis (e.g., schizophrenia).

The first part of this article draws on the leading control theories to describe the four major types of control: direct control, stake in conformity, beliefs condemning deviance, and self-control. These types of control are most often used to explain why some *individuals* are more likely than others to engage in deviance. The second part of this article describes several major extensions of control theory. One extension explains changes in the level of deviance over the life course of individuals; for example, it explains why most individuals substantially reduce their levels of criminal offending when they move from adolescence to adulthood. Another extension explains why some communities have higher rates of crime than others. And still other extensions explain group differences in crime and deviance, such as gender and age differences.

The Major Types of Control (or Restraints against Deviance)

I sometimes ask the students in my classes the following question: "Why are you not a criminal? That is, why do you refrain from engaging in acts such as theft and violence (at least most of the time)?" I get a variety of answers, including responses such as: "Because I am afraid of getting caught"; "My parents would kill me"; "My family would be greatly disappointed"; "It would look bad on my resume"; "The consequences could somehow affect my college career"; "I know the difference between what's right and what's wrong"; "I feel too guilty when I do something wrong"; and "I can control my anger instead of resorting to violence when I am in a conflict." These responses illustrate the different types of control or restraints against deviance. In particular, the major types of control include the following.

Direct Control

People subject to direct control refrain from deviance out of fear that they will be caught and sanctioned. Direct control is of course exercised by the criminal justice system, that is, the police, courts, and correctional agencies. The police patrol communities and respond to calls for service, sometimes catching and arresting suspected criminals. The police, however, are not very effective at exercising direct control. The large majority of crimes do *not* result in arrest. Most crimes are not reported to the police, and only about 20 percent of those crimes that become known to the police are cleared by arrest. The courts then sanction many of these arrested individuals, typically by placing them on probation (community supervision), but often by sending them to prison (about 1 out of every 100 adults in the United States is now incarcerated). Direct control by the criminal justice system is referred to as *formal* direct control, and research suggests that it has a *modest* effect on crime. In particular, areas where the certainty or likelihood of punishment is high are somewhat lower in crime. And people who believe the certainty of punishment is high are somewhat less likely to engage in crime. The severity of punishment has little or no effect on the likelihood of crime. Also, it appears that the *threat* of punishment is more important than the actual administration of punishment. People who are punished are about as likely, or perhaps somewhat more likely, to commit crimes in the future as are comparable individuals who are not punished or are punished less severely (Agnew 2009a; Nagin, Cullen, and Jonson 2009). One reason for this is that punishment by the criminal justice system has certain effects that are conducive to crime; for example, individuals with criminal records have more trouble getting jobs.

Informal direct control is far more common and effective than formal direct control.

Informal control is exercised by parents, friends, teachers, neighbors, employers, and others. Most such control is relatively mild, such as a disapproving glance by a friend or time-out by a parent when we misbehave. But such control may be more severe, such as expulsion from school, termination from employment, and shunning by neighbors. Informal control is more effective than formal because people such as our parents, friends, and teachers are much better able to monitor our behavior and apply sanctions when we misbehave. But if informal control is to be effective, it must have several elements. First, control agents such as parents must state clear rules that prohibit deviance and related behaviors (e.g., associating with delinquent peers). Second, control agents must carefully monitor behavior to make sure that these rules are obeyed. This monitoring may be direct, as when parents and teachers watch over the children in their care. And it may be indirect; for example, parents may regularly ask their children about their behavior and periodically talk with their children's teachers. Third, control agents must consistently sanction rule violations in a meaningful manner. The use of harsh or abusive sanctions, however, should be avoided. Such sanctions often backfire, alienating and angering the recipients, and thereby increasing the likelihood of further deviance (Patterson et al. 1992; Sampson and Laub 1993; Agnew 2009a).

Individuals differ a good deal in the level of direct control to which they are subject. For example, some juveniles are closely supervised by their parents, but others are free to do whatever they like. Their parents place few limits on their children, the juveniles spend much time away from home on the street, and they are seldom sanctioned by their parents or others when they misbehave. Elijah Anderson (1999) states that this was the case with a small percentage of the children in the poor, inner-city community that he examined in his classic book, *Code of the Street.*

> At an early age, often even before they start school and without much adult supervision, children from street-oriented families gravitate to the streets, where they must be ready to "hang," to socialize competitively with peers. These children have a great deal of latitude and are allowed to rip and run up and down the streets. They often come home from school, put their books down, and go right back out the door. On school nights many eight- and nine-year-olds remain out until nine or ten o'clock (teenagers may come home whenever they want to). (P. 69)

Parents may fail to exercise proper direct control for several reasons. They may lack the knowledge to be effective parents, perhaps because they did not experience effective parenting as children. They may suffer from problems, such as poverty, mental illness, drug abuse, and family violence, that interfere with their ability to parent. And they may have difficult children who frustrate and overwhelm them, causing them to give up on their efforts at effective parenting (Patterson et al. 1992; Agnew 2009a).

Much research has focused on direct control by parents, and research indicates that juveniles high in direct parental control are much less likely to engage in delinquency. Research also indicates that delinquency is lower in schools with high direct control, that is, schools where teachers and administrators clearly state rules for behavior, carefully monitor students, and consistently sanction rule violations in a meaningful, but not overly harsh, manner. Further, crime is also lower in neighborhoods where direct control is high, that is, neighborhoods where residents watch out for one another, and intervene when they witness criminal acts and other misbehavior (more later) (Patterson et al. 1992; Agnew 2009a; Sampson 2011).

Stake in Conformity

People are not equally responsive to direct control. Some individuals are readily deterred by the threat of sanction, while others do not seem to care that their deviant acts might result in sanction. For example, students in a school are more or less subject to the same level of direct control by teachers and administrators. But the students differ in their responsiveness to these controls: some generally conform and others misbehave on a regular basis. One reason for this is that individuals differ in their stake in conformity, which refers to those things that they have to lose if they are caught and sanctioned. Some people have a large stake in conformity. For example, some students have high grades, excellent reputations, close ties to teachers, and plans to attend prestigious colleges. These students have a great deal to lose if they are caught and sanctioned for deviance, especially serious deviant acts that might result in an official record and expulsion. Deviant acts could jeopardize their grades, ruin their reputations, hurt their educational plans, and lose their ties to teachers. Such students are usually responsive to direct controls. Other students, however, have failing grades, are known as troublemakers, plan to drop out of school, and have poor relations with teachers. These students have little to lose if they are caught and sanctioned, and so they are less responsive to direct controls.

There are two major types of stake in conformity. The first is known as *attachment,* and it involves strong emotional bonds to conventional others, such as parents, teachers, spouses, and religious figures. Individuals who are closely attached to these others are less likely to engage in deviance because doing so may hurt people they care about and jeopardize their ties to these significant others. For example, research suggests that juveniles who love and respect their parents are less likely to engage in crime (Hirschi 1969; Agnew 2009a). The second type of stake in conformity is known as *commitment,* which refers to the individual's actual or anticipated investment in conventional society. Individuals high in commitment have good grades; excellent reputations; extensive involvement in school and community activities; plans to attend college; and/or well-paid, prestigious jobs that are important to them. Such individuals refrain from deviance because these investments might be jeopardized if they are caught and sanctioned. Research suggests that crime is lower among those who are high in commitment (Hirschi 1969; Sampson and Laub 1993; Agnew 2009a).

Beliefs Condemning Deviance

People often find themselves in situations where there is little chance that deviant acts will be detected and sanctioned. Nevertheless, they refrain from deviance, even when it might be to their advantage. For example, suppose you are driving late at night, eager to get home, and encounter a red traffic light. You stop and look around, finding that the streets are completely deserted. Do you run the red light? Most people probably would not, even though there is virtually no chance that they would be caught and sanctioned. The reason is that they have been taught that doing so is wrong and they have adopted this belief. Parents, teachers, religious figures, and others often tell us that certain behaviors are wrong or immoral. And most of us end up adopting a set of beliefs that condemn deviance. These beliefs are frequently strong enough to prevent deviance, even when deviance might be to our advantage and the likelihood of getting caught is low.

Some individuals, however, do not develop strong beliefs condemning deviance. Perhaps their parents did not make a serious effort to instill such beliefs. Juveniles are more likely to adopt such beliefs when their parents establish a strong bond with them and effectively exercise direct control (e.g., clearly condemn and consistently sanction deviant acts). Individuals who do not learn to condemn deviance do not necessarily think that deviance is good. Rather, they are amoral or close to amoral in their orientation. They tend to believe that deviant acts are neither good nor bad. As such, they are more likely to engage in deviance when it is to their advantage. And research provides some support for this idea (Agnew 2009a). For example, juveniles are more likely to engage in delinquency when they agree with statements such as "Most things that people call 'delinquency' don't really hurt anyone" (Hirschi 1969:208–209).

Self-Control

The final type of control involves the personality traits of individuals. Some individuals have traits such that they can restrain themselves when tempted to engage in deviance. Other individuals, however, are low in self-control; they have trouble restraining themselves when tempted. Gottfredson and Hirschi (1990) developed self-control theory, and they state that people low in self-control have the following traits: they tend to act before thinking (are impulsive), are insensitive to others, prefer immediate over delayed rewards, like risky activities, have trouble controlling their anger, and have little ambition or motivation. Researchers have measured self-control by asking people whether they agree with statements such as: "I act on the spur of the moment without stopping to think," "I do things that bring me pleasure here and now," "I take risks just for the fun of it," and "I lose my temper pretty easily" (Grasmick et al. 1993). If you were to meet someone low in self-control, you might describe the person as "wild," "out-of-control," and having a "short fuse."

Much research indicates that low self-control is one of the leading causes of crime and deviance (Pratt and Cullen 2000; Goode 2008). However, certain of the particular claims that Gottrfedson and Hirschi (1990) make about self-control have been challenged. They state that one's level of self control is determined early in life, being a function of the extent to which parents exercise direct control. Children are said to be naturally low in self-control, inclined to satisfy their needs and desires in the most expedient manner possible—including deviance. Children develop high levels of self-control if their parents state clear rules for behavior, carefully monitor behavior, and consistently sanction rule violations. When parents fail to do this, their children remain low in self-control. Research does indicate that parents play an important role in the development of self-control, but it also suggests that other factors contribute to self-control. These include biological factors, particularly genetic inheritance (e.g., Wright and Beaver 2005). That is, our level of self-control is to some extent inherited from our parents. Also, others such as teachers, peers, and neighbors influence our level of self-control (e.g., Pratt, Turner, and Piquero 2004).

Gottfredson and Hirschi (1990) also state that levels of self-control are relatively stable after childhood, such that those relatively low in self-control at one point in time will be relatively low at a later point. While levels of self-control are fairly stable over time, research suggests that they do vary somewhat over the life course; perhaps because people such as teachers and peers can also impact self-control (e.g., Hay and Forrest 2006). Finally, Gottrfedson and Hrschi (1990) state that low self-control is the primary cause of deviance. Levels of direct control, stake in conformity, and beliefs condemning deviance are said to have little effect on deviance once level of self-control is taken into account. Gottfredson and Hirschi (1990), however, do state that it is important to consider the opportunity to engage in deviance. That is, those low in self-control cannot engage in deviance unless they also have the opportunity to do so. For example, they cannot engage in drug use unless they are also exposed to others who provide drugs. But aside from opportunity, level of self-control is said to be the sole cause of crime. The research, however, suggests that the other types of control, such as direct control, affect deviance even after self-control is taken into account. The same is true of factors associated with other theories, such as association with delinquent peers (e.g., Wright et al. 1999; Pratt and Cullen 2000). But despite these challenges, there is little doubt that low self-control is a major cause of deviance.

Extensions of Control Theory

While control theory is most often used to explain why some individuals are more deviant than others, it has been applied to other issues as well.

Explaining Crime over the Life Course

There has been much recent interest in explaining patterns of offending over the life course of individuals. Most notably, researchers have tried to explain why most offenders substantially reduce their levels of crime when they move from adolescence into adulthood, but some continue to offend well into the adult years. Sampson and Laub (1993) address this issue in their book, *Crime in the Making.* They argue that the major sources of control change over the life course. Ties to family and school are most important during childhood, while ties to spouse and work are most important during adulthood. They argue that those juvenile offenders who get involved in good marriages and form strong commitments to work are able to desist from crime. Those who fail to do so, however, continue to offend as adults. It is not entirely clear why some offenders are able to form strong bonds and others are not, but factors such as arrest and imprisonment may make it difficult to form such bonds. For example, having an arrest record makes it difficult to get a "good" job.

Explaining Community Differences in Crime Rates

A version of control theory known as *social disorganization theory* is perhaps the leading explanation of community differences in crime rates. Certain communities have much higher levels of crime than others. These high-crime communities tend to be economically deprived (e.g., high levels of poverty), have high rates of residential mobility (i.e., people frequently move into and out of the communities), and have high rates of family disruption (e.g., divorce, single-parent families). These factors are said to reduce the willingness and ability of community residents to exercise control over one another. In particular, the residents are frequently single parents struggling with economic and other problems, they often do not know their neighbors because of the high rates of mobility, and many are eager to move to more advantaged communities. As a consequence, they are less willing and able to intervene when they see crime and other misbehavior (i.e., exercise direct control). They are less supportive of community institutions that might help provide youth with a stake in conformity. They are less likely to help one another secure good educations and jobs, again reducing stake in conformity. And they are less likely to promote beliefs that strongly condemn deviance. Research provides substantial support for social disorganization theory (Kubrin, Stucky, and Krohn 2009; Sampson 2011).

Explaining Group Differences in Deviance, Such as Gender and Age Differences

Finally, control theory has also been used to explain other group differences in crime. I focus on gender and age differences, since gender and age are the two strongest correlates of crime—with young males having the highest rates of crime (Agnew 2009a). Regarding gender, there is evidence that females have lower rates of crime than males because they are more likely to be sanctioned for many deviant acts, are more strongly bonded to school, are more likely to condemn deviance, and are higher in self-control (Agnew 2009b). These differences are usually explained in terms of gender differences in socialization and social position. For example, it is said that parents frequently have a double standard of behavior, often sanctioning their female children for acts that they tolerate in their male children—such as staying out late and engaging in sexual intercourse. However, certain of these gender differences, such as that involving self-control, have been explained in terms of biological differences between males and females (e.g., Moffitt et al. 2001).

Likewise, control theory has been used to explain why adolescents have higher rates of crime than adults and children. Adolescents have higher rates of crime than adults partly because they are lower in self-control (that part of the brain involved in self-control is less developed in adolescents). Adolescents may also have a lower stake in conformity than adults, who have formed their own families and gotten heavily involved in work. And adolescents may have a higher rate of crime than children because they are less subject to direct control. In particular, adolescents spend much less time under the direct supervision of parents and other adults than do children. Adolescents may also have a lower stake in conformity than children; adolescents' bonds to parents are sometimes frayed and adolescents more often experience difficulties at school (Agnew 2005).

Conclusion

There is much evidence that levels of control play a major role in explaining deviance. In particular, individuals and groups that are low in direct control, stake in conformity, beliefs condemning deviance, and self-control are less likely to conform and more likely to engage in a range of deviant acts. At the same time, research indicates that these controls are not the only factors that explain levels of deviance. Despite the control theory assumption that all individuals are strongly motivated to engage in deviance, there is good evidence that the motivation for deviance differs among individuals and groups (Agnew 2005). Most other theories of deviance, including those described in this text, focus on those factors that explain such differences in motivation. For example, individuals who experience strains or stressors, such as financial hardship, are more strongly motivated to engage in deviance. Likewise, individuals who are reinforced for deviance—perhaps by social approval from peers—are more strongly motivated to engage in further deviance. A complete explanation of deviance, therefore, will have to consider both the restraints against deviance *and* the motivations for deviance.

Discussion Questions

1. Suppose you were conducting a survey of college students; what questions would you ask to determine their level of control (be sure to consider each of the four types of control and their components)?
2. It has been argued that control theory is not relevant to the explanation of white-collar and corporate crime, since individuals who commit these crimes are high in control. For example, they sometimes have degrees from top universities, prestigious jobs, excellent reputations, close ties to conventional others, and high levels of self-control. Do you think control theory can explain such crime? (Hint: consider each type of control in turn.) Do you think there are other types of deviance that control theory has trouble explaining?
3. What recommendations would control theorists make for controlling crime? Describe a program or policy that might increase one or more of the types of control listed earlier.

References

Agnew, Robert. 2005. *Why Do Criminals Offend? A General Theory of Crime and Delinquency.* New York: Oxford.

Agnew, Robert. 2009a. *Juvenile Delinquency: Causes and Control.* New York: Oxford.

Agnew, Robert. 2009b. "The Contribution of 'Mainstream Theories' to the Explanation of Female Delinquency." Pp. 7–29 in *The Delinquent Girl,* edited by Margaret A. Zahn. Philadelphia, PA: Temple University Press.

Anderson, Elijah. 1999. *Code of the Street.* New York; W.W. Norton.

Goode, Erich, ed. 2008. *Out of Control: Assessing the General Theory of Crime.* Stanford, CA: Stanford University Press.

Gottfredson, Michael R. and Travis Hirschi. 1990. *A General Theory of Crime.* Stanford, CA: Stanford University Press.

Grasmick, Harold G., Charles R. Tittle, Robert R. Bursik, Jr., and Bruce J. Arneklev. 1993. "Testing the Core Empirical Implications of Gottfredson and Hirschi's General Theory of Crime." *Journal of Research in Crime and Delinquency* 30:5–29.

Hay, Carter and Walter Forrest. 2006. "The Development of Self-Control: Examining Self-Control's Stability Thesis." *Criminology* 44:739–74.

Hirschi, Travis. 1969. *Causes of Delinquency.* Berkeley, CA: University of California Press.

Jones, Shayne and Neil Quisenberry. 2004. "The General Theory of Crime: How General Is It?" *Deviant Behavior* 25:401–26.

Kornhauser, Ruth R. 1978. *Social Sources of Delinquency.* Chicago, IL: University of Chicago Press.

Kubrin, Charis E., Thoas D. Stucky, and Marvin D. Krohn. 2009. *Researching Theories of Crime and Deviance.* New York: Oxford.

Maimon, David, Christopher R. Browning, and Jeanne Brooks-Gunn. 2010. "Collective Efficacy, Family Attachment, and Urban Adolescent Suicide Attempts." *Journal of Health and Social Behavior* 51:307–24.

Matza, David. 1964. *Delinquency and Drift.* New York: Wiley.

Moffitt, Terrie E., Avshalom Caspi, Michael Rutter, and Phil A. Silva. 2001. *Sex Differences in Antisocial Behaviour.* Cambridge, England: Cambridge University Press.

Nagin, Daniel S., Francis T. Cullen, and Cheryl Lero Jonson. 2009. "Imprisonment and Reoffending." *Crime & Justice* 38:115–200.

Nye, Ivan F. 1958. *Family Relationships and Delinquent Behavior.* New York: Wiley.

Patterson, Gerald R., John B. Reid, and Thomas J. Dishion. 1992. *Antisocial Boys.* Eugene, PR: Castalia.

Pew Center on the States. 2008. "One in 100." Washington, DC: Pew Charitable Trusts.

Pratt, Travis C. and Francis T. Cullen. 2000. "The Empirical Status of Gottfredson and Hirschi's General Theory of Crime." *Criminology* 38:931–64.

Pratt, Travis C., Michael G. Turner, and Alex R. Piquero. 2004. "Parental Socialization and Community Context: A Longitudinal Analysis of the Structural Sources of Low Self-Control." *Journal of Research in Crime and Delinquency* 41:219–43.

Sampson, Robert J. 2011. "The Community." Pp. 210–236 in *Crime and Public Policy*, edited by James Q. Wilson and Joan Petersilia. New York; Oxford.

Sampson, Robert J., and John H. Laub. 1993. *Crime in the Making.* Cambridge, MA: Harvard University Press.

Shaw, Clifford R., and Henry McKay. 1942. *Juvenile Delinquency and Urban Areas.* Chicago, IL: University of Chicago Press.

Tremblay, Richard E. 2006. "Tracking the Origins of Criminal Behavior: Back to the Future." *The Criminologist* 31(#1): 1, 3–7.

Wright, Bradley. R. E., Avashalom Caspi, Terrie E. Moffitt, and Phil A. Silva. 1999. "Low Self Control, Social Bonds, and Crime: Social Causation, Social Selection, or Both?" *Criminology* 37:479–514.

Wright, John P. and Kevin M. Beaver. 2005. "Do Parents Matter in Creating Self-Control in Their Children?" *Criminology* 43:1169–1202.

PART TWO

Constructionist Theories

Abortion has been legal since 1973, but it is getting harder to get one. Consider Lisa, a 22-year-old unmarried woman, who works in a restaurant. Several months ago she became pregnant and decided to have an abortion. But the abortion provider that was located 15 minutes from her home had just closed down. Only four doctors who performed abortions were left in the entire state of Missouri. The closest one to Lisa's hometown was at the Planned Parenthood clinic in St. Louis, an eight-hour round trip. Having no car, Lisa not only had to ask a friend to drive her, but also had to miss two days of work. She had to take the long trip again two weeks later for a follow-up exam that lasted five minutes. Her total expenditure, which included the clinic's bill, the abortion drug, gasoline, food, and incidentals, was more than $600. "It was all very frustrating," she said a month after her abortion. "I only recently paid everyone I borrowed money from."[1]

Besides Missouri, many other states have also made it more difficult to get an abortion. Not only have states created a hostile environment that has led to the closing of many abortion clinics, they have also imposed legal restrictions on abortion, such as requiring pre-abortion counseling, a waiting period, and parental consent or notification. In effect, states treat abortion as a deviant act. To constructionist sociologists, abortion is a deviant act only because society has socially constructed it to be. Moral entrepreneurs and people in power have the rhetoric and resources to construct a behavior as deviant. Thus, constructionists have developed theories about how people impute the notion of "deviance" to behaviors, such as abortion and what consequence this has for themselves and for others.

In this part of the reader, various constructionist theories are presented. In the first article, "Labeling," Mark Konty discusses how an audience's reaction determines if an act is considered deviant. In essence, it is society's reaction to behavior that results in a behavior being labeled. In the next article, "Conflict Theory: The Ongoing Battle," Addrain Conyers discusses the constant struggle among groups in society. The dominant group decides the legal code and cultural norms as the subordinate group struggles to abide and not be viewed criminal or deviant. The section concludes with Cannon's article, "Feminism and Deviance." She discusses concepts, such as feminism, patriarchy, and sexism to help one understand how societal views are male dominated and can cause women to be perceived as deviant.

Note

1. Tumulty, Karen, "Abortion: Where the Real Action Is." . . . *Time*, January 30, 2006, Pp. 50–53.

 ARTICLE 3

Mark Konty
Berea College

Labeling

We've all been to a party or reception where name tags that said "Hello my name is . . . " were handed out. We fill in our name and some of us add a flourish to the script, something that identifies us as more than our name, that we are unique, bold, or creative. Some of us just try to spell our names correctly, hoping the labels won't be necessary for long and we can peel them off. Certainly we all remove the label as soon as we leave the scene.

Most of us have been on a job interview or first date, the kind of interaction where we try to make a good first impression with our appearance. For a job interview we dress in business attire, something that signals our seriousness and professionalism. For the first date we select clothing, hairstyles, accessories, and even scents that improve our physical attractiveness, signal our social status, or use our style to signal something about our personality. "You never get a second chance to make a first impression," is a logically correct statement, but we never really stop managing the impression we want to make on others and our efforts to manage impressions continue long after the first impression is made.

Now imagine that you walk into a party and the host hands you a stick-on label that says "sex offender" on it. How will the other guests at the party respond to you? Will they treat you differently? What if you attend a reception and at the door you're given a label that says "drug addict"? Will people make polite conversation or ask you how the addiction is going? Or, will they just shun you so as to avoid the awkward conversation all together? With that stick-on label is there anything you can do or say that will cause people to see you in a positive light or is the negative label likely to override anything you can do or say? Does the label become the "master" of the situation, influencing everyone's opinion of you and how they act toward you? If you could, you would rip the label off before anyone could see it.

Suppose that when you went for your job interview or to meet your date for the first time you had to wear an orange jumpsuit just like the clothing worn by prisoners. What are your chances for getting that job? What kinds of inferences will the employer form about your character before even talking to you about your job skills? What about your date? What are the chances for a second date even if you are charming? How long will it take for you to convince your potential partner that you can be trusted—not just to avoid breaking the law, but to be a responsible and caring adult. It would take time, perhaps a long time, to convince the employer or romantic partner that there is more to you than the mistakes you made in your past.

Of course, few people would choose to wear labels like these in public. Even in jest we could anticipate others' responses to what these labels mean. When sociologists talk about *deviant labels* they refer to the meaning of the labels, others' responses to those meanings, the limitations the labels put on our social interactions, and finally what these social interactions signal to us about ourselves. When sociologists talk about *labeling* they refer to the processes by which we come to acquire, hold, and possibly remove the deviant labels. Labels and the labeling process are the subjects of what is broadly referred to as *labeling theory*.

To a sociologist, labeling is part of the process whereby people give meaning to an action or a person, and a "deviant" label is when that meaning refers to something that is "wrong," "bad," "immoral," "unpleasant," or any of the other dozen or so synonyms referring to a negative evaluation of an action or person. When an action is given a deviant label it implies that the community does not like that act, views it as harmful or unclean, will not trust a person who does such acts and are likely motivated to restrict the act with rules and punishments. When a person is given a deviant label it indicates that the individual has committed a deviant act and implies that the person's entire character is questionable. Labeling, as we will see, has negative consequences for both individuals' self-concept and their interaction with others.

Origins of the Labeling Concept

The concept that sociologists call "labeling" has its intellectual origins in pragmatist philosophy. Pragmatist philosophy first developed in the United States. The pragmatist philosophers addressed most of the great philosophical questions of the day but arguably their greatest contribution was their theory of epistemology—how do we know what we know?

Pragmatist philosophers, like William James, agreed with the naturalists that some knowledge is objective and can be known, but they also argued that human beings come to know things individually and not as part of a collective mind (James 1907). Because of this individuals often hold beliefs that are different from others' beliefs. While one belief may be true and another may be false, this distinction does not matter to the people holding the false (or true) beliefs. If someone believes something is true, then that person will act on that "truth" regardless of how "real" or "accurate" the belief is. This argument is often known in sociology as the Thomas Theorem: "If men define situations as real, they are real in their consequences (Thomas and Thomas 1928)."

George Herbert Mead (1934) applied this observation to how people come to know themselves. Mead referred to this knowledge as the "self." Self-meaning is not something we are born with, we learn it through interaction with others. It begins early in life when our parents talk to us, call us by name, and describe the things we do. As we age the source of our self-meanings expands and we come to understand ourselves by "taking the role of the other," by seeing ourselves through others' eyes. Eventually the audience of others includes an abstract "generalized other," which is the source we reference when we think about what "they" may say about us. This, for Mead, represents the final stage of development as we are now capable of seeing and defining ourselves through a specific other's eyes or through the eyes of the generalized other.

These intellectual developments, and the work of some other early sociologists, came to be known as *symbolic interactionism*. This perspective recognizes the importance of an individual's knowledge, of how a person comes to know about the world including his or her self, to explain both individual behavior and patterns of social interaction. For sociologists who study deviance, this perspective provides an explanation for how people come to know what behaviors are deviant (or not) and which people are deviant (or not). For the symbolic interactionist this knowledge is not a simple matter of what is true or false about a behavior or person, but rather what people think they know about a behavior or person and how that knowledge affects their interactions with others.

Consider our example of the would-be Romeo who wears an orange prison jumpsuit to his first meeting with a potential romantic partner. For Romeo the suit could be an unfortunate error, a faux pas from someone who had no experience, or poor judgment in selecting the proper attire for a first date. Or, Romeo could be trying to signal something about his personality or personal philosophy, that he is an independent person not afraid to violate social convention, a dramatic individual, and a daring stylist.

To the potential romantic partner, however, the orange jumpsuit could be interpreted as poor fashion sense, someone with poor judgment for how his date may feel sitting in public with someone dressed as a prisoner, perhaps Romeo has some kind of mental deficiency or illness, or in the most extreme case that Romeo is in fact an escaped prisoner! The point here is that the orange prison jumpsuit has meaning attached to it, a meaning that is most likely defined in a negative direction and says something about Romeo's general character.

The orange jumpsuit confers a "label" on Romeo, which not only affects his interaction with the potential romantic partner but also his interaction with others in the social setting and potential future interactions with others who hear about his absurd wardrobe selection. For Romeo's potential partner it doesn't matter what is "true" regarding the wardrobe selection; Romeo's date defines the situation and acts as if that definition is "true." This definition, or meaning, then has real consequences for Romeo's chances of any future romantic interactions. Once the label sticks it will be hard to remove and Romeo will have a hard time repairing his damaged reputation. Over time Romeo will come to define himself as he perceives others see him and the poor wardrobe selection becomes a self-fulfilling prophecy—he is a loser, a freak, a weirdo, and he continues down that path.

Development of the Labeling Concept

Now, substitute another label for the orange jumpsuit, a label like "delinquent" or "pot-head." Like a bright orange jumpsuit people know about the label and, whether true or not, deserved or not, act toward Romeo as if it is true. Because delinquency and drug use are generally evaluated as "bad" in our society, Romeo will be evaluated as "bad," a deviant. The community makes a big deal about Romeo's truancy and pot smoking, dramatizes the deviant behavior such that the community makes an example of Romeo, and holds him and his actions out as something the community must shun and put to an end.

Frank Tannenbaum (1938) referred to this process as the "dramatization of evil" and it pointed to the role that the audience plays in defining who Romeo is, what his character is and whether or not he is worthy of normal social interaction in the community. Tannenbaum's argument stood in stark contrast to other explanations for deviance at the time that focused on the defects of the rule breaker. Tannenbaum argued that the community, the audience, those reacting to and interacting with Romeo played as much a role in Romeo's behavior as anything that might be "wrong" with Romeo. In fact, Tannenbaum argued, the more the community reacts to Romeo's rule breaking, the more "wrong" Romeo becomes. Delinquents, in other words, are created, not born.

What happens if Romeo somehow evades detection? What if no one notices his shoplifting and glue sniffing? Will people treat Romeo as a deviant if they aren't aware that he is misbehaving? Of course not; people have to first have the knowledge before they can treat it as real and thus create real consequences for Romeo. Edwin Lemert (1951) explained that there is a real difference between primary deviance—a person's activities and self-meaning before detection, and secondary deviance—activities and self-meaning after detection. Prior to detection Romeo can construct his self-meanings however they suit him; he is a daredevil, not a shoplifter; a person who enjoys a good time, not a glue sniffer. After detection, after people act toward Romeo as a shoplifter or glue sniffer, he now must contend with that new self-knowledge.

So what will Romeo do? How will he respond? One outcome is that he will stop stealing things and stop huffing; he will be ashamed of his behavior and desire the good opinions of his fellows, so he stops stealing and sniffing. To the community this is the preferred outcome and labeling in this sense is an important aspect of social control. Emile Durkheim (1895) referred to this as "boundary maintenance." Observation tells us, however, that the preferred outcome is often not the actual outcome.

Being called a deviant, let's pick on Juliet, a "slut" for example, could have the exact opposite effect. Juliet will take the role of the other and, in turn, accept that self-meaning. She may say to herself, "well if people are going to treat me as a slut, I may as well act like one." The subsequent sexual relations, the secondary deviance, further the shaming and ostracization, which compels Juliet to even more of the kind of behavior the community is trying to prevent. Leona Tannenbaum (1999) studied three generations of women who were labeled "sluts" and found this to be a consistent description of their experience with the label.

So deviant labels are generally not something people want; like the smell of rotten eggs, the deviant label is noxious. People, then, go to some length to avoid detection or, if detected, to try and put a positive spin on their activity. Erving Goffman (1963), like Lemert, saw a clear distinction between those whose deviance is not known, the "discreditable," and those whose deviance is known, the "discredited." People try to avoid the "stigma" of deviance whether it is one's sexual proclivities or the fact that one is an atheist in a small Midwest town—either knowledge is potentially damaging to one's social interactions and self-concept. The reason stigma is so damaging is that it becomes a "master status," the social status that most defines who we are, superseding all other status in the eyes of others. Both the discredited and discreditable manage information about themselves to avoid, if they can, the noxious smell of the deviant label.

Does it matter if Juliet is actually sexually promiscuous? Will she be labeled a slut even if she has never had sex with anyone? Tannenbaum's research reveals that sexual activity has very little to do with the application of the slut label; a simple rumor will have people treating Juliet as a slut. This is consistent with the pragmatist epistemology that it doesn't matter whether or not a fact is true; if people believe it is true then the consequences of the false label are as real as the consequences of a true label. Howard Becker (1963) referred to Juliet's predicament as that of the "falsely accused" and as unjust as it seems there is very little Juliet can do once the label has been applied. This "fact" about Juliet becomes the reality that people believe and they will treat her accordingly. Juliet is now stigmatized, discredited, and faces the consequences of the noxious slut label.

In a just world Juliet would never be falsely accused and labels would be applied equally regardless of one's social status, but stratified societies are often unjust. Romeo, for example, will never be called a slut for hooking up with multiple females, in fact he may be praised with a "stud" label. Gender is one dimension of social status that determines how an identical behavior is differently labeled. In a seminal study whose results have been replicated again and again, William Chambliss (1973) documented how stratification can shield high-status persons from the noxious effects of deviant labels while condemning low-status individuals to accept whatever taint is put on them.

Chambliss' key finding was that two groups of teenagers, both engaged in rule breaking and sometimes dangerous behavior but from different sides of the proverbial tracks, experienced labeling differently. The "Saints" were routinely involved in deviance ranging from truancy to extremely reckless and drunken driving but were never punished by the town's social control agents (police, teachers, parents). Their behavior was attributed to boys "sowing their wild oats" through the shenanigans of youth. All of these boys went on to be successful.

The "Roughnecks" were also engaged in deviance including fighting and theft, but their behavior seemed visible to everyone and the town's control agents routinely busted them. Most of the Roughnecks' lives went bad, several died, and the only ones who escaped the label were two young men who went to college on athletic scholarships. Once they were away from the town that readily stigmatized them they were able to construct new self-meanings and they managed to put together successful lives.

Application of the Labeling Concept

Social status is not the only factor that affects how sticky a deviant label can be. Mental health professionals have long noted the second-class status of their clientele. People with mental health problems act strange; how else would we know they have a mental illness? Because of their weird activities we infer that they are also unpredictable and possibly dangerous. People with mental illnesses are difficult to cure, most never recover or get better—or so the common knowledge goes, and our common knowledge is often all we have. As a result people who exhibit behavior that is simply strange, odd, weird, but not criminal, are susceptible to a negative label: crazy, deranged, mad, disturbed, unhinged, and so on.

Thomas Scheff (1966) saw in labeling theory an explanation for his observations on the progression of mental illness. What may begin as simple eccentricity often seemed to devolve into a full-fledged commitment to one of the insane asylums of the time. Once committed to the mental health system no amount of normal behavior could remove the stigma of mental illness.

This fact was clearly demonstrated by Rosenhahn's (1973) novel quasi-experiment where "normal" people with no history of mental illness presented themselves at a psychiatric hospital complaining about headaches and hearing faint voices. They were immediately committed to the hospital with various diagnoses. While institutionalized the "sane" people acted completely normal, which in some cases was interpreted by the mental health professionals as further evidence of mental illness! Even upon release Rosenhahn's confederates, as normal and sane as you and I, were not "cured" of their illness that was in "remission." The "insane" label had stuck and nothing could remove the adhesive.

Link et al. (1989) offered a "modified labeling theory" of mental illness and provided substantial empirical evidence that the stigmatizing effects of labeling mental illness produced worse outcomes for those labeled. Critics of labeling theory often point to labeling theory's lack of an explanation for the origin, the etiology, of deviant behavior but concede that labeling theory's strength lies in what happens *after* the deviant labels are applied. Link and his colleagues demonstrated this in samples of mental health patients and members of the community. Once people discover that someone is diagnosed with a mental illness they form a stereotype of the afflicted person, apply a master status, and devalue and discriminate against the labeled person. Their data also demonstrated the lengths to which the "discreditable" will go to avoid detection as well as their use of information management once they are "discredited." It may not be the case that labeling *causes* mental illness, but it is clear from the data that labels make life harder for those trying to lead normal lives with the stigma of a mental disorder.

So it seems clear that deviant labels have powerful effects on people's social interaction and as a result their self-concept. It is also clear that people will go to great lengths to avoid the noxious effects of deviant labels. But how do people "manage information" once they are discredited? Goffman (1963) proposed that discredited people may take the opportunity to teach others about their misperceptions, to explain that the others' judgments and stereotypes are wrong. Link et al. (1989) found this was a common strategy among mental patients. Blinde and Taub (1992) observed similar strategies among female athletes facing the stereotype that they were "lesbians" because they acted like men, that is, enjoyed athletic competition. Although the female athletes are falsely accused, they are acutely aware of the stigma and often try to hide their athletic ability. If it is known they manage the information about themselves by either trying to present themselves as ultra-feminine with makeup and clothing choices or try to educate their audience regarding the inaccuracy of the stereotype by simply insisting that there is nothing wrong with being a lesbian.

Scott and Lyman (1968) proposed a theory of "accounts" to explain the various ways in which a discredited person may avoid the effects of stigma by "justifying" or "excusing" their untoward behavior. The deviant gets one chance to deflect the label and return things to normal. Romeo, for example, excuses his pot smoking by saying that his friends made him do it. He knew it was wrong but under the circumstances had little choice. Juliet may try to justify her sexual promiscuity by reminding everyone that men do not face the stigma. She chose to do what she did but if it is not wrong for men to do it then it is not wrong for her to do it. The key components to offering an account then are (1) whether or not the act should be defined as deviant and (2) whether or not the act was intentional. An excuse denies intention but accepts the definition of the act as wrong, while a justification accepts responsibility but denies the act was wrong.

We offer excuses and justifications all of the time for our minor transgressions—arriving late, forgetting something at the store, yelling at our children—but Scully and Marolla (1984) found that even the most vile deviants, convicted rapists, can easily access a culturally defined "vocabulary of motive" to excuse and justify their actions. They interviewed convicted rapists behind prison walls and found them ready to offer excuses ("I was high/drunk at the time") or justifications ("she aroused me with her dress and flirtation") that they anchored in culturally based reasoning regarding the role women play in perpetrating their own rapes. To be sure, these excuses and justifications did not sway the juries, thus the men's incarceration, but the manner in which the rapists accessed cultural beliefs about women's roles is highly suggestive of how these men were socialized to perceive women.

Status of the Labeling Concept

> . . . social groups create deviance by making rules whose infraction creates deviance, and by applying those roles to particular people and labeling them as outsiders. From this point of view, deviance is not a quality of the act the person commits, but rather a consequence of the application by other of rules and sanctions to an "offender." The deviant is one to whom that label has been successfully applied; deviant behavior is behavior that people so label. (Becker 1963:9)

Howard Becker's often quoted and cited statement on how to define deviant behavior (deviance) and deviant individuals (deviants) is the basis of the *reactive definition of deviance*. You will find this definition discussed in nearly every textbook on crime and deviance, usually juxtaposed with the "normative" definition (behavior that violates rules) or the "harm" definition (behavior that causes harm). Becker's definition puts him squarely in the tradition of the pragmatist epistemology; we know something is deviant by how people react to it and we know deviant people by how others react to them. The validity of the definition is not an issue; the only issue is simply whether or not people *believe* it to be true and act on that belief. This definition certainly has its detractors but there is no mistaking the tremendous impact it continues to make on the sociological study of deviance (see Konty 2006, 2007 for the current state of the debate).

Ross Matsueda (1992) and his colleague Karen Heimer (1994 with Matsueda) measured the "symbolic" components of labeling theory, "role-taking and role-commitment," and used statistical methods to demonstrate the effects deviant labels had on future acts of delinquency. Their "theory of differential social control" argued that the judgments of "significant others" carried significant weight with adolescents. The more a teenager values another's opinion, the more he or she is affected by the negative judgments, the stigmatizing, that come from deviant labels. Up to that point quantitative evidence for labeling theory had been difficult to find because researchers were looking for the effects in the labels of formal social control agents (police, courts, probation officers) rather than the effects of labels from significant others like peers, parents, or other important adults. It turns out, to no one's surprise, that teenagers are more affected by those closest to them rather than those whom they only occasionally see.

Another promising extension of labeling theory is the reintegration of criminals back into society after they have been detected, labeled, and punished. Everyone knows about the absurdly high recidivism rates of the current prison system. Braithwaite (1989) compared societies with lower recidivism rates to those with higher recidivism rates and observed that societies that worked to reintegrate their felons back into the society had lower recidivism rates than those who continue to stigmatize their felons. "Reintegrative shaming" works because after the label is applied the felon is readmitted to society and no longer shunned to the margins. Instead of sticking the deviant label to them with superglue, the label is removed after the punishment is served, thus making it easier for the felon to reintegrate into society.

Braithwaite's insights and application of labeling theory gave birth to a policy movement known as "restorative justice" that is showing remarkable results in lowering recidivism rates. The movement has a long way to go, however, as felons in the United State must wear their label forever, like the orange prison jumpsuit, and deal with the consequences of the master status—difficulty finding a job or a place to live, not being able to vote, and even finding themselves ineligible for most types of volunteer work. With access to conventional society denied it is little wonder that most felons commit further crimes and find themselves back in our expensive prison system.

Summary

In sociology the concept of labeling is used in two interrelated ways. One involves the labeling of people as *deviants*, and the other is the labeling of actions as *deviance*. When people are labeled as deviant, others infer that the deviant's general character is suspect, the deviant label is a "spoiled identity" and a "master status" that overrides all others. Even if the person is "falsely accused" the noxious effects are still the same. The deviant label affects a person's social interaction as well as his or her self-concept.

Behavior that is labeled as deviance is always a violation of some social convention—a rule, a norm, a law, a custom—but not every violation is labeled as deviance. A person's social status may affect whether or not his or her violations are deviance, as when the Saints' dangerous activities or Romeo's sexual conquests are attributed to normal male behavior, while Juliet's sexual promiscuity is attributed to her slutty character. Violations also must be visible before they can be labeled as deviance and thus the effects of deviance are different before and after the label is applied.

Research on labeling continues to demonstrate important social and psychological processes. Adolescents, and adults, are affected by the opinions of others with whom they are close; they "take the role of the other" and shape their self-meanings accordingly. Even people with diagnosed, organic mental illnesses are profoundly affected by the "reflected appraisals" of others. "Discreditable" people will go to great lengths to evade the noxious affects of the deviant label and we all have a ready arsenal of culturally appropriate "excuses" and "justifications" to avoid or attenuate becoming "discredited." Finally, labeling theory and research produced a movement of reform in criminal justice based on the concept of "reintegrative shaming" and is demonstrating bright promise for reducing society's recidivism problem.

Discussion Questions

1. Make a list of deviant labels, then rank the list with the worst deviants at the top. What criteria did you use to rank them? Would your ranking be different if someone you were close to had one of these labels? What if that person was someone you respected, like a pastor or minister, prior to labeling that person a deviant? Now do the same thing with deviance. What criteria did you use to rank these behaviors? Could your list change over time? Why or why not?
2. You may have heard the observation that "a terrorist to one person is a patriot to another." How does labeling theory help us understand this well-documented phenomenon?
3. What do you think about the "restorative justice" movement? Do a web search on it and read about the policy changes its advocates propose. Do you think this movement is too easy on deviants? Does the offender avoid punishment and retribution? Or, does the policy make sense because it reduces the cost to taxpayers, reduces future crime rates, and is consistent with the concept of forgiveness?

References

Becker, Howard. 1963. *Outsiders.* New York: Free Press.

Blinde, Elaine. M. and Diane. E. Taub. 1992. "Women Athletes as Falsely Accused Deviants: Managing the Lesbian Stigma." *The Sociological Quarterly* 33:521–33.

Braithwaite, John. 1989. *Crime, Shame and Reintegration.* Cambridge, MA: Cambridge University Press.

Chambliss, William. J. 1973. "The Saints and the Roughnecks." *Society* 11:24–31.

Durkheim, Émile 1982 (1895). *The Rules of Sociological Method.* New York: Simon and Schuster.

Goffman, Erving. 1963. *Stigma: Notes on the Management of Spoiled Identity.* Englewood Cliffs, NY: Prentice-Hall.

James, William. 1907. *Pragmatism: A New Name for Some Old Ways of Thinking.* New York: Longmans, Green.

Heimer, Karen and Ross L. Matsueda. 1994. "Role-Taking, Role Commitment, and Delinquency: A Theory of Differential Social Control." *American Sociological Review* 59:365–90.

Konty, Mark. 2006. "Of Deviants and Deviance." *Sociological Spectrum* 26:621–30.

Konty, Mark. 2007. "'When in Doubt Tell the Truth': Pragmatism and the Sociology of Deviance." *Deviant Behavior* 28:153–70.

Lemert, Edwin. M. 1951. *Social Pathology.* New York: McGraw-Hill.

Link, Bruce G., Francis E. Cullen, Elmer Struening, Patrick Shrout, and Bruce. P. Dohrenwend. 1989. "A Modified Labeling Theory Approach to Mental Disorders: An Empirical Assessment." *American Sociological Review* 54:400–23.

Matsueda, Ross L. 1992. "Reflected Appraisals, Parental Labeling, and Delinquent Behavior: Specifying a Symbolic Interactionist Theory." *American Journal of Sociology* 97:1577–1611

Mead, George. H. 1934. *Mind, Self, and Society.* Chicago, IL: University of Chicago Press.

Rosenhaun, David. L. 1973. "On Being Sane in Insane Places." *Science* 179(70):250–58.

Scheff, Thomas J. 1966. *Being Mentally Ill.* Piscataway, NJ: Aldine Transaction.

Scott, Marvin B. and Stanford Lyman. 1968. "Accounts." *American Sociological Review* 33:46–62.

Scully, Diana and J. Marolla. 1984. "Convicted Rapists' Vocabulary of Motive: Excuses and Justifications." *Social Problems* 31:530–44.

Tanenbaum, Leora. 1999. *Slut: Growing Up Female with a Bad Reputation.* New York: Harper Collins.

Tannenbaum, Frank. 1938. *Crime and the Community.* New York: Columbia University Press.

Thomas, William I. and Dorothy S. Thomas. 1928. *The Child in America: Behavior Problems and Programs,* pp. 571–72. New York: Knopf.

ARTICLE 4

Addrain Conyers
Marist College

Conflict Theory: The Ongoing Battle

During slavery times in America, legislation was enacted to define the roles of slaves and slave owners. These laws were known as slave codes. The codes gave the owners legal ownership and authority over their slaves. After slavery ended in America the slave codes were converted to black codes. Black codes were used to control the lives of the freed slaves. Eventually, the black codes were found unconstitutional and Jim Crow laws were created which allowed legal segregation of blacks and whites. Through time, these laws were also found unconstitutional. The constants throughout the change of laws were for one group to remain in power, another group to be subservient, and the subordinates fighting for equal rights. The constant struggle between the two groups is known as conflict.

The aforementioned struggle has not completely ceased. The laws became a part of the social norms that continue to plague race relations in America. This conflict has existed for centuries and serves as a historical and contemporary example of what conflict theorists examine: social and political mechanisms that create norms and deviance. Conflict theory is a point of view used to categorize a set of social structural theories with a common perspective: society is better categorized by conflict than consensus (Williams III and McShane 2010). Conflict theorists question the origins of laws and norms that define crime and deviance. The dominant group holds power in defining laws, norms, and values; consequently, the subordinate group will be viewed as deviant if they do not meet or pursue the dominant norms of society. The ruling class's goal is to maintain power at the cost of oppressing subordinate groups (Turk 1969; Quinney 1970); therefore, conflict theorists actually question the true intent and purpose of the laws and norms created (Turner 2003). Unlike other perspectives, conflict theorists do not focus their attention on the actual deviant behavior, but rather the norms and values that define deviance.

The Beginning

Conflict theory is founded in the work of Marx and Engels (1992 [1848]) and (Savur 1975). The Marxist perspective does not focus on deviant behavior itself, but the exploitative culture of capitalism. According to Marx, two social classes exist in a capitalist society, the bourgeoisie and the proletarians. Capitalism leads to this division and creates a small number of people in power and many people in subordination. The bourgeoisie are the ruling class. The proletarians are a class of laborers who are exploited by the bourgeoisie. Despite having less power, the proletarians are many in number. They become class conscious and aware of their social status. They mass together and fight against the exploitation of the powerful, hence the conflict. Capitalism is viewed as the cause of the conflict because of the economic and social disparity it creates.

Class consciousness is constant in a stratified society. This class consciousness not only causes conflict, but also leads to the proletarians desiring to be a part of the dominant group. The strength of the dominant group not only exists in their economic power, but their ability to have the working class believe and desire the dominant cultural norms. Marx and Engels did not address crime or deviance specifically, but their work guided future theorists to explore the high correlation between conflict and crime. There are other strands of power that can cause conflict besides economic class; however, many of the early conflict theorists assessed crime and deviance from the Marxist perspective and focused more on class struggle and how the law is an instrument of power for the dominant group (Spitzer 1975; Quinney 1977).

Class and Crime

Willem Bonger (1969) discusses how the economic conditions of capitalism will lead to an increase in crime rates. Capitalism will divide society into segments, and will consequently lead to egoism. This type of egoism brings about a criminal mind. An individual's position and skills will determine the type of crime he or she will commit. This is important because it introduces the idea that the upper class, as well as the lower class, is susceptible to this egoistic state of mind, which can lead to economic crimes. He states:

> A man who knows how to make counterfeit bank-notes will commit this crime, whenever he wishes for any reason to enrich himself in a dishonest fashion, but he will become neither an incendiary nor a procurer. A former prostitute, on the contrary, will not think of making bank-notes, but will become a procuress. The kind of economic crime committed by the person who has a mind to commit such a crime, depend principally upon chance (occupation, etc.). (1969:90)

Bonger clearly acknowledges that everyone in a capitalist society is liable to commit economic crimes due to their egoism. What differs is the type of crime one will commit because of his or her status and class. This can range from street crime to white-collar crime.

Group Conflict

Two rival gangs, the grizzlies and polars, meet at 12 a.m. on Saturday to decide who will rule the local turf. Never mind how the analogous names relate to their bear-like behavior. Never mind the fact they are dueling to decide whose gang members are going to sell illegal drugs in the streets. And most importantly, never mind the fact that many deaths will result from this night. All that matters is that they cannot share the same streets because they are affecting each others' goals to dominate the criminal activity of the streets. The battle begins. . . .

Group conflict theory changes the focus from capitalism and economics to conflict based on group interests (Vold 1958). Different groups come into conflict when there are opposing viewpoints, more specifically competition "in the same general field of interaction." If the groups do not have to interact, conflict will not occur. Groups are formed based on similarities and common goals between individuals. These individuals identify with one another and come together for the greater good of their group. Void argues that the conflict between opposing groups helps solidify the loyalty of group members and develops their *group-mindedness* attitudes. "The individual is most loyal to the group for which he has had to fight the hardest and to which he had to give the greatest measure of self for the common end of group achievement" (Vold and Bernard 1986:272). Groups can be segmented on a number of common traits such as race, gender, class, age, and religion. When the group is relatively subordinate, such as youth gangs, it is known as *minority power group*. Vold's conflict theory is distinctive because of the focus on group interest and not capitalism.

Social Reality of Crime

Richard Quinney (1970) is best known for his integrated social reality of crime theory. His focus on capitalism and power as the cause of crime grounds his theory in the conflict perspective; however, different aspects of the theory clearly integrate social constructionism, labeling, and differential association. His theory is best summarized in his six propositions (p. 15–23):

> Proposition 1 (Definition of Crime): Crime is a definition of human conduct that is created by authorized agents in a politically organized society.
>
> Proposition 2 (Formulation of Criminal Definition): Criminal definitions describe behaviors that conflict with the interests of the segments of society that have the power to shape public policy.
>
> Proposition 3 (Application of Criminal Definitions): Criminal definitions are applied by the segments of society that have the power to shape the enforcement and administration of criminal law.
>
> Proposition 4 (Development of Behavior in Relation to Criminal Definitions): Behavior patterns are structured in segmentally organized society in relation to criminal definitions, and within this context persons engage in actions that have relative probabilities of being defined as criminal.
>
> Proposition 5 (Construction of Criminal Conceptions): Conceptions of crime are constructed and diffused in the segments of society by various means of communication.
>
> Proposition 6 (The Social Reality of Crime): The social reality of crime is constructed by the formulation and application of criminal definitions, the developments of behavior patterns related to criminal definitions, and the construction of criminal conceptions.

Throughout the six propositions Quinney's reference to power and conflict is evident, but he also incorporates concepts of earlier established sociological and criminological theories. His first proposition focuses on the definition of crime as created by those in power. The manner in which one defines and constructs his or her reality is based on his or her personal background and experiences (Berger and Luckman 1966). In reference to the definition of crime, it is based on the formulation of those in power. Quinney's second and third propositions focus on the division of groups and specifically how the group in power will have the leverage to enforce their definitions. This is related to Vold's (1998) view on group conflict and how those in power will be able to control and dominate the law. The second proposition is also grounded in the labeling perspective due to the focus on moral entrepreneurs (Becker 1963). Quinney's fourth proposition references Sutherland's (1947) *Differential Association* theory as criminal behavior is learned based on one's surrounding norms. Quinney (1970) states: "Therefore all persons—whether they create criminal definitions or are the objects of criminal definitions—act according to normative systems learned in relative social and cultural settings" (p. 20). The fifth proposition also has roots in social construction and the labeling perspective due to the constructed conceptions being "diffused" throughout society. The diffusion refers to the media's ability to spread the constructed definitions of crime in a manner that disguises its dominant origins. His last proposition summarizes the focus of his theory: crime is socially constructed based on criminal definitions of the powerful.

Contemporary Trends

Liz, a young female college student working two jobs to make ends meet is riding the bus on her way home at 11 p.m. She cannot afford to live on campus, so she still lives with her family in the inner city. After a 45-minute ride, she finally arrives at her stop. She has three more blocks to walk before she is finally home to rest before her 8 a.m. class. As she turns on the block where her family resides, someone runs up from behind, hits her on the head with a bottle, and snatches her purse. She screams loud enough to startle a few neighbors. House lights turn on and the attacker flees. For Liz, this is not hypothetical, but reality.

Left Realist

Left realists emerged in the 1980s in Great Britain. Their main objective was to produce "real" policies to address the issue of crime. In essence, crime is a social problem that needs to be realistically addressed. Young (1992) argues that "criminology should be faithful to the nature of crime" (p. 26). Realists confront previous strands of conflict theory that focused on the definition of laws and norms:

> It is unrealistic to suggest that the problem of crime like mugging is merely the problem of mis-categorization and concomitant moral panics. If we choose to embrace this liberal position, we leave the political arena open to conservative campaigns for law and order . . . the reality of crime in the streets can be the reality of human suffering and personal disaster. (Young 1976:89)

Left realists focus their concerns on the impact of crime on the working class (Young 1986). The working class is viewed as the victim because they are the most vulnerable and constantly in position to be violated. Young (1992) argues there are four variables that should be used to explain crime: a victim, an offender, the public, and social control. The social relationships between these four variables can explain crime rates. In other strands of conflict theory the deviant is viewed as a victim, but in left realism the "real" victim is the vulnerable working class citizen.

Peacemaking Criminology

Quinney traveled from his Marxist roots to his current stance in peacemaking criminology (Anderson 2002). He is best known for his *Social Reality of Crime*, but he joined other theorists in a more recent movement known as "peacemaking" criminology (Pepinsky 1988, 1999; Quinney 1988; Pepinsky and Quinney 1991). The focus veers from traditional conflict theories by focusing on positive interaction, which can reduce conflict, and consequently reduce crime (Pepinsky 1999). Peacemaking encourages self-reflection of the individual to see how one can positively contribute to a peaceful community (Pepinsky and Quinney 1991). The government should be more concerned with the well-being of others, and not cause division by focusing on offenders. This division feeds the existing conflict. The justice system can promote positive interaction and community cohesiveness through changing the police, court, and correctional philosophies. For example, if police were to focus more on community policing rather than watchmen style they could promote positive interaction in the community. Overall, the peacemaking approach is designed to ameliorate the conflict.

Discussion

The conflict perspective is not limited to crime and law, but can also be applied to societal norms. For example, beauty norms (i.e., hair, complexion, and figure) in America are commonly associated with Euro-American physical characteristics—the dominant group in the country. Any deviation from the norms can result in a spoiled identity based solely on physical characteristics. A spoiled identity due to conflict is not always instantaneous; it can be a process. Turk (1969) in his *Criminality and Legal Order* focused on the criminalization process. This process acknowledges the role of authority in the criminalization process. Subjects who conflict with the norms and demands of authority are more likely to be labeled criminal; therefore, authority plays a bigger role in criminalizing behavior compared to subjects committing the behavior.

Overall, conflict theory has many different *perspectives*, which all view crime and deviance as a consequence of conflict. Conflict theorists, like labeling theorists, are not necessarily concerned with the cause of the behavior, but with who defines the cause. The focus, commonly, is the oppressive system. This oppressive system can vary based on the demographics of a population (e.g., race, class, gender, and religion) and which group possesses the power. Despite many theorists' attention to the dominant group's use of power, many have also directed their attention to conflict between groups of comparable power (Simmel 1950; Vold 1958; Dahrendorf 1958, 1959). It is also important to note that the conflict perspective has also led to the creation of a conflict resolution theory (Hansen 2008). The conflict perspective provides an overview and framework of what causes conflict and can help practitioners regulate conflict between opposing parties. The conflict perspective will always serve a purpose in addressing crime and deviance as long as social stratification is in existence. As society evolves the dynamics of the stratification may change, but this perspective will always be relevant in explaining the consequences of conflict.

Discussion Questions

1. Based on conflict theory, there are dominant and subordinate groups. The dominant group controls the laws and norms of a society. Can you identify both a dominant and subordinate group you are a member of? Which one is easier to identify? Why?
2. How does power shift when one group is more powerful and does everything to maintain that power?

References

Anderson, Kevin. B. 2002. "Richard Quinney's Journey: The Marxist Dimension", *Crime Delinquency*, 48:232–41.

Berger, Pete. L. and Thomas Luckman. 1966. *The Social Construction of Reality: A Treatise in the Sociology of Knowledge*. New York: Anchor Books.

Becker, Howard. S. 1963. *Outsiders: Studies in the Sociology of Deviance*. New York: The Free Press.

Bonger, William. 1969. *Criminality and Economic Conditions*. Bloomington, IN: Indiana University Press.

Dahrendorf, Ralf. 1958. "Out of Utopia: Toward a Reorientation of Sociological Analysis." *American Journal of Sociology*, 64:115–27.

Dahrendorf, Ralf. 1959. *Class and Class Conflict in Industrial Society*. Stanford, CA: Stanford University Press.

Hansen, Toran. 2008. "Critical Conflict Resolution Theory and Practice." *Conflict Resolution Quarterly* 25:403–27.

Marx, Karl and Friedrich Engels. 1992 (1848). *Communist Manifesto*. New York: Bantam.

Pepinsky, Harold. E. 1988. "Violence as Unresponsiveness: Toward a New Conception of Crime." *Justice Quarterly* 5:539–63.

Pepinsky, Harold. E. 1999. "Peacemaking Primer" In B. *Social Justice: Criminal Justice*, edited by, A. Arrigo. Belmont, CA: Wadsworth.

Pepinsky, Harold and Richard Quinney, eds. 1991. *Criminology as Peacemaking*. Bloomington, IN: Indiana University Press.

Quinney, Richard. 1970. *The Social Reality of Crime*. Boston, MA: Little, Brown.

Quinney, Richard. 1977. *Class, State and Crime: On the Theory and Practice of Criminal Justice*. New York: McKay.

Quinney, Richard. 1988. "Crime, Suffering, Service: Toward a Criminology of Peacemaking." *Quest* 1:66–75.

Savur, Manorama. 1975. "Sociology of Conflict Theory." *Social Scientist* 3:29–42.

Simmel, Georg. 1950. *The Sociology of Georg Simmel*. New York: Free Press.

Spitzer, Steven. 1975. "Towards a Marxian Theory of Deviance." *Social Problems* 22:638–51.

Sutherland, Edwin. H. 1947. *Principles of Criminology*, 3rd ed. Philadelphia, PA: Lippincott.

Turk, Austin. T. 1969. *Criminality and the Legal Order*. Chicago, IL: Rand McNally.

Turner, Jonathon. H. 2003. *The Structure of Sociological Theory*. 7th ed. Belmont, CA: Wadsworth.

Vold, George B. 1958. *Theoretical Criminology*. New York: Oxford University Press.

Vold, George. B. and Thomas J. Bernard. 1986. *Theoretical Criminology*, 3rd ed. New York: Oxford University Press.

Vold, George. B., Thomas. J. Bernard, and Jeffrey B. Snipes. 1998. *Theoretical Criminology,* 4th ed. New York: Oxford University Press.

Williams III, Frank. P. and Marilyn D. McShane. 2010. *Criminological Theory*, 5th ed. Upper Saddle River, NJ: Pearson Education.

Young, Jock. 1976. "Working Class Criminology." In *Critical Criminology,* edited by Ian Taylor, Paul Walton, and JockYoung. London: Croom Helm.

Young, Jock. 1986. "The Failure of Criminology: The Need for Radical Realism." In *Confronting Crime*, edited by Jock Young and Roger Matthews. London: Sage.

Young, Jock. 1992. "Ten Points of Realism." In *Rethinking Criminology: The Realist Debate*, edited by Jock Young and Roger Matthews. London: Sage.

 ARTICLE 5

Julie Ann Harms Cannon
Seattle University

Feminism and Deviance

Simply put, feminism is a movement to end sexism, sexist exploitation, and oppression. . . . As all advocates of feminist politics know, most people do not understand sexism, or if they do, they think it is not a problem.

(hooks 2000:1)

Although the field of deviance is firmly established within the discipline of sociology, deviance itself is both socially constructed and relative in nature. Rather than identifying deviance as a set of specific moral, ethical, or legal violations, the activity in question must simply be considered as any behavior that varies from the norm. While deviance has been studied from a variety of theoretical orientations, such as labeling theory, strain theory, differential association, control theory, and so on, feminist scholars have also contributed to our understanding of deviance, thus providing us with a more egalitarian view of deviant actors and participants.

Feminist Theories

It is important to note at the outset that while the following addresses many of the schools of thought within feminism, it is limited given the purpose of this article. Feminist theories are vast and varied and only a brief summation is given here. Even so, such an account will allow the reader to consider the many ways that feminist thought is applied to the myriad behaviors that are included within the field of deviance. Stated differently, these more general feminist theories while utilized to articulate a variety of oppressions related to race, class, gender, and sexuality can also illuminate our understanding of the specific area of gender and deviance.

Patriarchy and sexism are important concepts to understand if one is to apply a feminist critique to any behavior. First, *patriarchy* can be defined as "the assumption that they [men] are superior to females and should rule over us" (hooks 2000:ix). Although patriarchy causes disproportionate harm to women, hooks also argues that it is difficult to be in the position of dominance:

> In return for all the goodies men receive from patriarchy, they are required to dominate women, to exploit and oppress us, using violence if they must to keep patriarchy intact. Most men find it difficult to be patriarchs. Most men are disturbed by hatred and fear of women, by male violence against women, even the men who perpetuate this violence. But they fear letting go of the benefits. They are not certain what will happen to the world they know most intimately if patriarchy changes. So they find it easier to passively support male domination even when they know in their minds and hearts that it is wrong. (2000:ix)

In this sense, we can consider patriarchy the ideology that supports the unequal treatment of women, men, and others. This unequal treatment defines the second concept, *sexism*, "as a system of domination [that] is institutionalized" (hooks 1984:5) and restricts and oppresses women in their daily lives, although in different ways, depending on the racial/ethnic background, class, sexuality, and so on of diverse groups of women. Restated, patriarchy is the ideological support or foundation of institutionalized and individual sexism.

While earlier works necessarily addressed male biases in the field of deviance, emphasized the nature of the "deviant woman," described the specific sanctions against deviant women, and began to consider the interlocking nature of oppression (Miller 2001), the field of deviance is moving beyond this initial consideration of feminism. This movement is clearly indicated in Thio and Calhoun's (2001) earlier work, in which deviance is treated from a diversity of perspectives, including a diversity of feminist perspectives. Accordingly, this piece focuses on some of the more traditional schools of thought within feminism (even those that are less commonly used in scholarly research today) so that the reader can become better acquainted with the subject of feminism as it is more generally understood, and then moves to a more specific discussion of how different types of feminisms can be applied to specific case studies pertaining to women in the military and their portrayal in the media as victims or torturers (Tétreault 2006; Richter-Montpetit 2007; Lobasz 2008) and the reconfiguration of traditional "femininity" in the context of the rediscovered sport of women's roller derby (Carlson 2010; Finley 2010).

It should be noted that this line of thinking in no way diminishes earlier attempts to theorize deviance from a feminist standpoint. Rather, it is indicative of scholarly efforts to fully integrate feminism into the field of deviance rather than simply use an "add women and stir" approach (Ollenburger and Moore 1998; Tong 2009). Ideally readers will see feminism as a broad category of approaches that untangle the roles of patriarchy, race/ethnicity, social class, sexuality, and other forms of oppression as both backdrops and catalysts that explain and at times justify the deviant behavior of women and men in society.

In the following sections I describe the diversity of feminist thought and theories. Most importantly, the reader should note how each school of thought identifies the cause(s) of women's oppression, its proposed solutions, and the critiques of each. Although these frameworks have been hotly contested over the years, each has many adherents. When studying deviant behavior from a feminist perspective, consider which lens each scholar adopts. This is true for your own work as well.

Liberal Feminism

> In the liberal-feminist tradition, the cause of women's oppression is rooted in the individual or group lack of opportunity and education. The solution for change is for women to gain opportunities primarily through the institutions of education and economics. (Ollenburger and Moore 1998:17)

Although liberal feminism dates back to the eighteenth century, more contemporary liberal feminism deals with the "structural and attitudinal impediments to women's progress" (Tong 2009:35). Within this tradition three strains of thought have emerged. First, classical liberal feminists argue that changes in laws and policies are enough to create a more egalitarian society. Consequently, they favor both limited government intervention and a free market. "Freedom of expression, religion, and conscious play a major role in the psyches of classical liberal feminists" (Tong 2009:35). Second, welfare liberal feminists believe that it will take much more than policies, laws, and good intentions to eradicate gender inequality. Welfare liberals argue that feminism without the explicit backing of the government has no teeth. More specifically, the government must intervene on behalf of all citizens to provide equal "housing, education, health care, and social security" (Tong 2009:35). In addition, the government must intervene in the areas of taxation and profit if individuals, particularly women, will be able to "exercise their political and legal rights" (Tong 2009:35). Finally, some liberal feminists advocate androgyny as the solution to gender equality. From this perspective, if men and women were similar in terms of personality traits, interests, professions, and so on, there would be no logical reason for differential treatment on the basis of gender. In this way, both women and men could cultivate positive masculine and feminine traits. Consequently gender roles would be eliminated along with sex and gender discrimination. The major critique of liberal feminism is that it fails to embrace a systematic or institutionalized examination of patriarchy and sexism, particularly as related to diverse groups of women.

Marxist Feminism

> Traditional Marxist feminists trace the oppression of women to the beginnings of private property. The cause of women's oppression is linked to social organization of the economic order. (Ollenburger and Moore 1998)

Marxist feminists hold that capitalism is the primary source of women's oppression. In this respect, the only way to create gender equality is to dismantle capitalism as both an economic system and an ideology. Capitalism ties women to the home as producers of the working class. Additionally, women's work in the home helps to maintain the working class—their housework enables men to go out into the workforce to earn a wage. However, not all women are confined to the home. Because capitalism devalues the work of women and forces them to exist as reserve pools of cheap labor, women are relegated to lower-paying jobs, which ultimately brings down the wages of all workers and "establishes a sex-segregated workforce with differential pay scales" (Ollenburger and Moore 1998:20). Finally, within a capitalist system, women become consumers of goods that work to bolster the existing system and potentially further their own oppression—good examples would be wearing the latest style of shoes and clothes, using beauty care items, and getting breast implants. Of course, it is not only women but also men who suffer under such an economic system. However, Marxist feminists would argue that women are disproportionately oppressed under capitalism. The major critique of this perspective is that while capitalism is a very powerful tool of oppression, eliminating it will not necessarily free women. This will be discussed more fully later.

Radical Feminism

> Within the many radical-feminist perspectives, most fundamental of oppressions is patriarchy. In order for women to be free of oppression, the patriarchal structure of society must be changed. (Ollenburger and Moore 1998:21)

Within this perspective, the oppression of women is seen to be the oldest form of inequality, and furthermore, it is universal. Not surprisingly then, patriarchy is the most difficult form of oppression to eradicate (Jaggar and Rothenberg 1984). Within this school of thought the oppression of women is linked to the biological state of women in terms of childbirth and housework; the omnipresent threat of violence including but not limited to battering, rape, incest, sexual harassment, pornography; and to both heterosexism and homophobia—indeed, some lesbian feminists have argued that equality cannot exist as long as women's lives are tied to those of their oppressors via the patriarchal institution of marriage (Ollenburger and Moore 1998; Tong 2009). A powerful critique of this perspective relates to the pervasiveness of capitalism as an economic system and ideology. More specifically, even with the eradication of patriarchal ideology, as long as capitalism remains intact, women will never be free.

Socialist Feminism

> Among socialist feminists both patriarchy and class are regarded as primary oppressions. One form of oppression does not take precedence over the other. (Ollenburger and Moore 1998:23)

While some socialist feminists argued that an analysis of "production, reproduction socialization, and sexuality" is an appropriate beginning point for socialist feminism, others argued that an analysis of familial socialization, the institutional site where "the partnership of patriarchy and capitalism is legitimated" as being most essential (Ollenburger and Moore 1998:23). Regardless, this more inclusive definition of feminist thought identifies a two-pronged solution to women's oppression. Because socialist feminists argue that both capitalism and patriarchy are the primary sources of gender inequality, both must be eradicated to achieve a more equitable society. One critique of this perspective is that changing the deeply imbedded ideological values and practices, such as capitalism and patriarchy, will require a complex solution. Accordingly, Tong argued that "attitudes toward women will never really change as long as both female and male psychology are dominated by the phallic symbol" (Tong 2009:126). To be more specific, we must alter our understanding of what it means to be male and female in society using both nature (biology) and nurture (socialization) to understand the primary sources of women's oppression.

Cultural Feminism

> In a rejection of the masculine ideal and the devaluing labels placed on femininity by the patriarchal world, cultural feminists redefine femininity in a positive framework. (Ollenburger and Moore 1998:24)

Historically, cultural feminists idealized feminine traits over masculine traits. According to early cultural feminists, women naturally (or biologically) possess higher levels of nurturing, care, pacifism, community, that if properly recognized and channeled, would lead to more progressive and peaceful societies. However, because societies have overemphasized masculine qualities, such as physical strength, limited emotional expression, and aggression, societies have been stunted in terms of social progress and growth (Ollenburger and Moore 1998; Tong 2009).

While these earlier forms of cultural feminism have been criticized for their reliance on nature rather than nurture, later cultural feminists began to identify feminine and masculine traits as neither superior nor inferior, but rather different. More specifically, because women and men are socialized differently based on socially sanctioned gender roles, they are likely to respond differently in terms of their relationships, work lives, families, friendships, and so forth. Although contemporary cultural feminists consider gender in terms of socialization, this school of thought has been criticized for not challenging the reasoning behind these differences and working to dismantle a patriarchal system that fosters unequally valued roles for women and men (Ollenburger and Moore 1998; Tong 2009).

Multicultural, Global, and Postcolonial Feminism

> Sexism as a system of domination is institutionalized but it has never determined in an absolute way the fate of all women in this society. (hooks 1984:5)

Many feminists within and outside the United States have argued that women are differentially affected by sexism and patriarchy. The primary concept feminists have used to untangle the multifaceted nature of this oppression is intersectionality (Collins 1990). From this perspective, multiple oppressions cannot be treated individually, but rather must be considered as interlocking in nature. More specifically, one cannot consider race/ethnicity or culture without considering his or her relationship to gender—oppressions do not exist in isolation. While earlier feminists, such as liberal or cultural feminists, tried to create a sisterhood of women based on similarities, multicultural, global, and postcolonial feminists emphasize the diversity in women's lives—which oftentimes includes the importance of men's experiences of oppression related to race, class sexuality, and so on. From this perspective the term *women of color* came into being. However, this term has been critiqued for "othering" nonwhite feminists, while white women's experiences are taken as normative (Tong 2009). Additionally, many multicultural feminists argue that race/ethnicity is not necessarily the most salient identity of nonwhite women. Rather, questions of class, age sexuality, able-bodiedism, or other "self-identified cultures" become primary (Tong 2009).

Global and postcolonial feminists or "womanists" (Tong 2009) share much with their multicultural feminist counterparts, however; they address the ways that women's experiences are shaped by their global locations. As Tong (2009) notes, these theorists primarily focus on Third World women (women living in economically developing countries, usually found in the Southern Hemisphere) whose lives in many ways are controlled by the First World (more powerful and economically developed countries, usually found in the Northern Hemisphere). Major issues addressed by global and postcolonial feminists are reproduction, education, political involvement, family life, and so on. Additionally, global and postcolonial feminists find it important for First and Third World women to work together, recognizing both "diversity and commonality" (Tong 2009). However, an important critique of this perspective is that it is difficult "to strike a balance between universalism and relativism" (Tong 2009:233). Restated, women may have similar experiences of oppression, which should be identified, yet this does not make their experiences equivalent. Further, women who practice different cultures must respect one another, while perhaps disagreeing with particular elements of that culture.

Postmodern or Poststructuralist Feminism and Third-Wave Feminism

> Poststructuralist feminists reject traditional assumptions about truth and reality; in fact, they reject to the possibility of defining women at all. (Ollenburger and Moore 1998:25)

Although the term poststructuralist was used earlier to define this school of thought, postmodernism has become the more widely accepted term (Tong 2009). Postmodern feminism rejects dichotomous conceptions of social life such as gender (male/female), sexuality (gay/straight), privilege (oppressors/ oppressed), reason (objectivity/subjectivity), race/ethnicity (black/white), and reality (singular truths/multiple truths), to name a few. Postmodernists examine the sources of such dichotomous thinking in our textual realities and work to deconstruct them into more meaningful and accurate accounts of women's "everyday lives" (Smith 1987). Additionally, this school of thought works to deconstruct the categories noted earlier and articulate how and by whom they are defined (usually the more powerful). In this way women (and men) are given the power to define their own lives within a given particular institutional context such as the United States (Smith 1987; Ollenburger & Moore 1998; Tong 2009).

> Third-wave feminists are particularly eager to understand how gender oppression and other kinds of human oppression co-create and co-maintain each other. For third-wave feminists, difference is the way things are. (Tong 2009:284–285)

Much like multicultural, global, and postcolonial feminists, third-wave feminists embrace diversity in all its many forms, eschewing a monolithic or uniform conception of women. However, unlike earlier feminisms (those above would primarily be identified as part of the second wave), this particular school of feminist is known for its "messiness" (Dicker 2008; Tong 2009). However, this messiness is not accidental; third-wave feminism is messy by design. Third-wave feminists work to address all forms of oppression including but not limited to race/ ethnicity, class, gender, sexuality, nationality, culture, global location, and religion; consequently, their work invites and embraces many contradictions, including self-contradictions (Tong 2009). Because of the interlocking nature of these oppressions, third-wave feminists argue that individuals have very different experiences, depending on which facet of their lives is highlighted. Issues that were contentious for earlier feminists are moot for their third wave-counterparts. For example, "[i]f a woman wants to wear makeup, have cosmetic surgery, wear sexually provocative clothes, sell her sexual services, then, as far as many third-wave feminists she should feel free to do so, provided she feels empowered by her actions and not somehow demeaned, diminished, or somehow otherwise objectified by them" (Tong 2009:288). Third-wave feminism embraces the concept of choice more fully than any of its predecessors. However, this messiness is not fully embraced by all feminists. What seems to be most problematic is its attempt to include so much within its borders. More accurately, many would argue that third-wave feminism does not have enough of a platform or ideology to stand on. There is no singular vision. While third-wave feminists might argue that this is precisely the point, others are uneasy with this seemingly more casual approach to feminism. "The home of third wave feminists seems to be inhabited by a collection of strongly individual women, expressing each other's different feelings to each other and leaving it at that" (Dicker 2008; Tong 2009:289).

Feminist Theories and Deviant Behavior: A Case Study Approach

In what follows, I do not attempt to address each of the theories noted earlier. Rather, I have selected three themes that address elements of these works in very useful ways for the field of deviance—particularly those more "puzzling" areas that are not always easily defined as deviant (Thio and Calhoun 2001). To begin, I discuss the role of women in the Iraq War and the Abu Ghraib prison torture scandal, using three case studies related to a postmodern critique of liberal feminism and media presentations of women's roles as soldiers (Lobasz 2008), a postcolonial/multicultural critique of liberal feminism and the role of sexuality and women as torturers in the Abu Ghraib scandal (Richter-Montpetit 2007), and finally, a postmodern global feminist analysis of sexuality and the emasculation of "foreign" prisoners at Abu Ghraib (Tétreault 2006). Additionally, I present a postmodern, third-wave feminist analysis of two case studies of women's flat track roller derby (Carlson 2010; Finley 2010) and how this reinterpreted sport creates an alternative space for a newly imagined femininity.

Women Soldiers and War: Media Representations and Feminist Challenges

"Women in the military" has been a hotly contested topic in both society more generally and feminism more specifically. While many conservatives have argued that women cannot perform equally in battle conditions, liberal feminists have argued that women are just as capable as their male counterparts. However, diverse groups of feminists have been concerned with much more than the capabilities of women on the battlefield. They are equally concerned with media portrayals of women soldiers, women's roles as torturers, and also how sexism and homophobia have been used to humiliate men as prisoners of war (POW).

In the first case study presented here Lobasz (2008) addresses several important elements of women's role in the Iraq War. First, she argues that liberal feminists have argued that soldiers such as Pfc. (Private First Class) Jessica Lynch and Pfc. Lynndie England both performed as well as men under very harsh conditions. First, as a POW, Lynch was both injured and tortured (sodomized) and was presented in the media as going down with "guns blazing" (Lobasz 2008). According to liberal feminists this demonstrated her worth as a soldier. Yet very quickly, the media changed its tune. Very soon the media began to focus on her blonde hair, doe eyes, slight build, vulnerability, and innocence. Additionally, it turned out that she did not go down with a fight—she was merely captured and later rescued. While liberal feminists hoped that early depictions of Lynch would ensure women's equal treatment in the military, their hope backfired as Lynch was increasingly depicted as a "damsel in distress" (Lobasz 2008). This symbolic depiction of fragile femininity, a common media device, reinforced the negative views about women's capabilities on the battlefield (despite the fact that men were captured and rescued as well, a situation that was given a very masculine type of media attention). The Lynndie England story, although different, ended up being treated quite similarly in the media. Again although liberal feminists had hope that England's media representation regarding the Abu Ghraib prisoner torture scandal would demonstrate to the public that women were just as capable of abuse as men and therefore equal, the media spun the story in a much different direction. Unlike Lynch, the "damsel in distress," England was portrayed as a "fallen woman." Beyond the pictures linked to the abuse of prisoners, England was also portrayed as promiscuous, divorced, impregnated by her superior officer, and unable to make decisions for herself (she was just following orders). Though others (mostly men) were more highly involved in the prisoner abuse, England received far more media attention. This postmodern feminist approach provides a useful explanation for the differential treatment England received: "while feminists and gender traditionalists are likely to remain deadlocked on the subject of women's 'true' inner-nature, in the meantime the trope of the ruined woman is alive and well, and shaping our perceptions of gender roles and current events" (Lobasz 2008:329).

Richter-Montpetit (2007) agrees with Lobasz that a liberal feminist argument for gender equality was not the outcome of the prisoner abuse scandal at Abu Ghraib. This postcolonial, multicultural analysis of the scandal comes to very different conclusions. First the author argues that while the media and liberal feminists tended to downplay the extent of violence (including both murder and torture) at Abu Ghraib, they also neglected the sexual nature of the violence and the ways in which gender and sexuality were used in very traditional ways. Additionally, this violence committed against Third World "others" is part and parcel of a larger history of colonialism and violence on the part of the United States—violence that is carried out systematically based on race, class, gender, religious, and global inequality. While this does not detract from the accountability of individual soldiers, it does help us understand that such orders are commonplace occurrences although for the most part the public may be oblivious to these actions (Richter-Montpetit 2007). What makes average soldiers behave in such a manner? Ideologies of the superiority of whiteness, the need to save civilization itself, and militarized masculinity were all utilized to create such an environment (Richter-Montpetit 2007). Ideally, if you can convince soldiers that the civilized (read white) world rests on their shoulders, they will respond accordingly—this is not to argue that all soldiers will engage in torture, but it creates a climate in which torture, even murder, can be justified. Further, if you encourage a model of hyper-masculinity, you can conceive of torture that will both enlist the services of women soldiers and degrade the detainees by both humiliating and feminizing them. Dehumanization is also possible. "[T]o be feminized and sexualized by a female-identified soldier is deemed particularly humiliating for the colonized male body (and his nation). . . . I do not suggest that the 'female' soldiers were puppets in the service of racialized hetero-patriarchy, but rather that their motivations were located in colonial desires" (Richter-Montpetit 2007:47).

War photos are common—even those depicting dead enemies (Tétreault 2006). They have been used by soldiers as postcards as early as World War I. However, the types of photos captured at Abu Ghraib are not typically published, as "these are 'trophies' intended for limited distribution only" (Tétreault 2006:34). However, these photos were not merely souvenirs, they were criminal evidence—evidence that was at once sadistic, pornographic, and damning of the U.S. military. Consequently, the government worked hard to control what global and postmodern feminists call "orientalist spectacles" and the "masculine gaze." Stated differently, the government sought to limit our exposure to the highly ritualized, sexualized torture and murder of the "other" (in this case Muslim detainees). Women were used both within the walls of Abu Ghraib as torturers and outside as scapegoats to seemingly deemphasize the severity of the situation and make the scandal seem like nothing more than an aberration. But the use of women was strategic and purposeful. The military knew what it meant to torture and humiliate prisoners using sex, sexuality, and women soldiers. It was a deviant act. And more importantly, most condoned the actions of the guards. Only Specialist Joseph Darby resisted the violent and illegal acts he witnessed, so "yes, we are all torturers now" (Tétreault 2006:44).

Roller Derby, Postmodernist and Third-Wave Feminism: An Unconventional Femininity

Today's roller derby bears little resemblance to the early renditions first popularized in 1933 and coming back in the 1960s and 1970s (Carlson 2010; Finley 2010). In the early days, roller derby looked very much like our more contemporary depictions of professional wrestling—amusing, but not necessarily a serious sport. Most importantly, early on roller derby was contrived and full of amusing "high jinks" and stunts. It was designed to capture the attention of audience members and was never meant to be considered a serious athletic competition. Full of action and show it did just that, while in many ways still maintaining a traditional feminine sensibility for the skaters. Today's roller derby, while still theatrical in some respects, is a very high-speed, full-contact sport replete with serious strategies and very real injuries. Despite being very athletic in nature, roller derby is fraught with contradictions that appeal to third-wave feminist sensibilities. It is messy, individualistic in many ways, unconcerned with issues related to sexuality, sex, and fun—this is not your feminist mother's roller derby!

Finley (2010) takes issue with the hegemonic masculinity and hegemonic femininity required of "real" sports (the male role being more aggressive and the female role standing in as complementary) and argues that "derby girls" find ways to maneuver between the masculine world of contact sports, and the seemingly equivalent role set aside for women. Simply speaking there is no men's roller derby, so women do not occupy a complementary role. In this way, women are free to create "new spins" on old roles. More specifically, in roller derby, the role of the "pariah" (contaminated statuses for women such as "slut" or "bitch") does not stand in relation to men's roles and thus provides women with alternative forms of femininity (Finley 2010). Consequently, women are free to dress provocatively, dye their hair in unnatural hues, wear tattoos, use colorful language, and hit hard. They can take pride in their injuries and claim derby names that would otherwise be stigmatizing for women (e.g., Wicked Wonder, Bitch Barbie, Lola Fellonya, Naturally Blood, Maria Von Slap). And finally, in this realm women are free to maneuver in their relations with other women. Because "derby girls" work around traditional norms of masculinity and femininity, they often reject those women who work to support hegemonic masculinity by taking on the "girly girl" role. "Intragender competitions between women do not necessarily reproduce the gender order; they can undermine male dominance as well" (Finley 2010:379). Even the term *girl* works to subvert hegemonic masculinity because a "derby girl" is tough—even noting that she "skates like a girl" is a compliment; while a "girly girl" merely comes to show her panties to men without showing any regard for the rigors of the sport or the necessity of group practicing.

Carlson (2010) also examines the notion of emphasized femininity and the ways that the "Nowhere Roller Girls" (a roller derby league) contest this label through their actions on and off of the track. Additionally she addresses the "derby girl" as a "female significant" or someone who defies or undermines the norms of traditional femininity. Much like Finley (2010), Carlson (2010) concludes that women in roller derby challenge traditional expectations by flaunting the feminine in ways that subvert its oppression similarly to that of "punks" who participate in punk culture. "I explore how derby skaters, similar to punks, questioned socially meaningful relationships between the signified (i.e., emphasized femininity) and its different signifiers (namely, clothing, make-up, and sport practice)" (Carlson 2010:431). As noted earlier derby names are significant. Skaters are known only by their derby names and they are typically "playfully aggressive, menacing, raunchy, lewd, and clever, such as A Cup Killer, Chesstoserone, Lolita LeBruise, Brick shields, West Nile Iris, Lady Pain, Vicious Panties, and Clit Eastwood" (Carlson 2010:433). Derby girls dress "sexy," however; it is a sexuality that stands in stark contrast to the women's hyperaggression. While wearing bras, mini-skirts, fish net stockings, and so on, women proudly display their injuries, helmets, and padding—another way to subvert traditional norms of heterosexual beauty and femininity. Additionally, the "derby body" deviates from normative beauty standards. Women come to love a "big ass" so that they can perform the necessary "booty blocks" to help their team block the jammers (those who work to score points for the opposing team). While some women initially had hang-ups about their bodies, roller derby empowered them to embrace a larger feminine form. Finally, it is important to note that most "female significants" in the roller derby do not work toward institutional feminist ideals nor do they tend to consider race or social class in their analysis. Many simply skate to demonstrate that they are serious athletes and that roller derby should be considered a legitimate sport (Carlson 2010).

Conclusion

Deviance comes in many forms; however, many studies of deviance are amenable to a feminist theoretical framework. As you can see, feminist theories are diverse, are varied, and can describe a variety of social behaviors. Clearly, feminist theories within the field of deviance have worked to include a more systematic analysis of patriarchy and sexism and individual men are not actually the emphasis here. "When contemporary feminist movement first began there was a fierce anti-male faction. . . . As the movement progressed, as feminist thinking advanced, enlightened feminist activists saw that men were not the problem, that the problem was patriarchy, sexism, and male domination" (hooks 2000:67). It is this vision of feminism that must come to the forefront. Still negative images of feminism abound and much of this can be attributed to those who rejected men as comrades in struggle. The media had latched on to these depictions of feminists as man-haters and never fully let go. As more men and women begin to understand the necessity of deconstructing patriarchy and sexism and working together to do so, feminism stands a better chance of being recognized within an interdisciplinary context. Whether it is a more serious topic such as the Abu Ghraib scandal and the oppression and murder of detainees, or the lighter topic of women's roller derby, feminism has something to offer all areas of deviance. In this way, "feminism is for everybody" (hooks 2000).

Discussion Questions

1. Which feminist framework resonates more closely with your own worldview? How would you use this lens to study an area of deviance of interest to you?
2. How do feminist theories differ from more traditional theories of deviance? Do they function merely as frameworks or as testable theories for empirical studies?
3. How would a Marxist feminist explain Lynndie England's involvement in the Abu Ghraib incident? How might a liberal feminist explain the reemergence of the roller derby?

References

Carlson, Jennifer. 2010. "The Female Signifiant in All-Women's Amateur Roller Derby." *Sociology of Sport Journal* 27:428–40.

Collins, Patricia Hill. 1990. *Black Feminist Thought: Knowledge, Consciousness, and the Politics of Empowerment*. Boston, MA: Unwin and Hyman.

Dicker, Rory. 2008. *A History of U.S. Feminisms*. Berkeley, CA: Seal Press.

Finley, Nancy J. 2010. "Skating Femininity: Gender Maneuvering in Women's Roller Derby." *Journal of Contemporary Ethnography* 39:359–87.

hooks, bell. 1984. *Feminist Theory: From Margin to Center*. Boston, MA: South End Press.

hooks, bell. 2000. *Feminism Is for Everybody: Passionate Politics*. Cambridge, MA: South End Press.

Jaggar, Alice M. and Paula S. Rothenbug. 1984. *Feminist Frameworks: Alternative Theoretical Accounts of the Relation between Women and Men*, 2nd ed. New York: McGraw-Hill.

Lobasz, Jennifer K. 2008. "The Woman in Peril and the Ruined Woman: Representations of Female Soldiers in the Iraq War." *Journal of Women, Politics, & Policy* 29:305–34.

Miller, Jody. 2001. "Feminist Theory." Pp. 67–73 in *Readings in Deviant Behavior*, edited by Alex Thio and Thomas C. Calhoun, 2nd ed. Needham Heights, MA: Allyn & Bacon.

Ollenburger, Jane C. and Helen A. Moore. 1998. *A Sociology of Women: The Intersection of Patriarchy, Capitalism, and Colonization*, 2nd ed. Upper Saddle, NJ: Prentice Hall.

Richter-Monpetit, Melanie. 2007. "Empire, Desire and Violence: A Queer Transnational Feminist Reading of the Prisoner 'Abuse' in Abut Ghraib and the Question of 'Gender Equality.' " *International Journal of Politics*. 9:38–59.

Smith, Dorothy E. 1987. *The Everyday World as Problematic: A Feminist Sociology*. Boston, MA: Northeastern University Press.

Tétreault, Mary Ann. 2006. "The Sexual Politics of Abu Ghraib: Hegemony, Spectacle, and the Global War on Terror." *NWSA Journal* 18:33–50.

Thio, Alex and Thomas C. Calhoun, eds. 2001. *Readings in Deviant Behavior*, 2nd ed. Needham Heights, MA: Allyn & Bacon.

Tong, Rosemarie. 2009. *Feminist Thought: A More Comprehensive Introduction*, 3rd ed. Boulder, CO: Westview Press.

PART THREE

Physical Violence

Soon after 7:00 a.m. on April 16, 2007, the campus police at Virginia Tech University found two students in a dormitory who had been shot to death. About two hours later, the killer, a Virginia Tech senior, went to the school's engineering building. First he chained all the entrance doors shut. Then he headed to a German class and peered in as if he was looking for somebody. He left but soon returned. Quiet and purposeful, he shot the teacher in the head and methodically went around the room and took out the students one by one, pumping at least three bullets in each victim. He then went to three other rooms to carry out the massacre in the same way. After he killed 32 people, he committed suicide by shooting himself in the temple.[1]

Why do people commit such heinous acts of violence? This is a question that has been asked by the everyday citizen to the college professor. Stories of physical violence have always dominated our media headlines. Like a horror film, the public covers their eyes, but cannot resist following horrific events with questions of who? what? why? when? where? how? We cover two major topics in this part on physical violence: robbery and child abuse. Dee Wood Harper and Kelly Frailing discuss the different types of robbery from carjacking to residential robbery. Their article provides a historical and contemporary view on this violent crime. Elizabeth Mustaine covers the topic of violence in reference to the most innocent victims: children. She provides explanations of this form of deviance. She also goes on to discuss the fine line between corporal punishment and child abuse, offender demographics, and the long-term consequences of child abuse.

Note

1. Gibb, Nancy, "Darkness Falls: One Troubled Student Rains Down Death on a Quiet Campus." *Time*, April 30, 2007, 37–53.

ARTICLE 6

Dee Wood Harper
Loyola University New Orleans

Kelly Frailing
Texas A&M International University

Robbery

Introduction

The felony crime of robbery has enormous financial costs. In 2009, losses of an estimated $508 million were attributed to robberies (UCR 2009c). Robbery also has tremendous human and societal costs. This article introduces the crime of robbery. It begins by defining robbery and briefly describing trends in the crime, with a special focus on the type of robbery known as carjacking. A historical overview of robbery is provided and current patterns and trends in robbery are then discussed, followed by a description of both victim and offender characteristics. A number of different criminological theories on understanding robbery and why people commit this crime are explored in the next sections. This article concludes with a discussion on techniques used to prevent and control robbery. The aim of this article is to explore robbery from a variety of perspectives and to encourage readers to think critically about who commits robbery against whom and why and what can be done to curb this crime.

The Uniform Crime Reports (UCR), which are published every year by the Federal Bureau of Investigation (FBI), define robbery as "the taking or attempting to take anything of value from the care, custody, or control of a person or persons by force or threat of force or violence and/or by putting the victim in fear" (UCR 2009c). A slightly different definition is used internationally; in the Tenth United Nations Survey on Crime Trends and the Operations of Criminal Justice Systems, robbery "may be understood to mean the theft of property from a person, overcoming resistance by force or threat of force" and should also include purse- or bag-snatching and theft by violence (UNDOC 2008:10).

Robbery occurs most commonly on the streets and highways in the United States. In 2009, street and highway robberies in the United States accounted for 42.8 percent of the 408,217 robbery events known to the police (UCR 2009c). This was a decrease of 8 percent from 2008 and a 2.2 percent decrease from 2005. As alluded to in the definition mentioned earlier, these violent felony offenses involve the taking of anything of value from or under the control of another person by use of force or intimidation while the offender is armed with a dangerous weapon or when the offender leads the victim to believe he or she is armed with a dangerous weapon.

The second most common form of robbery in the United States is robbery of a residence, which includes home invasions and accounts for 16.9 percent of all robberies, followed by businesses at 13.7 percent. Gas station and convenience store robberies account for 7.8 percent. Bank robbery accounted for only 2.2 percent (8,981) of all robbery events, yet it yielded the greatest average return of $4,029 compared to the average robbery return of $1,244. Residential robbery (home invasion) was the only type of robbery that showed an increase (of 0.6 percent) from 2008 to 2009 (UCR 2009c).

FIGURE A6.1
Robbery Rate per 100,000 in the United States since 1990.

Source: UCR 1990–2009.

Figure A6.1 shows the robbery rate in the United States since 1990. The rate has been relatively stable since 2000, with an average of about 146 robberies per 100,000 people. The peak year during this time period was 1991, with a rate of about 273 per 100,000.

As mentioned earlier, there are different types of robbery (street, residential, etc.). A particularly modern form of armed robbery is carjacking. This section briefly describes this crime that combines auto theft with armed robbery. The term *carjacking* came into use via the media in the 1980s and some argue that the act of carjacking itself came into existence because of the development of more sophisticated auto theft prevention equipment that made it almost impossible to steal a car without the keys (Davis 2003). The U.S. federal statute forbidding carjacking was first enacted in 1992 and amended in 1994 and it currently reads as follows:

> Whoever, *with intent to cause death or serious bodily harm* takes a motor vehicle that has been transported, shipped, or received in interstate or foreign commerce from the person or presence of another by force and violence or by intimidation, or attempts to do so, shall (1) be fined under this title or imprisoned not more than 15 years or both, (2) if serious bodily injury results, be fined under this title or imprisoned not more than 25 years, or both, and (3) if death results, be fined under this title or imprisoned for any number of years up to life, or both *or sentenced to death* (18 U.S.C. § 2119; italics added to highlight the 1994 changes to the statute).

While the robbery rate in the United States has been relatively stable in recent years as seen earlier, the carjacking rate averaged 21 per 100,000 between 1993 and 1997 and dropped to 13 per 100,000 between 1998 and 2002 (Klaus 2004). Because of the potential for physical harm to the victim, carjacking is viewed as a serious crime that warrants severe penalties. As a felony offense, penalties for carjacking range from 3 years to 99 years at hard labor without benefit of parole, probation, or suspension of sentence, and under the federal statute, the penalty is death. Federal prosecution of carjacking in the United States usually involves a charge of carjacking, which carries a possible penalty of 15 years plus a $250,000 fine, with a mandatory consecutive sentence of seven years for using a firearm in a violent crime and another consecutive sentence of 10 years for being a felon in possession of a weapon, if applicable. The harshness of this prosecutorial strategy may have accounted for the decline in carjackings, as noted earlier.

Though it has received much media attention, carjacking has received little attention from criminologists. One exception includes Bruce Jacobs, Volkan Topalli, and Richard Wright's (2003) ethnographic study of 28 active carjackers in St. Louis, Missouri. The authors contend that the decision to commit carjacking is both mediated and shaped by participation in urban street culture.

Another exception is Linda Davis's (2003) study on carjacking in South Africa. She reports that South Africa leads the world in the carjacking rate. In 2000, the carjacking rate in South Africa was recorded at 34.1 per 100,000; by 2005, it had dropped to 26.5 per 100,000 (Carroll, 2006). Davis (2003) maintains that the country's history of apartheid and the associated culture of violence, rampart poverty, and unemployment, combined with the ineffectiveness of the criminal justice system to deal with the problem, accounts for the world's leading rate of carjacking. Davis interviewed a dozen imprisoned carjackers in South Africa and one of her more fascinating observations was that carjacking is a group activity executed by two to four males playing three distinctive roles, "namely, the 'pointer' (the individual pointing the weapon), the 'driver' (the individual who drives the vehicle), and the 'searcher' (the one responsible for searching the individual and the vehicle for weapons and anti-hijack devices)" (p. 175). Based on her interviews, Davis contends that carjacking is a large and rather lucrative business in South Africa. Cars are carjacked to be sold in other African nations and, quite frequently, simply to fill someone's order for car parts. At least in South Africa, the market for the vehicle or its parts in terms of make and model exists before the occurrence of the carjacking. Carroll (2006) maintains the drop in carjackings in South Africa between 2000 and 2005 may be indicative of the country adjusting to post-apartheid realities.

Efforts to combat carjacking have spawned an industry of technologies to make it difficult for carjackers to be successful car thieves. One such technology is a remote engine shutoff, which is designed to disable the automobile up to a quarter of a mile from the point where the theft occurred. The disabling of the car is tantamount to it running out of gas. A variant includes the vehicle sounding an alarm and blinking lights, thereby alerting bystanders. There are two parts to this antitheft system—the main control computer, which is mounted in the vehicle, and the reflector, which is worn by the authorized driver. The main control box receives a unique encrypted code from the reflector. Once the main control computer gets beyond a certain distance from the reflector, it triggers a series of relay actions that result in a fuel or ignition system disconnection. The driver maintains safe control over steering and braking but the vehicle will not start or back up (Forced Ignition Systems n.d.).

Another carjacking deterrent invented in South Africa, which as seen earlier is notorious for carjacking, is a vehicle-mounted flamethrower, patented by Charl Fourie in 1998. The device has a liquefied petroleum flamethrower that is mounted on each side of the vehicle below the doors. In a carjacking scenario, the car's owner flips a switch in the car, which directs a flame of approximately 20 feet. The inventor claims that the device would not kill but would probably blind a potential assailant. Of course, the potential victim would have to be aware of the carjacker in enough time to effectively use this deterrent; once the carjacker was very close to the potential victim, it would likely be too late. Another device with a potentially harmful component is the Auto Taser. This device looks like the Club, which is a locking bar that disables the steering wheel of a parked car, but contains a motion detector that sets off a 110–130 decibel alarm when a would-be thief enters the vehicle. If a potential thief touches the Auto Taser, he or she receives a 50,000 volt shock (Roche 1999).

Historical Overview of Robbery

Robbery is not a recent creation of urban society. The New Testament of the Bible tells of "a certain man . . . fell among thieves, which stripped him of his raiment, and wounded him, and departed, leaving him half dead" (Luke 10:30). This "certain man" was clearly the victim of an armed robbery. During the period when the territories of the Roman Empire in Europe were under relentless assault by the barbarian tribes from the east and the north, the Roman authorities were unable to control the dispossessed populations from "resorting to pillage and armed robbery" (McCall 1979:82). While there is little concrete evidence of the frequency of crimes such as armed robbery during the Middle Ages, there exists much anecdotal record of roving bands of marauding vagabonds. These bands were at least partially the result of the practice of barbaric kings of the day raising armies on the promise of plunder. Unsurprisingly, kings found it difficult to persuade their subjects in the intervals between royal campaigns "to contrive to live on some way other than by looting and rapine" (McCall 1979:83). Moreover, the medieval system of outlawry did little to control crime. Dating back to at least the sixth century, the practice of declaring someone an outlaw and thereby banishing him or her did nothing more than to displace the criminal element and allow it to move around.

Prosecution records of property crimes in England by the fifteenth century were sufficient to allow for analysis of some of the underlying causes of these crimes. For example, in Essex

> a sharp rises in the level of prosecuted property offences occurred during the years of bad harvests in the late 1590s, the period 1629–31 when a trade depression hit the country's cloth industry, the years 1648–52 and 1661, which were grave years of bad harvest and the years of dearth at the very end of the seventeenth century." (Sharpe 1996:23)

This pattern suggests a relationship between economic hardship and theft; it is reasonable to think that robbery may fit this same pattern. Another causal factor of increases in property crime was observed in the eighteenth century, namely, the discharge of large numbers of soldiers and sailors from service following the century's wars (Sharpe 1996:24). This thesis has also been postulated to account for the lawlessness of the American West during the 30 years following the end of the Civil War in 1865 (Macdonald 1975:12).

Contemporary Patterns and Trends

Street robbery is primarily an urban phenomenon, accounting for 52.8 percent of all robberies in cities with populations greater than 250,000 but accounting for only 24.4 percent in cities with populations of less than 10,000 (UCR 2009c:Robbery Table 2). The rate for reported robbery in the United States increased over fourfold in the three decades from 1960 (60 per 100,000) to 1990 (256 per 100,000), and as seen earlier, the rate declined throughout the decade of the 1990s to about 150 per 100,000 in 1999 (UCR 2009a). Also as seen earlier, after a short period of increase from 2004 through 2006, the robbery rate in the United States has begun to decrease again. It is currently at a 20-year low of 133 per 100,000.

International comparisons of robbery are difficult to make because despite the aforementioned United Nations Survey on Crime Trends, no uniform standards for defining or reporting the crime currently exist. For example, in some jurisdictions where an incident involves multiple crimes, only the most serious crime (which may or may not be robbery) is recorded. What may be called a simple robbery in one jurisdiction may be categorized as a first-degree or aggravated robbery in another. In some countries, burglary and robbery are lumped together into one category. The Czech Republic, which experienced a dramatic increase in robberies following the Velvet Revolution in 1989, treats robbery as a criminal offense against liberty. This means that robbery in the Czech Republic is conceived of as an attack on both property and freedom (Rozum, Kotulan, and Tomasek 2006). In the period following the dismantling of apartheid in South Africa in 1994, the number of robberies increased dramatically. Between 1997 and 2001, the number of robberies in South Africa increased 71 percent, from 122,369 to 208,932. This number has only recently begun to decline (Barclay and Tavares 2003). From this evidence, we can conclude that countries experiencing rapid rates of social and economic change also experience increasing rates of robbery (and in the case of South Africa, carjacking).

Robbery is becoming a growing problem in Europe. From 1997 to 2001, robbery increased in England and Wales by 92 percent, in Austria by 42 percent, in France by 75 percent, in the Netherlands by 48 percent, and in Poland by 72 percent. While Spain showed only a 1-percent increase for the time period, the volume of robberies there produced the highest rates for the entire continent (Barclay and Tavares 2003). A study of robbery in Croatia revealed that robberies increased threefold between 1994 and 2003 and that twofold of the increase occurred in just four years, between 1999 and 2003. Moreover, robbery in Croatia is becoming more of an urban problem. In 1994, the Croatian capital of Zagreb and Zagreb County accounted for less than 50 percent of robberies in the country; in 2004, they accounted for 74 percent (Dujmovic and Miksaj-Todorovic 2004).

Victim Characteristics

According to the National Crime Victimization Survey (NCVS), in which the crime victimization experiences of persons age 12 and older in the United States are recorded, 200 robberies were reported for every 100,000 persons in 2007; the UCR reports only 148 for that year. Because the UCR records only those crimes known to the police, the difference in these two data sets indicates that underreporting of robbery is about 25 percent. Nevertheless, both the NCVS and UCR reveal fairly low and stable robbery rates for the period from 2001 to 2008. In 2008, the robbery victimization rate was highest among the 12–15-year-old age group (55 per 100,000) and was also high for the 16–19 age group (48 per 100,000) and the 20–24 age group (54 per 100,000). More men (27 per 100,000) were victims of robbery than women (17 per 100,000) and far more African Americans were victims of robbery (55 per 100,000) than were whites (16 per 100,000). The perpetrator was a stranger in 61 percent of robbery incidents where the victim was male and 45 percent where the victim was female. Weapons were used in 40 percent of robberies, with firearms used in 24 percent of them (Rand 2008).

Perhaps surprisingly, gun robberies are the least likely to result in serious injury. They ordinarily eliminate the need for the robber to physically attack his or her victim in order to gain compliance. However, while the presence of a gun may lead to a lower injury rate, it tends to lead to a higher death rate (Cook 1978:185). Cook found that murders occurred in 7.66 per 1,000 robberies in which guns were used, compared to 2.71 per 1,000 robberies in which a gun was not known to be present.

Research indicates that the patterns in the use of force in a robbery are integral to transforming a normal situation into a robbery. According to Luckenbill (1980:365), force is used to establish the "robbery frame" as a special type of interaction setting. The robbery frame consists of two elements: first, the victim must not oppose and should even assist the perpetrator in taking his or her possessions to avoid death or injury and second, the offender should control the victim's conduct. The perpetrator employs some mode of force to signal a robbery is taking place and in order to compel the victim both to comply and to ratify the robbery frame.

Offender Characteristics

While robbery declined during the 1990s and continues to decline presently, it has yet to reach the low rates recorded in the 1960s. Arrests for robbery have increased in number and rate in recent years. For example, in 2000, 65,106 arrests were made for robbery in the United States and 77,290 arrests were made for robbery in 2009, reflecting an 18.7 percent increase in arrests. Sixteen percent of robberies reported to the police were cleared by arrest in 2000 and 18.9 percent were cleared by arrest in 2009 (UCR 2009d). Offender characteristics reveal that those arrested for robbery are typically young black males. Of offenders arrested for robbery in 2009, 42.8 percent were white and 55.5 percent were black. Nearly 90 percent were male and the peak ages for those arrested for robbery in 2009 were 18 (9,415), 17 (8,380), and 19 (8,001) (UCR 2009b).

One of the most difficult problems confronting social scientists is trying to explain the high incidence of robbery among young black males. According to LaFree (1995), the correlation between robbery and race is 98 percent and the majority of street robberies in large urban areas are committed by young black males. LaFree (1995:182) contends that the theories consistently advanced to explain black involvement in robbery are inadequate. Social disorganization theory, for example, links black crime rates to high rates of female-headed households and low marriage rates but comparative research does not consistently support this view. For example, some European countries have high levels of divorce and female-headed households and low crime rates. Other theorists argue that although everyone is exposed to the goals of monetary success, access to the means of achieving these goals through conventional means is structured unequally. Crime is committed in order to achieve monetary success outside the legitimate means. Given the relatively dire economic situation for many blacks, this theory seems to have merit. However, an examination of unemployment and income measures revealed that neither had a significant effect on black crime rates (LaFree, 1995:182–186). According to LaFree, the most promising line of inquiry is the effect of intraracial inequality. The widening gap between successful middle-class blacks and a growing black underclass results in the further isolation of this segment of the black population. Moreover, this division may account for more than just a high robbery rate among the urban black and poor.

Katz (1988:241) argues that the overrepresentation of blacks in robbery statistics is a result of blacks embracing the seductions of the stickup and the social construction of the "hardman" as a street robber. Katz contends that within the modern poor black urban community, being "bad" is often a collectively celebrated way of being that has emotional resonance and transcends good and evil. Of course, insofar as Katz's explanation accounts for robbery among blacks, it accounts for only a certain type, namely, the street robbery.

Understanding Robbery

No treatise on robbery is complete without a discussion of John Conklin's (1972) typology of robbery, which examines the degree to which the robber is committed to robbery as a source of livelihood. Conklin identified four types of robbers: professionals, opportunists, addicts, and alcoholics. He concludes that the professionals, those who specialize in planned bank robberies, for example, are on the decline and that presently, professional robbers do not significantly differ from opportunist robbers. The opportunist robber acts randomly, although victim vulnerability, the potential yield, and consideration of both location and escape do indicate some thought in committing the act.

In street robberies, young males ranging in age from early teens to early 20s often operate as a small team. Younger members of the team approach a potential victim to ask for directions, the time, a cigarette, or spare change. This approach is a ploy designed to stop the target person and "connect" with him or her. The older member of the team approaches the victim from behind with a gun or weapon and announces the stickup. The younger members of the team relieve the victim of money, jewelry, purses, cell phones, and other valuables (Harper 2005).

In some instances, victims unintentionally set themselves up for robbery. For example, a robber (male or female) may pose as a friendly stranger who approaches a person drinking alone in a bar. The robber engages the person in conversation, even buying or offering to buy him or her drinks. After a rapport is established, the robber asks if the intended victim would like sex or drugs. If the intended victim answers in the negative, the relationship is terminated by the robber. If the answer is in the affirmative, the robber offers to accompany the victim to some unknown but not-too-distant location. In the case of a female robber, she usually has a male accomplice who has left the bar and is waiting at a previously arranged location where the robbery can be safely accomplished. In the case of the male robber working alone, the victim is simply led to a quiet location a short distance from the bar and robbed (Harper 2005).

Conklin's (1972) typology also includes addict and alcoholic robbers who engage in robbery to support their habits. These robbers are not committed to robbery as a favored type of crime, but they are committed to theft in general. Physical force rather than a weapon is more often used to take money from victims. In recent years, aggressive panhandling has been employed as a robbery strategy in large urban areas by addicts, alcoholics, and in some instances, so-called gutter punks. Aggressive panhandlers acting individually or in small groups ambush pedestrians in hotel districts, near convention center facilities, and near tourist attractions, pushing and threatening them and demanding money. If the pedestrians are not forthcoming with money or valuables, they are often shoved, hit, or kicked and cursed (Harper 2005).

Why Do People Commit Robbery?

The simple answer is that robbery is a quick way to secure money. However, there are many irrational elements to the crime. For example, the legal penalty for robbery does not depend on the amount taken and the monetary return from a typical street robbery is not great. Even when tourists are targeted, the take is rarely more than $300 in cash (Harper 2005). Given the inverse relationship between high risk and the low rate of return, why does the robber persist in this crime? Viewing robbery from the robber's perspective, Katz (1988:167) distinguishes three phases in the robber's experience, which leads to a customary style of attack and a particular understanding of self. The would-be robber must achieve a moral advantage over the target (gaining control of the situation), he or she must commit to the act by declaring the crime ("Give it up!"), and he or she must commit to the crime beyond reason (given the potential negative consequences). In other words, the robber must become a hardman. Katz argues that the offender constructs the causes of the crime and that the causes he or she constructs move the offender toward committing further crime; this is what Katz calls the attraction of doing evil. Rapidly spending the money taken during a robbery, the chaotic experience of the crime itself, the ability to control the situation, and the varieties of illicit action that comprise a robbery make up the life of the robber and contribute to his or her sense of self, which in turn account for his or her persistence in this particular crime.

As reported earlier, blacks, males, and youths primarily commit robbery. Messerschmidt (1993) suggests that an "opposition masculinity" accounts for the disproportionate number of marginalized racial minority boys being involved in robbery. He argues that this violent crime is a means of expressing their masculinity. Expression of masculinity through robbery flows from their disconcerting school experiences as well as from their life experiences with poverty, racism, negated futures, and the lack of power accorded them. He argues that because of these detrimental conditions, young racial minority boys are more likely to commit certain types of street crime and, in the process, construct a different type of masculinity outside that constructed in the school setting. Robbery provides an ideal opportunity for them to act tough and male. According to Messerschmidt (1993), robbery becomes a rational practice of "doing gender" for these young racial minority boys.

In an effort to more fully explain the crime of armed robbery, Wright and Decker (1997) conducted semi-structured interviews with 86 active armed robbers on the streets of St. Louis, Missouri, the majority of whom were black and male. When asked why they committed robbery, the robbers said they did so in order to obtain fast cash and further maintained that legitimate opportunities to earn enough money to live on (and in many cases also support their drug, alcohol, and gambling habits) were impossible to obtain due to limitations on education and desirable skills. They chose victims who were in proximity and, in many cases, were also involved in the criminal lifestyle, such as drug dealers; when seemingly law-abiding citizens were chosen as victims, it was because their appearances or demeanors indicated they might have money on them. Interestingly, the robbers believed white victims would offer less resistance than black ones. In order to successfully complete robberies, the robbers used a combination of a surprise approach of their victims, tough talk, and the use of a deadly weapon. When victims offered resistance, the robbers often used brute but nonlethal violence to secure compliance. In addition to the financial rewards, the robbers noted that committing robberies gave them a sense of control in a world where they otherwise had none. Especially this last finding supports Katz's (1988) contentions as seen earlier.

Prevention and Control of Robbery

Due to potential harm to victims as well as the potential financial losses associated with the crime of robbery, numerous countermeasures have been developed and implemented in an attempt to deter or at least displace robberies. These countermeasures have been employed primarily at fixed-location businesses and have been designed to accomplish several things singularly or in combination, namely, reduce the potential rewards of a robbery, increase the likelihood of failure of a robbery attempt, and/or increase the effort needed to achieve the reward. These countermeasures can be classified into two general types: environmental and administrative.

Environmental countermeasures are generally concerned with deterring robbers by increasing the effort needed to successfully complete the robbery and increasing the likelihood of identification and apprehension through physical alterations and adaptations. Commonly employed environmental robbery countermeasures include:

1. *Alarms:* These are devices that either manually or automatically alert law enforcement to a robbery in progress at a location, such as a convenience store. The alarm system can be hand or foot operated in the case of a button or it can be linked to the cash register keys or to bills situated within the cash drawer (Ekblom 1987; Loomis et al. 2002).
2. *Bullet resistant barriers (BRB):* These physical barriers come in several forms, including pass-through windows, pop-up screens, and enclosed sales counter areas, and are designed to separate employees from potential robbers. The barriers can either prevent customers from entering a retail business or allow entry into the business, but in that case, they enclose the employee within a bullet resistant space (Kube 1988; Grandjean 1990; Butterworth 1991).
3. *Closed circuit television (CCTV):* CCTV is a video recording system in which video cameras are strategically placed around businesses' points of entry and interaction with customers. The presence of CCTV can increase a robber's likelihood of being identified and arrested. In addition, some locations employ dummy cameras that do not video record activity but are designed to give potential robbers the impression that the location is under constant surveillance (Crow and Bull 1975; Swanson 1986; Figlio and Armaud 1991).
4. *Door annunciators:* These devices announce a person's entry into a business location. They alert the employee of the person's entry via an audible signal (Swanson 1986; Jeffery, Hunter, and Griswold 1987).
5. *Height strips:* A particularly innovative countermeasure, height strips are color-coded markings in a doorway of a business that can assist victims in properly quantifying robber's height. The presence of the height strip has the added countermeasure of serving as a warning signal to potential robbers that the location is prepared for the possibility of a robbery (OSHA 1998; Hendricks et al 1999).
6. *Lighting (in terms of both quality and quantity):* The presence of bright lighting provides for increased formal and informal surveillance of the location (Crow and Bull 1975; Jeffery et al. 1987; Hunter 1988; Butterworth 1991; Painter 1994; Erickson 1996; Farrington and Welsh 2002).
7. *Time-accessed safes (often referred to as time-accessed cash controller safes or TACC safes):* These safes are equipped with a time-delay feature. The delay, which is usually 10 minutes, requires that a robber would have to remain at the location for at least that long to gain access to cash in the safe (Dunckel 1988; OSHA 1998).
8. *Traffic flow devices:* These are physical structures designed to impede a robber's ability to flee after the crime. They include fencing, landscaping, electronically controlled doors, and a small number of exits (Crow and Bull 1975; Swanson 1986; Jeffery et al. 1987; Hunter 1988; Erickson 1996).
9. *Visibility both into and out of a business:* Unobstructed visibility into and out of a building is thought to reduce robbery attempts because both formal and informal surveillance can occur. Additionally, potential robbers may be deterred by unobstructed visibility as they may observe a large number of people within a location (Crow and Bull 1975; Hunter 1988; Butterworth 1991; Bellamy 1996; Hendricks, Amandus, and Zahm 1997).

Administrative countermeasures are also designed to deter robbers by increasing the effort needed to complete the robbery, by reducing the amount of potential reward, and by increasing the likelihood of identification and apprehension. These measures are implemented through workplace policies and procedures. Commonly employed administrative robbery countermeasures include the following:

1. *On-hand cash limits:* This refers to the reduction of available cash (e.g., $35–$50) in late night retail businesses, such as convenience stores or gas stations, to reduce a location's attractiveness as a robbery target (OSHA 1998; Hendricks et al. 1999).
2. *Hours of operations/hours of operation of BRB:* This refers to the decision by management to reduce access to a business, either by closing the establishment completely or by utilizing a BRB to reduce access to the employee during the late night hours (Kube 1988; Grandjean 1990; Butterworth 1991).
3. *Multiple staffing:* Multiple staffing refers to the belief that the presence of more than one employee will cause a potential robber to select another target. This is often referred to as the "two clerk rule" (Crow and Bull 1975; Jeffery et al. 1987; Vogel 1990; Figlio and Armaud 1991).
4. *Robbery prevention training:* Robbery prevention training is mandatory instruction for employees that occurs before a robbery. Among other things, this training reminds employees to pay attention to people entering the business and instructs them on how to react if a robbery attempt does appear imminent (OSHA 1998).
5. *Signage:* *Signage* refers to public display of information that advises potential offenders of the robbery countermeasures in place at the location, such as "Cashier does not have access to safe" and "Store is under video and audio surveillance." In the United States, these signs are often posted in both English and Spanish (OSHA 1988).

Certain businesses and industries have implemented robbery countermeasures that are related to their specific operations. One such countermeasure taken by clothing retailers employs the concept of benefit denial. Expensive clothing may be equipped with a dye pack that will ruin the clothes via ink stains if the dye pack is not deactivated at the cash register. The theft attempt may be successful but the reward has been greatly if not totally negated. In countries where private armored car officers are not authorized to carry weapons, a system has been implemented in which an acid pack deploys and destroys the cash in the delivery bag if that bag is stolen or otherwise not delivered to its destination.

Robbery countermeasures are probably most easily brought to mind in the context of the banking industry. Similar to those used by some clothing retailers, banks have implemented the use of dye packs that are designed to explode and saturate bills with brightly colored dye. This both reduces the potential reward of the robbery and increases the risk of apprehension. Banks have also placed limits on the amount of cash that can be withdrawn from automated teller machines (ATM) and many banks have installed cameras at their ATMs. Other bank robbery deterrents are similar to those mentioned earlier, that is, CCTV, lighting, unobstructed view, and so on; additional measures more specific to banks include having an employee or a security guard greet customers upon their arrival and an immediately accessible connection with the police so that robbers' details may be communicated as quickly as possible (Best Practices 2003).

Based on interviews with victimized bank tellers and with bank robbers, the FBI determined that bank robberies could be prevented and successful robbers could be apprehended if policies were changed. The SafeCatch program reflects these changes. SafeCatch encourages bank employees to be more observant of customers' behavior and to rely on their instincts when they believe something is "not quite right." In these situations, tellers are encouraged to be overly friendly to potential robbers, as the potential robbers are expecting a confrontation and may become uncomfortable enough to abort their felonious plans when approached in a friendly way. When a robbery does occur, SafeCatch procedure dictates that the victimized teller should contact the police immediately without using the alarm (which delays law enforcement's arrival) and without waiting for authorization from a superior. Another technique banks can employ to increase the chances of apprehending successful robbers is to lower the CCTV camera on the exit door so it takes head-on (instead of bird's eye) shots of those leaving the bank. SafeCatch developer Larry Carr credits the program for a drop in bank robberies in the Seattle area, in large part, because bank robbers tend to commit a host of robberies. Once they are apprehended, their contribution to the number of bank robberies is negated (Fields 2009).

Finally, as seen previously, less than one in four of all robberies are cleared by arrest. The conviction rate for arrested robbers, however, rose from 39 percent in 1994 to 46 percent in 2004 (Durose and Langan 2007). This means that those who are arrested for robbery have almost a one in two chance of being convicted of the crime and, once convicted, have a very high chance (78 percent) of being incarcerated. The potential threat of severe sanction coupled with the judicial targeting of repeat offenders may have some, although unknown, deterrent effect on potential robbers.

To summarize, this article has explored a number of different facets of the crime of robbery. In the United States, the reported robbery rate is currently at a 20-year low; it is about half of what it was in the early to mid-1990s. There has been a similar decline in the carjacking rate; this decline may be due to the invention of more sophisticated anticarjacking devices, the harsh penalties that carjacking can incur, or both.

Robbery is by no means a new crime. Anecdotal reports of robbery are found throughout the historical record and robbery may have occurred with greater frequency in times of bad harvest or economic depression, as did property crime; it is similarly reasonable to infer from the evidence that robbery increases at times of social upheaval. Contemporarily in the United States, street robbery is primarily an urban phenomenon. International comparison of robbery rates is difficult owing to a lack of standard definition and measurement of the crime, but it is known that many European countries have seen an increase in robbery in recent years.

The NCVS indicates that robberies are underreported in the UCR by about 25 percent. Victims of robbery tend to be young, male, and black. Robbery offenders also tend to be young, male, and black. Sociologists and criminologists have struggled to explain this trend. Various explanations include the isolation of a growing black underclass (LaFree 1995) and the opportunity to be "bad" and in so doing gaining a culturally valued status (Katz 1988).

Conklin (1972) identified four categories of robbers in his typology, one of which is the opportunistic robber. Three scenarios in which the opportunistic robber might operate are described, that involving a robber or team of robbers targeting a victim or victims on the street, a robber or a team of robbers targeting a single person at a bar, and aggressive panhandling. The crime of robbery has a low yield, especially relative to the risk involved. Explanations of why people continue to commit robbery are advanced by Katz (1988), who contends robberies and their elements become part of the robber's sense of self, by Messerschmidt (1993), who contends that robbery is a way for young black males to "do gender" and by Wright and Decker (1997), who contend that robbers persist in their crime in order to obtain quick cash and to exercise control in the world.

There are several familiar robbery-prevention strategies. Environmental forms of robbery prevention include alarms, bullet proof barriers, CCTV, door annunciators, height strips, bright lighting, time-accessed safes, traffic control devices, and manipulation of visibility.

Administrative forms of robbery prevention include on-hand cash limits, limits on hours of operation, multiple staff on duty, robbery prevention training, and signage. Robbery prevention strategies specific to the banking industry include dye packs, security guards on hand to greet customers, immediate access to the police when needed, and more recently, the SafeCatch program, which relies on the experience of tellers to act when situations seem unusual by being overly friendly to potential robbers. All these strategies, plus the high chance of incarceration upon apprehension for a robbery, may have a deterrent effect on this crime.

Discussion Questions

1. As seen in this article, there is a disparity between the number of robberies reported to the police as measured by the UCR and the number of people who indicate they have been robbery victims as measured by the NCVS. What do you think accounts for this disparity?
2. A wide variety of robbery prevention techniques are detailed in this article. These techniques are most relevant for businesses, but as you know, most robberies are street robberies. What robbery prevention measures can you think of that may be effective against street robberies?

References

Barclay, Gordon and Cynthia Tavares. 2003. *International Comparisons of Criminal Justice Statistics 2001.* London: Home Office. Retrieved February 10, 2011 (http://www.observatorioseguranca.org/pdf/01%20(23).pdf).

Bellamy, Lisa. 1996. "Situational Crime Prevention in Convenience Store Robberies." *Security Journal* 7:41–52.

Best Practices. 2003. Bank Robbery "Best Practices." Retrieved February 10, 2011 (http://www.bankersonline.com/security/robbery_bestpractices.html).

Butterworth, Robert. 1991. *Study of Safety and Security Requirements for "At-Risk" Businesses.* Tallahassee, FL: Office of Attorney General.

Carroll, Rory. 2006. "Carjacking: The Everyday Ordeal Testing South Africa." *The Guardian*, March 1. Retrieved November 10, 2011 (http://www.guardian.co.uk/world/2006/mar/02/film.oscars2006 on).

Conklin, John E. 1972. *Robbery and the Criminal Justice System.* Philadelphia, PA: Lippincott.

Cook, Phillip J. 1978. "The Effect of Gun Availability on Robbery and Robbery Murder: A Cross-Section Study of Fifty Cities." In Hearings before the Sub-Committee on Crime of the Committee of the Judiciary. House of Representatives, May 4 and 18. Washington, DC: U.S. Government Printing Office.

Crow, Wayman and James Bull. 1975. *Robbery Deterrence: An Applied Behavioral Science Demonstration.* La Jolla, CA: Western Behavioral Science Institute.

Davis, Linda. 2003. "Carjacking: Insights from South Africa to a New Crime Problem." *Australian and New Zealand Journal of Criminology* 26:173–91.

Dujmovic, Zvonimir and Ljiljana Miksaj-Todorovis. 2004. "Basic Problems of Robbery Detection. Pp. 1–7 in *Policing in Central and Eastern Europe: Dilemmas of Contemporary Criminal Justice*, edited by Gorazd Mesko, Milan Pagon, and Bojan Dobovsek. Slovenia: University of Maribor.

Dunckel, Kenneth. 1988. "Holdup Delay Locks: Deterrent or Encouragement?" *Security Management* 32:70–73.

Durose, Matthew R. and Patrick A. Langan. 2007. "Felony Sentences in State Courts, 2004." Bureau of Justice Statistics. Retrieved February 10, 2011 (http://bjs.ojp.usdoj.gov/content/pub/pdf/fssc04.pdf).

Ekblom, Paul. 1987. "Preventing Robberies at Sub-Post Offices: An Evaluation of a Security Initiative." *Crime Prevention Unit Paper No. 9.* London: Home Office.

Erickson, Rosemary. 1996. *Armed Robbers and Their Crimes.* Seattle, WA: Athena Research.

Farrington, David and B. Welsh. 2002. "Effects of Improved Street Lighting on Crime: A Systematic Review." *Home Office Research Study 251.* London: Home Office.

Fields, Tom. 2009. "SafeCatch: How to Deter Bank Robberies." Retrieved February 10, 2011 (http://www.bankinfosecurity.com/articles.php?art_id=1747&opg=1).

Figlio, Robert and Steven Armaud. 1991. "An Assessment of Robbery Deterrence Measures at Convenience Stores." In *Convenience Store Security: Report and Recommendations*. Alexandria, VA.: NACS.

Forced Ignition Systems. n.d. "How Does the Forced Ignition System Work?" Retrieved February 10, 2011 (http://www.forcedignition.com/fiworks.html).

Grandjean, C. 1990. "Bank Robberies and Physical Security in Switzerland: A Case Study of the Escalation and Displacement Phenomena." *Security Journal* 3:155–59.

Harper, Dee Wood, Jr. 2005. "The Tourist and His Criminal: Patterns in Street Robbery." Pp. 125–38 in *Tourism, Security and Safety: A Case Approach*, edited by Yoel Mansfield and Abraham Piazam. Burlington, MA: Butterworth-Heinemann.

Hendricks, Scott, Douglas Landsittel, Harlan Amandus, Jay Malcan, and Jennifer Bell. 1999. "A Matched Case-Control Study of Convenience Store Robbery Risk Factors." *Journal of Occupational and Environmental Medicine* 41:995–1004.

Hendricks, Scott, Harlan Amandus, and D. Zahm. 1997. "Convenience Store Robberies in Selected Metropolitan Areas and Risk Factors for Employee Injury." *Journal of Occupational and Environmental Medicine* 39:1233–39.

Hunter, Ronald. 1988. *The Effects of Environmental Factors upon Convenience Store Robbery in Florida.* Tallahassee, FL: Florida Department of Legal Affairs.

Jacobs, Bruce A., Volkan Topalli, and Richard Wright. 2003. "Carjacking, Street Life and Offender Motivation." *British Journal of Criminology* 43:673–78.

Jeffery, C. Ray, Ronald Hunter, and Jeffery Griswold. 1987. "Crime Prevention and Computer Analysis of Convenience Store Robberies in Tallahassee." *Florida Police Journal* 34:65–69.

Katz, Jack. 1988. *Seductions of Crime*. New York: Basic Books.

Klaus, Patsy. 2004. "Carjacking, 1993–2002." Bureau of Justice Statistics Crime Data Brief. Retrieved February 10, 2011 (http://bjs.ojp.usdoj.gov/content/pub/pdf/c02.pdf).

Kube, Edwin. 1988. "Preventing Bank Robbery: Lessons From Interviewing Robbers." *Journal of Security Administration* 11:78–83.

LaFree, Gary. 1995. "Race and Crime Trends in the United States, 1946–1990." Pp. 169–93 in *Ethnicity, Race and Crime*, edited by Darnell F. Hawkins. Albany, NY: State University of New York Press.

Loomis, Dana, Stephen Marshall, Susanne Wolf, Carol Runyan, and John Butts. 2002. "Effectiveness of Safety Measures Recommended for Prevention of Workplace Homicide." *The Journal of the American Medical Association* 287:1011–17.

Luckenbill, David F. 1980. "Patterns of Force in Robbery." *Deviant Behavior* 1:361–78.

Macdonald, John M. 1975. *Armed Robbery*. Springfield, IL: Thomas.

McCall, Andrew. 1979. *The Medieval Underworld*. London: Hamish Hamilton.

Messerschmidt, James. 1993. *Masculinities and Crime.* Lanham, MD: Rowman & Littlefield.

OSHA. 1998. "Occupational Safety and Health Administration Recommendations for Workplace Violence Prevention Programs in Late-Night Retail Establishments." Washington, DC: U.S. Department of Labor.

Painter, Kate. 1994. "The Impact of Street Lighting on Crime, Fear, and Pedestrian Street Use." *Security Journal* 5:116–24.

Rand, Michael R. 2008. "Criminal Victimization, 2008." Bureau of Justice Statistics Bulletin. Retrieved February 10, 2011 (http://bjs.ojp.usdoj.gov/content/pub/pdf/cv08.pdf).

Roche, Thomas. 1999. "Steal This Car: High Impact Automobile Security." Retrieved February 10, 2011 (http://www.gettingit.com/article/69).

Rozum, Jan, Petr Kotulan, and Jan Tomasek. 2006. "Robbery Crime in Prague." *Selected Results of Research Activities of ICSP in the Years 2004–2007.* Retrieved February 10, 2011 (http://www.ok.cz/iksp/docs/359.pdf).

Sharpe, James A. 1996. "Crime in England: Long-Term Trends and the Problem of Modernization." Pp. 17–34 in *The Civilization of Crime,* edited by Eric A. Johnson and Eric H. Monkkonen. Urbana, IL: University of Illinois Press.

Swanson, R. 1986. *Convenience Store Robbery Analysis: A Research Study of Robbers, Victims, and Environment.* Gainesville, FL: Unpublished report to the Gainesville Police Department.

UCR. 1990–2009. Data available from home page: http://www.fbi.gov/about-us/cjis/ucr/ucr.

UCR. 2009a. Estimated Robbery Rate. Retrieved February 10, 2011 (http://www.ucrdatatool.gov/Search/Crime/State/RunCrimeTrendsInOneVar.cfm).

UCR. 2009b. Offender Characteristics of Those Arrested for Robbery. Age table: Retrieved February 10, 2011 (http://www2.fbi.gov/ucr/cius2009/data/table_38.html). Race table: Retrieved February 10, 2011 (http://www2.fbi.gov/ucr/cius2009/data/table_43.html). Gender table: Retrieved February 10, 2011 (http://www2.fbi.gov/ucr/cius2009/data/table_42.html).

UCR. 2009c. Robbery. Retrieved February 10, 2011 (http://www2.fbi.gov/ucr/cius2009/offenses/violent_crime/robbery.html).

UCR. 2009d. Ten-Year Arrest Trends. Retrieved February 10, 2011 (http://www2.fbi.gov/ucr/cius2009/data/table_32.html).

United States Federal Statute. n.d. "Carjacking, 18 U.S.C. § 2119." Retrieved February 10, 2011 (http://www.justice.gov/usao/eousa/foia_reading_room/usam/title9/crm01110.htm).

UNDOC. 2008. "Questionnaire for the Tenth United Nations Survey of Crime Trends and Operations of Criminal Justice Systems." Retrieved February 10, 2011 (http://www.unodc.org/pdf/crime/tenthsurvey/10th_CTS_form_English.pdf).

Wright, Richard T. and Scott H. Decker. 1997. *Armed Robbers in Action: Stickups and Street Crime.* Boston, MA: Northeastern University Press.

Vogel, Robert. 1990. *Convenience Store Robbery.* DeLand, FL: Volusia County Sheriff's Office.

 ARTICLE 7

Elizabeth Ehrhardt Mustaine
University of Central Florida

Child Abuse

Child Abuse and Neglect: An Overview

While many forms of deviance are not especially harmful to those who participate in them, and many do not have "victims" per se, child abuse is a serious form of deviance. The abuse of children can cause delayed or stunted social and cognitive development, physical and psychological injury that can last a lifetime, and possibly even death as most children are defenseless against abuse, are dependent on their caretakers, and are unable to protect themselves from these acts. Consequently, child abuse is a very real and prominent social problem today.

The Children's Defense Fund reported that each day in America in 2009, 2,175 children were confirmed as abused or neglected, 4 children were killed by abuse or neglect, and 78 babies died before their first birthdays (although not all may die due to abuse), and 1,240 public school students were corporally punished (Children's Defense Fund 2011). These daily estimates translate into tremendous national figures. In 2009, case workers substantiated an estimated 763,000 reports of child abuse or neglect (U.S. Department of Health and Human Services 2010). Of these, 78.3 percent suffered neglect, 17.8 percent were physically abused, 9.5 percent were sexually abused, 7.6 percent were emotionally or psychologically maltreated, and 2.4 percent were medically neglected (percentages add to more than 100 percent because some children experienced more than one type of abuse). In addition, 9.6 percent of the victims experienced "other" types of maltreatment, such as "abandonment," "threats of harm to the child," and "congenital drug addiction." Obviously, this form of deviance is a substantial one.

Estimates of Child Abuse: Methodological Limitations

Several issues arise when considering the amount of child abuse that occurs annually in the United States. Child abuse is very hard to estimate because much (or most) child abuse is not reported. Children who are abused are unlikely to report their victimization because they may not know any better, they still love their abusers and do not want to see them taken away (or themselves be taken away from their abusers), they have been threatened into not reporting, and/or they do not know to whom they should report their victimization. Still further, children may report their abuse only to find the person to whom they report does not believe them or take any action on their behalf. Continuing to muddy the waters, child abuse can be disguised as legitimate injury, particularly because young children are often somewhat uncoordinated and are still learning to accomplish physical tasks, may not know their physical limitations, and are often legitimately injured during regular play. In the end, children rarely report child abuse; most often it is an adult (e.g., teacher, counselor, doctor) who makes a report based on suspicion.

Even when child abuse is reported, social service agents and investigators may not follow up or substantiate reports for many reasons. Parents can pretend, lie, or cover up injuries or stories of how injuries occurred when social service agents investigate. Further, there is not always agreement about what should be counted as abuse by service providers and researchers. Additionally, social service agencies/agents have huge caseloads and may be able to deal only with the most serious forms of child abuse, leaving the more "minor" forms of abuse unsupervised and unmanaged (and uncounted in the statistical totals).

Child Abuse and Neglect: The Legalities

One of the most difficult legal issues is balancing the right of parents to use corporal punishment when disciplining a child, while not crossing over the line into the realm of child abuse. Generally, state statutes use phrases such as "reasonable discipline of a minor," "causes only temporary, short-term pain," may cause "the potential for bruising," but not "permanent damage, disability, disfigurement or injury" to the child as ways of indicating the types of discipline behaviors that are legal. However, corporal punishment that is "excessive," is "malicious," and "endangers the bodily safety of" "an intentional infliction of injury" is not allowed under most state statutes (e.g., State of Florida child abuse statute) (Children's Defense Fund 2011).

While most laws about child abuse and neglect fall at the state levels, federal legislation provides a foundation for states by identifying a minimum set of acts and behaviors that define child abuse and neglect. The Federal Child Abuse Prevention and Treatment Act (CAPTA), which stems from the Keeping Children and Families Safe Act of 2003, defines child abuse and neglect as, at minimum, "(1) any recent act or failure to act on the part of a parent or caretaker which results in death, serious physical or emotional harm, sexual abuse, or exploitation; or (2) an act or failure to act which presents an imminent risk or serious harm" (42 U.S.C.A. §5106g).

Using these minimum standards, each state is responsible for providing its own definition of maltreatment within civil and criminal statutes. When defining types of child abuse, many states incorporate similar elements and definitions into their legal statutes. For example, neglect is often defined as failure to provide for a child's basic needs. Neglect can encompass physical elements (e.g., failure to provide necessary food or shelter, or lack of appropriate supervision), medical elements (e.g., failure to provide necessary medical or mental health treatment), educational elements (e.g., failure to educate a child or attend to special educational needs), and emotional elements (e.g., inattention to a child's emotional needs, failure to provide psychological care, or failure to prevent the child from using alcohol or other drugs). Failure to meet needs does not always mean a child is neglected, as situations such as poverty, cultural values, and community standards can influence the application of legal statutes. Additionally, several states distinguish between failure to provide based on financial inability and failure to provide for no apparent financial reason (Haley's Rights 2011).

Statutes on physical abuse typically include elements of physical injury (ranging from minor bruises to severe fractures or death) as a result of punching, beating, kicking, biting, shaking, throwing, stabbing, chocking, hitting (with a hand, stick, strap, or other object), burning, or otherwise harming a child. Such injury is considered abuse regardless of the intention of the caretaker. Additionally, many state statutes include allowing or encouraging another person to physically harm a child (such as noted earlier) as another form of physical abuse in and of itself (Children's Defense Fund 2011; Haley's Rights 2011).

Sexual abuse usually includes activities, such as fondling a child's genitals, penetration, incest, rape, sodomy, indecent exposure, and exploitation through prostitution or the production of pornographic materials, by a parent or caretaker (Children's Defense Fund 2011; Haley's Rights 2011).

Finally, emotional or psychological abuse typically is defined as a pattern of behavior that impairs a child's emotional development or sense of self-worth. This may include constant criticism, threats, or rejection, as well as withholding love, support, or guidance. Emotional abuse is often the most difficult to prove and, therefore child-protective services may not be able to intervene without evidence of harm to the child. Some states suggest harm may be evidenced by an observable or substantial change in behavior, emotional response, or cognition, or by anxiety, depression, withdrawal, or aggressive behavior. Practically, emotional abuse is almost always present when other types of abuse are identified (Children's Defense Fund 2011; Haley's Rights 2011).

Some states include an element of substance abuse in their statutes on child abuse. Circumstances that can be considered substance abuse include (1) manufacturing of a controlled substance in the presence of a child or on the premises occupied by a child (Colorado, Indiana, Iowa, Montana, South Dakota, Tennessee, and Virginia); (2) allowing a child to be present where the chemicals or equipment for the manufacture of controlled substances are used (Arizona, New Mexico); (3) selling, distributing, or giving drugs or alcohol to a child (Florida, Hawaii, Illinois, Minnesota, and Texas); (4) using a controlled substance by a caregiver that impairs the caregiver's ability to adequately care for the child (Kentucky, New York, Rhode Island, and Texas); and (5) exposing a child to drug paraphernalia (North Dakota); involving a child in the criminal sale or distribution of drugs (Montana, Virginia); or involving a child in a drug-related activity (District of Columbia) (Haley's Rights 2011).

Corporal Punishment versus Child Abuse

Many parents use corporal punishment (e.g., spanking) when disciplining their children (Straus 2001). Surprisingly though, most research finds that the use of physical punishment (most often spanking) is not an effective method of discipline. The literature on this issue tends to find that spanking stops misbehavior, but no more effectively than other firm measures. Further, it seems to hinder rather than improve general compliance/obedience (particularly when the child is not in the presence of the punisher) (Straus 2001).

The question arises, why is physical punishment no more effective at gaining child compliance than other nonviolent forms of discipline? The answer is that some of the problems that arise when parents use spanking or other forms of physical punishment include that spanking does not teach what children should do, nor does it provide them with alternative behavior options should the circumstance arise again. Spanking also undermines reasoning, explanation, or other forms of parental instruction because children cannot learn, reason, or solve problems well while experiencing threat, pain, fear, or anger. Further, the use of physical punishment is inconsistent with nonviolent principles, or parental modeling. Additionally, the use of spanking chips away at the bonds of affection between parents and children, and tends to induce resentment and fear. And, it hinders the development of empathy and compassion in children, and they do not learn to take responsibility for their own behavior (Pitzer 1997).

One of the biggest problems with the use of corporal punishment, though, is that it can escalate into much more severe forms of violence. Usually parents spank because they are angry (and somewhat out of control) and they cannot think of other ways to discipline. When parents are acting out of emotional triggers, the notion of discipline is lost while punishment and pain become the foci. The next section includes a public service message that makes this point clear.

Child Abuse Victims: The Patterns

In 2009, of the children who were found to be victims of child abuse, nearly 75 percent of them were first-time victims (or had not come to the attention of authorities prior). A slight majority of child abuse victims were girls (51.1 percent), compared to 48.2 percent of abuse victims being boys. The younger the child, the more at risk he or she is for child abuse and neglect victimization. Specifically, the proportion of infants to age three who experienced abuse was 33.4 percent (12.6 percent of infants, 7.4 percent of one-year-olds, 7 percent of two-year-olds, and 6.4 percent of three-year-olds. After age three, rates of child abuse by age decreased substantially. To elaborate, 23.3 percent of 4–7-year-olds, 18.8 percent of 8–11-year-olds, 17.8 percent of 12–15-year-olds, and 6.3 percent of 16–17-year-olds are victims of child abuse (U.S. Department of Health and Human Services 2010).

There are patterns regarding race and ethnic groups also. Whites, African Americans, and Hispanics comprise 87 percent of all child abuse victims (44 percent, 22.3 percent, and 20.7 percent, respectively), but African American, American Indian, Alaska Native children, and children of multiple races have the highest rates of victimization (15.1, 11.6, and 12.4 per 1,000 children in the population of the same race or ethnicity, respectively). Asian and Pacific Islander children had the lowest rates of child abuse and neglect victimization with 0.9 and 0.2 percent, respectively (U.S. Department of Health and Human Services 2010).

Regarding living arrangements, nearly 27 percent of victims were living with a single mother, 20 percent were living with married parents, while 22 percent were living with both parents, but the marital status was unknown (this reporting element had nearly 40 percent missing data, however). Regarding disability, nearly 11 percent of child abuse victims had mental retardation, emotional disturbance, visual or hearing impairment, learning disability, physical disability, behavioral problems, or other medical problems (U.S. Department of Health and Human Services 2010).

Children who had been prior victims of maltreatment were 94.6 percent more likely to experience a recurrence than those who were not prior victims. Further, child victims who were reported with a disability were 52 percent more likely to experience recurrence than children without a disability. Finally, the oldest victims (16–21 years of age) were the least likely to experience a recurrence, and were 51 percent less likely than were infants (younger than age one) (U.S. Department of Health and Human Services 2006).

Child fatalities are the most serious form of maltreatment. The patterns associated with child fatalities basically mirror those of child maltreatment. Researchers find that younger children are more likely to be killed as a result of abuse, with nearly 40 percent of murdered children being less than one-year-old. And, again, we find that as children get older, their risk for fatality decreases substantially (e.g., 16–17-year-olds make up 1.4 percent of murdered children). Similarly, race and ethnicity show corresponding patterns with child fatalities. For instance, again research identifies that more than 80 percent of child fatalities were of African American, Hispanic, and white children. However, one exception to the corresponding patterns between maltreatment and fatality is gender: girls had a rate of fatality of 2.12 and boys had a rate of 2.36 per 100,000 girls/boys in the population (U.S. Department of Health and Human Services 2010).

One question to be addressed regarding child fatalities is, why do infants have such higher rates of death when compared to older toddlers and adolescents? Children under one year old pose an immense amount of responsibility for their caretakers: they are completely dependent and need constant attention. Children this age are needy, impulsive, and not amenable to verbal control or effective communication. This can easily overwhelm vulnerable parents.

Another difficulty associated with infants is that they are physically weak and small. Injuries to infants can be fatal, while similar injuries to older children would not. The most common cause of death in children less than one year is cerebral trauma (often the result of shaken baby syndrome). Exasperated parents can deliver shakes or blows without realizing how little it takes to cause irreparable and fatal damage to an infant. Research informs us that two of the most common triggers for fatal child abuse are crying that will not cease and toileting accidents. Both of these circumstances are common in infants and young toddlers whose only means of communication often is crying, and who are limited in mobility and cannot use the toilet.

Finally, very young children cannot assist in injury diagnoses. Children who have been injured due to abuse or neglect often cannot communicate to medical professionals where it hurts, how it hurts, and so on. Also, nonfatal injuries can turn fatal in the absence of care by neglectful parents or parents who do not want medical professionals to possibly identify an injury as being the result of abuse.

Child Abuse Perpetrators: The Patterns

Child abuse perpetrators were more likely to be younger individuals, with slightly over 33 percent of them in their 20s, slightly less than 33 percent in their 30s, and approximately 16 percent in their 40s. Perpetrators of maltreatment were overwhelmingly parents of the abused child (81 percent). Of those perpetrators who were parents, over 85 percent were biological parents, 4 percent were stepparents, and 1 percent were adoptive parents (the remaining 10 percent were of unknown parental relationship). Other relatives of the children were 6.3 percent of the abusers and 4.3 percent of them were the unmarried partner of the child's parent. Child daycare providers, foster parents, friends and neighbors, legal guardians, group home staff, and other professionals individually all comprised less than 1 percent of the child abusers (U.S. Department of Health and Human Services 2010).

Regarding gender, approximately 58 percent of perpetrators were women and 42 percent were men. Women are typically younger than men. Women abusers were, on average, 31 years old, while on average, men were 34 years old. Forty percent of women who abused were younger than 30 years of age, compared with 33 percent of men being under 30 years of age (U.S. Department of Health and Human Services 2010).

The racial distribution of perpetrators is also similar to that of victims. Nearly half of the perpetrators were white (48.5 percent), 20 percent were African American, and 19 percent were Hispanic/Latino (U.S. Department of Health and Human Services 2010).

Regarding fatalities, estimates reveal that approximately 76 percent of perpetrators were parents of the victim. Other relatives accounted for nearly 5 percent, and unmarried partners of parents made up 3 percent of perpetrators (U.S. Department of Health and Human Services 2010).

Explanations for Child Abuse

As with many forms of deviance, questions about why people abuse children are pervasive. Many of these explanations are tantamount to theories of deviance in general. Some of the more common/well-accepted explanations for child abuse are individual pathology, parent–child interaction, past abuse in the family (or social learning), situational factors, and cultural support for physical punishment along with a lack of cultural support for helping parents here in the United States (Crosson-Tower 2008).

The first theory centers on the individual pathology of a parent or caretaker who is abusive. This explanation centers on the idea that people who abuse their children have something wrong with them, biologically or personality wise. Such psychological pathologies may include having anger control problems, being depressed or having postpartum depression, having a low tolerance for frustration (e.g., children can be extremely frustrating: they don't always listen, they constantly push the line for how far they can go, and once the line has been established, they are constantly treading on it to make sure it has not changed). They are dependent and self-centered, so caretakers have very little privacy or time to themselves), being rigid (e.g., having no tolerance for differences, such as, what if your son wanted to play with dolls? A rigid father would not let him, laugh at him for wanting to, punish him when he does, etc.), having deficits in empathy (parents who cannot put themselves into the shoes of their children cannot fully understand what their children need emotionally), and being disorganized, inefficient, and ineffectual (parents who are unable to manage their own lives are unlikely to be successful at managing the lives of their children, and since many children want and need limits, these parents are unable to set them and/or adhere to them).

Biological pathologies that may increase the likelihood of child abuse include having substance abuse or dependence problems, or having persistent or reoccurring physical health problems (these types of health problems can be extremely painful, and can cause a person to become more self-absorbed, both qualities can give rise to a lack of patience, lower frustration tolerance, and increased stress).

A second common explanation for child abuse centers on the interaction between the parent and the child, noting that certain types of parents are more likely to abuse, and certain types of children are more likely to be abused, and when these less skilled parents are coupled with these more difficult children, child abuse is the most likely to occur. Discussion here then focuses on what makes a parent less skilled, and what makes a child more difficult?

Characteristics of unskilled parents are likely to include traits such as only pointing out what children do wrong and never giving any encouragement for good behavior and failing to be sensitive to the emotional needs of children. Less skilled parents tend to have unrealistic expectations of children. They may engage in role reversal—where the parents make the child take care of them, and viewing that the parent's happiness and well-being is the responsibility of the child. Some parents view the parental role as extremely stressful and experience little enjoyment from being a parent. Finally, less skilled parents tend to have more negative perceptions regarding their child(ren). For example, perhaps the child has darker skin than they expected, they may feel the child is being manipulative (long before children have this capability), or they may view the child as the scapegoat for all the parents' or family's problems. Theoretically, given these characteristics, parents would be more likely to abuse their children, but if unskilled parents are coupled with a difficult child, they would be especially likely to be abusive.

So, what makes a child more difficult? Certainly, through no fault of their own, children may have characteristics that are associated with child care that is more demanding and difficult than in the "normal" or "average" situation. Such characteristics can include having physical and mental disabilities (autism, Attention Deficit Hyperactivity Disorder, hyperactivity, etc.), they may be colicky, be frequently sick, be particularly needy, or cry more often; some babies are simply happier than other babies for reasons that cannot be known. Further, infants are difficult even in the best of circumstances. They are unable to communicate effectively, and they are completely dependent on their caretakers for everything, including eating, diaper changing, moving around, entertainment, and emotional bonding. Again, these types of children, being more difficult, are more likely to be victims of child abuse.

Nonetheless, each of these types of parents and children alone cannot explain the abuse of children, but it is the interaction between them that becomes the key. Here, unskilled parents may produce children who are happy and not as needy, and even though they are unskilled, they do not abuse because the child takes less effort. At the same time, children who are more difficult may have parents who are skilled and are able to handle and manage with aplomb the extra effort these children take. Risks for child abuse increase than when unskilled parents must contend with difficult children.

Social learning or past abuse in the family is a third common explanation for child abuse. Here, the theory concentrates not only on what children learn when they see or experience violence in their homes, but additionally on what they do not learn as a result of these experiences. Social learning theory in the context of family violence stresses that if children are abused or see abuse (toward siblings or a parent), those interactions and violent family members become the representations and role models for their future familial interactions. In this way, what children learn is just as important as what they do not learn. Children who witness or experience violence may learn that this is the way parents deal with children, or that violence is an acceptable method of child rearing and discipline. They may think when they become parents that "violence worked on me when I was a child, and I turned out fine." They may learn unhealthy relationship interaction patterns; they may witness the negative interactions of their parents and they may learn the maladaptive or violent methods of expressing anger, reacting to stress, or coping with conflict.

What is equally as important, though, is that children are unlikely to learn more acceptable and nonviolent ways of rearing children, interacting with family members, and working out conflict. Here it may happen that a child who was abused would like to be nonviolent toward his or her own children, but when the chips are down and the child is misbehaving, this abused-child-turned-adult does not have a repertoire of nonviolent strategies to try. This parent, then, is more likely to fall back on what he or she knows as methods of discipline.

Something important to note here is that not all abused children grow up to become abusive adults. Children who break the cycle were often able to establish and maintain one healthy emotional relationship with someone during their childhoods (or period of young adulthood). For instance, they may have received emotional support from a nonabusing parent, or they received social support and had a positive relationship with another adult during their childhood (e.g., teacher, coach, minister, neighbor). Abused children who participate in therapy during some period of their lives can often break the cycle of violence. And, adults who were abused but are able to form an emotionally supportive and satisfying relationship with a mate can make the transition to being nonviolent in their family interactions.

Some common situational factors influence families and parents and increase the risks for child abuse. Typically, these factors are those that increase family stress or social isolation. Specifically, such factors may be families that receive public assistance or have low socioeconomic status (a combination of low income and low education), or individuals in families who are unemployed, underemployed (working in a job that requires lower qualifications than an individual possesses), or employed only part time. These financial difficulties cause great stress for families in meeting the needs of the individual members. Other stress-inducing familial characteristics are single-parent households and larger family size. Finally, social isolation can be devastating on families and family members. Having friends with whom we can talk, rely, drop kids off with occasionally is tremendously important for our personal growth and satisfaction in life. Additionally, social isolation and stress can cause individuals to be quick to lose their tempers, cause people to be less rational in their decision making and make mountains out of molehills. These situations can lead families to be at greater risk for child abuse.

Finally, cultural views and supports (or lack thereof) can lead to greater amounts of child abuse in a society such as the United States. One such cultural view is our societal support for physical punishment. This is problematic because there are similarities between the way we deal with criminals and the way we deal with errant children. We advocate the use of capital punishment for seriously violent criminals, and we are quick to use idioms such as "spare the rod and spoil the child" when it comes to the discipline/punishment of children. In fact, it was not until quite recently that parenting books began to encourage parents to use other strategies than spanking or other forms of corporal punishment in the discipline of their children. Only in recent years has the American Academy of Pediatrics recommended that parents do not spank or use other forms of violence on their children because of the deleterious effects such methods have on children and their bonds with their parents (http://www.aap.org). Nevertheless, regardless of recommendations, the culture of corporal punishment persists.

Another cultural view in the United States that can give rise to greater incidents of child abuse is the belief that after getting married, couples, *of course*, should want and have children. Culturally, we consider that children are a blessing, raising kids is the most wonderful thing a person can do, and everyone should have children. Along with this notion is the idea that motherhood is always wonderful, it is the most fulfilling thing a woman can do, and the bond between a mother and a child is strong, glorious, and automatic—all women love being mothers. So, culturally (and theoretically), society nearly insists that married couples have children and that they will love having children. But, after children are born, there is not much support for couples who have trouble adjusting to parenthood, or who do not absolutely love their new roles as parents. We look askance at parents who need help, and we cannot believe parents who say anything negative about parenthood. As such, theoretically, society has set up a situation where couples are strongly encouraged to have kids, are told they will love kids, but then turns a blind or disdainful eye when these same parents need emotional, financial, or other forms of help or support. It is these types of cultural viewpoints that increase the risks for child abuse in society.

The Consequences of Child Abuse and Neglect

The consequences of child abuse are tremendous and long lasting. Research has shown that the traumatic experience of childhood abuse is life-changing. These costs may surface during adolescence or they may not become evident until abused children have grown up and become abusing parents or abused spouses. Early identification and treatment is important to minimize these potential long-term effects. Whenever children say they have been abused, it is imperative that they be taken seriously and their abuse reported. Suspicions of child abuse must be reported as well. If there is a possibility that a child is or has been abused, an investigation must be conducted.

Children who have been abused may exhibit traits such as the inability to love or have faith in others. This often translates into adults who are unable to establish lasting and stable personal relationships. These individuals have trouble with physical closeness and touching as well as emotional intimacy and trust (Thomas 2003). Further, these qualities tend to cause a fear of entering into new, as well as the sabotaging of any current, relationships.

Psychologically, children who have been abused tend to have poor self images, are passive, are withdrawn, or are clingy. They are angry individuals who are filled with rage, anxiety, and a variety of fears. They are often aggressive, disruptive, and depressed. Many abused children have flashbacks and nightmares about the abuse they have experienced, and this may cause sleep problems as well as drug and alcohol problems. Posttraumatic stress disorder and antisocial personality disorder are both typical among maltreated children. Research has also shown that most abused children fail to reach "successful psychosocial functioning," and are, thus, not resilient and do not resume a "normal life" after the abuse has ended (Thomas 2003).

Socially, (and likely because of these psychological injuries), abused children have trouble in school, will have difficulty getting and remaining employed, and may commit a variety of illegal or socially inappropriate behaviors. Many studies have shown that victims of child abuse are likely to participate in high-risk behaviors, such as alcohol or drug abuse, the use of tobacco, and high-risk sexual behaviors (having unprotected sex, having large numbers of sexual partners). Later in life, abused children are more likely to have been arrested and homeless. They are also less able to defend themselves in conflict situations and guard themselves against repeated victimizations (Childhelp 2011).

Medically, abused children likely will experience health problems due to the high frequency and often occurring physical injuries they receive. Additionally, abused children experience much emotional turmoil and stress, which can also have a significant impact on their physical condition. These health problems are likely to continue occurring into adulthood. Some of these longer-lasting health problems include headaches; eating problems; problems with toileting; and chronic pain in the back, stomach, chest, and genital areas. Some researchers have noted that abused children may experience neurological impairment and problems with intellectual functioning, while others have found a correlation between abuse and heart, lung, and liver disease, and even cancer (Thomas 2003).

Victims of sexual abuse show an alarming number of disturbances as adults. Some dislike and avoid sex, or experience sexual problems or disorders, other victims appear to enjoy sexual activities that are self-defeating or maladaptive, normally called "dysfunctional sexual behavior" and have many sexual partners (Children's Defense Fund 2011).

Abused children also experience a wide variety of developmental delays. Many do not reach physical, cognitive, and/or emotional developmental milestones at the typical time, and some never accomplish what they are supposed to during childhood socialization. In the next section, these developmental delays are discussed as a means of identifying children who may be abused (Crosson-Tower 2008).

Changes in Attitudes Can Help Abused Children

Scholars often suggest changes in attitudes and culture as ways that deviant behavior can be handled. These types of changes can increase tolerance of deviance or can work in opposition to it. For example, seeking attitudinal changes may include providing education and experiential opportunities to create greater acceptance of differences among societal members. In this way, behaviors grow to be seen as more acceptable and less deviant. Cultural and attitudinal changes can also work in defiance of deviant behavior. In these instances, education and experience can create greater awareness of problematic deviant behaviors in order to highlight the harmful quality of the behavior in question, thereby reducing its commission. For child abuse, both types of educational efforts can help abused children.

One of the most difficult issues with which society must contend is the cultural practice of parents or other authority figures using corporal punishment to discipline children. In this way then, some more minor forms of child abuse may not be seen as deviant at all, but fully acceptable. Some parents may abuse their children under the guise of discipline, and many instances of physical child abuse arise from angry parents who go too far when disciplining their children with physical punishment. In support of physical punishment, though, many grandparents will argue, "Spare the rod and spoil the child"; while parents may believe that, "I was smacked/spanked/hit with a belt as a child and I turned out fine." We must institute more educational efforts about issues such as punishment and discipline styles and strategies, having greater respect for children, as well as informing the community about what child abuse is, and how to recognize it. Here, then, greater awareness of the harm corporal punishment produces and its potential to escalate into abuse may begin to minimize its occurrence as well as make it less acceptable among members of society.

Additionally, we must alter our cultural orientation about child bearing and rearing. We must work to normalize choosing to be child-free. Society must allow couples who wish to remain child-free to do so without disdain. And, we must acknowledge that raising children is very difficult, is not always gloriously wonderful, and that parents who seek help should be lauded and not looked on with askance. These kinds of efforts may reduce the number of couples or individuals who reluctantly have children due to societal pressure and then mistreat them. This, in turn, will increase the number of children who are raised in nonviolent emotionally satisfying families, thereby becoming better adjusted adults.

Discussion Questions

1. How would you draw the line between child abuse and corporal punishment? Consider both the physical and emotional elements of punishment. Think about how the law could reflect your ideas.
2. Consider the demographic and social patterns associated with child abuse perpetrators and the various theories explaining child abuse. Pick out several patterns you find particularly interesting. Which theories are better at explaining these patterns, and which are less satisfying?
3. How can we begin to change societal attitudes regarding children? What particular attitudes are the most important to change?

References

42 U.S.C.A. §5106g. 1998. The Child Abuse Prevention and Treatment Act.

Childhelp: Prevention and Treatment of Child Abuse. Retrieved April 10, 2011 (http://www.childhelp.org/resources/learning-center/statistics).

Children's Defense Fund. 2011. Retrieved April 14, 2011 (http://www.childrensdefense.org/child-research-data-publications/each-day-in-america.html).

Crosson-Tower, Cynthia. 2008. *Understanding Child Abuse and Neglect,* 7th ed. New York: Allyn & Bacon.

Haley's Rights. Retrieved April 10, 2011 (http://www.haleysrights.org/).

Pitzer, Ronald L. 1997. "Corporal Punishment in the Discipline of Children in the Home: Research Update for Practitioners" paper presented at the National Council on Family Relations Annual Conference, Washington DC. Retrieved March 14, 2011 (http://www.extension.umn.edu/distribution/familydevelopment/DE7266.html).

Straus, Murray A. 2001. *Beating the Devil Out of Them: Corporal Punishment in American Families and Its Effects on Children.* New Brunswick, NJ: Transaction Publishers.

Thomas, Peter M. 2003. "Protection, Dissociation, and Internal Roles: Modeling and Treating the Effects of Child Abuse." *Review of General Psychology* 7(4) 364–80.

U.S. Department of Health and Human Services, Administration for Children and Families, Children's Bureau. 2006. *National Child Abuse and Neglect Data System* (NCANDS). Retrieved March 14, 2011 (http://aspe.hhs.gov/hsp/06/catalog-ai-an-na/NCANDS.htm).

U.S. Department of Health and Human Services, Administration for Children and Families, Administration on Children, Youth and Families, Children's Bureau. 2010. *Child Maltreatment 2009.* Retrieved March 14, 2011 (http://www.acf.hhs.gov/programs/cb/stats_research/index.htm#can).

PART FOUR

Substance Use and Abuse

In 2010, senior U.S. district judge Jack T. Camp, Jr., pleaded guilty to unlawful possession and use of cocaine, marijuana, and Roxicodone, a prescription pain reliever. He bought his drugs from a stripper who had a federal drug trafficking conviction. Their relationship began with a table dance a few months earlier, which evolved into sex and drugs being a part of their regular interaction. Camp was appointed by President Ronald Regan and was part of a U.S. district court for over 20 years. As a part of his plea, he resigned from his judicial position.[1]

The 67-year-old Camp did not fit the typical media profile of a drug user, neither did his drug usage. Substance abusers come from various backgrounds and use various stimulants to achieve their highs. This part discusses some of the different types of substance abuse. Erich Goode provides an overview of drug use as a form of deviant behavior. He discusses everything from alcohol to psychoactive drugs. Articles 9 and 10 in this part discuss substance abuse on college campuses. Jenkot provides empirical findings on the various types of substance abuse, from marijuana to Ecstasy to cocaine, that are common on college campuses. Ford and Schroeder end this part by discussing how academic strain has led many college students to a common venue for substance abuse: prescription drugs.

Note

1. Rankin, Bill. 2010. "U.S. Judge Pleas Guilty to Drug Charges." *The Atlanta Journal-Constitution*, November 19. Retrieved May 12, 2011 (http://www.ajc.com/news/atlanta/u-s-judge-pleads-747336.html).

ARTICLE 8

Erich Goode
Professor Emeritus at Stony Brook University

Drug Use as Deviant Behavior[1]

Substances that stimulate pleasure centers in the brain belong to a category of drugs that pharmacologists refer to as *psychoactive*. Over the millennia, humans have discovered the psychoactive quality in plants, such as marijuana, opium, psychedelic mushrooms, the peyote cactus, coca leaves, as well the fermented product of rotten fruit and other vegetable substances, in the form of alcohol. Archaeologists and ethnobotanists (Schultes and Von Reis 1995; Merlin 2003) believe that the human use of psychoactive substances dates back tens of thousands of years, long before the end of the Stone Age, even before the discovery of agriculture, permanent settlements, and the forging of metals. It is almost certain that the earliest use of drugs was sacred and ceremonial, only later, medicinal, and later still, for hedonistic purposes. Just as importantly, throughout more than 99 percent of human history, the alteration of the human consciousness by chemical means has been culturally approved, conventional, and normative. Using drugs to communicate with the gods and heal the body are *instrumental* activities. In contrast, getting high is a *recreational* activity—an end in itself. It was probably only when significant numbers of renegades, apostates, and miscreants wandered away from socially approved pathways and culturally licit interpretations of reality that some members of humanity were inspired to take up the practice of getting intoxicated specifically for the purpose of achieving a sought-after psychic state. Hence, drug use was both *cause* and *consequence* of deviant behavior.

The overlapping territory between drug use and deviance is immense and diverse; we can divide it into three spheres. First, from a *constructionist* perspective, both have been condemned and negatively sanctioned behaviors; more specifically, by taking illicit drugs, or taking specific drugs immoderately or inappropriately, the user has, at times and in certain societies, been socially and legally *defined* as a disreputable person as well as a criminal. Second, from a *predispositional* perspective, drug use and deviant behavior and crime are acts that have a similar, even mutual, genesis—that is, they can be seen as *effects of a common cause*. And third, considering their overlap from a *causal* perspective, drug use can be seen as *triggering* deviant—specifically, violent and criminal—behavior.

Drug Use: An Introduction

Pharmacologists classify psychoactive drugs according to their effects on the mind. In such a classification, they locate four broad categories of drugs, and identify two specific drugs that are unique unto themselves. People tend to take psychoactive drugs recreationally to get high, to achieve euphoria, or to achieve a pleasurable mental state. Not all drugs activate the same pleasure centers in the brain, nor do they articulate with deviance and crime in the same ways.

Stimulants speed up signals passing through the central nervous system (CNS), that is, the brain and spinal column. They cause users to feel more alert and awake, and increase their overall behavioral output. Representatives include powder and crack cocaine, amphetamine, and methamphetamine.

Sedatives or *general depressants* decrease the activity and functioning of a wide range of organs. They tend to facilitate relaxation, inhibit anxiety and, at higher doses, induce sleep. The most well-known of the general depressants is alcohol, which scientists refer to as ethyl alcohol or ethanol; other sedatives include barbiturates, methaqualone (Quaalude and Sopor) and GHB, as well as tranquilizers, such as Valium, Xanax, Librium, lorazepam, and Rohypnol ("roofies"). In sufficiently high doses, general depressants induce mental clouding, drowsiness, and a physical dependence; an overdose can produce unconsciousness, coma, and even death. The depressants are physically dependency producing.

Narcotics, or "narcotic analgesics," diminish the brain's perception of pain. This category includes the opiates—opium and its derivatives, including morphine, heroin, and codeine—as well as the synthetic narcotics, called opioids (or "opium-like" drugs), such as Percodan, Dilaudid, methadone, meperidine (or Demerol), oxycodone (including OxyContin), and fentanyl. All narcotics are also physically addicting: They generate a physical dependency with regular, long-term use. In addition, their effects include mental clouding and euphoria. It is their euphoria-generating property that causes many people to use narcotics recreationally—that is, for the purpose of getting high.

Hallucinogens (once referred to as psychedelics) have effects on the CNS that cannot be reduced to a simple stimulation-depression continuum. These drugs induce profound sensory alterations. They include lysergic acid diethylamide (LSD), peyote and mescaline, and psilocybin or "magic mushrooms" ("shrooms"). The principal effect of the hallucinogens is extreme psychoactivity, that is, capable of inducing sensations that do not correspond with external reality—at the most extreme end, outright hallucinations—along with a loosening of the imagination and an intensification of emotional states. The hallucinogens do not produce a physical dependence—in fact, their effects tend to minimize their chronic use—and they are not toxic; that is, there are no known cases of death by overdose.

Phencyclidine (PCP) or Sernyl is a *disassociative-anesthetic*, a minor drug type with only two major representatives. Ketamine ("special K") is a milder version of PCP. These drugs produce drowsiness, discoordination, a distorted sense of the reality of one's physical surroundings, and a feeling of invulnerability.

3,4-Methylenedioxymethamphetamine (MDMA or Ecstasy) is sometimes referred to as a hallucinogen, but it does not produce sensory alterations; a more accurate term to describe it would be *empathogen*; that is, it is capable of inducing empathy, or an emotional identification with others.

Marijuana has, at different times and in different places, been classified as a depressant, a stimulant, and, as late as the 1970s, a hallucinogen. It is a vegetable substance, typically consisting of the buds, resin, and leaves of the *cannabis* plant; hashish, a related substance, is made up exclusively of the resin of this plant. Nowadays, most observers feel that the marijuana products belong in a category by itself. Cannabis, usually smoked, induces a dreamy, mind-wandering, semi-somnolent, and impaired cognitive condition, along with some discoordination. The drug is not addictive or physically dependency producing, and does not cause overdose deaths.

The Use of Psychoactive Drugs

In its World Drug Report for 2010, the United Nations Office on Drugs and Crime (UNODC) estimated that about 200 million people worldwide (or roughly 4.5 percent of the population age 15 to 64) used one or more illicit substance at least once in 2008, of whom about 160 million used marijuana. UNDOC estimated that amphetamine is the world's second most commonly used illegal substance, followed by cocaine and the opiates. The world's total opium and cocaine cultivation and production declined roughly from 10 to 15 percent since 2007. Of the people who use illicit drugs, about 10 to 15 percent are problem users; that is, they either inject drugs or are physically dependent on illicit drugs. The two drugs with the most substantial North American representation are cocaine (40 percent of the global cocaine market) and cannabis (just under 20 percent of the total).

How do we know about the use of psychoactive drug use in the general population? More specifically, if the possession and distribution of a substance are illegal and its use is disapproved of, wouldn't respondents in a survey lie about their illicit drug use and sale? The answer is, no, not quite. Most people give answers to such surveys truthfully enough for researchers to make use of their responses and give observers a reasonably accurate approximation of their use. Moreover, making use of multiple sources of information ("triangulation") increases the researcher's confidence that responses to surveys are reliable and accurate. With respect to the incidence of drug use in the United States, we can make use of four principal data sources: the National Survey on Drug Use and Health (NSDUH), which studies the drug use of samples of the population as a whole; Monitoring the Future (MTF), a survey on drug use among samples of eighth, tenth, and twelfth graders (Johnston et al. 2010); ADAM, or the Advanced Drug Abuse Monitoring program, which draws national urban samples of arrestees, drug-tests them, and questions them about their drug use; and the two Drug Abuse Warning Network, or DAWN programs, which look at drug-related hospital emergency department (ED) admissions and drug-related overdose deaths or mortalities, as determined by medical examiners (ME).

The two drug use surveys (NSDUH and MTF) show that alcohol is by far the most commonly used recreational drug in America. Over half of the United States population (52 percent) has drunk an alcoholic beverage during the prior month; four out of ten high school seniors have done so (43 percent), and over a quarter of 12th graders (28 percent) say that during the previous 30 days, they have gotten drunk. Keep in mind, among adolescents, the younger the age, the lower the use: nearly all categories of drug use for 10th graders is lower than for 12th graders, and nearly all use for eighth graders is lower than for tenth graders. Among illicit drugs, marijuana is without peer in popularity. More episodes of marijuana use take place than for all the other illegal drugs combined. Roughly 100 million people in the United States have tried marijuana at least once, and of these, 15 million have used it in the past month. While 6 percent of the population above the age of 12 has used marijuana during the past month, only 3.4 percent have used any and all other drugs during the same time period. During the past month, among high school seniors, the at least one-time use of drugs such as LSD, Ecstasy, amphetamines, and cocaine is in the 1 to 3 percent range; for marijuana it is nearly a fifth (19 percent). Hence, most illegal drug use is marijuana use. As a general rule, the more deviant and socially disapproved the drug, the lower the percentage of the population that uses it.

Moreover, *legal* drugs tend to be used much more often on a continued basis, while *illegal* drugs tend to be used more infrequently and episodically and are more likely to be given up after a period of time. Of all drugs, legal or illegal, alcohol attracts the greatest user loyalty: roughly six persons in ten who say that they ever drank did so in the past month. For *illegal* drugs, marijuana tends to be "stuck with" the longest—15 percent of all Americans who have tried it have remained users. In other words, the more legal the drug, the more loyal users are to it—the more they stick with it, the more likely they are to *continue* using it over time, and the less likely they are to give up its use. Turning the equation around, the more illegal or illicit the drug, the less likely it is that one-time users will stick with it or continue using it. Hence, marijuana, the "least illicit" of the illicit drugs, is the one that users are most likely to continue using. For cocaine and methamphetamine, the figure is 6 percent and 4 percent, respectively, and for heroin, it is 4 percent; only six-tenths of 1 percent of at least one-time users have taken PCP in the past month (SAMHSA 2010.)

Drug Use *as* Deviance and Crime

At certain times and places, the illicit drug user has been socially and legally constructed as disreputable and criminal. Nineteenth-century America "could quite properly be described as a dope fiend's paradise" (Brecher et al. 1972:3). Psychoactive substances were freely available from a variety of different sources, and the public consumption of these substances was immense—in all likelihood, on a per population basis, equaling or surpassing today's volume of use. Users and addicts were not socially marginalized, stigmatized, or regarded as deviants or criminals. What stimulated such high levels of use a century or so ago? How did tolerance for drug taking emerge? And what brought about a change in attitudes and public policy? How did we get from a society in which no one was imprisoned on drug charges to one in which hundreds of thousands—indeed, several million—are? What does history have to teach us about changes in the drug laws and the climate of public opinion?

Such a historical investigation should encompass all drugs—including alcohol, narcotics, and cocaine. Alcohol was the first drug to be controlled by both the law and public opinion. In 1830, the per capita consumption of absolute alcohol stood at 7.10 gallons per year, a literally staggering sum. Beer, wine, and distilled spirits freely flowed, and was consumed at all manner of occasions, including breakfast, during work breaks, in the field, and during political campaigns. Saloons were virtually unregulated, and were magnets of a host of vices, including prostitution, chronic drunkenness, gambling, and political corruption (Lender and Martin 1987:103–104). Because of efforts of the temperance movement, specifically the Women's Christian Temperance Movement (WCTU), local ordinances and public opinion began moderating the consumption of alcohol, and by the early 1900s, consumption had dropped to roughly 2 gallons per annum per adult age 15 and older (Lender and Martin 1987). In comparison, narcotics legislation lagged a generation or more behind. In 1900, because of practically nonexistent regulation and primitive medical practices, there were over 300,000 narcotic addicts in the United States, most of them female and middle-aged and of iatrogenic and medical, rather than recreational, origin. Dozens of companies marketed cocaine-based soft drugs. It was not until 1906 that the law required the label on a medication to list the ingredients contained therein. In 1914, Congress passed the Harrison Narcotic Act, and President Woodrow Wilson signed it into law; legislators pledged that the federal law would bring some control over the traffic in opiates and cocaine (Musto 1999:61). While several physicians challenged the law by maintaining their addict-patients on narcotics, in several key decisions, the Supreme Court ruled that maintenance of the addict was a "plain perversion" of the Harrison Act (Musto 1999:132). In 1918, local, state, and federal authorities set up roughly 50 maintenance clinics to treat the addict, and by 1923, largely because of the efforts of crusading journalistic exposés, all had been closed down by federal authorities.

Interestingly, during the period from the late 1800s to the mid-nineteen-teens, the shift to a new addict population had already been taking place. The middle-aged female medical addicts taking morphine for an ailment had already largely been withdrawn from narcotics, and, increasingly, the representative or typical addict was younger, criminal, a mainliner, and specifically a heroin abuser. By the early 1920s, the addict was a criminal by law, and a deviant by public opinion.

Early in the twentieth century, again, as a result of the efforts of the temperance movement, local, state, and federal laws restricted the hours of bars and where they could be located, which brought the consumption of alcohol under social and legal authority. However, the anti-alcohol movement of the early twentieth century was satisfied only by complete prohibition, which was accomplished in 1920. But by criminalizing alcohol distribution, Prohibition only further deviantized and criminalized drinking, forcing drinkers to seek out illicit operations, making a mockery of the law, energizing organized crime, and leaving quality control up to illegal distilleries (Lender and Martin 1987). Sensibly, by 1930, the American government repealed the Eighteenth Amendment (the Volstead Act) and attempted to *domesticate* and *conventionalize* drinking, bringing alcohol distribution under some semblance of legal and social control. Alcohol consumption went on a roller-coaster ride, from the high of the early 1800s (7.10 gallons of absolute alcohol per year per drinking age adult), to a drastic decline by the nineteen-teens (1.96 gallons), to a further decline during the Prohibition era (0.90 gallons), to an initial post-Prohibition low of between 1 and 2 gallons per adult. After the 1960s, alcohol consumption has wiggled around somewhere between 2 and 3 gallons per capita per year (Lender and Martin 1987: 205–206). In other words, between the 1990s and the early 2000s, for the typical drinker, alcohol consumption had remained fairly moderate (Goode 2012).

As we saw, the nineteenth-century saloon was a den of iniquity and corruption (Lender and Martin 1987; Duis 1999); social and legal controls, as well as the entry of women into bars (Murdock 1998), have brought the institution into the mainstream. In contrast, increasingly, into the 1930s and 1940s, the user of narcotics was a street person, a criminal, a deviant; the urban "shooting gallery" never developed as a legitimate meeting place for addicts. This process of deviantization began taking place even before the passage of the Harrison Narcotic Act (Courtwright 1982). For the most part, medical addicts died off or stopped using, and the Chinese opium culture, so prominent in American folklore during the nineteenth century, faded from the American scene, its devotees growing increasingly old and dying off. At the same time that drinking and drinkers grew increasingly mainstream and nondeviant, the status of the narcotic addict moved in precisely the opposite direction. Methadone maintenance programs have attempted to redefine enrolled narcotic addicts as "clients" and "patients," have drastically reduced the addicts' criminal behavior, and virtually eliminated their euphoric, addled states as well as blocked withdrawal, overdoses, and the intravenous use of narcotics. But relatively few methadone-maintained clients hold a full-time, year-round job, a fairly high proportion turn in "dirty" samples—indicating that "cheating" by taking other drugs is common—and conservatives continue to be successful in stalemating the expansion of the program. While the attempt of prohibitionists to drive alcohol out of mainstream American society proved to be a catastrophic failure, the meliorist attempt to incorporate the addict into the mainstream has met with extremely limited success. It seems that in American society, the narcotic addict will remain something of a deviant.

Of the illicit drugs, marijuana maintains the most diverse and least stigmatized clientele. Its widespread use, partial decriminalization in more than a dozen states, and the tepid public acceptance of the validity of its criminal status ensure that its users will not be regarded as pariahs or outcasts. While not entirely mainstream, smoking marijuana does not cast the user beyond the pale of respectability in the same way that using narcotics or cocaine does.

The Empirical Relationship between Drug Use and Crime

The statistical relationship between the consumption of psychoactive drugs and engaging in criminal behavior is one of the most robust and firmly established in the criminological literature. It is in fact completely unproblematic;

hardly any criminologists or sociologists of deviance or drug use question that drugs and crime are empirically related. In nearly every systematic study ever conducted, persons who use illicit drugs, drink alcohol, and smoke cigarettes are statistically more likely to engage in criminal or delinquent behavior, especially frequently, than persons who do not use drugs, drink, or smoke. And the more frequently persons use drugs for recreational purposes the greater the likelihood that they engage in criminal behavior, the greater the likelihood that they will do so frequently, and the more serious the criminal behavior they engage in. While most drinkers and cigarette smokers do not commit crime, drinking and smoking are statistically related to criminal behavior.

James Inciardi refers to the drugs-crime nexus as "the riddle of the sphinx" (2002:182)—an intellectual puzzle that seems fiendishly difficult, that demands an answer upon pain of death, yet whose answer may be simpler than we realize. Logically, the relationship between these two variables could be drug use causes crime; crime causes drug use; both are the effects of a common cause. But in real-world terms, what exactly do these mechanistic causal sequences *mean*? There is a spectrum of possibilities.

As all researchers know, convincingly establishing a precise cause-and-effect relationship between two or more variables is tricky and troublesome. With respect to the relationship between drug use and crime, this problem may be even more problematic than usual not only because of the complexity of the variables but also the quality of the research. Among many vexing issues we might consider the relationship between drug use and criminal behavior is "probabilistic, not deterministic. Most drug users are not otherwise criminally active, and the vast majority of drug-using incidents neither cause nor accompany other forms of criminality." Moreover, the drugs-crime link "varies across individuals, over time, . . . across situations," and, very possibly, "over time periods," as well as from one neighborhood or community and demographic group to another (MacCoun, Kilmer, and Reuter 2003:65, 66).

In addition, drugs are differentially linked to crime, on a drug-by-drug basis. With respect to sheer volume, alcohol is implicated in more criminal behavior than any other psychoactive drug, but it is consumed on a monthly-or-more basis by more than half the American population, and the overwhelming majority of drinking episodes result in no criminal behavior whatsoever. On an episode-by-episode basis, cocaine and heroin are, compared with other illicit drugs, *extremely* intimately linked with criminal offending; in contrast, the use of Ecstasy hardly ever appears in police records as implicated in criminal events. And lastly, the role of drug use in *being* criminally victimized further complicates the drugs-crime picture. Persons under the influence of alcohol and illicit drugs stand a significantly greater chance of becoming a victim of a predatory crime than persons not under the influence. The issue of victimization is especially important for women (MacCoun, Kilmer, and Reuter 2003: 71; Goode 2011:155–157).

Empirically, the drugs-crime relationship is so strong, consistent, and statistically significant that documentation seems almost superfluous. Nonetheless, the Youth Risk Surveillance study, a nationally representative survey of 15,000 teenagers in grades 9 through 12, provides ample evidence that the two behaviors are intimately related.

To choose a few relationships almost at random, consider the fact that females who smoked more than 20 cigarettes a day in the month prior to the survey were 125 times more likely to say they drove under the influence of alcohol six or more times during the previous month (50 percent) than was true of those who did not smoke at all (0.4 percent); males who smoked 20 or more cigarettes were 45 times more likely to have done so (17.9 percent versus 0.4 percent).

Females who drank five or more drinks on 20 or more days during the prior 30 days were

26 times more likely to carry a weapon to school on six or more days (44 percent) than those who never drank five or more drinks during that same period (1.7 percent); males who drank five or more drinks were just shy of 10 times more likely to have done so (75 percent versus 7.6 percent).

Females who used cocaine more than 10 times during their lives were 51 times more likely to have gotten into 12 or more fights during the previous year (36 percent) than was true of those who did not use cocaine at all (0.7 percent); males who used cocaine 10 or more times were 16 times more likely to have done so (36 percent versus 2.3 percent).[2]

These relationships are consistent and remarkably robust. It hardly matters which indicator of drug use, legal or illegal (the purchase of alcohol is illegal to persons under 21 and the purchase of cigarettes is illegal to everyone under the age of 18), or which indicator of crime and delinquency we choose, the two dimensions are so intimately related they almost seem to be measures of the same phenomenon. Precisely the same relationship holds between drug use and risky sexual behavior (e.g., having sex at an early age, having sex without the use of a condom, drinking alcohol before having sex, getting pregnant or causing a pregnancy, having sex with multiple partners), as well as between delinquency and risky sexual behavior. In addition, as we see, the correlation between the use of alcohol and tobacco, which are inexpensive, and delinquent behavior, is extremely strong, on par with that between illicit drugs and delinquency. These findings are entirely consistent with Gottfredson and Hirschi's (1990) contentions about the drugs-crime nexus.

These data are illustrative but not definitive. But the sheer weight of the available evidence, from multitudinous sources, including survey data—whether based on randomized samples or not—arrest data, overdose data, and data drawn from drug tests, confirms precisely the same generalization: people who use psychoactive drugs—both legal and illicit—for recreational purposes are substantially and significantly more likely to commit criminal offenses, and vice versa. "Many data sources," say policy analysts MacCoun, Kilmer, and Reuter (2003), "establish a raw correlation between drug use and other criminal offenses" (p. 65). At this point, further documentation seems redundant.

The ADAM is based on a sample of arrestees for violent crimes, property crimes, drug crimes, driving while intoxicated, and domestic violence crimes; it is drawn in 10 counties in which several of the nation's large cities are located. The 2008 sample, all male, was made up of about 4,000 booked arrestees who agreed to supply a urine sample—about 85 percent of all arrestees who were approached. What is so useful about ADAM is that it accesses populations that would be inaccessible by means of more conventional research methods, such as the surveys. This is the case because many of ADAM's samples do not live in conventional households, nor can they be located in a conventional institution, such as a school or place of employment. For someone interested in the relationship between drug use and crime, ADAM is a crucial source (Yacoubian 2000).

The first story ADAM's data tells is that arrestees—presumably, all or almost all of whom are criminal offenders—are *extraordinarily* highly likely to use drugs. In 2008, a median of 40 percent of arrestees urine-tested positive for marijuana; the median was 30 percent for cocaine. In stark contrast, only 6 percent of the American population says that they used at least one illicit drug once or more during the past *month*. With most tests employed, no drug (except, possibly, marijuana) can be detected a month or more since most recent use—most are detectable only within two to three days. The chances are, if that 6 percent figure is accurate, less than 3 percent of the American population would test positive for an illegal drug; that is, in any given moment in time, they used recently enough to have traces in their bodies. Compared with a cross-section of the population at large—most of whom are *not* criminals—criminal offenders are *extremely* likely to use psychoactive drugs, *hugely* more likely to do so than is true of nonoffenders.

The second tale that ADAM tells is that the use of methamphetamine, a drug that in the late 1980s, the media claimed was "sweeping the country," becoming the America's number one "drug of choice," remains highly regionalized. Tests were much more likely to be positive for arrestees in West Coast cities such as Sacramento (35 percent) and Portland (15 percent) than in cities, such as New York, Atlanta, and Charlotte, located in states on the East Coast (less than 0.5 percent).

A third important story: opiates (mainly heroin) are fairly rarely used. Only in Chicago (29 percent) and Washington (12 percent) did more than 1 in 10 arrestees test positive for the presence of one or more opiates. Only 1 in 20 arrestees, on average, tested positive for any of the opiates.

A fourth important lesson that ADAM teaches is that marijuana and cocaine are by far the two premier drugs that arrestees have taken recently. In fact, marijuana seems to have become the "drug of choice" of the nation's criminals, especially among the young (Golub and Johnson 2001).

A fifth lesson from the ADAM II data is that in a relative sense, self-reports for drug use very roughly correspond to testing positively for the presence of drugs; for the most part, a high proportion of people who use drugs admit to having done so. When the researchers asked, then tested, arrestees for use and presence of marijuana, the same percentage (44 percent) indicated that they had taken the drug in the past 30 days as had tested positive for the drug. Drugs that were less likely to have been used—such as opiates and methamphetamine—were correspondingly low in the self-report survey (2.5 percent and 0.5 percent, respectively) as well as the drug test (5.5 percent and 2 percent). The ADAM II team estimated that, overall, respondents admitted to having used a specific drug about half as frequently as tested positive for that substance.

Researchers agree that ADAM's data are unique and valuable. But they do have limitations. Most important, by definition, arrestees are offenders who get caught. Many offenders are able to escape detection; those who do may differ from arrestees in important ways, including their drug use patterns. In spite of this and other limitations, ADAM's sample of arrestees is as good as any sample is likely to be, and data from its tabulations are crucial to an understanding of the drugs and crime picture.

Are Drug Users Predisposed to Engage in Criminal Behavior?

The predisposition model argues against and opposes the enslavement or medical model, which holds that ordinary people become entrapped or "enslaved" to narcotic addiction (Lindesmith 1965, 1968). According to the proponents of the predisposition model, addicts do not engage in criminal behavior because they are forced into a life of crime by their drug use, and they were not law-abiding people before they became involved in the use of narcotics. In fact, most of the people who became addicted were already engaged in a life of crime, even before they became involved with drugs. The drugs-crime connection exists because criminals are deviant, because antisocial people have a predisposition for both crime and drug use, and because criminals and users of illicit drugs are pretty much the same people—they constitute strongly overlapping sectors of the population. This predisposition is reinforced by the fact that in the social circles in which criminals inhabit and move about, drug use is accepted, encouraged, and widespread. And as a result of this predisposition, legalizing drugs would be futile. Under legalization, criminal behavior would remain high among the people who become addicts—whether or not they become addicts—because they engaged in a life of crime even before they began using drugs, and they will continue to do so, though at a higher level, after they habitually use drugs. The predisposition hypothesis was promulgated in the 1950s and early 1960s by representatives of the Federal Bureau of Narcotics and the FBI. Currently, it is supported by Gottfredson and Hirschi's (1990) "general theory of crime." This perspective is also referred to as the "criminal model."

A predisposition to engage in risky, hedonistic behavior that manifests low self-control, Gottfredson and Hirschi (1990) argue, is what fuses these two behaviors in the same individuals. The relation between drug use and delinquency and crime "is not a causal question," they state (p. 93). The two are correlated because they are in fact *one and the same behavior*—at least, manifestations of one and the same underlying tendency—not two separate and independent dimensions. Drug use and crime "are the same thing—that is, manifestations of low self-control. If we are correct," they say, "longitudinal research designed to determine the causal relationship between crime and drug use is a waste of time and money" (1990: 233–234). There is no conceptual or theoretical distinction between the two; one does not cause the other—they are manifestations of exactly the same tendency.

What generates this underlying predisposition, this impulse to engage in these two interlocked behaviors is, as we've seen, low self-control—the tendency to seek short-term, easy, simple, immediate gratification of desires, as the authors say, "money without work, sex without courtship, revenge without court delays," acts that are "*exciting, risky, or thrilling,*" that provide "*few or meager long-term benefits,*" that require "*little skill or planning,*" and often result in "*pain or discomfort for the victim*" (1990:89). In other words, low impulse control is the mechanism, vehicle, or *means* by which the tendency to engage in criminal behavior and drug use is expressed. And what breeds low self-control is, as we've seen, poor, inadequate parenting, that is, the inability or unwillingness of parents to monitor or sanction the untoward behavior of their children. Low self-control is a lifelong characteristic of the individual, modified but not substantially altered by the aging process, which prevails for males and females separately and independently.

In sum, the link between drug use and criminal behavior is forged by their common, inherent appeal, by the fact that they both satisfy the same impulse, the thirst for immediate gratification, which is appealing for persons lacking self-control. Both are risky behaviors, often entailing harm both to the actor and to victims, but both get the actor what is desired in the short run. Gottfredson and Hirschi's answer to the "Why?" question—why is the link between drug use and criminal behavior so empirically robust?—is that there is a *predisposition* to engage in both behaviors. They are both manifestations of the same underlying tendency; no other explanation explains as many aspects of this empirical link as does self-control theory. Accordingly, any other models, especially Lindesmith's "enslavement" theory, that explain their correlation, say Gottfredson and Hirschi, are wrong (1990:41).

The consumption of alcohol and the use of illicit psychoactive drugs are likewise related in revealing and important ways. But since many fewer people use illicit drugs than use alcohol, the relationship is far from perfect. Let us express their relationship in the following two generalizations. First: *most people who drink don't use illegal drugs.* And second: *people who drink alcohol are more likely to use illegal drugs than people who don't drink.* Drinking is a correlate of illicit drug use, which in turn is a correlate of criminal behavior; in addition, drinking is independently statistically correlated with criminal behavior.

Does Drug Use Lead to Deviant and Criminal Behavior?

The most commonsensical and traditional explanation of why drugs and violence are connected is the psychopharmacological model. Proponents of this line of thought hold that it is the psychological and physical effects of psychoactive substances that cause users to become criminally inclined and violent toward others. As a result of ingesting one or more substances, users "may become excitable, irrational, and may exhibit violent behavior" (Goldstein 1985: 494). In the 1930s, this was precisely the model the Federal Bureau of Narcotics promulgated with respect to marijuana (Anslinger 1937). Although the effects of opiates tend to be soothing and soporific, the "irritability associated with the withdrawal syndrome ... may indeed lead to violence" (Goldstein 1985:495). And, as we saw, someone is more likely to be victimized when under the influence of one or more psychoactive substances, and hence, in that sense, the effects of drugs may lead, albeit indirectly, to violence.

Another explanation for drug use often leading to violence is the *economic-compulsive* model. Some researchers argue that because addicts need to raise large sums of money quickly, they engage in high-risk crimes, including theft, robbery, and burglary, that often escalate into acts of physical harm against the victim. (Robbery is, of course, *itself* a crime of violence, as well as an economically motivated crime.) For instance, in a given robbery, both the perpetrator and the victim may be nervous; the victim may resist, struggle, attempt to retaliate against the offender, and the victim may be accidentally stabbed or shot. In a burglary, the resident may confront the offender, resulting in a struggle; suddenly, a crime of stealth becomes assault or even murder. Economic crimes undertaken to support a drug habit don't always remain simple property crimes; inadvertently, a certain proportion turn into crimes of violence.

The world of drug dealing is saturated with violence. Lacking recourse to the protection of the law, dealers often resort to taking the law into their own hands. Drug sellers carry or stash drugs—a commodity far more valuable on the streets than gold—and handle large sums of cash. The temptation for street people is to rob dealers of both the cash and the drugs. Drug sellers are vulnerable to arrest, and informers often turn them in to avoid long prison sentences; violence is a common response to such a betrayal. Drug sales may result in disputes over the quality and quantity of the goods sold. One gang may decide to "muscle into" the territory of an established gang, resulting in violent retaliation. Buyers may receive a shipment of drugs, use most of it themselves, and be unable to pay for what they consumed.

Systemic violence, then, refers to "the traditionally aggressive patterns of interaction within the system of drug distribution and use." In the *systemic violence model*, systemic violence is "normatively embedded in the social and economic networks of drug users and sellers. Drug use, the drug business, and the violence connected to both of these phenomena are all part of the same general lifestyle. Individuals caught in this lifestyle value the experience of substance use, recognize the risks involved, and struggle for survival every day. That struggle is clearly a major contributor to the total volume of crime and violence in American society" (Goldstein 1985:497, 503).

A team of researchers who examined the dynamics of criminal homicide in New York City during the height of the crack crisis tackled the question of which of these three models best explains the strong relationship between drug use and violence (Goldstein et al. 1989). They classified a homicide as "drug related" if both the researchers and the police decided that drugs contributed to the killing "in an important and causal manner" (p. 662). The researchers drew a sample of roughly a quarter of all criminal homicides that took place in 1988. It was made up of 414 "homicide events," since some of these "events" involved more than one perpetrator and more than one victim. Just over half (53 percent) of these "events" were classified as primarily drug related; just under half (47 percent) were deemed not to be drug related. Studying each event on a case-by-case basis, the researchers and the police determined that 60 percent of the drug-related homicides involved crack cocaine; an additional 22 percent involved powder cocaine.

Which of the three models best explains the connection between drugs and criminal homicide? The psychopharmacological model, which during the crack epidemic in the late 1980s attracted so much media attention and is so intuitively appealing to much of the public, did not offer an adequate guide to reality. The team deemed that of the 118 crack-related homicides, only 3 (3 percent) had been caused by the psychoactive effects of the drug. They judged that only 8 (7 percent) were economic-compulsive in origin. Except for a few "multidimensionally" caused homicides, they decided that all of the remainder (100 out of 118, or 85 percent) could be explained by the *systemic* model. The circumstances of systemic homicides included territorial disputes, the robbery of a drug dealer, efforts to collect a drug debt, disputes over a drug theft, and reactions to a dealer selling poor, weak drugs. Typically, killings connected to crack (and powder cocaine as well) were caused *not* by the effects of the drug but by the violent and conflictual nature of the crack *business.*

What makes the crack business an especially disputational enterprise? Why was the crack trade, for example, in comparison with the heroin business, an arena in which murder took place with special frequency? The authors trace the volatile nature of the crack trade to its unstable, unorganized distribution system. Since cocaine can be extremely easily converted into crack, there is no hierarchy or organizational structure to hold dealing networks together. The marketplace is made up of many small-scale entrepreneurs, independents who are able to start up a business for themselves and compete in the same territory for a clientele. Hence, boundary disputes are plentiful, and there are no higher-ups—indeed, no organization at all—capable of controlling violence when it does threaten to erupt.

Notes

1. A few paragraphs in this chapter have been adapted from Goode (2008, 2011, 2012).

2. I would like to thank Jo Anne Grundbaum at the Centers for Disease Control and Prevention (CDC) for providing me with the raw data which enabled me to make these tabulations.

Discussion Questions

1. What are the various ways drugs are connected to deviance? Which is most harmful to society?
2. If illegal drugs were legalized, what effect would it have on society?

References

Anslinger, Harry J., with Courtney Riley Cooper. 1937. "Marihuana—Assassin of Youth." *American Magazine*, July, pp. 18–19, 150–53.

Brecher, Edward M., and the Editors of *Consumer Reports*. 1972. *Licit and Illicit Drugs*. Boston, MA: Little, Brown.

Courtwright, David T. 1982. *Dark Paradise: Opiate Addiction in America Before 1940*. Cambridge, MA: Harvard University Press.

Duis, Perry R. 1999. *The Saloon: Public Drinking in Chicago and Boston, 1880–1920*. Urbana, IL: University of Illinois Press.

Goldstein, Paul J. 1985. "The Drugs/Crime Nexus: A Tripartite Conceptual Framework." *Journal of Drug Issues* 15(fall):493–506.

Goldstein, Paul, Henry H. Brownstein, Patrick Ryan, and Patricia A. Bellucci. 1989. "Crack in Homicide in New York City, 1988: A Conceptually Based Event Analysis." *Contemporary Drug Problems* 16(winter):651–87.

Golub, Andrew and Bruce D. Johnson. 2001. "The Rise of Marijuana as the Drug of Choice among Youthful Adult Arrestees." *Research in Brief*, National Institute of Justice, June, pp. 1–19.

Goode, Erich. 2011. *Deviant Behavior*. Englewood Cliffs, NJ: Pearson Prentice Hall.

Goode, Erich. 2012. *Drugs in American Society*, 8th ed. New York: McGraw-Hill.

Gottfredson, Michael R. and Travis Hirschi. 1990. *A General Theory of Crime*. Stanford, CA: Stanford University Press.

Inciardi, James A. 2002. *The War on Drugs III*. Boston, MA: Allyn & Bacon.

Johnston, Lloyd D., Patrick O'Malley, Jerald G. Bachman, and John E. Schulenberger. 2010. *Monitoring the Future: National Results on Adolescent Drug Use, Overview of Key Findings 2009*. Bethesda, MD: National Institute on Drug Abuse.

Lender, Mark Edward and James Kirby Martin. 1987. *Drinking in America*, rev. and exp. ed. New York: Free Press.

Lindesmith, Alfred. 1965. *The Addict and the Law*. Bloomington, IN: Indiana University Press.

Lindesmith, Alfred. 1968. *Addiction and Opiates*. Chicago, IL: Aldine.

MacCoun, Robert J., Beau Kilmer, and Peter Reuter. 2003. "Research on Drugs-Crime Linkages: The Next Generation." Pp. 65–95 in *Toward a Drugs and Crime Research Agenda for the 21st Century*. Washington, DC: National Institute of Justice.

Merlin, M. D. 2003. "Archaeological Evidence for the Tradition of Psychoactive Plant Use in the Old World." *Economic Botany* 57(3):295–323.

Murdock, Catherine Gilbert. 1998. *Domesticating Drink: Women, Men, and Alcohol in America, 1870–1940*. Baltimore, MD: Johns Hopkins University Press.

Musto, David F. 1999. *The American Disease: Origins of Narcotic Control*, 3rd ed. New York: Oxford University Press.

Schultes, Richard Evans and Sin Von Reis, eds. 1995. *Ethnobotany: Evolution of a Discipline*. Portland, OR: Dioscorides Press.

Substance Abuse and Mental Health Services Administration (SAMHSA). 2010. *Results from the 2008 National Survey on Drug Use and Health: National Findings*. Rockville, MD: U.S. Department of Health and Human Services.

Yacoubian, George S., Jr. 2000. "Assessing ADAM's Domain: Past Problems and Future Prospects." *Contemporary Drug Problems* 2(spring):121–35.

ARTICLE 9

Robert B. Jenkot
Coastal Carolina University

"What's Goin' On?": Illicit Drug and Alcohol Use among College Students

My ongoing interest in drug and alcohol use among college students was compounded in the fall of 2009, when I overheard a conversation between two female students. One woman said, "I really didn't want to go out with him, but then he gave me a handful of pills, so I was like, OK."

Understanding the correlation between alcohol and drug use with sexual assault, my concern for the student was piqued. To hear firsthand that a woman would place herself in a position of potential peril due solely (since she did not want to date the man originally) to the proffering of a handful of unknown pills was curious behavior to say the least. It is important to note that the woman did not say a "handful of Adderall," or even a "handful of uppers." Drug users are familiar with the drugs they use. Drug users know the drugs they like and dislike on sight. Pills are perhaps the easiest to identify as they have distinct markings, colors, and shapes. Yet this woman gave the impression that she was offered a handful of various unknown pills and accepted the man's offer based upon that alone.

This woman's statement caused the initiation of this study into what is happening more generally on our campuses regarding drug and alcohol use. Was this woman's behavior normal for a college campus, or was her behavior simply an anomaly? This article seeks to explore the relationships in which drugs are used, misused, and abused on college campuses.

Literature Review

Any discussion of drugs necessitates some method of qualifying which drugs are considered. There are a wide variety of psychoactive substances available to the American public. Some of these drugs are legal, legal by prescription, legal according to status, or legal in certain circumstances. Some drugs are obviously illegal regardless of the social context. This research will consider drugs including alcohol, for those under 21 years of age, as well as all currently available illicit drugs (marijuana, lysergic acid diethylamide (LSD), heroin, etc.), and the misuse of prescription medication (Adderall, Ritalin, etc.). Tobacco is not included in this study.

Alcohol Use by College Students

Alcohol and other drug use on college campuses has been an area of concern for a long time. Many current faculty and administrators surely recall the near-obligatory "beer bash" of their own undergraduate years. However, "the way in which students are drinking has changed ... students drink more alcohol, more often, and for the sole purpose of getting drunk" (CESAR 1994). Further, CESAR (1994) (the Center for Substance Abuse Research) also reports that in 1993 one-third of women drank alcohol with the intended goal of getting drunk. Importantly, that number was three times higher than in 1977

(CESAR 1994). These changes are not university specific, but uniform throughout the national college student population.

In response to the "new student drinking culture," there has been a rising chorus to lower the drinking age in and around campuses, if not nationally. The rationale of the leading group, the Amethyst Initiative, revolves around the idea that maintaining the illegality of alcohol for underage college students pushes them to take part in other illegal activity (e.g., using fake identification to enter bars) as well as frequenting locations that might offer other drugs such as house parties (CESAR 2008, Amethyst Initiative 2010). The idea seems ludicrous to many, but must be taken seriously when we consider that there are currently 135 signatories (all university and college presidents and chancellors) supportive of the initiative (Amethyst Initiative 2010). The Amethyst Initiative is apparently staking its claim for student safety in the harm reduction model. If we realize that the drinking is taking place, we should work to limit the harm that can come from it.

We must also be aware that students reach their 21st birthdays while being members of the college community. Brister, Wetherill, and Fromme found that 68 percent of college students who had planned to drink as part of their 21st birthday celebrations consumed more than anticipated (2010:183). Of those who drank alcohol as part of their celebration, 22 percent of men and 12 percent of women consumed more than 21 drinks on their 21st birthday (Rutledge, Park, and Sher 2008:515). Such a high level of alcohol consumption is regularly linked to many negative outcomes (driving under the influence, sexual assault, assaults and battery, etc.).

The culture of alcohol consumption described has led to many problems for college students nationwide. We may be familiar with being hungover, vomiting, missing classes, or injuring one's self (falling or getting into fights); however, perhaps the most important harm to students is being victimized. CESAR (1995a) reports that 3.9 percent of college students were sexually assaulted or raped, and these crimes were committed in connection with an alcohol-related event. Further, 3.6 percent of college students have had suicidal ideation while intoxicated (CESAR 1995a). Another report indicates that alcohol-related sexual assault/date rape by someone who has been drinking affected 71,379 students in 2002 (Hingson et al. 2002:135–136). Furthermore, 1,445 students died as a result of their alcohol-related behavior (Hingson et al. 2002:135–136). These numbers, arguably, pose the greatest threat to the students. Certainly intoxicated students missing classes, performing poorly, or even taking part in a variety of vandalism is not desirable behavior; but sexual assault and death have ramifications beyond the victim/survivor.

Taken a step further, nearly half of all college students (47 percent) believe that alcohol use "facilitates sexual opportunities" (Presley et al. 1997; Dermen, Cooper, and Agocha 1998). This means that alcohol use and abuse is tied, for some college students, to their sexual behavior. Importantly, one's sexual behavior is linked to his or her sexual identity. Creation, maintenance, and reification of one's identity are important in sustaining association with relevant social groups. Therefore, the student's identity as a student, connected with various groups, a gender, and potentially his or her beliefs regarding alcohol and sexual behavior can lead to severely problematic behaviors like sexual assault.

Further, Miller, Hemenway, and Wechsler (1999) found that college students with serious alcohol problems are more likely to own guns compared to those students who do not have such problems. In the post–Virginia Tech campus atmosphere, this finding is troublesome. Simply owning a gun is not remarkable taken alone. However, combined with the various alcohol-related problems, and the belief that alcohol provides a connection with students' sexuality/sexual behavior, we further complicate the problem of alcohol consumption among students on college campuses. Unfortunately, college students do not use only alcohol. Empirical evidence leads to the understanding that students are using prescription medications, but misusing them as well.

Illicit Drug Use and Prescription Drug Misuse by Students

Beyond the dangers that problem-drinking bring to campuses nationwide, the use of Adderall increased the likelihood of other multidrug use among college-aged students (CESAR 2006). According to the National Institutes of Health (NIH 2007), Adderall is one of the most commonly used drugs among people aged 18–24 (after alcohol, tobacco, and marijuana). Here we begin to understand the compounding effect of drug use and misuse. The Drug Early Warning System (DEWS) states that prescription stimulants (Adderall, Ritalin, etc.) are the "New Caffeine" for college students (DEWS 2005).

Again, faculty and administrators surely recall pulling all-nighters for exams where coffee was guzzled in hopes to stay awake and sharpen their focus. Today, the student's response to the same need is often different. In one study, 58 percent of the students responding stated that they used prescription stimulants to help them concentrate, with an additional 43 percent using them to increase their alertness (Teter et al. 2005). The drug preferences among college students who reported prescription stimulant use in the last year demonstrate a clear preference for the use of Adderall (75.8 percent of the sample) (Teter et al. 2006).

The Substance Abuse and Mental Health Services Administration (SAMHSA) found that full-time college students who have used Adderall nonmedically are more likely to have also used other illicit drugs or misused other prescription medication (SAMHSA 2009). Among the other results regarding college student drug use, they found 79.9 percent also used marijuana, 44.9 percent used analgesics (pain relievers), 32.2 percent used hallucinogens (LSD, "Magic Mushrooms"), 28.9 percent used cocaine, 24.5 percent used tranquilizers, 14.8 percent used Ecstasy (MDMA), and 9.4 percent used inhalants (SAMHSA 2009). Importantly, many of these drugs have synergistic effects with one another and with alcohol. These synergistic effects can amplify the effects of one or both drugs taken, resulting in the potential for greater harm to individuals, their fellow students, as well as the larger community.

Teter et al. (2003) support these findings and clarify the polydrug use among college students. Of those students who used misused methylphenidate (i.e., Ritalin), 100 percent also used marijuana, 98 percent took part in binge drinking in the past two weeks, 77 percent used cigarettes, and 58 percent used Ecstasy ($n = 2{,}250$) (Teter et al. 2003:610).

Focus on Marijuana Use

Throughout this discussion, marijuana has consistently been reported as a common drug being used among college students. Additionally, marijuana (and/or alcohol) is often the initial drug used by people regardless of their connection to any college. It is worth noting that about one-third of college students do not begin to use marijuana regularly until age 18 or older (Gledhill-Hoyt, Strote, and Wechsler 2000). Obviously, this is also when most students begin their college careers. However, what is the effect of marijuana on these students?

Students at the University of Maryland College Park who reported marijuana use in the past month tended to have lower grade point averages (Hsu et al. 1995). Nearly 40 percent had a GPA below 2.5, and 20 percent had less than a 3.0 (Hsu et al. 1995). Beyond often earning lower grades, there are more serious problems that have been found to be related to marijuana use. The largest problems students have reported are that 40.1 percent have concentration problems, 24.3 percent regularly put themselves in physical danger, 18.6 percent drive after using the drug, 14.4 percent give up important activities, and 13.9 percent oversleep and miss classes (Caldeira et al. 2008).

Drug Using Culture

Given that there is a "new drinking culture" among college students, and that students are also using a wide variety of drugs often in problematic combinations, what is the student culture that leads to these behaviors? Are these drugs easy to obtain? DEWS and CESAR both found that alcohol, prescription medications, and a variety of other drugs are easily available for both high-risk and low-risk college students (CESAR 2006; DEWS 2006).

The evidence clearly points to the availability of a wide array of drugs and alcohol to college students. These, perhaps not so, surprising reports lead to two final problematic reports regarding college students and drug-related behavior: Rohypnol and the use of inhalants.

In the early 1990s several emerging drugs were found directly linked with sexual assaults and rape in particular (CESAR 1995b). These drugs are gamma-hydroxybutyric acid (GHB), and Rohypnol (aka roofies). These drugs largely replace the "Mickey Finns" that have been unfortunately popular on college campuses in years gone by. These substances are essentially colorless, odorless, and quickly dissolved in liquids and are used to drug (mostly) women who are later sexually assaulted. There is very little research on its use on campuses, and even less on its prevalence. However, it is a drug of concern that is known to be present on college campuses nationwide (CESAR 1995b).

The use of inhalants by college students is especially troubling. Glue and paint "huffers" are expected to be adolescents; research has shown that most adolescent users are white or Latino (CESAR 1997). However, the growth of this form of drug use is known to lead to short-term memory loss, permanent brain damage, and death (even at initial use). Clearly, these specific consequences can be linked to the college-related behaviors of reading, studying, and test taking.

It is within this context that the present research is located. Clearly, something is happening with the students, but what that is has yet to be uncovered. Are students simply more bent on using drugs and alcohol? Is student proximity to bars and other unsupervised nightlife leading to such behavior? Or, perhaps a combination of these and other factors leaves us with students who have easy access to a variety of drugs, who misuse prescription drugs to facilitate studying (and partying), and who combine these drugs with alcohol.

Methodology

This project surveyed college students' drug-using behavior at a mid-sized southeastern university. The study was approved through the Institutional Review Board of the university. The survey used both open- and closed-ended questions to provide both demographic and qualitative data. The survey was distributed between April 2010 and January 2011. The survey was distributed via a Web site external to the university, and the options regarding the completed surveys enabled respondents to ensure that no one could identify who viewed the page, who downloaded the survey, who completed the survey, and who delivered a completed survey.

A snowball sampling method was employed to gain respondents and aid in the confidentiality of all respondents. Several current students were very open about their own alcohol- and drug-using behavior and volunteered to assist in obtaining voluntary participants. The sample size was 60 participants, all of whom currently use or had used or misused drugs or alcohol.

While the sample size is small, the results are indicative of patterned behavior.

Furthermore, the results illuminate an often forgotten aspect of alcohol and drug use—the relationships in which the behavior takes place.

Results

The percentages provided in this section do not always equal 100 percent due to multiple answers being provided for several questions. With a sample size of 60, the following image of the average student respondent emerges. The student is a psychology major (40 percent of respondents), in either his or her first or fourth year in college (both categories at 33.3 percent), is 21 years old (20.9 years average age), is from South Carolina (53.3 percent of the respondents), self categorizes himself or herself as white or of European ancestry (93 percent), is female (53.3 percent), and has a 50-percent chance of being currently employed (both categories of employment were 50 percent).

Regarding this person's drug-using behavior, she would not use tobacco (46.6 percent), but would drink beer (86.6 percent), not drink wine (60 percent), would drink hard liquor (86.6 percent), but not have a current prescription for any medication (66.6 percent). She will have used multiple drugs over her life (see Table A9.1). If she currently uses drugs, the drug she most often uses is marijuana (46.4 percent). If she still uses any drug, her drug of choice is also marijuana (46.4 percent). The first drug she ever used was marijuana (66.6 percent). The drug she first tried at college was marijuana (53.3 percent). The last drug that she used was also marijuana (66.6 percent).

Table A9.1 details the kinds of drugs that the student sample reported using over their lifetimes:

TABLE A9.1
Lifetime Use of Drugs (excluding alcohol)

Drug	Frequency	Percentage Using
Cocaine and Crack Cocaine	12	20
MDMA (Ecstasy)	8	13.3
Heroin	4	6.6
Percocet, Oxycodone, Vicodin, and Oxycontin	44	73.3
Xanax and Klonopin (benzodiazapines)	8	13.3
Salvia Divinorum	4	6.6
2CE	4	6.6
Adderall	20	33.3
LSD and Mushrooms (psilocybin)	40	66.6
Marijuana	40	66.6

Note: Percentages do not equal 100 percent as some respondents reported multiple drug use.

The drugs that the responding students reported as being used most often are marijuana (46.4 percent), Adderall (20 percent), and painkillers (which include opiates, analgesics, sedatives, and benzodiazepines 13.3 percent). The respondent's drugs of choice are marijuana (33.3 percent), alcohol/beer (20 percent), Ecstasy (6.6 percent), and Adderall (6.6 percent). The first drug that these respondents ever used was marijuana (66.6 percent), alcohol/beer (6.6 percent), and Adderall (6.6 percent).

The respondent's top three rationales for using an illicit drug the first time are curiosity/saw it being used (46.6 percent), peer pressure (33.2 percent), and a friend was using the drug (26.6 percent). The most common circumstance for initial drug use while at college was being with friends who were using (79.8 percent).

When requested to report what circumstances might exist when they were *most likely* to use drugs, the respondents who used drugs stated that "Chillin with Friends/in Apartment/Dorm Room/Smokin' a Blunt in a Car" was most popular (40 percent). The remaining categories each had four respondents reporting (6.6 percent): need energy, before work, bored, after test/paper/homework, stressed, any time at home, backstage, at night, and "Surrounded" (it is unclear what that response means).

To elicit a contrary circumstance, respondents were asked when they were least likely to use drugs. Their responses centered on three main categories and each had eight respondents (13.3 percent in each category): before test, around family, and in class. The remaining responses were out of weed, out of country, project due, day, and with friends.

Respondents were asked when they had last used a drug. Sixteen respondents (26.6 percent) stated "a few hours ago." The remaining categories each had eight respondents (13.3 percent in each category): one year, minutes ago, and now.

Concerning the availability of illicit drugs on campus, students responded that a variety of drugs were easily available. Twenty-eight (46.4 percent) said that "if they were on campus and wanted to get marijuana," they could get some in minutes. Similarly, eight (13.3 percent) respondents to the survey stated that they could get Adderall within minutes, and it would cost $10.00. LSD was reported to take 45 minutes to obtain on campus (four respondents, 6.6 percent). Four respondents (6.6 percent) said it would take hours to get illicit drugs on campus. Four more respondents (6.6 percent) stated that it would take "less than a day" to get their drug of choice. Twelve respondents (20 percent) stated that it would take "more than one day" to get their drug of choice. Lastly, 16 respondents (26.6 percent) did not answer the question.

Taking part in the sort of drug and alcohol consumption noted in this article is sure to result in some problems. When queried on the survey if the respondents had ever experienced any problem due to their drug or alcohol use, the overwhelming response was *no* (60 percent). The 12 respondents (20 percent) who did say that they had experienced a problem due to alcohol or drug use resulted in two categories of "problems" being reported. Eight (13.3 percent) respondents stated that drugs or alcohol had "negatively affected school work." The remaining four respondents (6.6 percent) who reported a problem due to drug or alcohol use experienced property being stolen from them. Twelve respondents (20 percent) did not answer the question.

Thirty-two (46.4 percent) of the student respondents stated that they believe that there is "no drug problem" at the university. For those respondents who did report that there was a drug problem (40 percent), their five responses provide a rationale for drug use/misuse among students and are categorized as: majority of students use drugs (20 percent), problem on all campuses (6.6 percent), police not harsh enough (6.6 percent), addiction (6.6 percent), and trying to fit in (6.6 percent).

In an effort to determine the respondents' involvement with campus, they were asked if they had attended campus activities such as athletic matches, concerts, plays, and speakers. Thirty-six respondents (60 percent) stated that they did take part, twenty (33.3 percent) did not, while four (6.6 percent) stated that they took part only in tailgating activities. On a related note, the students were asked if they took part in campus activities while under the influence of drugs or alcohol; 32 (53.3 percent) said that they had taken part while under the influence of drugs or alcohol, 24 (40 percent) said that they had not, and 4 (6.6 percent) did not answer the question.

The final question of the survey sought to understand why the students currently used illicit drugs. Importantly, 20 students (40 percent) reported that they did not currently use drugs. Of the remaining respondents, the following rationales were reported for why they currently use drugs: eight (13.3 percent) stated that they enjoy the high. The remainder four (6.6 percent) respondents' rationale: makes me smile, socially, self medicating, don't see a problem with it, am human and young, it's fun, helps me study, and yes (which is unclear what that response means).

Discussion

The use rates detailed in the results of this study are similar to those nationwide. We can expect that students who drink more, and more often, would be prone to using other drugs. Indeed, higher use rates for stimulants also make sense as it would allow a drinker to stay awake longer to drink more. The desire for this effect may be the rationale for current alcoholic drinks mixed with "energy drinks," and the recent efforts to regulate them.

Another area of concern might be the perception of others and of one's self by the students. Using the ideas regarding sexiness (does alcohol make males, females, and/or me sexier), we see some expected results for heterosexual students. First, heterosexual men who are using alcohol tend to think women are sexier. This result ties in with the fact that males are the offenders of most sexual assaults. Women who are using alcohol, not surprisingly, are less apt to think that men are sexier. The effects of alcohol are often reported to reduce inhibitions, so women may demonstrate a more open persona, refusing or minimizing the inhibition for self-defense (watching for strangers, avoiding drinking unattended drinks, and possibly "hooking up" with an unknown person). The more open persona exhibited by women may be viewed as sexier. Males, on the other hand, are more apt to be involved in violent acts (fights, yelling, etc.), which may not be seen as "sexy." If we combine these ideas with the use of stimulants and/or hallucinogens (e.g., MDMA/Ecstasy, LSD), especially for women and steroid use for men, we get a compounded effect of the drugs. Stimulant and hallucinogen use often make the user more sensitive to tactile sensations, or "touchy-feely," often giving innocent hugs and kisses to others. These effects can be considered sexy by the alcohol-using male. At the same time, steroid use by men has been shown to increase their aggressiveness, and hostility, which is probably not considered "sexy" by heterosexual women.

One's sexuality, and his or her reflexive ideas about himself or herself and others, leads us to the clear connection that alcohol and drug use in college is inextricably tied to group association. Initial exposure to drug use, to initial drug use, to continued drug-using behavior is tied to friends and friends' using behavior. Whether they are "chillin with friends," or "smoking a blunt in a car," the behaviors are social. However, four respondents did state that they were least likely to use drugs around friends (6.6 percent). The response by these four may reflect the method of ingestion of the drug, or the type of drug itself, but the data did not provide any details. Intravenous drug users regularly try to hide this form of ingestion from others as many view it as extreme and undesirable. Similarly, heroin users may try to hide their use as it is often considered a "hard drug" compared to the wider acceptance of a drug like marijuana.

The understanding of college student alcohol and drug use as social behaviors leads to a conception of the behaviors as tied to group association, and social learning as means to explain the initiation into drug use, and maintenance of drug use as potentially a norm of that group. If the students want to remain a part of their social groups, they must conform to the norms of those groups. Exposure to new behaviors (e.g., underage drinking, illicit drug use, prescription drug misuse) can be viewed as a norm, and the initiate must learn the ways (norms) of the group.

While this study does have some limitations, primarily that the sample size is far too small to be representative of the entire student population, the survey instrument was able to shed some light onto the context of drug use by the students. Importantly, a third of the sample claimed that they no longer used any illicit drugs. Of those who reported still using drugs, the survey provided some important ideas that can be used to modify or halt future student's drug using behaviors. For example, the students who stated that they were "curious," "needed energy," or "peer pressure" tell us that there are ways to counter the "drug message." Working with students who face peer pressure, but extending the work to explain methods of limiting, or terminating the influence could be beneficial.

Historically, colleges have tried to provide a variety of nonacademic events to prevent students from roaming to parties, bars, or other potential hazards off campus. This survey demonstrates that, of the respondents, students simply come to the events high—and are likely to attend the event, but are then free to visit bars, house parties, or use drugs in their dorm/apartment afterward. Perhaps the money and time spent coordinating these events could be better directed toward the nondrug-using population, leading them to continue their drug-free lifestyle versus changing the learned behavior of student peer groups.

Discussion Questions

1. What are the common consequences of student drug use? Do you feel benefits outweigh the costs? Why or why not?
2. What do you feel is the best way to address this issue of substance abuse? In which manner, will students be more receptive?

References

Amethyst Initiative. 2010. Retrieved July 17, 2010 (http://www.amethystinitiative.org/).

Brister, H. A., R. R. Wetherill, and K. Fromme. 2010. "Anticipated Versus Actual Alcohol Consumption During 21st Birthday Celebrations." *Journal of Studies of Alcohol and Drugs* 71(2): 180–83.

Caldeira, K. M., A. M. Arria, K. E. O'Grady, K. B. Vincent, and E. D. Wish. 2008. "The Occurrence of Cannabis Use Disorders and Other Cannabis-Related Problems among First-Year College Students." *Addictive Behaviors* 33(3):397–411.

CESAR (Center for the Evaluation of Substance Abuse Research). 1994. "Alcohol Abuse the Number One Problem on College Campuses." *CESAR Fax* 3(31).

CESAR. 1995a. "An Estimated 12,000 UMCP Students Report Experiencing One to Four Alcohol-Related Problems Within the Past Year." *CESAR Fax* 4(47 [rev.]).

CESAR. 1995b. "Drug Abuse Alert: Rohypnol." *CESAR Fax* 4(24).

CESAR. 1997. "Drug Abuse Alert: Inhalants." *CESAR Fax* 6(33).

CESAR. 2006. "Alcohol, Marijuana, Adderall, and Ritalin, Perceived to Be Most Easily Available Drugs Misused Among Undergraduates. *CESAR Fax* 15(43).

CESAR. 2008. "Amethyst Initiative Statement Calls for Dialogue About the National Minimum Drinking Age." *CESAR Fax* 17 (35).

Dermen, Kurt, M. Lynne Cooper, and V. Bede Agocha. 1998. "Sex-Related Alcohol Expectancies as Moderators of the Relationship between Alcohol Use and Risky Sex in Adolescents." *Journal of Studies on Alcohol* 59(71):71–77.

DEWS.2005. "New Student Drug Research (SDR) Survey Examines Prescription Stimulant Misuse Among College Students." *DEWS (Drug Early Warning System) Investigates*, July. College Park, MD: University of Maryland College Park.

DEWS. 2006. "Perceptions of Prescription Stimulant Misuse among College Students at High and Low Risk of Drug Use." *DEWS (Drug Early Warning System) Investigates*, October. College Park, MD: University of Maryland College Park.

Gledhill-Hoyt, J., H. Lee, J. Strote, and H. Wechsler. 2000. "Increased Use of Marijuana and Other Illicit Drugs at US Colleges in the 1990s: Results of Three National Surveys."*Addiction* 95(11):1655–67.

Hingson, R. W., T. Heeren, R. C. Zakocs, A. Kopstein, and H Wechsler. 2002. "Magnitude of Alcohol-Related Mortality and Morbidity among U.S. College Students Aged 18–24." *Journal of Studies on Alcohol* 63:136–44.

Hsu, M., E. Wish, J. Gan, R. Brown, and M. Bridwell. 1995 (revised). *1994 UMCP Student Drug Survey*. College Park, MD: University Health Center & University of Maryland College Park.

Miller, Matthew, David Hemenway, and Henry Wechsler. 1999. "Guns at College." *Journal of American College Health* 48:7–12.

Presley, Cheryl, Philip W. Meilman, Jeffery R. Cashin, and Jami S. Leichliter. 1997. "Alcohol and Drugs on American Campuses: Issues of Violence and Harassment." Carbondale, IL: Core Institute, Southern Illinois University Carbondale.

Rutledge, P. C., A. Park, and K. J. Sher. 2008. "21st Birthday Drinking: Extremely Extreme." *Journal of Consulting and clinical Psychology* 76(3):511–16.

SAMHSA (United States Substance Abuse and Mental Health Services Administration). 2009. "Nonmedical Use of Adderall among Full-Time College Students." *The NSDUH Report*. April 7.

Teter, C. J., S. Esteban, C. Boyd, and S. Guthrie. 2003. "Illicit Methylphenidate Use in an Undergraduate Student Sample: Prevalence and Risk Factors." *Pharmacotherapy* 23(5):609–17.

Teter, C. J., S. E. McCabe, J. A. Cranford, C. J. Boyd, and S. K. Guthrie. 2005. "Prevalence and Motives for Illicit Use of Prescription Stimulants in and Undergraduate Student Sample." *Journal of American College Health* 53(6): 253–62.

Teter, C. J., S. E. McCabe, K. LaGrange, J. A. Cranford, and C. J. Boyd. 2006. "Illicit Use of Specific Prescription Stimulants among College Students: Prevalence, Motives, and Routes of Administration." *Pharmacotherapy* 26(10):1501–10.

 ARTICLE 10

Jason A. Ford
University of Central Florida

Ryan D. Schroeder
University of Louisville

Academic Strain and Prescription Stimulant Misuse among College Students

Introduction

In recent years, there has been a substantial increase in the prevalence of prescription drug misuse, generally defined as the use of prescription medications that are not prescribed or the use of prescription medications solely for the feeling or experience. In 2000, 20 percent of young adults aged 18–25 years reported prescription drug misuse at some point in their lifetime (SAMHSA 2001). The prevalence of lifetime prescription drug misuse in this population increased to 29 percent in 2009 (SAMHSA 2010a). Prescription drug misuse is widely recognized as a major public health concern. In 2009 approximately 3.5 million drug-related emergency department visits were attributed to prescription drug misuse, including both adverse reactions to prescription drugs and the misuse or abuse of prescription drugs (SAMHSA 2010b). That is, 77 percent of all drug-related emergency department visits in the United States involved prescription drugs.

Much of the existing research on prescription drug misuse is epidemiological in nature and focuses on samples of high school or college students. Prevalence rates and trends in prescription drug misuse have been studied extensively (Blanco et al. 2007; McCabe et al. 2007a; Johnston et al., 2010; SAMHSA 2010a). Research has identified demographic characteristics of users (Simoni-Wastila and Strickler 2004; McCabe et al. 2005; Arkes and Iguchi 2008; Ford and Rivera 2008) and other risk factors for misuse (Simoni-Wastila and Strickler 2004; Kroutil et al. 2006; Herman-Stahl et al. 2007; Ford and Arrastia 2008). In addition, researchers have studied sources of diversion (McCabe et al. 2006; Inciardi et al. 2007; McCabe et al. 2007b), motives for misuse (Teter et al. 2005; McCabe et al. 2007b), and routes of administration (Teter et al. 2006; McCabe et al. 2007b). Research has also examined the co-ingestion of prescription drugs with other substances (McCabe 2006; McCabe et al. 2009) and negative outcomes associated with prescription drug misuse (Huang et al. 2006; Ford 2008; McCabe 2008; McCabe et al. 2009).

However, very little research to date has applied criminological theories to the study of this emerging form of substance use. The current research applies concepts from Agnew's (1992) general strain theory to prescription drug misuse in a national sample of college students. Given the academic demands placed on today's college students, the immense pressures to succeed that college students face on a regular basis, and the instrumental coping capabilities of prescription stimulants specifically to help meet these demands, general strain theory is a particularly useful framework to foster a theoretical grasp on the processes leading to prescription medication misuse among college students. To the degree that colleges and universities are subcultures with a distinct set of values and norms within the dominant culture, academic achievement is a particularly salient goal unique to academic settings.

General Strain Theory

Agnew's (1992) general strain theory outlines three nonmutually exclusive sources of strain. The first source is failure to achieve positively valued goals. Within the college culture academic success is one particularly salient goal that students are expected to strive for and achieve. Strain results from the failure to achieve this culturally defined goal. Prior research highlights poor grades as a form of strain from this perspective (Agnew 1992; Agnew and White 1992; Sharp et al. 2001; Vowell and Chen 2004). The second source of strain is the removal of positively valued stimuli. In the context of college life, the removal of positively valued stimuli might include receiving poor grades, loss of scholarship money, negative encounters with faculty, and perceived discrimination. The third source of strain according to general strain theory is the presence of noxious stimuli. In academic settings, noxious stimuli might include decrepit physical infrastructural conditions, physical and verbal abuse by peers, and faculty who are overly harsh in interactions with students. For the purposes of the current research, we also maintain that poor grades, in certain circumstances, can be interpreted as an example of the presence of noxious stimuli.

Taken together, the failure to achieve academic success and the inability to meet the academic demands at college fit nicely within the three sources of strain identified by the general strain theory and academic strain is therefore likely to lead to deviance and crime. General strain theory, however, does not postulate a direct relationship between strain and criminal activities. Rather, strain increases the probability that an individual will endure negative affective states, such as anger, anxiety, fear, or depression (Agnew 1992; Agnew and White 1992). College is an excessively stressful period for many young adults caused by heavy academic workloads, fear of failure, and competition for the highest grades (Cottrell 1992; Patrick, Grace, and Lovato 1992), and this stress contributes too many of the problems common among college student populations, including depression (Cottrell 1992; Patrick et al. 1992).

The negative affective states caused by strain cause pressure for corrective action (Agnew 1992). Deviance and crime are possible methods of alleviating strain and the negative emotionality associated with strain, as deviance can aid in achieving desired goals, protect valued stimuli, or help escape from noxious situations (Agnew 1992; Agnew and White 1992). More importantly to the current research, adolescents who experience strain may try to manage the negative affect through substance use. Crime and violence are unlikely to be instrumental methods of achieving desired academic goals or avoid losing positively valued stimuli within academic settings, but the negative affect associated with academic strain can be easily remedied through the use of illicit drugs or even heavy alcohol use. Prior research has indicated that college students often turn to illicit drugs (Sax 1997; Eitle 2002) and/or alcohol (Perkins 1999; Leeman and Wapner 2001) in response to stress in academic settings.

Tests of general strain theory have shown support for the theory in explaining juvenile delinquency and violent crime (Agnew and White 1992; Paternoster and Mazerolle 1994; Hoffman and Cerbone 1999; Piquero and Sealock 2004), but tests have not always supported the theoretical connection between strain and substance use (Agnew and White 1992; Aseltine, Gore, and Gordon 2000). It is possible that substance use is an effective method of emotional coping or escape from noxious stimuli for many individuals, but there are very little instrumental uses for drugs to solve the problems that cause strain. Prescription stimulant misuse, however, provides individuals experiencing strain within academic settings instrumental (more alert, staying up late to study, increased focus) as well as emotional coping strategies (escape, fun, socializing). By shifting the focus of research to a specific stressor among a specific subgroup, academic strain among college students, and a specific class of substance use that has both instrumental and emotional coping qualities, prescription stimulants, we hope to elucidate the general strain theory processes that link strain to substance use.

Substance Use among College Students

College students have historically been at the forefront of changes in substance use that later materialize within the general population. Using data from the College Alcohol Study, Mohler-Kuo, Lee, and Wechsler (2003) report significant increases in the prevalence of prescription drug misuse between 1993 and 2001 across several classes of prescription medication. Findings from the 2009 National Survey on Drug Use and Health estimate that 16 percent of college students age 18–22 misused prescription drugs in the past year, and that college students have higher past-year prevalence rates of prescription stimulant misuse than their counterparts in the same age range not enrolled in college (4.96 percent and 3.69 percent, respectively), but the difference is not significant (SAMHSA 2010a).

The primary motivations for prescription drug misuse among college students include relieving pain, experimentation, getting high, and relaxation (Low and Gendaszek 2002; Teter et al. 2005; Quintero et al. 2006; McCabe et al. 2007b) as well as an aid to sleep, pain control, and weight loss (Quintero et al. 2006). Most importantly to the current research, college students report misusing prescription medication, specifically stimulants, to help meet academic demands by improving intellectual performance and increasing concentration/alertness (Babcock and Byrne 2000; Low and Gendaszek 2002; Teter et al. 2005; Quintero et al. 2006).

Anecdotal evidence points to the widespread use of prescription stimulants such as Adderall, Ritalin, and Dexedrine without a prescription by both high school and college students. These so called homework drugs help students focus on course material and study for longer periods of time, and use is more common at schools with more competitive admission standards and generally peaks during finals week. There are many possible explanations for the widespread use of these "homework drugs." First, students may feel compelled to use these drugs as a way to manage a hectic schedule including a full-time course load, part-time employment, extracurricular activities, and social activities. Second, these drugs are widely available and their use as a "study aide" is socially acceptable. Students may feel that using prescription stimulants is a way to achieve a socially approved goal, good grades, and is therefore more acceptable than using other drugs simply to get high.

College life has traditionally been associated with experimentation, including high rates of substance use (Kett 1977; Horowitz 1987; Baer 2002). The growing trend of prescription drug misuse among young adults generally, and among college students specifically, is cause for concern given the addictive potential of such medication and the health consequences that misuse of these substances can cause. An especially troubling aspect of the prevalence and growing popularity of misusing prescription medication is the putative advantages of using prescription drugs compared to "street" drugs. Cicero, Inciardi, and Munoz (2005) argue that prescription drugs are easier to obtain, there is less likelihood of arrest, use is more socially accepted, and there is a perception that prescription drugs are safer. Prescription drugs then are ideal candidates for misuse in a college environment. Prescription medications are pure, having a known chemical composition and predicable dose dependent effects, and are widely available on college campuses (Quintero et al. 2006). Using prescription medication for recreational and instrumental purposes has become normalized among certain social groups on college campuses.

The misuse of prescription medication is clearly a growing problem in our society, particularly among college students. Understanding the theoretical processes involved in the misuse of prescription medication is an essential first step in slowing the spread of this unique form of substance use on college campuses. Based on the prior research and the theoretical processes postulated by the general strain theory, we hypothesize that academic strain will be associated with depression among college students, which will then be associated with the prescription stimulant misuse.

Method

The data for this study were obtained from the Harvard School of Public Health's College Alcohol Study, which examined substance use and other health risk behaviors of more than 14,000 college students. The sample is representative of students enrolled full time at four-year schools in the United States, including students from private and public schools; nonreligiously and religiously affiliated schools; large, medium, and small schools; schools located in urban, suburban, and rural settings; all female schools; and historically black institutions.

The dependent variable is prescription stimulant misuse in the past year. Respondents were asked, "How often, if ever, have you used any of the drugs listed below?" One option was prescription-type stimulants and respondents were instructed to not include anything used under a doctor's orders.

Our measure of academic strain is operationalized as a disjunction between academic aspirations and outcomes, and is a combination of two items: importance of academic work and GPA. Importance of academic work was assessed using one survey question, "How important is academic work?" (0 = somewhat or not at all important, 1 = important or very important). GPA was measured to distinguish below-average students (0 = GPA under 3.0) from above-average students (1 = GPA of 3.0 or higher). Using these items, we constructed a four-category academic strain measure, conceptualized as a disjunction between academic goals and outcomes. The variable was coded 1–4, with higher values indicating greater levels of academic strain. First, *determined achievers* believe their academic work is important/very important and have a GPA above 3.0, and therefore would experience little academic strain (coded 1). Second, *apathetic achievers* believe their academic work is somewhat/not at all important but have a GPA above 3.0 (coded 2). Third, *apathetic underachievers* believe their academic work is somewhat/not at all important and have a GPA below 3.0 (coded 3). Fourth, *determined underachievers* believe their academic work is important/very important but have a GPA below 3.0, which suggests that these students experience a high level of academic strain (coded 4).

Our measure of negative affect is depression, with a higher score indicating a higher level of depression. The measure of *depression*, past 30 days, includes the following nine items: feel full of pep, been very nervous, felt so down that nothing could cheer you up, felt calm and peaceful, have a lot of energy, felt downhearted and blue, feel worn out, been a happy person, feel tired.

Several controls, measured as dichotomous variables, are included in the analyses: gender, race, ethnicity, and age. We also include controls for other types of substance use: binge drinking, marijuana use, and hard drug use. The analytical models also include controls for elements of Travis Hirschi's social control theory (1969) and Ronald Akers' social learning theory (1985), important controls when testing general strain theory.

Results

Our analysis begins with a discussion of the characteristics of the sample. Nearly 4 percent of the sample reports prescription stimulant misuse in the past year. The sample had approximately 39 percent male, 76 percent white, 7 percent Hispanic, with an average age of nearly 21. Based on our measure of academic strain, roughly 61 percent of respondents are *determined achievers*, 15 percent are *apathetic achievers*, 9 percent are *apathetic underachievers*, and 15 percent are *determined underachievers*. Roughly 44 percent of the sample reports binge drinking in the past two weeks, 27 percent reports the use of marijuana in the past year, and 10 percent reports the use of "hard" drugs in the past year.

The second step in our analysis is to examine the relationship between academic strain, depression, and prescription-stimulant misuse. As articulated by strain theorists, there is no direct connection between academic strain and prescription-stimulant misuse; the connection is indirect via negative affect. According to the theory, students who experience higher levels of academic strain should be more likely to report the presence of negative affect states. In our study, academic strain is significantly associated with depression, as students under greater levels of academic strain are more likely to report higher levels of depression than respondents who report lower levels of academic strain. The theory then stipulates that individuals who experience negative affect states, such as depression, are more likely to engage in deviant behavior in an attempt to cope with strain. In our study depression is significantly associated with prescription stimulant misuse, as students who report higher levels of depression are at an increased risk for prescription stimulant misuse. These findings provide support for general strain theory, as the impact of academic strain on prescription stimulant misuse is completely indirect, via our measure of negative affect. Students who experience academic strain report higher levels of depression, and students who report higher levels of depression are more likely to report prescription stimulant misuse.

Discussion

In recent years there has been a dramatic increase in prescription drug misuse. In addition, several national surveys of substance use indicate that the prevalence of prescription drug misuse is now greater than the prevalence of other illicit drug use, not including marijuana. While there is an abundance of research on substance use, the research on prescription drug misuse is relatively sparse in comparison. A significant limitation to the existing research in this area is a lack of theoretically based studies.

Consequently, we know very little about the theoretical reasons for prescription drug misuse. The current research seeks to fill this important gap in the literature by conducting one of the first theoretical-based examinations of prescription drug misuse. With a national sample of college students, we created a measure of academic strain based on Agnew's general strain theory to determine if academic strain is significantly associated with prescription drug misuse. We hypothesized that academic strain is significantly associated with prescription stimulant misuse based on the abundance of support for Agnew's strain theory and a limited number of studies that cite academic enhancement as a motivation for prescription stimulant misuse (Babcock and Byrne 2000; Low and Gendaszek, 2002; Teter et al. 2005; Quintero et al. 2006).

Findings from the current study provide support for general strain theory. Academic strain is indirectly associated with prescription stimulant misuse. In accordance with general strain theory, academic strain is significantly associated with depression (our measure of negative affect), and depression is significantly associated with prescription stimulant misuse. Previous tests of the general strain theory have not shown convincing support for the relationship between strain and substance use (see Agnew and White 1992), but the current research highlights the utility of shifting the focus of general strain theory research away from comprehensive measures of strain and indiscriminate offending outcomes to specific forms of strain (e.g., academic strain) associated with specific deviant outcomes (e.g., prescription drug misuse).

Our research highlights that academic strain that results in negative affective states is a key process leading to the misuse of prescription medication on college campuses. College and university administrators and health officials, therefore, should use this information to create and implement more effective programs to address the nonmedical use of prescription medication among college students. Firstly, college students hold generally favorable views of illicit prescription drugs (Cicero et al. 2005; Quintero et al. 2006), so administrators should create education programs designed to change these positive perceptions of these drugs. Secondly, stress on college campuses is at an all-time high (UCLA Higher Education Research Institute 2000), so specific programs should be developed that identify students who are falling behind academically and intervene in this process to lessen the negative consequences of this strain. Lastly, because depression is an important mediating factor in the process academic strain leading to the misuse of prescription stimulants, a greater emphasis on college campuses should be placed on identifying and treating students experiencing emotional distress. Most colleges and universities nationwide are reporting a staggering increased demand for counseling services over the past decade and 38 percent of colleges and universities do not offer any psychiatric services at all (Gallagher 2001). University officials must create programs that meet the demand for increased psychological services on campuses around the country, not only to treat those students who are in search of such help but also to identify those students who are struggling with emotional distress but do not actively seek help. In sum, programs that change attitudes and perceptions of nonmedical prescription medication use among college students, identify students experiencing academic strain, and develop counseling services able to meet increasing demands and identify those students in need of psychological help will all be important steps toward curbing the misuse of prescription stimulants on college campuses.

Discussion Questions

1. How do you deal with the everyday strains in your life? Would any of your coping mechanisms be considered deviant?
2. Why has prescription drug use become a common practice?

References

Agnew, Robert. 1992. "Foundation for a General Strain Theory of Crime and Delinquency." *Criminology* 30:47–87.

Agnew, Robert and Helene Raskin White. 1992. "An Empirical Test of General Strain Theory." *Criminology* 30:475–99.

Akers, Ronald L. 1985. *Deviant Behavior: A Social Learning Approach.* Belmont, CA: Wadsworth.

Arkes, Jeremy and Martin Y. Iguchi. 2008. "How Predictors or Prescription Drug Abuse Vary by Age." *Journal of Drug Issues* 38:1027–43.

Aseltine, Robert H., Jr., Susan Gore, and Jennifer Gordon. 2000. "Life Stress, Anger and Anxiety, and Delinquency: An Empirical Test of General Strain Theory." *Journal of Health and Social Behavior* 41:256–75.

Babcock, Quinton and Tom Byrne. 2000. "Student Perceptions of Methylphenidate Abuse at a Public Liberal Arts College." *Journal of American College Health* 49:143–45.

Baer, John S. 2002. "Student Factors: Understanding Individual Variation in College Drinking." *Journal of Studies on Alcohol, Supplement* 14: 40–53.

Blanco, Carlos, Donald Alderson, Elizabeth Ogburn, Bridget F. Grant, Edward V. Nunes, Mark L. Hatzenbuehler, and Deborah S. Hasin. 2007. "Changes in the Prevalence of Non-Medical Prescription Drug Use and Drug Disorders in the United States: 1991–1992 and 2001–2002." *Drug and Alcohol Dependence* 90:252–60.

Cicero Theodore J., James A. Inciardi, and Alvaro Munoz. 2005. "Trends in Abuse of OxyContin and Other Opioid Analgesics in the United States." *Journal of Pain* 6:662–72.

Cottrell, Richard. 1992. *Stress Management*. Guilford, CT: The Dushkin Publishing Group, Inc.

Eitle, David J. 2002. "Exploring a Source of Deviance-Producing Strain for Females: Perceived Discrimination and General Strain Theory." *Journal of Criminal Justice* 30: 429–42.

Ford, Jason A. 2008. "Non-Medical Prescription Drug Use and Delinquency: An Analysis with a National Sample." *Journal of Drug Issues* 38:493–16.

Ford, Jason A. and Fernando I. Rivera. 2008. "Non-Medical Prescription Drug Use among Hispanics." *Journal of Drug Issues* 38:285–310.

Ford, Jason A. and Meagan Arrastia. 2008. "Pill-Poppers and Dopers: A Comparison of Non-Medical Prescription Drug Use and Other Illicit/Street Drug Use among College Students." *Addictive Behaviors* 33:934–41.

Gallagher, Robert P. 2001. "National Survey of Counseling Center Directors, International Campus." *American Journal of Psychiatry* 124:303–10.

Herman-Stahl, Mindy A., Christopher P. Krebs, Larry A. Kroutil, and David C. Heller. 2007. "Risk and Protective Factors for Methamphetamine Use and Nonmedical Use of Prescription Stimulants among Young Adults Aged 18 to 25." *Addictive Behaviors* 32:1003–15.

Hirschi, Travis. 1969. *Causes of Delinquency*. Berkeley, CA: University of California Press.

Hoffmann, John P. and Felicia G. Cerbone. 1999. "Stressful Life Events and Delinquency Escalation in Early Adolescence." *Criminology* 37:343–74.

Horowitz, Helen Lefkowitz. 1987. *Campus Life: Undergraduate Cultures from the End of the Eighteenth Century to the Present*. New York: Alfred A. Knopf.

Huang, Boji, Deborah A. Dawson, Frederick S. Stinson, Deborah S. Hasin, June W. Ruan, Tulshi D. Saha, Sharon M. Smith, Rise B. Goldstein, and Bridget F. Grant. 2006. "Prevalence, Correlates, and Comorbidity of Nonmedical Prescription Drug Use and Drug Use Disorders in the United States: Results of the National Epidemiologic Survey on Alcohol and Related Conditions." *The Journal of Clinical Psychiatry* 67:1062–73.

Inciardi, James A., Hillary L. Surratt, Steven P. Kurtz, and Theodore J. Cicero. 2007. "Mechanisms of Prescription Drug Diversion among Drug-Involved Club- and Street-Based Populations." *Pain Medicine* 8:171–83.

Johnston, Lloyd D., Patrick M. O'Malley, Jerald G. Bachman, and John E. Schulenberg. 2010. *Monitoring the Future National Survey Results on Drug Use, 1975–2009: Volume II, College Students and Adults Ages 19*–50 (NIH Publication No. 10-7585). Bethesda, MD: National Institute on Drug Abuse.

Kett, Joseph F. 1977. *Rites of Passage: Adolescence in America 1790 to the Present*. New York: Basic Books.

Kroutil, Larry A., David L. Van Brunt, Mindy A. Herman-Stahl, David C. Heller, Robert M. Bray, and Michael A. Penne. 2006. "Nonmedical Use of Prescription Stimulants in the United States." *Drug and Alcohol Dependence* 84:135–43.

Leeman, Robert F. and Seymour Wapner. 2001. "Some Factors Involved in Alcohol Consumption of First-Year Undergraduates." *Journal of Drug Education* 31:249–62.

Low, Kathryn G. and A.E. Gendaszek. 2002. "Illicit Use of Psychostimulants among College Students: A Preliminary Study." *Psychology, Health and Medicine* 7:283–87.

McCabe, Sean Esteban. (2006). "Simultaneous and Concurrent Polydrug Use of Alcohol and Prescription Drugs: Prevalence, Correlates, and Consequences." *Journal of Studies on Alcohol* 67 529–37.

McCabe, Sean Esteban. 2008. "Screening for Drug Abuse among Medical and Nonmedical Users of Prescription Drugs in a Probability Sample of College Students." *Archives of Pediatric and Adolescent Medicine* 162:225–31.

McCabe, Sean Esteban, B. T. West, and H. Wechsler. 2007a. "Trends and College-Level Characteristics Associated with the Non-Medical Use of Prescription Drugs among US College Students from 1993 to 2001." *Addiction* 102:455–65.

McCabe, Sean Esteban, Carol J. Boyd, and Christian J. Teter . (2009). "Subtypes of Nonmedical Prescription Drug Misuse." *Drug and Alcohol Dependence* 102:63–70.

McCabe, Sean Esteban, Christian J. Teter, and Carol J. Boyd. (2006). "Medical Use, Illicit Use and Diversion of Prescription Stimulant Medication." *Journal of Psychoactive Drugs* 38:43–56.

McCabe, Sean Esteban, Christina J. Teter, Carol J. Boyd, John R. Knight, and Henry Wechsler. (2005). "Nonmedical Use of Prescription Opioids among U.S. College Students: Prevalence and Correlates from a National Survey." *Addictive Behaviors* 30:789–805.

McCabe, Sean Esteban, J. A. Cranford, C. J. Boyd, and C. J. Teter. 2007b. "Motives, Diversion and Routes of Administration Associated with Nonmedical Use of Prescription Opioids." *Addictive Behaviors* 32:562–75.

Mohler-Kuo, Meichun, Jae Eun Lee, and Henry Wechsler. 2003. "Trends in Marijuana and Other Illicit Drug Use among College Students: Results from 4 Harvard School of Public Health College Alcohol Study Surveys (1993–2001)." *Journal of American College Health* 52:17–24.

Paternoster, Raymond and Paul Mazerolle. 1994. "General Strain Theory and Delinquency: A Replication and Extension." *Journal of Research in Crime and Delinquency* 31:235–63.

Patrick, Kevin, Ted W. Grace, and Chris Y. Lovato. 1992. "Health Issues for College Students." *Annual Review of Public Health* 13:253–68.

Perkins, H. Wesley. 1999. "Stress Motivated Drinking in Collegiate and Postcollegiate Young Adulthood: Life Course and Gender Patterns." *Journal of Studies on Alcohol* 60:219–27.

Piquero, Nicole Leeper and Miriam D. Sealock. 2004. "Gender and General Strain Theory: A Preliminary Test of Broidy and Agnew's Gender/GST Hypotheses." *Justice Quarterly* 21:125–58.

Quintero, Gilbert, Jeffrey Peterson, and Bonnie Young. 2006. "An Exploratory Study of Socio-Cultural Factors Contributing to Prescription Drug Misuse among College Students." *Journal of Drug Issues* 36:903–31.

Sax, Linda J. 1997. " Health Trends among College Freshman." *Journal of College Health* 45:243–50.

Sharp, Susan F., Toni L. Terling-Watt, Leslie A. Atkins, Jay Trace Gilliam, and Anna Sanders. 2001. "Purging Behavior in a Sample of College Females: A Research Note on General Strain Theory and Female Deviance." *Deviant Behavior* 22:171–88.

Simoni-Wastila, Linda, Grant Ritter, and Gail Strickler. 2004. "Gender and Other Factors Associated with the Non-Medical Use of Abusable Prescription Drugs." *Substance Use & Misuse* 39:1–23.

Substance Abuse and Mental Health Services Administration. 2001. *Results from the 2000 National Household Survey on Drug Abuse: Volume I. Summary of National Findings* (Office of Applied Studies, NHSDA Series H-17, DHHS Publication No. SMA 02-3758). Rockville, MD.

Substance Abuse and Mental Health Services Administration. 2010a. *Results from the 2009 National Survey on Drug Use and Health: Volume I. Summary of National Findings* (Office of Applied Studies, NSDUH Series H-38A, HHS Publication No. SMA 10-4586Findings). Rockville, MD.

Substance Abuse and Mental Health Services Administration, Center for Behavioral Health Statistics and Quality. 2010b. *The DAWN Report: Highlights of the 2009 Drug Abuse Warning Network (DAWN) Findings on Drug-Related Emergency Department Visits.* Rockville, MD.

Teter, Christian J., Sean Esteban McCabe, James A. Cranford, Carol J. Boyd, and Sally K. Guthrie. 2005. "Prevalence and Motives for Illicit Use of Prescription Stimulants in an Undergraduate Student Sample." *Journal of American College Health* 53:253–62.

Teter, Christian J., Sean Esteban McCabe, LaGrange, K., James A. Cranford, and Carol J. Boyd. 2006. "Illicit Use of Specific Prescription Stimulants among College Students: Prevalence, Motives, and Routes of Administration." *Pharmacotherapy* 26:1501–10.

UCLA Higher Education Research Institute. 2000. *The American Freshman: National Norms for 1999.* Los Angeles, CA: UCLA Graduate School of Education and Information Studies.

Vowell, Paul R. and Jieming Chen. 2004. "Predicting Academic Misconduct: A Comparative Test of Four Sociological Explanations." *Sociological Inquiry* 74:226–49.

PART FIVE

Sexual Deviance

Removal of both testicles during surgical castration has been the punishment for approximately 100 convicted sex offenders in the Czech Republic over the past 10 years. It is the only country in Europe that surgically castrates offenders. It is a punishment that is irreversible and in the United States considered cruel and unusual. Historically, castration dates back thousands of years and is one of society's many responses to sexual deviance.[1] The historical relevance of this punishment also sheds light on how long abnormal sexual behavior has caught the public's attention.

Sexual deviance is a broad concept with a plethora of behaviors under its conceptual umbrella. There is not one universal definition of the concept because the concept varies based on cultural context. Today, these behaviors commonly include, but are not limited to, prostitution, nonheterosexuality, rape, sexual assault, child molestation, and sexual sadomasochism. Many of these topics are discussed in various sections of this reader. In this part of the reader we will discuss sexual deviancy in reference to pornography, sexual coercion, and prostitution. Kernsmith and Kernsmith discuss the relationship between pornography and female sexual coercion. It is hypothesized that women who report more frequent use of pornography will also report higher levels of perpetrating sexual coercion. Ronald Weitzer discusses the prohibitionist movement to abolish prostitution. He provides an overview of the movement by providing its justification, broad generalizations, and flawed empirical support. This part concludes with an article by Sharon S. Oselin on leaving street prostitution. Oselin conducted 36 interviews with individuals who have left prostitution, providing their reasons, turning points, and their use of prostitution-helping organizations.

Note

1. Cendrowicz, Leo. 2009. "The Unkindest Cut: A Czech Solution for Sex Offenders." *Time*, February 11. Retrieved May 12, 2011 (http://www.time.com/time/world/article/0,8599,1878462,00.html).

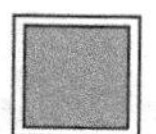 ARTICLE 11

Poco D. Kernsmith
Wayne State University

Roger M. Kernsmith
Eastern Michigan University

Female Pornography Use and Sexual Coercion Perpetration

Sexual coercion refers to the behaviors used to convince or pressure an unwilling partner into having sex. These behaviors include things such as threats, verbal bullying, guilt, and manipulation (Struckman-Johnson and Struckman-Johnson 1994; Hogben, Byrne, and Hamberger 1995). Although less severe and violent than sexual assault, each ultimately results in an unwanted sexual experience. Recent literature has identified that females may behave in sexually coercive and manipulative ways at nearly the same rate as males (Struckman-Johnson and Struckman-Johnson 1994).

The relationship between pornography and sexual aggression among males has been researched extensively (Allen et al. 1995; Oddone-Paolucci, Genuis, and Violato 2000). However, little research has explored the impact of pornography use on female behavior. Due to the changing nature of women's use of pornography and the use of coercive sexual behavior by females, it may be important to examine this relationship among females as well. The goal of this study is to examine the relationship between women's use of pornography and their sexually aggressive and coercive behavior.

Gender Differences in Sexual Coercion

Some research indicates that females' report rates of sexual ***coercion*** are nearly as high as those reported by males (Struckman-Johnson and Struckman-Johnson 1994; Hogben et al. 1995), while others report rates of coercion by females to be lower (O'Sullivan, Byers, and Finkelman 1998). However, contextual factors, such as resistance and negative response, indicate that the exposures of males and females to coercive sexual victimization may be different (O'Sullivan et al. 1998).

Risk Factors for Coercion Perpetration

Several factors related to school involvement and activities have been found to relate to sexual coercion and violence. These include having fraternity or sorority membership, participating in college athletics, and living in residence halls (Boswell and Spade 1996; Schwartz and DeKeseredy 1997; Mustaine and Tewksbury 2002; Mohler-Kuo et al. 2004). Alcohol and other drugs (Harrington and Leitenberg 1994; Abbey et al. 2004;) and promiscuous, or impersonal, sex (Malamuth 1998; Malamuth, Addison, and Koss 2000) are also frequently associated with these factors, as well as aggressive sexual behavior. A history of exposure to violence has been found to be an important predictor of physical violence perpetration in relationships among both males (Henning et al. 1996; Gortner, Golan, and Jacobson 1997; Mihalic and Elliot 1997) and females (Kernsmith 2006).

Pornography and Violence

Assessing the impact of pornography on sexual violence has been a controversial issue for several decades. Some argue that exposure to sexually explicit materials, particularly violent pornography, can increase the likelihood of perpetrating rape and other forms of sexual violence (Malamuth and Check 1984; Demare, Lips, and Briere 1993). Several feminist theorists have argued that pornography trivializes the impact of rape and increases the dehumanization of women as sexual objects (Morgan 1980; Dworkin 1988; MacKinnon 1992).

While the research on pornography is varied in its conclusions, the largest body of literature supports the perspective that the relationship between violence and pornography is a complex one (Fisher and Grenier 1994; Malamuth et al. 2000). Many of the previous studies of pornography and sexual aggression have focused on laboratory experiments in which participants, usually males, are exposed to sexually explicit materials or to control stimuli. Participants are then assessed on rape-supportive attitudes or laboratory aggression (Allen et al. 1995; Malamuth et al. 2000). A meta-analysis of laboratory studies indicated that only if pornography links violence and sex, is it likely to be related to increases in rape myth acceptance (Allen et al. 1995; Oddone-Paolucci et al. 2000), although the results were somewhat mixed.

Women and Pornography

Males have been identified as more frequent consumers of pornography (Boies 2002; Itzin 2002; Stack, Wasserman, and Kern 2004). However, studies of pornography use among college students found that rates of pornography use among females are increasing, with nearly half of female adolescents reporting viewing pornography in the past 6 months (Peter and Valkenburg 2006). The pornography industry is largely driven by males for male consumption, with dramatic differences in the types of erotica females prefer to consume (Salmon 2004). Females report preference for sexually explicit materials in which males and females are equally aggressive (Glascock 2005). Additionally, women are more likely to use pornography with a partner and without masturbation, while males typically use pornography with masturbation while alone. These differences may have implications for the impact on sexual behavior, but that relationship has not been researched.

Research Goals and Hypotheses

The goal of this study is to examine the relationship between use of pornography and female sexual aggression among college students. It is hypothesized that women who report more frequent use of pornography, whether from print, video, or online sources, will also report higher levels of perpetrating sexual coercion. However, it was expected that a relationship between pornography and physical forms of sexual aggression would not be found for females as it has been among males. This relationship is examined, controlling for a variety of factors including demographics; school involvement; prior victimization or exposure to violence; alcohol and drug use; and sexual behaviors and attitudes. It is anticipated that pornography use will remain an important predictor of coercion, controlling for all of these factors.

Research Methods

Data Collection

Data for this study were collected in surveys of undergraduate students enrolled in "Introduction to Sociology" and "Social Problems" courses at two mid-sized Midwest universities. The subjects were asked questions about their experience with sexual aggression and its correlates. The questionnaires were administered by the authors in class and required roughly 25 minutes for most students to complete.

Measures

Dependent Variables

Focus groups were held to discuss experiences with sexual coercion to develop new scales for coercion, perpetration, and victimization. The sexually coercive strategies were selected for inclusion by findings from three focus groups, made up of students at one of the schools participating in the study. The scale was found to be largely similar to others used in previous research with the addition of some types of behaviors (Struckman-Johnson and Struckman-Johnson 1994). In these groups, the participants discussed the ways that they thought men and women would try to convince someone to have sex who was not interested or initially said ***no***. The commonly mentioned items were included in the scale of sexual coercion.

Five subscales and one overall measure of total self-reported sexual coercion perpetration were created from the respondents' answers to 41 questions about the frequency of their sexually coercive behaviors. Respondents to the survey were asked to select a frequency from a five-point, Likert-type scale, ranging from "never" to "often," in reply to the question "Thinking about all the times in the past year you wanted someone to have sex with you, or do something sexual with you, how often did you do each of the following to get them to do something they were reluctant to do?"

The first subscale measures the use of extortion and bargaining as a coercive strategy used by the respondents, based on their reported frequency of tactics, such as threatening to break up or have sex with another person, and nagging or pestering. Next, the respondents' use of "sweet talk" and/or deceit is measured by the respondents' reported frequency of behaviors, such as "telling them what they want to hear" and promising that it will not be "just one time." The third subscale measures the perpetrator's insistence on the victim's obligation to perform the desired sexual acts. The self-reported coercive behaviors in this scale include calling the victim a tease or stating that the victim "owes" it to him or her for reasons such as having done it before or being in a relationship. The respondents' use of emotional manipulation through guilt or belittlement was measured, with reports of the behavior such as comparing them to past partners, crying or pouting, and making them feel guilty. Lastly, the use of physical force and intimidation was measured through the respondents' self-reported frequency of physically hurting or restraining the victim or threatening to do so, physically restraining them, shouting or yelling, hitting things, and getting angry. Purposefully getting them drunk or otherwise intoxicated was included in the measure of physical force, because drinking impedes the ability of the victim to physically resist or consent, and is therefore included in the legal definition of forcible rape (Schwartz and Leggett 1999). The response items used to measure all five of these subscales (all 41 items) were also combined into a measure of the mean frequency of total coercive behavior.

Independent Variables

It was expected that those who more frequently used pornography would also be more likely to engage in coercive behavior. Pornography use was measured with the mean of the respondents' answers to four questions regarding their self-reported frequency in which they had "looked at pornographic pictures in a magazine," "watched pornographic movies on video or DVD," "downloaded or looked at pornographic pictures online," and "downloaded or watched pornographic videos online" in the past year. Responses were measured on a five-point, Likert-type scale ranging from "never" to "more than 10 times a month."

Control Variables

Several other variables that were thought might be associated with increased sexual coercion were included in this study. First, respondent

TABLE A11.1
Self-reported coercion behaviors.

Extortion Behaviors ($\alpha = 0.71$)*	Percentage
Withheld emotional affection	24
Withheld other sex acts	19
Nag or pester them	14
Offered to buy them things	11
Threatened to "break up"	8
Threatened to have sex with other people	6
Threatened to stop paying for things	2
Threatened to cause a public scene	2
Threatened to embarrass them	1
Threatened to take away children	1
Deceit Behaviors ($\alpha = 0.72$)*	
Said nice things	32
Said they were special	17
Told them whatever they wanted to hear	11
Said it will be good	9
Promised it would not be only one time	4
Propose marriage	2
Obligation Behaviors ($\alpha = 0.68$)*	
Call them a "tease"	26
Told them you "need it"	16
Said they "owed" it to you	12
Said "we have done it before"	6
Said "we are in a serious relationship"	6
Said "everyone else is doing it"	3

Emotional Manipulation Behaviors ($\alpha = 0.81$)*	Percentage
Pouted	37
Made them feel guilty	29
Cried	26
Accused them of cheating	22
Compared them to past partners	21
Said they were mean	15
Criticized their appearance	13
Said mean things	8
Said they don't love you	8

Said they must be homosexual	4
Said you would stop loving them	3
Threatened to hurt yourself	2
Force and Intimidation Behaviors ($\alpha = 0.67$)*	**Percentage**
Got angry	26
Shouted or yelled	10
Hit things	6
Got them drunk or otherwise intoxicated	6
Physically restrained them	5
Physically hurt them	3
Threatened to physically hurt them	1

* At least once in the past year to get someone to do something sexual that he or she did not want to do.

age, race (white/nonwhite), and sexual orientation (lesbian and bisexual/heterosexual) were included as demographic controls. Also, the respondents' level of university involvement, prior exposure to violence, and frequency of the respondents' use of intoxicating substances were controlled for in the analysis. For this study, school involvement includes such factors as fraternity or sorority membership, participation in college athletics, and living in residence halls. History of exposure to violence, including experiencing childhood physical and/or sexual abuse, witnessing domestic violence, experiencing sexual assault, and dating violence, was also examined. Additionally, sexual attitudes and behaviors, including frequency of sexual activity, age of first sexual experience, and perceived importance of relationships and sexual activity, are predicted to be related to both pornography and sexual coercion.

Sample

As shown in Table A11.2, of the 512 women included in our sample, the median reported age was 19 and it ranged from 18 to 43 years old. White students comprised 63 percent of the sample, 24 percent was African American, and none of the other remaining race and/or ethnic categories identified in the survey instrument accounted for more than 5 percent of the students in the sample. Approximately 5 percent reported involvement in a sorority, while 3 percent reported participation on a college athletic team, and the mean self-reported GPA was 3.1 on a 4-point scale.

Findings

Descriptive Statistics

With respect to the use of pornography, 43 percent of respondents reported using some form of pornography measured for this study at least once in the previous year. Approximately 28 percent reported using print media, 18 percent reported using pornographic pictures online, 33 percent reported using pornographic videos (VHS or DVD), while only 10 percent reported using pornographic video online. Among those who used any pornography, most (76 percent) reported using it less than once a month.

Table A11.1 provides the prevalence of self-reported sexual coercion perpetration among females in our sample for each of the subscales. Approximately 65 percent of the

TABLE A11.2
Sample characteristics and reported porn use.

Sample Characteristics				
Sample size (N)	512			
Median age	19			
Whites	63 percent			
African American	24 percent			
Sorority	5 percent			
percent on Athletic team	3 percent			
Mean GPA	3.1			
Self-Reported Pornography Use (Per Month in the Past Year)	Never	<1	1–2	3+
Print pornography	72 percent	21 percent	5 percent	3 percent
Online pornographic photos	82 percent	14 percent	3 percent	1 percent
VHS or DVD adult videos	68 percent	26 percent	4 percent	3 percent
Online adult videos	90 percent	8 percent	1 percent	1 percent

women in our sample reported employing at least one of the measured sexual coercion strategies in the previous year in order to get someone to do something sexual that the other person did not want to do. The coercion strategies most commonly used by female respondents included pouting (37 percent), saying nice things (32 percent), making their partner feel guilty (29 percent), getting angry (26 percent), calling the partner a tease (26 percent), withholding emotional affection (24 percent), accusing him of cheating (22 percent), comparing him to past partners (21 percent), and withholding other sex acts (19 percent). The least likely strategies to be used by these same respondents included proposing marriage (2 percent), threatening to stop paying for things (2 percent), threatening to physically hurt their partner (2 percent), threatening to hurt themselves (2 percent), threatening to embarrass the partner (1 percent), and threatening to take away their children (1 percent).

Pornography Use and Sexually Coercive Behavior

As shown in Table A11.3, pornography use is positively related to total sexual coercion, extortion/bargaining, sweet talk/deceit, obligation, and the use of emotional manipulation. In these four models, it is notable that pornography use has quite a strong and consistent relationship to the coercion measures. This indicates that those who are using pornography more often are also more likely to engage in coercive behaviors.

One coercion subscale, the use of physical force and intimidation, was not significantly related to pornography use. Considering the relatively low level of physical coercion reported by these female respondents, this finding is not surprising.

Discussion

The findings indicate that those women who use pornography more frequently are also more likely to use sexual coercion, regardless

TABLE A11.3
Pornography use on sexual coercion measures with controls.

Variables	All Coercion *Beta*	Extortion/ Bargaining *Beta*	Deceit *Beta*	Obligation *Beta*	Manipulate *Beta*	Force *Beta*
Pornography use	0.23**	0.18**	0.24**	0.21**	0.21**	0.09**
Drug and alcohol use						
Alcohol use	–0.07	–0.12*	–0.06	0.01	–0.02	–0.12
Marijuana use	–0.01	0.02	–0.09	–0.01	0.02	0.07
Other drug use	0.07	0.07	0.09	0.07	0.02	0.03
Sex and dating behavior						
Number of sex partners in past year	–0.03	–0.03	0.02	–0.03	–0.01	–0.01
Number of sex acts in average month	–0.04	0.01	–0.03	–0.12*	–0.04	–0.02
Importance of relationship satisfaction	–0.07	–0.04	–0.19**	–0.03	–0.03	–0.03
Importance of regular sex	0.13*	0.10	0.12	0.18**	0.10	0.07
Current relationship satisfaction	–0.03	0.01	–0.01	–0.04	–0.04	0.01
Current sex satisfaction	–0.12	–0.14*	–0.05	–0.05	–0.16*	–0.09
Sex frequency relative to others	0.16**	0.16*	0.15*	0.10	0.12*	0.17**
Age at first consensual sex	–0.06	–0.03	–0.04	0.01	–0.09	–0.07
Not in relationship or dating	–0.07	0.07	–0.10	–0.10	–0.09	–0.01
History of Abuse						
Witness parent verbal abuse	–0.05	–0.05	–0.06	–0.03	–0.05	–0.02
Witness parent physical abuse	0.03	0.04	0.05	0.01	0.02	–0.01
Physically abused by parent	–0.03	0.01	0.01	–0.02	–0.06	–0.08
Molestation (no penetration)	–0.07	–0.09	–0.03	–0.09	–0.05	–0.09
Sexually assault < age 12	0.06	0.07	0.02	0.11	0.04	0.07
Sexually assault age 13–17	–0.05	–0.02	–0.01	–0.03	–0.09	–0.05
Physical dating violence	0.10	0.04	0.04	0.09	0.13*	0.09

(continued)

■ TABLE A11.3 (*continued*)

Variables	All Coercion *Beta*	Extortion/ Bargaining *Beta*	Deceit *Beta*	Obligation *Beta*	Manipulate *Beta*	Force *Beta*
Emotional dating violence	0.05	0.05	0.03	0.03	–0.06	0.11
Demographics						
Age	–0.10	–0.14	0.01	–0.08	–0.17**	–0.09
White	–0.18**	–0.07	–0.10	–0.21**	–0.19**	–0.14**
Lesbian or bisexual	–0.02	–0.03	–0.01	–0.02	–0.03	0.01
Residential student	0.09	0.07	0.11	0.10	0.06	0.06
GPA	–0.04	–0.04	0.02	–0.01	–0.06	–0.09
Sorority	0.03	0.08	–0.01	–0.02	0.02	0.03
Athletic team	–0.04	–0.06	–0.04	–0.02	–0.03	–0.04
Adjusted R^2	0.15	0.08	0.11	0.11	0.17	0.09
Significance of F	0.00	0.00	0.00	0.00	0.00	0.00

* Significant at $p < .05$ ** Significant at $p < .01$

of their level of drug and alcohol use, sex and dating behavior, history of abuse or demographics. Pornography use was significantly related to perpetration of all forms of coercion, except physical force and intimidation (which is the least likely form of coercion reported to be used by the women in our sample.)

Several studies have explored the role of pornography in teaching boys about sexual norms and behaviors (Boies 2002; Beggan and Allison 2003). These studies indicate that pornography provides a significant, though often distorted, source of sexual information, second only to the influence of peers (Trostle 2003). Similarly, research indicates that females learn what is expected of them in terms of beauty and behavior from media, including pornography (Jeffreys 2005). Females are increasingly targeted as a new sexual market (Attwood 2005). Thus, it is likely that young women who use pornography may also learn about sexual expectations and norms from pornography, including the desirability of promiscuity in females.

This fact may be supported by the finding that sexual coercion is also more common among women who report that frequent sex is important to them ($r = .198$, $p < .000$) and among those who believe they engage in sex more frequently than their peers ($r = .223$, $p < .000$). This is similar to the findings of Peter and Valkenburg (2006) that identified that females exposed to sexually explicit materials in a laboratory setting showed an increase in recreational attitudes toward sex, which among males has been found to be related to increased sexual aggression (Malamuth 1998; Malamuth et al. 2000). These women may also be attempting to replicate the model of desirable female sexuality they see depicted in pornographic depictions of sex.

The finding that pornography use was not related to physical forms of coercion may lend further support to this "imitation" explanation. Pornography rarely portrays females as physically overpowering males. Therefore, it is unlikely that a female who consumes pornography would find models of physically aggressive female sexuality to imitate. Instead, aggressive female seduction is increasingly portrayed as positive for both the sexually assertive and sophisticated female aggressor and as a reflection on the male partner's desirability and sexual prowess (Brosius, Weaver, and Staab 1993). However, these actions are based on the myths that males cannot be sexually victimized and that men's sexual desire is unremitting (Burt 1980, 1983). A meta-analysis of pornography studies has found significant relationship between pornography and rape-myth acceptance (Oddone-Paolucci et al. 2000). Although these studies focused on females as victims, it is possible that these results could also be true when females are perpetrators against males, with regard to the acceptance of incorrect and exaggerated views of male sexuality.

One limitation of the study was the limited data available on the nature of the pornography used by the females. The content or nature of the pornography, such as violence, domination, or more egalitarian sexuality, is not known. In addition, it is unknown if the pornography was used alone or with a partner. Each of these variables could be important to consider in future research.

Additionally, although the model was significant, it explained only 17 percent of the variable in coercive behavior. As human sexual behavior is complex, it is likely that other variables not measured in the present study may add to the predictive ability of the model. These may include religious beliefs, feminist attitudes, and temperament and personality characteristics. These provide important avenues for further research that could be explored in the future.

Although exploratory in nature, these findings may have important implications for the prevention of sexual coercion in dating relationships. Prevention programs have primarily targeted males as the perpetrators and females as the victims. These approaches, based in traditionally gendered sexual scripts, may not go far enough in promoting healthy sexuality among college students. Female perpetrators may perceive prevention programs to be inapplicable to their own coercive behaviors, and males may inadvertently learn that they cannot be considered victims of sexual coercion.

Prevention programs that fail to acknowledge the possibility of male victimization serve to perpetuate the myth that males always want sex and that coercion of males is acceptable. These myths discourage men from seeking help when they have been victimized because they may fear that they won't be believed or that services are not available for them (Mezey and King 1990; Donnelly and Kenyon 1996). Males may also be unlikely to report their sexual victimization to a friend, the police, or a counselor because they are afraid that their sexual self-identity might be jeopardized. Pino and Meier (1999) found that males were least likely to report being raped when they felt their masculinity would be challenged. Reporting becomes even less likely since this statistically rare event is seldom discussed openly and is typically viewed as an aberration (Groth and Burgess 1980; Kaufman et al. 1980). Although women are more likely than males to be victims of sexual assault, education regarding incidence of coercion and assaults against males is crucial to encouraging healthy relationships and providing needed services and support to male victims. Given the strong relationship between pornography and perpetration among females, it may be valuable to discuss the messages and models about male and female sexuality found in pornography. Challenging the myths perpetuated in these materials may help decrease female sexual coerciveness.

Discussion Questions

1. Why do you think that women who use pornography might also be more likely to pressure someone to have sex? What other risk factors do you think there might be for coercive behavior by females?

2. How do you think people would respond to a man who sought help for being pressured to have sex? Would it be the same for a woman? Why or why not?
3. How do you think norms about sexual behavior among women have changed in the past 20 years? Why do you think they have changed?

References

Abbey, Antonia, Tina Zawacki, Philip O. Buck, A. Monique Clinton, and Pam McAuslan. 2004. "Sexual assault and alcohol consumption: What do we know about their relationship and what types of research are still needed?" *Aggression and Violent Behavior* 9:271–303.

Allen, Mike, Tara Emmers, Lisa Gebhardt, and Mary A. Giery. 1995. "Exposure to pornography and acceptance of rape myths." *Journal of Communication* 45:5–26.

Attwood, Feona. 2005. "Fashion and Passion: Marketing Sex to Women." *Sexualities* 8:392–406.

Beggan, James K. and Scott T. Allison. 2003. "'What Sort of Man Reads Playboy?' The Self-Reported Influence of Playboy on the Construction of Masculinity." *The Journal of Men's Studies* 11:189–206.

Boies, Sylvain C. 2002. "University Students' Uses of and Reactions to Online Sexual Information and Entertainment: Links to Online and Offline Sexual Behaviour." *Canadian Journal of Human Sexuality* 11:77–89.

Boswell, A. Ayres and Joan Z. Spade. 1996. "Fraternities and Collegiate Rape Culture: Why Are Some Fraternities More Dangerous Places for Women?" *Gender & Society* 10:133–47.

Brosius, Hans-Bernd, James B. Weaver, and Joachim F. Staab. 1993. "Exploring the Social and Sexual 'Reality' of Contemporary Pornography." *Journal of Sex Research* 30:161–70.

Burt, Martha R. 1980. "Cultural Myths and Supports for Rape." *Journal of Personality and Social Psychology* 38:217–30.

Burt, Martha R. 1983. "Justifying Personal Violence: A Comparison of Rapists and the General Public." *Victimology* 8:131–50.

Demaré, Dano, Hilary M. Lips, and John Briere. 1993. "Sexually Violent Pornography, Anti-Women Attitudes, and Sexual Aggression: A Structural Equation Model." *Journal of Research in Personality* 27(3):285–300.

Donnelly, Denise A. and Stacy S. Kenyon. 1996. "Honey, We Don't Do Men: Gender Stereotypes and the Provision of Services to Sexually Assaulted Males." *Journal of Interpersonal Violence* 11(3):441–48.

Dworkin, Andrea. 1988. *Letters from a War Zone.* New York: E. P. Dutton.

Fisher, William A. and Guy Grenier. 1994. "Violent Pornography, Antiwoman Thoughts, and Antiwoman Acts: In Search of Reliable Effects." *Journal of Sex Research* 31(1):23–38.

Glascock, Jack. 2005. "Degrading Content and Character Sex: Accounting for Men and Women's Differential Reactions to Pornography." *Communication Reports* 18:43–53.

Gortner, Eric T., Jackie K. Gollan, and Neil S. Jacobson. 1997. "Psychological Aspects of Perpetrators of Intimate Partner Violence and their Relationships with the Victims." *Psychiatric Clinics of North America* 20:337–350.

Groth, A. Nicholas and Ann W. Burgess. 1980. "Male Rape: Offenders and Victims." *The American Journal of Psychiatry* 137:806–10.

Harrington, Nicole Turillon and Harold Leitenberg. 1994. "Relationship between Alcohol Consumption and Victim Behaviors Immediately Preceding Sexual Aggression by an Acquaintance." *Violence and Victims* 9(4):315–24.

Henning, Kris, Harold Leitenberg, Patricia Coffey, Todd Bennett, and M. Kay Jankowski. 1997. "Long-Term Psychological and Social Impact of Witnessing Physical Conflict between Parents." *Journal of Interpersonal Violence* 11:35–51.

Hogben, M., D. Byrne, and M. E. Hamburger. 1995. "Coercive Heterosexual Sexuality in Dating Relationships of College Students: Implications of Differential Male-Female Experiences." *Journal of Psychology and Human Sexuality* 8(1–2):69–78.

Itzin, Catherine. 2002. "Pornography and the Construction of Misogyny." *Journal of Sexual Aggression* 8:4–42.

Jeffreys, Sheila. 2005. *Beauty and Misogyny: Harmful Cultural Practices in the West.* New York: Routledge.

Kaufman, Arthur. 1980. "Male Rape Victims: Noninstitutionalized Assault." *The American Journal of Psychiatry* 137:221–23.

Kernsmith, Poco. 2006. "Gender Differences in the Impact of Family of Origin Violence on Perpetrators of Domestic Violence." *Journal of Family Violence* 21:163–71.

MacKinnon, Catharine A. 1992. "Francis Biddle's Sister: Pornography, Civil Rights, and Speech." Pp. 261–321 in *Gender Constructs and Social Issues,* edited by T. L. Whitehead and B. V. Reid. Champaign, IL: University of Illinois Press.

Malamuth, Neil M. 1998. "An Evolutionary-Based Model Integrating Research on the Characteristics of Sexually Coercive Men." Pp. 151–84 in *Advances in Psychological Science, Vol. 1: Social, Personal, and Cultural Aspects,* edited by J. G. Adair, D. Bélanger, and K. L. Dion. Hove, England: Psychology Press/Erlbaum (UK) Taylor & Francis.

Malamuth, Neil M., Tamara Addison, and Mary Koss. 2000. "Pornography and Sexual Aggression: Are There Reliable Effects and Can We Understand Them?" *Annual Review of Sex Research* 11:26–91.

Malamuth, Neil M. and James V. Check. 1984. "Debriefing Effectiveness Following Exposure to Pornographic Rape Depictions." *Journal of Sex Research* 20:1–13.

Mihalic, Sharon Wofford and Delbert Elliott. 1997. "A Social Learning Theory Model of Marital Violence." *Journal of Family Violence* 12:21–47.

Mohler-Kuo, Meichun, George W. Dowdall, Mary P. Koss, and Henry Wechsler. 2004. "Correlates of Rape While Intoxicated in a National Sample of College Women." *Journal of Studies on Alcohol* 65:37–45.

Morgan, Robin. 1980. Theory and Practice: Pornography and Rape. Pp. 134–40 in *Take Back the Night,* edited by Laura Ledere. New York: William Morrow.

Mustaine, Elizabeth Ehrhardt and Richard Tewksbury. 2002. "Sexual Assault of College Women: A Feminist Interpretation of a Routine Activities Analysis." *Criminal Justice Review* 27:89–123.

O'Sullivan, Lucia F., E. Sandra Byers, and Larry Finkelman. 1998. "A Comparison of Male and Female College Students' Experiences of Sexual Coercion." *Psychology of Women Quarterly* 22:177–95.

Oddone-Paolucci, Elizabeth, Mark Genuis, and Claudio Violato. 2000. "A Meta-Analysis of the Published Research on the Effects of Pornography." Pp. 48–59 in *The Changing Family and Child Development.,* edited by C. Violato, E. Oddone-Paolucci, and M. Genuis. Aldershot, England: Ashgate Publishing Ltd.

Peter, Jochen and Patti M. Valkenburg. 2006. "Adolescents' Exposure to Sexually Explicit Online Material and Recreational Attitudes toward Sex." *Journal of Communication* 56:639–60.

Pino, Nathan W. and Robert F. Meier. 1999. "Gender Differences in Rape Reporting." *Sex Roles* 40:979–90.

Salmon, Catherine. 2004. "The Pornography Debate: What Sex Differences in Erotica Can Tell About Human Sexuality." Pp. 217–30 in *Evolutionary Psychology, Public Policy and Personal Decisions,* edited by C. Crawford and C. Salmon. Mahwah, NJ: Lawrence Erlbaum Associates Publishers.

Schwartz, Martin D. and Walter S. DeKeseredy. 1997. *Sexual Assault on the College campus: The Role of Male Peer Support.* Thousand Oaks, CA: Sage Publications.

Schwartz, Martin D. and Molly S. Leggett. 1999. "Bad Dates or Emotional Trauma? The Aftermath of Campus Sexual Assault." *Violence Against Women* 5:251–71.

Stack, Steven, Ira Wasserman, and Roger Kern. 2004. "Adult Social Bonds and Use of Internet Pornography." *Social Science Quarterly* 85:75–88.

Struckman-Johnson, C. and D. Struckman-Johnson. 1994. "Men Pressured and Forced into Sexual Experience." *Archives of Sexual Behavior* 23:93–114.

Trostle, Lawrence C. 1993. "Pornography as a Source of Sex Information for University Students: Some Consistent Findings." *Psychological Reports* 72:407–12.

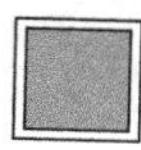

ARTICLE 12

Ronald Weitzer
George Washington University

The Prohibitionist Critique of Prostitution

Influential activists and some academics regard prostitution as a harmful institution. They can be called prohibitionists because their ultimate objective is to abolish prostitution. Their views are shaped by what I call the *oppression paradigm,* which defines all prostitution as a means of subordinating of women (see Weitzer 2009). Here, I will critically evaluate the main claims of the prohibitionist perspective.

Claims without Evidence

Prohibitionist writers claim that prostitution is the epitome of male domination and exploitation of women. Such a claim is presented as self-evident, absolute truth, without being supported by evidence. The prohibitionists define prostitution in a one-dimensional manner—as a form of violence or, more generally, as inherently exploitative and harmful to all sex workers everywhere. This definition is contrary to the findings of many evidence-based studies, which show that violence to prostitutes varies considerably across time and place. Violence does not occur throughout the sex trade. Not all the prostitutes at any time and at any place are subjected to violence. In upscale brothels, for example, relatively few workers experience trouble from clients, because of the presence of gatekeepers and coworkers who serve a social control function.

Without relying on solid evidence to support their claims, prohibitionists typically make far-reaching assertions about the fundamental character of sex work. The following are some examples. They argue, for instance, that prostitution is an expression of men's power against women, that is, paying for sexual services enables men to assert power and control over women in a way which would be deemed unacceptable in any other sphere. Prostitution is defined as harmful not only to the women who sell sex but also to all women inasmuch as its very existence reinforces larger patterns of sexual objectification and women's commodification.

Prohibitionists also construe prostitution negatively by equating it with other condemned practices, such as domestic violence, sexual slavery, pedophilia, rape, and other crimes. They argue that prostitutes should be called "prostituted women," victims, or "survivors." These labels clearly indicate that prostitutes lack human agency and the capacity to choose this kind of work, and are instead passive victims of predatory males.

The prohibitionist's use of those labels and definitions obscures what research has discovered in the relationships between prostitutes and their customers, which are complex and varied. Moreover, many customers and prostitutes themselves reject those derogatory labels. In a study of 294 street prostitutes in Miami, for instance, almost all of them "prefer the terms *sex worker* and *working woman* and refer to themselves as such" (Kurtz et al. 2004). Others call themselves escorts or providers. In contrast to the demonization of clients in the writings of prohibitionists, a comparative study found few differences between prostitutes' customers and a nationally representative sample of American men (Monto and McRee 2005).

Many prohibitionists also make specific empirical claims that are simply false. It is asserted that *most* prostitutes enter the sex trade when they are very young (13 to 14 years old), were physically or sexually abused as children, were tricked or forced into prostitution by pimps or traffickers, use or are addicted to drugs, and desperately want to exit the sex trade. Each of these claims holds true for a sector of the population (especially those engaged in survival sex on the streets), but are not necessarily true for the majority of other street prostitutes or of indoor sex workers. Studies have reported very different percentages of individuals who started selling sex when they were minors. In some, only a minority entered prostitution before age 18 and an even smaller percentage at age 13 to 14. Similarly, although many prostitutes want to leave the sex trade, others prefer this kind of work, for various reasons. A study of Thai sex workers, for example, found that only 15 percent wanted to quit selling sex, whereas the rest wanted to keep working in the sex trade, and 69 percent said they thought sex work was a good job (Steinfatt 2002). Finally, there is no doubt that a percentage of prostitutes were abused as children, now have pimps, and are drug addicted, but, again, the evidence does not support the notion that this is true for most sex workers.

Sweeping Generalizations

Prohibitionists tend to select the most disturbing instances of abuse and present them as typical or representative throughout the sex trade. They also insist that there are no differences between the distinct types of prostitution. Instead of grouping all prostitutes into one undifferentiated category, the evidence points to significant differences among those who sell sex. Street walkers, for example, differ from indoor prostitutes in important ways and the different kinds of indoor workers differ among themselves as well. Many studies have found that prostitution is a *segmented market*—with different strata organized in different ways (see Weitzer 2009).

Victimization is one area in which prohibitionist writers frequently make unwarranted generalizations. They claim that extremely high percentages (80 to 100 percent) of prostitutes are assaulted, robbed, raped, and otherwise victimized. These victimization figures are typically much higher than those reported by mainstream researchers (see Weitzer 2009). Moreover, prohibitionists fail to point out that victimization varies from one type of prostitution to another. Specifically, street walkers are more likely than indoor prostitutes to be victimized. As one study concludes, "When sex markets are directly compared, the harms introduced by sex work are overwhelmingly concentrated in street sex markets" (Cusick 2006:4; see also Church et al. 2001). This does not mean that indoor work is risk-free, but it does challenge the claim that victimization is high throughout the sex industry.

Flawed Data Collection

The procedures for collecting data in studies by prohibitionists are often either invisible or problematic. Some of these studies make grand generalizations about "prostitution" based on small, unrepresentative samples, usually of a few street prostitutes in one city. Other studies by prohibitionists fail to provide sufficient detail about sampling methods (how subjects were located and contacted, what they were told about the study, etc.) or fail to disclose the questions asked of respondents. As anyone involved in survey research knows, the way in which the questionnaire is worded can make a huge difference in the responses obtained, and standard practice is to provide the reader with the most important items verbatim, especially on sensitive topics like deviant behavior.

Some prohibitionist writers are frank about their biases. For example, before Melissa Farley (2007:22) began interviewing women in Nevada's legal brothels, she revealed: "I knew that they would minimize how bad it was.

We were asking the women to briefly remove a mask that was crucial to their psychological survival." In other words, Farley assumed that working conditions were "bad" at the outset and also that the workers would deny or "mask" this. Likewise, a Chicago study by Jody Raphael and Deborah Shapiro *began* from the premise that prostitution is harmful: "This research project was designed within a framework of prostitution as a form of violence against women and not prostitution as a legitimate industry" (Raphael and Shapiro 2004: 132). The 12 interviewers in this study were former prostitutes who shared that view. They were "survivors of prostitution who did not see their own [prior prostitution] experiences as 'work' or a 'choice'," and, remarkably, the authors acknowledged this "bias of the surveyors" (Raphael and Shapiro 2002: 9, 33). When both the lead researchers and interviewers hold such strong antiprostitution biases, the study's findings must be questioned.

Discrediting Inconvenient Findings

If prohibitionist writers come across findings that they did not expect, they tend to go to great length to discredit these findings. One example of this is downplaying or questioning the voices of sex workers themselves when they disagree with writers' opinions. Consider, for example, this statement by Janice Raymond, a leading prohibitionist activist: "There is no doubt that a small number of women say they choose to be in prostitution, especially in public contexts orchestrated by the sex industry" (Raymond 2003:325). By claiming that the number is small and by using the words *say* and *orchestrated,* Raymond clearly tries to cast doubt on the veracity of the women's testimony.

Prohibitionists sometimes distort other researchers' findings that they disagree with, and sometimes they invert what another researcher has found. Farley, for example, claimed that regular customers "strongly endorsed rape myths" (i.e., false notions about rapists and their victims) and cited a study by Marin Monto and Norma Hotaling (2001) to support this claim. But Monto and Hotaling reported only that repeat customers were more likely than other customers to accept rape myths, not that they strongly endorsed these myths. Farley also failed to mention the most important finding of the Monto-Hotaling study—that there were "low levels of rape myth acceptance" among the large sample of clients studied (Monto and Hotaling 2001:275).

In trying to make the case that indoor prostitution victimizes women to the same extent as street prostitution, one prohibitionist writer reported that a British study by Stephanie Church and her colleagues (2001) found that workers in indoor venues (private residences, saunas) reported more attempted rapes than street walkers. In fact, the Church study reported *the opposite:* that 28 percent of street workers said they had ever experienced an attempted rape, compared with 17 percent of indoor workers. Moreover, the prohibitionist writer failed to mention that street prostitutes were *11 times* more likely to have actually been raped. According to the Church study, 22 percent of the street sample compared with only 2 percent of the indoor sample had ever been raped while at work. This example is a clear case of both inverting and ignoring findings that inconveniently contradict the prohibitionist view that indoor prostitution is as dangerous as street-level prostitution.

Claiming That Legalization Is Perilous

Prohibitionists have been very critical of nations that have decriminalized prostitution (removing it from the criminal law) or have adopted some form of legalization (e.g., registration of business owners, licensing of sex workers, mandatory condom use or STD exams, zoning restrictions). Prohibitionists argue that decriminalization and legalization will only make the situation worse than where prostitution is illegal. They also believe that legalization gives an official stamp of approval to a contemptible institution and creates a culture in which sex-for-pay is rendered acceptable. As Janice Raymond (2003:322) states:

> When legal barriers disappear, so too do the social and ethical barriers to treating women as sexual merchandise. Legalization of prostitution sends the message to new generations of men and boys that women are sexual commodities and that prostitution is harmless fun.

Raymond adds that legalization is inherently a "failed policy," one that can never be successful.

In addition to the growth of a culture that allegedly degrades women, prohibitionist writers believe that levels of violence and exploitation will inevitably rise if prostitution is legalized. As prohibitionist Mary Sullivan writes, "Legitimizing prostitution as work has simply worked to normalize the violence and sexual abuse that workers experience on a daily basis. . . . Legalized prostitution is government-sanctioned abuse of women. . . . Prostitution can never be made safe" (Sullivan 2005:23, 18).

Such a pronouncement is an article of faith, not a conclusion from scientific, empirical evidence. Note the use of the sweeping terms *never* and *failed policy,* which are rather dogmatic, unscientific predictions. In fact, there is evidence challenging Sullivan's claim regarding safety. A decade of research on legal brothels in Nevada by Kathryn Hausbeck and Barbara Brents (2010:272) concluded that "Nevada's legal brothels offer the safest environment available for women to sell consensual sex." An investigation by the Ministry of Justice in the Netherlands found that the "vast majority" of workers in Dutch brothels reported that they "often or always feel safe" (Daalder 2004:30). Likewise, in Queensland, Australia, according to a government report, "there is no doubt that licensed brothels provide the safest working environment for sex workers in Queensland. . . . Legal brothels now operating in Queensland provide a sustainable model for a healthy, crime-free, and safe legal licensed brothel industry" and are a "state of the art model for the sex industry in Australia" (Crime and Misconduct Commission 2004:89). In New Zealand, decriminalization in 2003 extended numerous rights to sex workers, "increased [their] confidence, well-being, and a sense of validation," and made them more willing to report problems to the police, according to a government report (PLRC 2008:50). These assessments do not mean that legalized prostitution is a panacea or that it is free of problems in the nations where it exists; research on legal prostitution systems shows that they often confront unanticipated problems in the postlegalization period and that they vary considerably in their effects on workers and owners of erotic businesses (Weitzer 2012). But the evidence from a variety of settings where prostitution is legal and regulated by the government indicates that legalization *can* be superior to criminalization in terms of harm-reduction and the protection of workers' interests (Weitzer 2012), and that prohibitionists' claims are grounded in their opposition to prostitution *in general* rather than anything inherent in decriminalization and legalization.

In conclusion, we can see that there are several major deficiencies in the oppression paradigm and the blanket prohibitionist approach to sex work. More often than not, the writings of those who subscribe to these views are based on staunch ideological positions and/or seriously flawed "research" that is terribly biased toward supporting predetermined conclusions. A superior framework for understanding the wide variation that exists in the world of prostitution is what is called the *polymorphous paradigm* (Weitzer 2009, 2012), which recognizes that commercial sex can range from extremely harsh and exploitative types, at one pole, to much more rewarding practices where the sex workers control their working conditions and are able to minimize or avoid problems and risks.

Discussion Questions

1. Is prostitution necessarily oppressive of women? Describe the arguments on both sides of the debate.
2. In terms of the rules of sound social science research, what are two of the problems with the studies conducted by those who endorse the prohibitionist approach or the oppression paradigm?
3. Can the legalization of prostitution decrease incidents of violence and other abuses in this kind of work?

References

Church, Stephanie, Marion Henderson, Marina Barnard, and Graham Hart. 2001. "Violence by Clients towards Female Prostitutes in Different Work Setting." *British Medical Journal* 32: 524–26.

Cusick, Linda. 2006. "Widening the Harm Reduction Agenda: From Drug Use to Sex Work." *The International Journal of Drug Policy* 17: 3–11.

Daalder, A. L. 2004. *Lifting the Ban on Brothels: Prostitution in 2000—2001.* The Hague, Netherlands: Ministry of Justice.

Farley, Melissa. 2007. *Prostitution and Trafficking in Nevada.* San Francisco: Prostitution Research and Education.

Hausbeck, Kathryn and Barbara Brents. 2010. "Nevada's Legal Brothels." Pp. 255–84 in *Sex for Sale: Prostitution, Pornography, and the Sex Industry*, 2nd ed., edited by R. Weitzer. New York: Routledge.

Kurtz, Steven, Hilary Surratt, James Inciardi, and Marion Kelly. 2004. "Sex Work and Date Violence." *Violence Against Women* 10: 357–85.

Monto, Martin and Nick McRee. 2005. "A Comparison of the Male Customers of Female Street Prostitutes with National Samples of Men." *International Journal of Offender Therapy and Comparative Criminology* 49:505–29.

Monto, Martin and Norma Hotaling. 2001. "Predictors of Rape Myth Acceptance among the Male Clients of Female Street Prostitutes." *Violence Against Women* 7: 275–93.

PLRC [Prostitution Law Review Committee]. 2008. Report of the Prostitution Law Review Committee on the Operation of the Prostitution Reform Act 2003. Wellington, New Zealand: Ministry of Justice.

Raphael, Jody and Deborah Shapiro. 2002. *Sisters Speak Out: The Lives and Needs of Prostituted Women in Chicago.* Chicago, IL: Center for Impact Research.

Raphael, Jody and Deborah Shapiro. 2004. "Violence in Indoor and Outdoor Prostitution Venues." *Violence Against Women* 10: 126–39.

Raymond, Janice. 2003. "Ten Reasons for *Not* Legalizing Prostitution and a Legal Response to the Demand for Prostitution." *Journal of Trauma Practice* 2: 315–22.

Steinfatt, Thomas. 2002. Working at the Bar: Sex Work and Health Communication in Thailand. Westport, CT: Ablex.

Sullivan, Mary. 2005. What Happens When Prostitution Becomes Work? An Update on Legalization of Prostitution in Australia. North Fitzroy, Australia: Coalition Against Trafficking in Women.

Weitzer, Ronald. 2009. "Sociology of Sex Work." *Annual Review of Sociology* 35:213–34.

Weitzer, Ronald. 2012. Legalizing Prostitution: From Illicit Vice to Lawful Business. New York: NYU Press.

ARTICLE 13

Sharon S. Oselin
California State University, Los Angeles

Exiting Street Prostitution: A Combination of Internal and External Factors

Sex workers elicit much curiosity among academics and the general public because their work violates prevalent social norms, and therefore is often considered deviant. Prostitution, most commonly defined as an exchange of sex for compensation, is one of the oldest recorded types of sex work and continues to prosper throughout the world. In the social sciences there is a significant amount of research on prostitution, concerning the daily lives of prostitutes, stigma management, and the political and social forces that shape their lives (Alexander 1987; Pearl 1987; Chapkis 2000; Weitzer 2000). Surprisingly, there are few studies on how and why women leave sex work and prostitution in particular.

While there is a lack of overall research conducted on individuals who transition out of the trade, there are two prevailing explanations on this topic. First, certain scholars emphasize individuals who work in prostitution do so because it is the best available option as most occupy a low socioeconomic status (Miller 1986; Brock 1998; Bernstein 2007). Therefore, structurally based class concerns would need to be addressed to help sex workers quit prostitution. The second approach turns to internal factors as they prompt exits, such as having personal reasons and motivations to leave (Dalla 2006; Sanders 2007) and experiencing turning points that cause cognitive changes (Månsson and Hedin 1999).

On top of these concerns, existing research on prostitutes also contends leaving is more difficult due to labeling, stigma, and the associated deviant and criminal status of the work. Because of these conditions, quitting may be both a desirable goal and more difficult to achieve single-handedly. Prostitution-helping organizations (PHOs) are nongovernmental programs that provide resources and aid to prostitutes, and many aspire to help prostitutes leave the trade altogether. In this study, I examine the factors that cultivate an exit from street prostitution as prostitutes enroll in PHOs.

Methodology

I rely on rich, qualitative data in order to examine which factors are tied to leaving prostitution. In order to gain access to this population, I served as an intern at four different PHOs in the United States where I had frequent contact with street prostitutes. I completed this research between 2002 and 2006, and spent an average of three months at each site, conducting participant observations and interviews. I rely primarily on the in-depth interviews I conducted with 36 female prostitutes across these sites in this study. These women ranged in age from 20 to 55, with an average age of 34.

The interviews focused on the following topics: past histories in prostitution, life course events, experiences on the streets, family relationships, identity, reasons for leaving prostitution and entering the program, interactions with the criminal justice system, and future goals. I conducted the tape-recorded interviews in a private setting to ensure confidentiality, and assigned each interviewee a pseudonym for protection. Throughout these interviews, the women espoused stories that contained fairly simplistic cause-and-effect narratives (Tilly 2006).

After completing all the interviews, I transcribed and coded them in order to examine which themes were important to the transition out of prostitution. I did not find there to be any significant differences across these four samples, in terms of how and why prostitutes initially left prostitution, even though they were associated with four distinct PHOs.

Factors Leading to an Exit

My research concludes that leaving street prostitution, at least for the women included in this study, is not only a process but is also the result of a combination of factors. Specifically, I find both internal (reasons for leaving, turning points) and external factors (learning of a PHO, bridge parties) lead women to initially exit prostitution as they enter PHOs. I will examine each of these factors in the following sections.

Reasons for Leaving Prostitution

A central factor that facilitates leaving prostitution is to have reasons (or motivations) to do so. The women in this study all cited reasons for quitting, with an average of 2.55 reasons given per woman. Others scholars have noted the variety of reasons women want to exit the trade, including relational factors, restrictive factors, spirituality, cumulative burdens, being in a transitional context, violence, sobriety, and health issues (Dalla 2006; Sanders 2007). As I analyzed their reasons for wanting to exit, I also noticed many of these reasons were formulated based upon their personal backgrounds and past experiences.

For instance, one common theme that emerged among motivations for quitting centered on religious beliefs that persisted over the life course. A 41-year-old woman, who worked in prostitution for 15 years, highlighted the important role a Higher Power played throughout her life even while she worked on the streets. She explained how religion was a big part of her childhood and her faith eventually became a primary motivation to leave as an adult:

> My mom was a Jehovah witness and that's the religion I was raised in. I always had faith. When I was working on the streets, I kept praying to God: This is not me. Why do I keep doing this? Why can't I stop? God help me stop. . . . He was always there knocking I just had to open up the door to allow him to come in and help me stop.

Another motivation for leaving related to violence that occurred in these street environments. Although prostitutes' experiences with violence varied considerably, for some individuals fear of violence and death was their motivation to get out. The following statement by Jenna, a prostitute for 27 years, illustrates this reason: "I was almost killed by my last john [client] and I ran for my life. It was at that point that I knew I needed to get help and quit. It was bad out there. . . . I was raped many times and left for dead, having people cut my face up and damage my eye."

Other prostitutes emphasized how sex work took a physical, mental, and physical toll on them over time. Elaine felt 17 years as a prostitute burdened her with many mental and emotional problems. She claimed to be exhausted from the work and declared that most girls who leave prostitution are also motivated by this factor: "If they are really, really ready to change their lives [and leave] mostly it's because they are tired. That's the main reason you will hear the girls give. They are just burned out by the work."

Interpersonal relationships with family members, partners, or close friends likewise became a reason to leave the trade. In certain cases, sex work threatened an existing relationship and therefore served as a motivation to quit. Upon discovering what she did for a living, Rosaria summarized how her fiancée responded: "He didn't like the drugs, alcohol or prostitution . . . the way I was living. So to be with him, I needed to change."

Turning Points of Change

Beyond reasons for leaving, women also emphasized a turning point event that prompted them to place exiting prostitution as a central goal. Turning points can cultivate a shift within a person that brings a new set of priorities and goals to the forefront (Stark and Lofland 1965). Previous research finds turning point events were an important step to leave street prostitution (Månsson and Hedin 1999; Sanders 2007). In this study, I find that although there is some overlap between turning point events and reasons for leaving, most women spoke of them as two distinct categories. Typically, prostitutes cite reasons for exiting that vary from their turning point event, and as a result of experiencing this event, their reasons become more important to them. I find that three types of events prompted a turning point: arrests, hospitalizations, and childbirth.

Arrests and Jail

Given that street prostitutes are highly visible to law enforcement, it is not surprising that all the women in this study have been arrested for prostitution at some point throughout their career. This finding corroborates previous work that claims street prostitutes have among the highest arrest rates of all sex workers (Alexander 1987). As a result of these arrests, a majority of women in this study served jail or prison sentences. Those who had a history of multiple arrests and extensive criminal records spoke of their heightened fears of returning to prison and the prospect of serving long-term sentences. When these fears became a reality, rearrests and potential imprisonment became a turning point event.

Shondra explained how her imprisonment evoked a turning point in her life as it made her motivation for leaving skyrocket:

> God finally rescued me the last time I went to jail, and it finally clicked after I was arrested that this was God's way of helping me out. I prayed for God to strengthen my faith in Him and to put Him in my life. . . . To feel what I knew was right and what I was raised to believe in. I embraced that and ran with it because that was my lifeline and I knew with no doubt in my mind that if I would have kept going the way I was going I would end up dead. After I was released I went right into the program because I knew this was my one shot.

Another woman, who entered prostitution at the age of nine, had a substantial history of arrests and imprisonment and recently violated her parole. Upon this violation, the prospect of serving a lengthy prison sentence was extremely likely, and became a turning point event for her: "I was on parole and I got busted for prostitution again. I knew I was going back to prison for a long time, so I called my parole officer and asked her to help me quit for real. At that point, I knew something had to change."

Hospitalization

Another event that cultivated a turning point for prostitutes was when they experienced extreme psychological duress that resulted in hospitalization. In these situations, the women attribute their change in thinking to their time spent in the hospital, where they were able to take stock of their situation and formulate alternative career options.

Even though Evette had a variety of reasons for wanting to leave prostitution, it was the time she spent in a hospital due to a "mental breakdown" that provided a catalyst for quitting. She felt her mental instability was a result of her excessive drug use, which was fueled by her work in the trade:

> I never really thought about stopping [prostitution] until the drug thing really took a toll on me mentally. I started hallucinating and began losing my mind and it wasn't fun. That's when I really wanted out. When I was in the hospital I recognized that this was it—now or never—I had to leave. Something just clicked inside me.

After this realization, Evette stated she could not return to prostitution.

Tiffany also suffered from mental illness, which she attributed to her intense drug addiction, and attempted suicide. Her motivations for quitting revolved solely around having a "spiritual awakening," but it was not until she ended up in the hospital that she began to take the necessary steps to exit:

> I tried to smoke myself to death, drink myself to death, and take pills and had to go to the psychiatric unit for six days. It was during this time that I had the clarity to know that I needed help. When I was released I came right to this program.

Childbirth

Pregnancy and childbirth were the final turning point events that occurred among prostitutes. Amy stated feelings of exhaustion made her want to leave the trade for years, yet it was pregnancy and the birth of her son that produced a turning point in her life that altered her priorities. She recalled her changed perspective after her son was born:

> I want my kids back. I realized it was time to stop when I was pregnant with my son and I didn't want to be doing that anymore since he needed a mother. At that point, I started trying to figure out how I could leave ... what else I could do instead.

For prostitutes in this study, turning points created a newfound sense of purpose and priorities, where they felt getting out of prostitution was paramount. In order for a PHO to be perceived as a viable option to exit, prostitutes first had to learn about the program and what it offered.

Learning of a PHO

In addition to internal factors, such as motivations and turning points, external factors shape the process of exiting prostitution. The first of these is having an awareness of a PHO as an avenue through which to leave. Indeed, knowing about a program and the services it provides can make leaving more appealing and appear attainable because one can expect certain provisions through this association. Prostitutes in this study learned about PHOs through a variety of sources: outreach services of PHOs, staff associated with affiliated institutions, family members or friends, and the media.

For instance, Janise first heard of the local PHO when she began using its temporary crisis shelter years earlier: "See I was just a client coming in and out of their crisis shelter, getting meals or sleeping." Other clients claimed they first heard of a PHO when they came across its mobile outreach unit, whose purpose was to provide condoms, information, and safety tips to street prostitutes. For instance, one prostitute explained:

> I had always known about them as far as passing out condoms and stuff. . . . I even knew the staff on a first name basis . . . but did I go in for the help and all that? No, I did not. I even lived really close to the residential house but I never once thought about going there because in my mind there was no help for me. But, it was a seed planted. I knew in the back of my head the program was there for me when I was ready to quit.

Another way the women learned of PHOs was through social workers affiliated with other institutions, such as jails or hospitals. Tiffany stated it was her hospital social worker who informed her about the PHO:

> I was in the hospital for eight days and the social worker, Mr. Green, came and spoke about this program. He said it was peaceful and there were counselors there and all that ... that was about two and a half years ago, and that's how long it took me before I actually ended up here. But it was at that point that the seed was planted.

Other women found out about PHOs through their family members or friends. Monique attributed learning about the program to her sister and a fellow prostitute, both of whom had enrolled years before:

> I had seen the evidence of the program through my sister, who graduated from the program a few years back. And another lady in my neighborhood was also a prostitute and really bad off. She went to the program too and they both did well.

Likewise, a friend in jail told Mary about a PHO for the first time: "I heard about it at least a year and a half ago from a friend while I was in jail. I always kept that in mind."

Women also acquired information about PHOs from advertisements or articles in local newspapers. Around the same time she learned of the program from her friend, Mary also saw a newspaper article about it that featured the history of the program, the services it offered, and its contact information. Similarly, another client came across an ad in a local newspaper that "stuck in her mind." She recited the title of the ad that resonated with her: "Do you want to get out of the life of prostitution?"

Interestingly, in spite of learning about the PHOs, few women attempted to immediately enroll in them because they felt they were not yet ready to exit altogether. For many women, this knowledge became a "seed planted" that they acted on at a later date.

Third-Party Bridges

The final external factor tied to exiting is based on a specific type of social network—third-party bridges—or individuals who connect prostitutes to PHOs. In the social network literature, this third-party bridge is referred to as a "broker," an actor who mediates exchanges between two other actors not directly linked (Fernandez and Gould 1994). In this study, I find women not only learn about these programs through their social networks but they rely on these "bridges" to facilitate their entrance into PHOs.

There are two types of bridges that help women enroll in PHOs. The first type is comprised of individuals who act as professional bridges, or those who have shared interests with PHOs. Simply put, they are largely motivated to facilitate prostitutes' placement in PHOs based on their occupational goals and duties. The second type is personal bridges, individuals primarily concerned with the desires of the prostitutes rather than the organizations.

Professional Bridges

The most common professional bridges who link women with PHOs are individuals affiliated with the criminal justice system, such as public defense attorneys, parole officers, and the police. These bridges are especially salient for those prostitutes entangled within the criminal justice system, and based upon their power, advocate for this sentence in lieu of imprisonment. While a judge often makes the final decision, attorneys and parole officers certainly influence these outcomes. After learning of a PHO, Tisha, a prostitute for nine years, asked her parole officer to plead with the judge for her placement there. As a bridge party, who had significant power over her sentencing, it was up to her parole officer's discretion whether she would be able to enter the PHO. Tisha explained:

> I heard about the PHO the third time I went to jail through a chaplain who told me there are programs for prostitutes. I've never heard of one before that. Because I did a crime—prostitution— I was on parole and I was looking at serving a minimum of 18 months in jail. I didn't know if I was going to get into the program, not because they wouldn't accept me but because my parole officer wouldn't recommend it. ... I had to go through her first. So I called my parole officer and I told her about the program. ... I didn't know if she would recommend it for me or not. Finally, she granted me permission and I was able to enter.

Tisha's story was a common explanation of how bridges help prostitutes enroll in PHOs rather than go to prison.

In rare instances, the police serve as the bridge between street prostitutes and PHOs. Although the police have no legal authority to force a woman to enter a PHO, in circumstances where a woman is willing to accept their suggestion, they serve as the effective bridge. Amy, who entered prostitution as a 13-year-old runaway, was one of these individuals:

> The cops picked me up and they brought me here, and that was the first time I heard about this program. I thought the program wouldn't take me but they did because the cops knew the director so I got in. And now I haven't worked in prostitution for six months.

Social workers also function as bridges to PHOs, and they are especially instrumental for the women who experience traumatic events and land in the hospital. For example, when Tiffany was in a psychiatric hospital after she attempted suicide, the on-site social worker recommended she enter a PHO and orchestrated her placement into the program.

Lawyers, parole officers, police, and social workers all act as professional bridges because they share a mutual interest with the PHOs, which is to get the women out of prostitution and discourage further involvement with the criminal justice system. Acting as brokers between prostitutes and PHOs is beneficial for the workers professionally, as these placements can ultimately help accomplish occupational goals. One police captain summarized the mutual benefits:

> The police became an advocate for this program, not only by distributing information to the prostitutes who we were directly involved in the criminal justice system, but also to other agencies, such as courts. You know, if we could keep her from going on the street again by connected her to this program, we've not only helped her, but we've accomplished our goal for the community as well. I think it worked as a real good win/win situation for both of us.

Personal Bridges

Family and friends also become bridges between prostitutes and PHOs but their motivation is to help prostitutes achieve their goals. For example, after Monique learned of the PHO and experienced a turning point in jail, she turned to her sister, who had graduated from the PHO a few years prior, for help:

> I went to call my sister and asked her if they will help me. I asked her, "Will they have a spot for me?" She told me more about them, provided their number, and put in a word for me with the director. I called them and they said as soon as you get released you can come.

Likewise, Chanelle, who worked as a prostitute for 10 years, emphasized how her friend became a crucial link to her entrance into a PHO:

> Apparently, the director of the program would go to the prison and give presentations about the program, what you had to do to qualify and so on. So a friend I had in jail saw that, kept that information and would pass it on to other women in jail who wanted another chance at life but were serious about it. After we became friends, she told me about the program and gave me the phone number. I called them and told them I heard about it through a woman who met the director in jail, said I sincerely wanted to quit prostitution, and asked for an interview. Once my sentence was up I came right here.

Prostitute Perceptions of PHOs

Exiting with the help of PHOs is certainly not the only pathway out of street prostitution. However, given the difficulties associated with the trade, many of the women in this study claimed they would not have been able to quit if it were not for resources and support of a PHO. Debbie stated she had thought about leaving prostitution before but it never happened until she finally entered a program:

> Yes, I couldn't do it alone. I tried before but it didn't work. I started to get back on drugs. Or I'd find myself in a predicament that I couldn't handle and I needed money. Or I would be staying someplace and they would tell me that I had to get out. Where was I going to go? And the only thing I knew was to go and get money from men [through sex] and once I started doing that I started using drugs too. The program offered me a different way out. I knew they helped you get an education, a job, and maintain sobriety.

Loretta also believed that a PHO could teach her how to live a life outside of prostitution:

> So I knew it was just time to stop and I didn't know how and I felt that this place was definitely going to show me how. They provided me with so many tools I didn't have or couldn't get on my own. They offered me an education so I could get a job and support myself.

In short, many of these women perceived they could not surmount the barriers to exit prostitution on their own. Therefore, they felt by utilizing the services and resources of a PHO their transition would be easier, as they would acquire skills and structure, which would ultimately improve their chances of success.

Conclusions

Most people think of prostitutes as criminals and deviants, a type of role that does not have much prestige or value in our society. Indeed, such sociolegal circumstances likely exacerbate the difficulties of working in prostitution (Sanders 2007). Prior studies also find those who occupy deviant roles experience unique circumstances (labeling, stigma, and other hardships), which can make leaving those roles more challenging (Brown 1991; Sanders 2007).

While prior research points to structural (e.g., poverty) or individually based changes as they prompt exits from prostitution, this research finds it is a combination of factors that pull women out of street level sex work. I find that although internal factors are important because they imply mental and emotional changes and a willingness to leave, it is also one's knowledge of available "helping" programs and third-party bridges that facilitate such exits. My findings do not discount previous theories, but they enrich those theories by emphasizing it is *both* internal and external factors together that enable exits from street prostitution.

Although there are other pathways out of prostitution that are not covered in this analysis, PHOs indeed provide one avenue through which women can leave sex work. To that end, the role of these organizations was paramount to this process, as the women in this sample felt their affiliation with a PHO offered future possibilities and opportunities they otherwise would not have had. While this study examines the relevant factors associated with leaving prostitution via PHOs, I do not argue that upon enrollment these women have fully or indefinitely exited that role. In fact, I contend that this transition is sure to involve a longer, more complex process of change that is shaped by these organizations and their staff members. Such an analysis, however, extends beyond the scope of this study.

Because this study is solely based on street prostitution within U.S. cities, these conclusions may not be generalizable to sex workers in other contexts or countries that maintain a different sociolegal approach to prostitution. Moreover, this research includes only female street prostitutes, and the factors that are relevant to their exits may not apply to male prostitutes. Future research should continue to examine this topic to assess how the exiting process unfolds among different types of sex workers.

Discussion Questions

1. Can these findings about exiting prostitution be used to understand how people leave other types of deviant roles? If so, in what ways?
2. Select another population and describe how you would design a study to test this theory.

References

Alexander, Priscilla. 1987. "Prostitution: A Difficult Issue for Feminists." Pp. 184–214 in *Sex Work: Writings by Women in the Sex Industry*, edited by F. Delacoste and P. Alexander. Pittsburg, PA: Cleis Press.

Bernstein, Elizabeth. 2007. *Temporarily Yours: Intimacy, Authenticity, and the Commerce of Sex.* Chicago, IL: University of Chicago Press.

Brock, Deborah. 1998. *Making Work, Making Trouble: Prostitution as a Social Problem.* Toronto: University of Toronto Press.

Brown, J. David. 1991. "The Professional Ex-: An Alternative for Exiting the Deviant Career." *Sociological Quarterly* 32(2):219–30.

Chapkis, Wendy. 2000. "Power and Control in the Commercial Sex Trade." Pp. 181–201 in *Sex for Sale*, edited by R. Weitzer. New York: Routledge.

Dalla, Rochelle. 2006. Exposing the "Pretty Woman" Myth: A Qualitative Investigation of Street Level Prostituted Women. Lanham, MD: Lexington.

Fernandez, Roberto M. and Roger V. Gould. 1994. "A Dilemma of State Power: Brokerage and Influence in the National Health Policy Domain." *American Journal of Sociology* 99(6):1455–91.

Månsson, Sven-Axel and Ulla-Carin Hedin. 1999. "Breaking the Matthew Effect: On Women Leaving Prostitution." *International Journal of Social Welfare* 8(1):67–77.

Miller, Eleanor. 1986. *Street Woman.* Philadelphia, PA: Temple University Press.

Pearl, Julie. 1987. "The Highest Paying Customers: America's Cities and the Costs of Prostitution Control." *Hastings Law Journal* 38(4):769–800.

Sanders, Teela. 2007. "Becoming an Ex-Sex Worker: Making Transitions Out of a Deviant Career." *Feminist Criminology* 2(1):74–95.

Stark, Rodney and John Lofland. 1965. "Becoming a World-Saver: A Theory of Conversion to Deviant Perspective." *American Sociological Review* 30(6):862–75.

Tilly, Charles. 2006. Why? What Happens When People Give Reasons and Why. Princeton, NJ: Princeton.

Weitzer, Ronald. 2000. "Why We Need More Research on Sex Work." Pp. 1–3 in *Sex for Sale*, edited by R. Weitzer. New York: Routledge.

PART SIX

Physical Manifestations of Deviance

On YouTube one can find many videos on how to physically injure one's body. The videos commonly involve teens demonstrating how they physically harm themselves via cutting, burning, and hitting. The individuals in the videos argue this physical harm is a coping mechanism to deal with pressure in their lives. The videos can also serve as an instruction manual to anyone else interested in exhibiting the same type of behavior. The strain of life, historically shown to lead to crime and deviance, has physically manifested itself and now individuals physically take it out on themselves.[1]

In Article 14, "The Relationship between Tattooing and Deviance in Contemporary Society," Joshua Adams investigates the relationship between tattoos and deviance. He covers important topics such as the history of tattooing, the debate over deviance or art, and the social demographics of tattooed individuals. In Article 15, we go a bit further than physical artwork; we examine self-mutilation and body modification. Jimmy Taylor takes us into the world of self-injurers. He discusses the key areas of cutting, piercing, and self-mutilation. In Article 16, Richard Tewksbury and colleagues cover the different types of teenage suicide. They analyze suicide notes and categorize these notes based on the typologies of suicide established by Emile Durkheim: anomic, altruistic, egoistic, and fatalistic.

Note

1. Szabo, Lisa. 2011. "Teens Share Self-Injury, 'Cutting' Videos on YouTube." *USA Today*, February 21. Retrieved June 17, 2011 (http://yourlife.usatoday.com/parenting-family/teen-ya/story/2011/02/Teens-share-Internet-injury-videos/43962874/1).

Joshua Adams
State University of New York, Fredonia

The Relationship between Tattooing and Deviance in Contemporary Society

The subjectivity of deviance, as well as the fluid nature of what is and what is not considered deviant at any given time, is a fundamental insight of sociology. A prime example of this is the practice of tattooing. The history of tattooing in the United States reveals that the labeling of a behavior as deviant is contingent upon the assessments and subsequent reactions of others. Cultural evaluations of behavior as deviant shift as prevailing norms change and evolve. In the United States, tattooing has been both a popular and a stigmatized practice subject to changes in fashion and cultural norms. The past two decades have seen tattooing experience a growth in popularity and mainstream attention. Academics have noticed the cultural changes surrounding tattooing, moving away from the traditional characterization of the tattoo as an indicator of deviance and focusing on the tattoo as an expression of identity (Atkinson 2002) and a serious art form (Vail 1999). This article examines tattooing as a practice that, in recent history, has been closely associated with deviant behaviors and groups. The changing cultural uses of tattooing, as well as shifting perceptions of tattooed individuals, reinforces our understanding of deviance as temporally and spatially contextual. This article considers how those changes have affected our overall understanding of the practice of tattooing in addition to how, and to what degree, the status of certain practices transitions between deviance and normative acceptability.

Since it first achieved a degree of mainstream popularity in the West, particularly Western Europe and the United States, in the late eighteenth century, tattooing has at times been considered fashionable and exotic. More often than not, however, it has been evaluated as overwhelmingly deviant. Associated with sailors (Bradley 2000), criminals (Govenar 2000), "savage" races (Oettermann 2000), and circus entertainers (Mifflin 1997), tattooing was firmly positioned as the domain of those labeled socially undesirable. Those in the medical community have suggested it as an indicator of low self-esteem (Braithwaite et al. 1998), drug and alcohol abuse (Braithwaite et al. 2001), and impulsiveness; deviant sexualities; or any variety of "underlying psychiatric conditions" (Raspa and Cusack 1990:1481). Given such negative social connotations, a thriving "deviant subculture" emerged in the United States—a culture that provides support for those who are tattooed and that attempts to redefine the tattoo as a positive characteristic (Sanders 1990). Indeed, marketers mining these subcultures searching for the next big trend are partially responsible for the heightened visibility of tattooing and have perhaps led to a greater acceptance and understanding of body art.

Deviant Practice or Fashionable Art?

The practice of permanently marking the body can be found across cultures and historical contexts, often as normatively sanctioned, socially integrating customs (Rubin 1988a). After the reintroduction of tattooing to Europeans in the eighteenth century, the practice fluctuated between fad and novelty, but was not regarded as an overt sign of deviant or criminal inclinations until the end of the nineteenth century (Bradley 2000). By the beginning of the twentieth century, attitudes toward tattooing were being influenced by the sociobiological perspectives of criminologists such as Cesare Lombroso who effectively pathologized tattooing as a primitive and degenerate trait of criminals and the lower classes (Bradley 2000).

Despite the association of tattooing with criminals, tattooing quickly became popular among the American and British upper classes in the late 1880s (Bradley 2000). Tattoos were also popular among soldiers during the Civil War as an expression of patriotic sentiment (Oettermann 2000). These seemingly contradictory attitudes toward tattooing exemplify the trajectory of tattooing as both fashionable and transgressive. This illustrates the power dynamics involved defining deviant behavior. While tattooing was the height of upper-class fashion at the close of the nineteenth century, for members of the lower classes, being tattooed remained a stigmatizing and deviant behavior (Fisher 2002). Furthermore, with the invention of the electric tattoo machine, tattoos became relatively more accessible and popular among the lower classes, diminishing the interest of the fashionable elite (Fisher 2002). The increasing association of tattoos with marginal social groups cemented its status as an indicator of deviance so that "by the mid-twentieth century tattooing was firmly established as a definedly deviant practice in the public mind" (Sanders 1989:18).

Tattooing experienced a dramatic shift in the 1960s with advances in technique and style as well as renewed public interest. A transition known as the "tattoo renaissance" encompassed a diversification and improvement of artistic styles, experimentation with design, the growth of custom tattooing, and a professionalization of standards and attention to sanitation of equipment (Rubin 1988b). There was also a demographic shift that saw an increase in female clients, professionals, and those with more disposable income with greater interest in the compositional aesthetics of the tattoo (Rubin 1988b). This was in sharp contrast to predominantly white, blue-collar, working-class clientele of previous decades who got tattoos of the standardized "flash" designs that lined the walls of tattoo studios (Steward 1990). Additionally, many tattooists have begun defining themselves as artists, creating custom pieces of art for clients (Sanders 1989; Irwin 2003). The transformation of the tattoo industry in conjunction with broader cultural changes that led to increased interest in tattooing by a wider demographic helped to move body art closer to mainstream acceptance and away from its association with deviance.

As the tattoo renaissance progressed into the 1980s and 1990s, marking the body has expanded to a vast array of social groups. Contemporary frameworks for interpreting the tattoo have expanded beyond the simple heuristic of deviance. DeMello (2000) suggests that tattooing is often imbued with a range of spiritual meanings and notions of reconnection with the primitive. Body modification is also used as a means of asserting individual identity by transgressing normative expectations; some have noted the use of female body modification to reclaim the body from abuse or illness through the processes of body marking (Pitts 2003). These reassessments have contributed to the transition of tattooing away from deviance and recontextualized it as a more commonly practiced and acceptable avenue for self-expression.

Gender has played a prominent role in recent scholarship on body modification, in part because tattooing has traditionally been understood as a male pursuit. Tattoos have long been the domain of the working class, the serviceman, and the criminal: an outward sign that, according to Steward (1990), "leaves no doubt as to one's masculinity" (p. 57). For Pitts (1998), transgressive body modifications can signify a reappropriation of the body and rejection of gendered constraints. Indeed, tattooing often confounds mainstream beauty ideals, and for women "tattooing can also be a rather flamboyant way to violate diffuse cultural rules about the gendered body" (Atkinson 2002:228). Whatever the purpose, tattooing among women has dramatically increased during the past quarter-century, with some research seeing women account for nearly half of tattoo clients (Laumann and Derick 2006).

While the prevailing attitudes toward tattooing may have shifted and social scientists now note the positive, prosocial, socially integrating function of body modification, others remain skeptical. Many remain unconvinced that body modifications are performed in a sanitary environment and that recipients are prepared for the lasting effects. In an article on the prevalence of tattooing among college students, Armstrong et al. (2002) suggest that "education should be aimed at dissuading the prevalence and perceived value of the product in a matter-of-fact manner while incorporating the major barriers (permanent marks, costs, and hepatitis) in a young adult perspective for decision making" (p. 322). Stirn et al. (2006) note that both body piercing and tattooing "create a lasting body modification, which counters, generally speaking, the established norms of beauty" (p. 531). Additionally, because of its historical relationship with criminals, and because there exists a separate culture of prison tattooing, the role of tattooing among prisoners is a common theme. Tattoos are used within the institutional setting as a means of communicating status, ethnicity, and gang affiliations to create what DeMello (1993) terms the "convict body," where the tattoos themselves become signifiers of the individual's identity as a convict.

As tattooing becomes more widely practiced among diverse populations, particularly in the United States, researchers have often pointed to the commodification of subcultural practices as one of the primary engines driving this surge in popularity. The commodification of tattooing represents the practice as simultaneously fashionable and rebellious. Pitts (2003) observes this process, noting that "some of the practices, especially tattoos and body piercings, were appropriated by MTV and the catwalk, and by the late 1990s, these had become wholly acceptable, if alternative and hip, forms of fashion" (p. 12). Kosut (2006b) suggests that tattoos have been "pulled from their sub-cultural roots (blue-collar, deviant, underground) and replanted in the mainstream" yet "have a certain aura of cool and rebellion about them" (p. 1043).

Methods

The data for this study were collected via a telephone survey administered through the Public Opinion Laboratory at Northern Illinois University, between February and April 2004. The nationally representative sample was composed of 500 adults between the ages of 18 and 50 living within the contiguous United States. Respondents were selected and contacted using random digit dialing. This dataset was originally collected as part of a health-oriented research project to "provide US tattooing and body piercing prevalence, societal distribution, and medical and social consequence data" (Laumann and Derick 2006:413). Additionally, this sample allows for a reasonable comparison between tattooed and nontattooed respondents. The analyses that follow focus specifically on the sociological implications of tattooing within the United States, the transitioning demographics, and the ostensible shift of tattooing from an overwhelmingly deviant to a more acceptable, or at least tolerated, social practice.

Given the possibility of a tattoo renaissance and the widening array of individuals who become tattooed (DeMello 2000), it seems reasonable to expect that those who are tattooed will be more educated and have a higher, and therefore disposable, income. However, as tattooing currently enjoys a surge in popularity among college students (Armstrong et al. 2002), it is likely to occur with greater frequency among a younger demographic. Similarly, while tattooing has traditionally been perceived as a male-dominated pursuit, recently, more women have been modifying their bodies through tattooing and body piercing for a variety for personal, spiritual, and political purposes (Atkinson 2002; Pitts 2003). Additionally, Laumann and Derick (2006) found that tattooing was equally common among both men and women.

Several researchers have also noted the influence of friends and family on whether an individual becomes tattooed (Armstrong et al. 2004). Others have found that religious affiliation and employment, as measures of social integration, are negatively associated with being tattooed (Stirn et al. 2006). As such, it appears that social connections should play a distinct role in the decision to be tattooed.

Drawing from the previous research on tattooing—research that notes historical and contemporary associations with criminal behavior as well as that indicating tattooing's greater levels of social acceptability over time—one might expect that being tattooed is no longer a valid indicator of criminal behavior. Additionally, if tattooing is indeed gaining broader social acceptance, or at least being practiced more widely, it is expected that tattooing will also have little or no relationship with other traditionally deviant practices. However, taking into account DeMello's (1993) arguments that tattoos serve a specific social function within prisons, that prison tattoos are qualitatively different from professional tattoos, and that visible prison tattoos "particularly those on the face, neck, and hands" (p. 10) mark one in an external fashion and are more likely to be socially stigmatizing in general, it is expected that having served time in jail will be a significant predicator of whether an individual has a tattoo on his or her face, neck, or hands.

Findings

The findings presented here counter some of the assumptions about the degree to which tattooing has changed. Table A14.1 shows the social characteristics of both tattooed and nontattooed respondents. Within the entire sample ($N = 500$), 120 respondents report having a minimum of one tattoo, with men and women being tattooed at roughly equivalent levels.

TABLE A14.1
Social Characteristics of Tattooed and Non-tattooed Respondents[a]

	Tattooed Respondents	Nontattooed Respondents
	120 (24 percent)	380 (76 percent)
Gender		
Male	64 (53.3 percent)	183 (48.2 percent)
Female	56 (46.7 percent)	197 (51.8 percent)
*Race**		
White/Caucasian	86 (71.7 percent)	306 (80.5 percent)
Black/African American	16 (13.3 percent)	41 (10.8 percent)
Asian/Pacific Islander	0 (0.0 percent)	6 (2.0 percent)
Native American/Alaskan Native	2 (1.7 percent)	5 (1.0 percent)
Some other race	15 (12.5 percent)	19 (5.0 percent)

(continued)

TABLE A14.1 (continued)

	Tattooed Respondents	Nontattooed Respondents
*Age****		
20–29	39 (32.5 percent)	66 (18.0 percent)
30–39	42 (34.9 percent)	104 (28.3 percent)
40–49	26 (21.6 percent)	137 (37.3 percent)
Above 50	11 (9.1 percent)	60 (16.3 percent)
*Marital Status**		
Ever married	67 (56.8 percent)	251 (66.1 percent)
Never married	51 (43.2 percent)	126 (33.2 percent)
*Educational Attainment***		
Less than high school diploma	11 (9.3 percent)	15 (4.0 percent)
High school diploma	46 (39 percent)	99 (26.1 percent)
Some college	21 (17.8 percent)	65 (17.1 percent)
Associates or bachelor's degree	32 (27.1 percent)	142 (37.4 percent)
Some graduate study/graduate degree	8 (6.7 percent)	57 (15.0 percent)
Total Household Income		
Less than $10,000	9 (8.7 percent)	19 (6.4 percent)
$10,000–$20,000	10 (9.6 percent)	17 (5.7 percent)
$20,000–$30,000	13 (12.5 percent)	34 (11.4 percent)
$30,000–$40,000	20 (19.2 percent)	39 (13.1 percent)
$40,000–$50,000	10 (9.6 percent)	33 (11.1 percent)
$50,000–$75,000	20 (19.2 percent)	61 (20.5 percent)
$75,000–$100,000	9 (8.7 percent)	46 (15.5 percent)
$100,000–$150,000	7 (6.7 percent)	34 (11.4 percent)
$150,000 or more	6 (5.7 percent)	14 (4.7 percent)
Employment Status		
Currently Employed	87 (73.7 percent)	286 (76.1 percent)
Not Currently Employed	31 (26.3 percent)	90 (23.9 percent)
*Religious Affiliation***		
Yes	61 (52.6 percent)	259 (69.4 percent)
No	55 (47.4 percent)	114 (30.6 percent)
*Have Friends or Family with Tattoos****		
Yes	108 (90.0 percent)	238 (63.1 percent)
No	12 (10.0 percent)	141 (37.2 percent)

[a]Not all categories total to 100 percent due to missing values and non-responses.
*$p < .05$, **$p < .01$, ***$p < .001$.

Of those who are tattooed, whites account for nearly 72 percent of the sample, while income and education levels are distributed relatively evenly across categories. The majority of tattooed respondents (73.7 percent) are employed. Tattooed respondents also overwhelmingly report having close friends or family members who are also tattooed (90 percent). This observation ties in closely to Sander's (1988) typology of tattoo client motivations, specifically as participation in a group or as a symbol of interpersonal relationships, as well as with Armstrong et al.'s (2004) finding that the support and encouragement of friends was related to whether one would consider being tattooed.

Additionally, Table A14.1 indicates a negative relationship between education and being tattooed, suggesting that those with more education are less likely to be tattooed. The negative association between age and being tattooed indicates that older respondents are less likely to have tattoos. While the tattoo renaissance often receives credit for expanding the appeal of tattooing to a more diverse clientele, these findings suggest that there has still been a lag in an overall social acceptance of tattooing. Moreover, the popularity tattooing currently enjoys among younger individuals appears to be an effect of gradual changes in attitudes toward tattooing as well as its contemporary reputation as fashionable and trendy (DeMello 2000).

Having friends and family who are tattooed is positively associated with the respondent being tattooed. Also, these findings indicate a negative relationship between religious affiliation and being tattooed, while employment status shows a weak relationship. These are also consistent with prior findings that indicate a relationship between the assessment of friends and family and an individual's decision to become tattooed (Armstrong et al. 2002, 2004). Similarly, Stirn et al. (2006) argued that lack of religious affiliation and unemployment among tattooed individuals indicated poor social integration. Perhaps rather than indicating a lack of social integration among tattooed respondents, the negative religious affiliation instead indicates the presence of religious prohibitions against tattooing among nontattooed respondents. Gender is not significantly associated with being tattooed, consistent with the notion that men and women are getting tattooed with relatively comparable frequency.

To test more explicitly the linkages between tattooing and deviance, particularly criminality, Figure A14.1 shows the percentage distribution of respondents who are nontattooed, are tattooed, and have tattoos in "extra-stigmatizing" areas, specifically the face, neck, hands, and fingers by time spent in jail, recreational drug use, and alcohol use. The findings indicate that nearly 25 percent of tattooed respondents have spent three or more days in jail; furthermore, about 72 percent of respondents with the extra-stigmatizing tattoos report serving time in jail, compared to roughly 6 percent of the nontattooed population. Similarly, just under 50 percent of tattooed respondents report using recreational drugs, nearly double that of the nontattooed population, while 83 percent of the extra-stigmatized tattooed population report recreational drug use. Alcohol use is relatively constant across categories.

Conclusion

This article examines the transitioning status of tattooing away from its deviant roots and stereotypical associations with criminality. Despite a growing popularity, wider social acceptance, and diversified clientele (Pitts 2003), the practice of tattooing still appears to retain some of its marginal characteristics. The persistent association of tattooing with time spent in jail suggests that it maintains its currency among marginal groups even as it experiences a resurgence of interest among young people. Indeed, Atkinson (2003) notes that despite prior associations with deviance, throughout the 1950s and 60s tattooing became thoroughly entrenched as a deviant

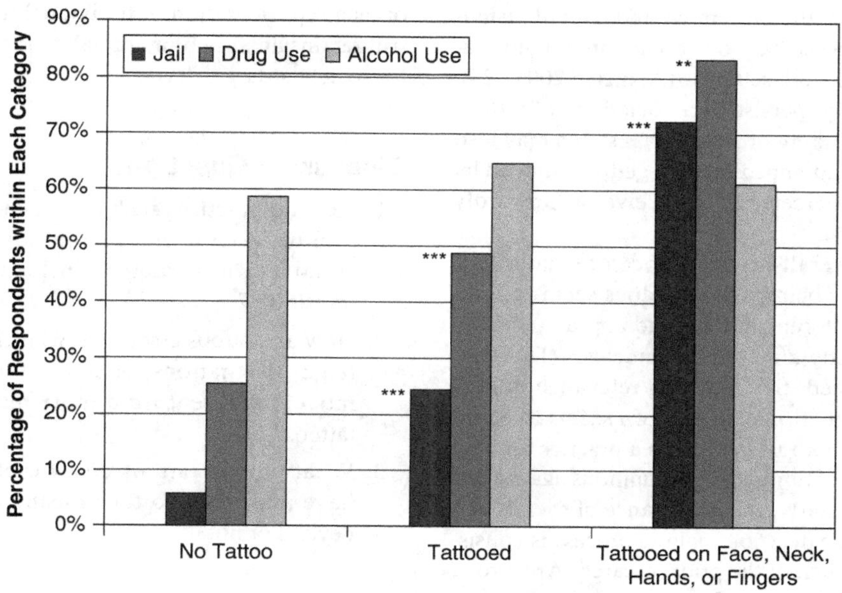

FIGURE A14.1
Jail Time, Recreational Drug Use, and Alcohol Use by Tattoo Status.

practice, popular among prisoners and motorcycle gangs, and that by the 1970s tattoos were generally regarded as a voluntarily inscribed signifier of deviance. Notwithstanding the changes within the industry, embodied in the notion of a tattoo renaissance, it is understandably difficult to shed the negative associations with tattoos after generations of active stigmatization.

Similarly, these findings suggest that the overall scope of the tattoo renaissance is rather limited to a narrow group of serious collectors (Vail 1999; Irwin 2003) and that tattooing has not been overwhelmingly embraced by those who are older, with higher levels of education or higher incomes. For older populations, traditional characterizations of tattooing as the domain of the lower-class or deviant groups most likely remain salient, regardless of how body art is reframed in the popular media. Likewise, as Kosut (2006b) has observed, much of the commodification of tattoo has been oriented toward youth culture, repositioning the practice as "a sign of rebellion, youth, trendiness, or some amalgam of coolness" (p. 1039) and distancing it from more negative associations. As tattooing is increasingly used as a marketing device and fashionable expression of individuality for younger consumers, one would expect a comparable expansion of the practice among a younger demographic as well as more relaxed attitudes about its level of social acceptability. The negative relationship between education and tattooing is probably more closely related to one's anticipated career trajectory and normative expectations. Even among tattoo enthusiasts, the potential for occupational constraint often informs both the placement and overall visibility of tattoos as "tattooed bodies are not normative in most work settings" (Atkinson 2003:124). Additionally, persistent associations of tattooing with working or lower-class status may also function as an impediment to getting tattooed by those who perceive of themselves as upwardly mobile.

The overall insignificance of gender as a predictor of being tattooed does seem to indicate that tattooing has a broad appeal and is no longer strictly a masculine endeavor (DeMello 2000). Indeed, the declining relevance of gender to whether one has a tattoo seems to be indicative of both its growth as a practice and the weakening of normative prohibitions against tattooing. Similarly, the importance of friends and family to the decision-making process is consistent with much of the prior research. Armstrong et al. (2002) found that among nontattooed college students, one's parents' assessment was the second most significant barrier to getting a tattoo. For tattooed respondents, negative comments from significant others were the third most important barrier to obtaining more tattoos. While individuals may or may not be influenced by the assessments of society-at-large, the risk of social sanction from one's close peers and family is enough to affect the decision to become tattooed. Conversely, the finding here suggests that having friends or family who are tattooed will be positively associated with the respondent also being tattooed, indicating that the judgment and behavior of key reference groups often outweighs the general normative constraints and stigma associated with tattooing.

This article has explored the degree to which tattooing has moved away from its traditionally deviant associations. As Kosut (2006a) has noted, "longstanding and commonplace associations between tattoo and criminals or psychopaths still linger, yet they reside alongside new representations and discourses" (p. 91). This observation appears to be true; even when tattooing is being explored as a high-art medium or as a representation of individual identity, it still retains an aura of marginality and, perhaps for society-at-large, deviance.

Discussion Questions

1. How do practices such as tattooing transition between deviance and normativity? What cultural factors influence these transitions?
2. How are tattoos associated with criminality (e.g., gang tattoos, prison tattoos) qualitatively different from more mainstream tattoos?
3. What type of tattoos do your classmates have and what do they mean? Are these deviant or not?

References

Armstrong, Myrna, Alden Roberts, Donna Owen, and Jerome Koch. 2004. "Toward Building a Composite of College Student Influences with Body Art." *Issues in Comprehensive Pediatric Nursing* 27:277–95.

Armstrong, Myrna, Donna Owen, Alden Roberts, and Jerome Koch. 2002. "College Tattoos: More Than Skin Deep." *Dermatology Nursing* 14:317–23.

Atkinson, Michael. 2002. "Pretty in Ink: Conformity, Resistance, and Negotiation in Women's Tattooing." *Sex Roles* 47:219–35.

Atkinson, Michael. 2003. *Tattooed: The Sociogenesis of a Body Art*. Toronto: University of Toronto Press.

Bradley, James. 2000. "Body Commodification? Class and Tattoos in Victorian Britain." Pp. 136–155 in *Written on the Body: The Tattoo in European and American History*, edited by J. Caplan. Princeton, NJ: Princeton University Press.

Braithwaite, Ronald, Alyssa Robillard, Tammy Woodring, Torrence Stephens, Kimberly Jacob Arriola. 2001. "Tattooing and Body Piercing among Adolescent Detainees: Relationship to Alcohol and Other Drug Use." *Journal of Substance Abuse* 13:5–16.

Braithwaite, Ronald, Torrance Stephens, N. Bowman, M. Milton, and Kisha Braithwaite. 1998. "Tattooing and Body Piercing: Examining the Public Health Implications of These Risky Behaviors." *Corrections Today* 60:120–22.

DeMello, Margo. 1993. "The Convict Body: Tattooing among Male Prisoners." *Anthropology Today* 9:10–13.

DeMello, Margo. 2000. Bodies of Inscription: A Cultural History of the Modern Tattoo Community. Durham, NC: Duke University Press.

Fisher, Jill. 2002. "Tattooing the Body, Marking Culture." *Body and Society* 8:91–107.

Govenar, Alan. 2000. "The Changing Image of Tattooing in American Culture, 1846–1966." Pp. 212–33 in *Written on the Body: The Tattoo in European and American History*, edited by J. Caplan. Princeton, NJ: Princeton University Press.

Irwin, Katherine. 2003. "Saints and Sinners: Elite Tattoo Collectors and Tattooists as Positive and Negative Deviants." *Sociological Spectrum* 23:27–57.

Kosut, Mary. 2006a. "Mad Artists and Tattooed Perverts: Deviant Discourse and the Social Construction of Cultural Categories." *Deviant Behavior* 27:73–95.

Kosut, Mary. 2006b. "An Ironic Fad: The Commodification and Consumption of Tattoos." *The Journal of Popular Culture* 39:1035–48.

Laumann, Anne. and Amy Derick. 2006. "Tattoos and Body Piercings in the United States: A National Data Set." *Journal of the American Academy of Dermatology* 55:413–21.

Mifflin, Margot. 1997. Bodies of Subversion: A Secret History of Women and Tattoo. New York: Juno Books.

Oettermann, Stephan. 2000. "On Display: Tattooed Entertainers in America and Germany." Pp. 193–211 in *Written on the Body: The Tattoo in European and American History*, edited by J. Caplan. Princeton, NJ: Princeton University Press.

Pitts, Victoria. 1998. "'Reclaiming' the Female Body: Embodied Identity Work, Resistance and the Grotesque." *Body and Society* 4:67–84.

Pitts, Victoria. 2003. *In the Flesh: The Cultural Politics of Body Modification*. New York: Palgrave Macmillan.

Raspa, Robert and John Cusack. 1990. "Psychiatric Implications of Tattoos." *American Family Physician* 41:1481–86.

Rubin, Arnold. 1988a. *Marks of Civilization*. Regents of the University of California.

Rubin, Arnold. 1988b. "The Tattoo Renaissance." Pp. 233–264 in *Marks of Civilization*, edited by A. Rubin. Regents of the University of California.

Sanders, Clinton. 1988. "Drill and Fill: Client Choice, Client Typologies, and Interactional Control in Commercial Settings." Pp. 219–32 in *Marks of Civilization*, edited by A. Rubin. Regents of the University of California.

Sanders, Clinton. 1989. *Customizing the Body: The Art and Culture of Tattooing*. Philadelphia, PA: Temple University Press.

Sanders, Clinton. 1990. "'A Lot of People Like It': The Relationship between Deviance and Popular Culture." Pp. 3–14 in *Marginal Conventions: Popular Culture, Mass Media, and Social Deviance*, edited by C. Sanders. Bowling Green, OH: Bowling Green State University Popular Press.

Steward, Samuel. 1990. Bad Boys and Tough Tattoos: A Social History of the Tattoo with Gangs, Sailors, and Street-Corner Punks 1950–1965. New York: The Haworth Press.

Stirn, Aglaja, Andreas Hinz, and Elmar Brahler. 2006. "Prevalence of Tattooing and Body Piercing in Germany and Perception of Health, Mental Disorders, and Sensation Seeking among Tattooed and Body-Pierced Individuals." *Journal of Psychosomatic Research* 60:531–34.

Vail, D. Angus. 1999. "Tattoos Are Like Potato Chips . . . You Can't Have Just One: The Process of Becoming and Being a Collector." *Deviant Behavior* 20:253–73.

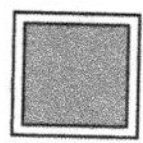

ARTICLE 15

Jimmy D. Taylor
Ohio University Zanesville

Self-Mutilation and Body Modification

The private worlds of self-injurers are elusive and somewhat mysterious to social researchers. In addition to the frequently secretive nature of these and related activities, rapid social and technological change, cultural diversity, and unclear categorical lines serve to complicate research efforts in this highly controversial and philosophically contested area. The purpose of this exploration is to address some of the more frequently registered concerns, key issues, and innovations in research in the areas of cutting, piercing, and self-mutilation. There is significant overlap in these three areas of research; however, this article will focus on relevant research developments in each of the three areas.

Agreeing on a definition for self-injury frequently poses a problem for social scientists. Similar to other socially constructed forms of deviance, cultural relativity and the susceptibility to change serve to make it difficult for researchers to agree on fixed definitions of self-injury–related areas of deviant behavior. One aspect of self-injury that is widely agreed upon is that there are multiple reasons for these physical acts. Common reasons cited for engaging in related activities are as dissimilar as unifying and include depression; past sexual abuse; fitting in; standing out; simultaneously fitting in while standing out; cathartic release; expressions of emotional turmoil, anger, grief, and other forms of dissatisfaction to others; peer pressure; identity crises; narcissism; self-loathing; to feel euphoric; and to experience a form of self-nurturing as wounds literally heal. It has been estimated that as many as 4 percent of adults and 23 percent of adolescents practice some form of self-injury (Holmes 2000; Jacobson and Gould 2007). These practices are more frequent among adolescent to early-adult women, although increased instances of self-injury by teenage boys and young adult males have been reported from the mid-1990s to present (Williams 2008).

Research involving self-injury has evolved primarily from medical and psychiatric studies. Various studies (Solomon and Farrand 1996; Guertin et al. 2001; Adler and Adler 2005; Bates 2005) indicate that this has resulted from the refuted but once widely held notion that self-injury is a type of suicidal tendency that always requires medical treatment or intervention. Although the "deliberate harming of skin tissue" of one's own body is often referred to as "body modification" (Myers 1992; Featherstone 1999; Pitts 2003), "self-mutilation" (Ross and Heath 2002; Holmes 2000:8; Williams 2008), "self-cutting" (Levenkron 1998; Bates 2005), "self-harm" (Gardner 2001; Cohn 2004; Schmidt and Davidson 2004), and "self-injury" (Hodgson 2004; Adler and Adler 2005; Walsh 2005), prominent deviant behavior scholars such as Adler and Adler (2005) and Thio (2009) have appealed to scholars researching related topics to adopt the term *self-injury*. It is their contention that the other terms for these patterns of behavior are too judgmental, less applicable, and too closely tied to widely held notions of extreme violence or even evil. The term *self-injury* is also said to resonate more strongly with the actual practitioners of these activities (Adler and Adler 2005), such as intentional bone-breaking, branding, burning, cutting, pricking, scratching, hair pulling and skin picking, to name a few.

Durkheim and the Sociological Origins of Self-Injury

Emile Durkheim (1965 [1915]) helped to elevate the priority of analyzing the cultural significance of marking the human body as a means of expression and shared meaning. He noted that "the best way of proving to one's self and to others that one is a member of a certain group is to place a distinctive mark on the body" (p. 265). The body, and not just written or spoken forms of communication or other cultural products, is used to convey meaning to the social world. This has been reiterated by Shilling (2005), who suggested that the literal, physical symbols left on the body as the result of practices such as cutting, scarification, tattooing, painting, and other means of "decoration" serve an integrating role by enabling members of a common, shared, but often obscured culture to recognize one another as kindred (p. 29).

It is important to make a distinction between the type of body markings and self-injury noted by Durkheim—which occur among highly homogenous and cohesive (mechanical) cultures, that emphasize the good of the collective—and those that occur within highly specialized (organic), more diverse cultures that espouse individuality and freedom of expression. Contemporary ethnographers such as Clifford (1988) and Mascia-Lees and Sharpe (1994) highlight the significance of the tentative symbolic value placed on different body alterations. The meanings assigned to some of the markings/alterations that are tied to deep cultural roots remain relatively intact over time, whereas more fleeting meanings were noted for alterations within modern societies.

Other scholars (Maguire 2002) have focused on how the practice of body modification is positioned to thrive in modern, capitalist social systems, in that the body is adorned in response to market changes and demands. The body becomes something of an artistic canvas, or billboard, for sending out messages to a target audience. This process is said to be facilitated by the rapid interpretation and reinterpretation of the "normal" body, based, in part, on constantly updated and highly circulated popular media images (Shilling 2005). Other researchers (Pitts 1999, 2003; DeMello 2000; Kosut 2006) have chosen to focus on the influence of media outlets in casting certain forms of body modification in a deviant light.

A last key social force that has a profound influence on modes of self-injury is technology. Cerulo (1997), Foster (1997), Adler and Adler (2008) have emphasized the significance of evolving technology and how this impacts forms and functions of deviant behaviors related to self-injury. They report that innovations in information technology (particularly personal digital assistants and other Web-based technologies) are changing the way deviance is defined and performed by individual actors and their deviant communities. Now deviant actors can simultaneously find other deviant subculture participants in order to interact and foster group solidarity—instead of remaining in "loner" isolation as was more often the case with previous generations of deviants—while also being afforded the ability to maintain strict anonymity whenever desired.

Cutting

The reasons frequently cited for engaging in self-injury practices by cutting are varied and highly complex. Although scientific studies pertaining to cutting practices are limited in terms of the number of studies published and also in their scope, existing literature suggest substantial variation among cutters in terms of function and form of cutting practices. It is also important, however, to consider the rapid change in public perception and awareness of cutting activities, and the social forces driving this dynamic form of deviance.

Inside the Social Structure and Organization of Cutting

Forms of deviant behavior are often identified and defined according to recognizable or predictable ways in which they are organized, maintained, transmitted, and conducted. Seminal studies on cutting conducted by sociologists Patricia and Peter Adler (2005, 2008) have helped to illuminate the tentative nature of cutters and fragility of cutting categories. Adler and Adler (2005) analyzed cutting categories by adopting and applying Best and Luckenbill's (1982) theoretical typology of "individual" and "loner" deviance.

According to Best and Luckenbill's (1982) typology, "individual" deviants have gained all of the skills necessary to enable them to enact and participate in forms of deviance by themselves and for themselves. Some of the distinguishing characteristics of individual deviants center on the notion that although they (the cutters) are independent in the sense that they are free to engage in their choice forms of deviance on their own, it is not necessary that they remain isolated from other like-minded deviants (Deshotels and Forsyth 2007). Individual deviants, such as skydivers (Anderson and Taylor 2010), military gun collectors (Taylor 2009), and the homeless (Snow and Anderson 1993), to name a few, may operate within support networks conducive to their deviant tastes and needs and even commit their independent acts of deviance in the presence of subcultural supporters. This would also include acts of deviance that are performed on the body of the individual deviant participant, such as the self-injury practice of cutting.

In contrast to "individual deviants," the "loners" or "loner deviants" are those individuals who dwell primarily in social isolation, without notable support networks to share in their deviant experiences or lifestyle choices. Consequently, loner deviants commit deviant acts on their own, without training, assistance, or support from other deviants who perform similar or identical acts. Similar to other loner deviants, such as drug addicts who work in medical or related professions (Dabney and Hollinger 1999), those with eating disorders (O'Shaughnessy and Dallos 2009), and even child pornographers (Jenkins 2001), individuals who self-injure are not likely to be associated (to their knowledge) with others who are engaged in the same or similar forms of self-injury. Therefore, loner deviants must typically seek out and develop the skills necessary to perform their acts of deviance on their own, in relative isolation.

Adler and Adler (2005 and 2008) illuminate rapid change in the cutting world due to ways in which public awareness and technology—more specifically, Internet resources and chat room–style support networks—have informed a broader population about the ways of cutting. They found that as cutting populations have begun to "find" one another, and talk more openly about their self-injury practices, a slow-moving destigmatization campaign has ensued. As the stigmatizing stronghold on cutting has begun to weaken, it has fostered a new era of possibility for those who cut. Among the most promising of these possibilities is the burgeoning subcultural networking component ushered in by the Internet. The cyber world has made it increasingly more practical for the practitioners of cutting—a group who were once primarily limited to carrying on their cutting practices in extreme isolation, with the widespread (and persistent) belief that the practice is a shameful, dirty secret (Holmes 2000; Adler and Adler 2008; Kibler 2009; Klonsky 2009)—to feel more normal and find groups that help meet their individual needs (McKenna and Green 2002).

As a result of these changes, cutters are more difficult to situate in one specific category of deviance, including the "individual," "loner" typology. Instead, cutters appear to be constantly negotiating the boundaries of their new options and possibilities. On the one hand, it is still a highly stigmatized form of deviance; however, the rapidly growing network systems and public information available to cutters make the transition from loner to individual deviant (and back) far more feasible. Additionally, the technologically evolved modern state of cutting sets the stage for a cutter to simultaneously hide his or her cutting life from the non-cutting world (and from the online community by remaining anonymous), while engaging in the deviant social support network and information banks. A tech-savvy cutter can quite literally be simultaneously alone and interacting with countless others. Also, depending on the desire and needs of a cutter, Internet and other deviant support networks may be used to self-educate for the purposes of disengaging from self-injury, or to seek support and self-educate for the purposes of continuing cutting as a type of life maintenance (Whitlock, Powers, and Eckenrode 2006). The later perspective assumes that cutting is a reasonable and legitimate, multipurpose coping strategy (Adler and Adler 2008).

Cutting and Suicide

The topic of suicide is prominent in most of the studies on cutting. This persistent focus is primarily due to a long-standing (and seemingly false) assumption that all cutters are simply practicing for their eventual suicide attempts (Solomon and Farrand 1996; Bates 2005). On the contrary, as more detailed data unfold, it has been suggested that many or most cutters do so more frequently as an extreme effort to self-heal, rather than destroy (Guertin et al. 2001; Bates 2005; Klonsky 2009; Whitlock et al. 2009). As the respondents of one study who had engaged in self-injury and attempted suicide explained, they relied on cutting and other forms of self-mutiliation to cope, or as a sort of patchwork self-treatment. They considered their suicide attempt to be exactly the opposite—cutting was set aside as an aspect of renewal and restoration, while the suicide attempt was compartmentalized as expressly for total self-destruction (Adler and Adler 2005).

As a logical outcropping of these and related findings, a move toward separate classifications of self-injury, based on the presence of suicidal intent has been proposed and recently implemented (Muehlenkamp 2005; Lloyd-Richardson et al. 2007). Accordingly, Muehlenkamp (2005) has appealed to the field of psychiatry to list non-suicidal self-injury (NSSI) disorder as a unique category of disorder in the next edition of the *Diagnostic and Systematic Manual for Mental Illness (DSM),* due to the notable lack of suicidal intent among cutters and other self-injurers. Similarly, Lloyd-Richardson et al. (2007) suggested new official names for the proposed categorization scheme: non-suicidal self-injury (NSSI) and suicidal self-injury (SSI). It is important to note that this new form of categorization does *not* imply that no cutters are at risk of suicide. The focus is simply on intent. Even among cutters with no obvious, conscious suicidal intent, there remains a concern over the persistent link between self-injurers who exhibit signs of depression and suicide (Holmes 2000; Adler and Adler 2005; Kibler 2009).

Body Piercing

Although it has been noted in the discussion of other forms of self-injury up to this point that classification schemes and typologies pertaining to self-injury remain a source of contention and uncertainty, nowhere is this more evident than in research exploring the social world of body piercers. Although body piercing is often referred to as a form of self-injury or "self-mutilation" in popular media outlets (Mascia-Lees and Sharpe 1994; Pitts 2003), academic treatment of body piercing studies more typically rely on a body modification (BM) framework (Favazza 1996; Shilling 2005). Leading research on body piercing as BM reveals less about deviant behavior, and more about the constant interpretation and reinterpretation of the meaning of the human body (Featherstone 1987) and attempts to communicate with the social world using the flesh as a working canvas (Shilling 2005). In this light, piercings are tantamount to a "body project," both responsive to and representative of the changing foci of social institutions—especially consumer media images (Pitts 2003; Shilling 2005).

Of all forms of BM, body piercing and tattooing are the most common globally (Favazza, 1996; Stirn 2003). BMs cover a wide variety of decorative body practices, ranging from the highly dangerous and pathological to seemingly harmless peer group fashion statements (Stirn and Andreas 2008). Although media attention given to body piercing and other BM practices remains overwhelmingly negative (DeMello 2000; Pitts 2003), a few studies have indicated high instances of a few negative traits among body piercers, such as an "anger trait" (Carroll and Anderson 2002); thrill seeking (Roberti, Storch, and Bravata 2004), and risky adolescent sexual behavior (Roberts, Auinger, and Ryan 2004).

Concluding Comments

Self-injurers are far more diversified in their activities and reasons for engaging in their choice forms of deviance than is typically depicted in research studies. While self-injury studies are in their infancy, a growing body of research in this area continually highlights the difficulties of situating self-injurers within specific analytical frameworks. These difficulties hinge on the influence of rapidly evolving and expanding technological resources, shifting public awareness and media-driven fluctuations in the perception of the body and identity (which help to shape these self-injury and body modification practices). All of these social factors make it difficult to situate self-injurers within tidy categories, or fix a permanent, meaningful definition.

What remains unclear is the point at which BM or self-injury practices such as cutting, piercing and tattooing transition from being a form of pseudoartistic expression on a living canvas (and/or attempts to signal individuality to the social world and efforts to simply fit in) to something intended to do legitimate, self-inflicted harm. Future research objectives are clear. In order to promote research that continues to explore the new worlds that self-injurers are creating for themselves, we must be more proactive about countering media-driven misconceptions about self-injury, as a collective effort to destigmatize these activities. This will benefit self-injurers, by making it easier for those who need help to seek it out, while also fostering a better sense of trust and openness among the research community and self-injurers and, subsequently yield richer data.

Discussion Questions

1. What are common "self-injury" practices?
2. Why are "cutters" so difficult to categorize?
3. How have innovations in technology been used to collect information on cutters?

References

Adler, Patricia A. and Peter Adler. 2005. "Self-Injurers as Loners: The Social Organization of Solitary Deviance." *Deviant Behavior* 26(4):345–78.

Adler, Patricia A. and Peter Adler. 2008. "The Cyber Worlds of Self-Injurers: Deviant Communities, Relationships, and Selves."*Symbolic Interaction* 31(1):33–56.

Anderson, Leon and Jim Taylor. 2010. "Standing Out While Fitting In: Serious Leisure Identities and Aligning Actions Among Skydivers and Gun Collectors." *Journal of Contemporary Ethnography* 39(1):34–59.

Bates, Betsy. 2005. "Cutting May Be More Widespread Than Imagined." *Family Practice News* 35(6):50.

Best, Joel and David F. Luckenbill. 1982. *Organizing Deviance*. Upper Saddle River, NJ: Prentice-Hall.

Carroll, L. and R. Anderson. 2002. "Body Piercing, Tattooing, Self-Esteem, and Body Investment in Adolescent Girls." *Adolescence* 37(147):627–37.

Cerulo, Karen A. 1997. "Reframing Sociological Concepts for a Brave New (Virtual?) World." *Sociological Inquiry* 67:48–58.

Clifford, James. 1988. *The Predicament of Culture: Twentieth-Century Ethnography, Literature and Art.* Cambridge, MA: Harvard University Press.

Cohn, Leigh. 2004. *Self Harm Behaviors and Eating Disorders.* London: Routledge.

Dabney, Dean A. and Richard C. Hollinger. 1999. "Illicit Prescription Drug Use among Pharmacists: Evidence of a Paradox of Familiarity." *Work and Occupations* 26:77–106.

Deshotels, Tina H. and Craig J. Forsyth. 2007. "Postmodern Masculinities and the Eunuch." *Deviant Behavior* 28:201–18.

Demello, Margo. 2000. *Bodies of Inscription: A Cultural History of the Modern Tatoo Community.* Durham, NC: Duke University Press.

Durkheim, Emile. 1965 [1915]. *The Elementary Forms of Religious Life.* Los Angeles, CA: The Free Press.

Favazza, Armando. 1996. *Bodies Under Siege: Self-Mutilation and Body Modification in Culture and Psychiatry.* Baltimore, MD: Johns Hopkins University Press.

Featherstone, Mike. 1999. "Body Modification: An Introduction." *Body and Society* 5:1–13.

Foster, Derek. 1997. "Community and Identity in the Electronic Village." Pp. 23–27 in *Internet Culture*, edited by D. Porter. New York: Routledge.

Gardner, Fiona. 2001. *Self-Harm: A Psychotherapeutic Approach.* London: Routledge.

Guertin, Tracey. 2001. "Self-Mutilative Behavior in Adolescents Who Attempt Suicide by Overdose." *Journal of the American Academy of Child & Adolescent Psychiatry* 40(9):1062–69.

Hodgson, Sarah. 2004. "Cutting through the Silence: A Sociological Construction of Self-Injury." *Sociological Inquiry* 74(2):162–79.

Holmes, Ann. 2000. *Cutting the Pain Away: Understanding Self-Mutilation.* Philadelphia, PA: Chelsea House.

Jacobson, Colleen and Madelyn Gould. 2007. "The Epidemiology and Phenomenology of Non-Suicidal Self-Injurious Behavior among Adolescents: A Critical Review of the Literature." *Archives of Suicide Research* 11(2):129–47.

Jenkins, Philip. 2001. *Beyond Tolerance: Child Pornography on the Internet.* New York: New York University Press.

Kibler, Jackie. 2009. "Self-Injury in the Schools: An Exploratory Analysis of Midwest School Counselors' Knowledge and Experience." *North American Journal of Psychology* 11(2):309–22.

Klonsky, David E. 2009. "Assessing the Functions of Non-suicidal Self-injury: Psychometric Properties of the Inventory of Statements about Self-injury (ISAS)." *Journal of Psychopathology and Behavioral Assessment* 31(3):215–19.

Kosut, Mary. 2006. "An Ironic Fad: The Comodification and Consumption of Tattoos." *The Journal of Popular Culture* 39:1035–48.

Levenkron, Steven. 1998. *Cutting: Understanding and Overcoming Self-Mutilation.* New York: Norton.

Lloyd-Richardson E. E., N. Perrine, L. Dierker, M. L. Kelley. 2007. "Characteristics and Functions of Non-Suicidal Self-Injury in a Community Sample of Adolescents." *Psychological Medicine* 4:1–10.

Maguire, Jennifer. 2002. "Body Lessons: Fitness Publishing and the Cultural Production of the Fitness Consumer." *International Review for the Sociology of Sport* 37:449–64.

Mascia-Lees, Frances and Patricia Sharpe. 1994. "The Anthropological Unconscious." *American Anthropologist* 96(3):649–60.

McKenna, Katelyn Y. A. and Amie S. Green. 2002. "Virtual Group Dynamics." *Group Dynamics: Theory, Research and Practice* 6:116–27.

Muehlenkamp, J. J. 2005. "Self-injurious Behavior as a Separate Clinical Syndrome." *American Journal of Orthopsychiatry* 75(2):324–33.

Myers, James. 1992. "Nonmainstream Body Modification: Genital Piercing, Branding, Burning and Cutting." *Journal of Contemporary Ethnography* 21:267–306.

O'Shaughnessy, Ruth and Rudi Dallos. 2009. "Attachment Research and Eating Disorders: A Review of the Literature." *Clinical Child Psychology and Psychiatry* 14(4):559–74.

Pitts, Victoria. 1999. "Body Modification, Self-Mutilation and Agency in the Media Accounts of a Subculture." *Body and Society* 5:291–303.

Pitts, Victoria. 2003. *In the Flesh: The Cultural Politics of Body Modification.* New York: Palgrave Macmillan.

Roberti, J. W., E. A. Storch, and E. A. Bravata. 2004. "Sensation Seeking, Exposure to Psychosocial Stressors, and Body Modifications in a College Population." *Personality and Individual Differences* 37:1167–77.

Roberts, T. A., P. Auinger, and S. A. Ryan. 2004. "Body Piercing and High-Risk Behavior in Adolescents." *Journal of Adolescent Health* 34:224–29.

Ross, Shana and Nancy Heath. 2002. "A Study of the Frequency of Self-Mutilation in a Community Sample of Adolescents." *Journal of Youth and Adolescence* 31(1):67.

Schmidt, Ulrike and Kate Davidson. 2004. *Life After Self-Harm: A Guide to the Future*. New York: Routledge.

Shilling, Chris. 2005. *The Body in Culture, Technology and Society*. Los Angeles, CA: Sage.

Snow, David A. and Leon Anderson. 1993. *Down on Their Luck: A Study of Homeless Street People*. Berkeley, CA: University of California Press.

Solomon, Yvette and Julie Farrand. 1996. "Why Don't You Do It Properly?: Young Women Who Self-Injure." *Journal of Adolescence* 19(11):10–19.

Taylor, Jimmy D. 2009. *American Gun Culture: Collectors, Shows and the Story of the Gun*. New York: LFB.

Thio, Alex. 2009. *Deviant Behavior*, 10th ed. New York: Pearson.

Walsh, Barnet. 2005. *Treating Self-Injury*. New York: Guilford.

Whitlock, J., J. Powers, and J. Eckenrode. 2006. "The Virtual Cutting Edge: The Internet and Adolescent Self-Injury." *Developmental Psychology* 42(1/2):407–17.

Whitlock, Janis, Greg Eells, Nina Cummings, and Amanda Purington. 2009. "Nonsuicidal Self-Injury in College Populations: Mental Health Provider Assessment of Prevalence and Need." *Journal of College Student Psychotherapy* 23(3): 172–83.

Williams, Mary. 2008. *Self-Mutilation: Opposing Viewpoints*. Thomson Gale.

 ARTICLE 16

Richard Tewksbury
University of Louisville

Ronald M. Holmes
University of Louisville

David Patrick Connor
University of Louisville

Typologies of Teenage Suicide: Analyzing Suicide Notes through Durkheimian Categories

Introduction

It is no secret some individuals in our society decide to intentionally end their own lives. In 2010, there were more than 34,000 suicides reported in the United States, ranking suicide as the 11th most common cause of death for all Americans (Centers for Disease Control and Prevention 2010). Of all 2006 suicides, 79 percent were by men (Centers for Disease Control and Prevention 2009). In taking their own lives, more than half (56.0 percent) of men were likely to utilize firearms, while the majority of women (40.3 percent) selected poisoning. These numbers may be underestimates, however, as the official number of suicides is also commonly believed to be underreported (Holmes and Holmes 2005).

Prior to their engagements in such lethal acts, individuals contemplating suicide sometimes record their last form of written communication. These suicide notes, which contain a diverse variety of content, have the potential to reveal valuable information concerning suicidal individuals and their states of mind. Determined to express their last thoughts to the world, writers of suicide notes invite readers into their consciousness, typically moments before their deaths.

All original names have been removed to ensure confidentiality.

Suicide Notes

Contrary to popular belief, only a minority of suicides involve leaving of a suicide note. Suicide notes are found in only about 25 percent to 35 percent of suicides (O'Donnell, Farmer, and Catalan 1993; Holmes and Holmes 2005; Shioiri et al. 2005). This rate has been consistent regardless of the number of suicides in a community or culture. One other factor that has been shown to be related to whether individuals leave suicide notes include where the suicide occurs. Suicides in the home have a greater likelihood of a note being left (O'Donnell et al. 1993; Ho et al. 1998).

Also, an individual's characteristics and behaviors may influence the likelihood of a suicide note being left. Drug users are less likely to leave notes (Beck, Morris, and Lester 1974), those drinking at the time of suicide are more likely to leave notes (Kuwabara et al. 2006),[1] and less educated persons are less likely to leave notes. Additionally, individuals who commit suicide for reasons of physical illness or psychiatric disorders are less likely to leave notes (Kuwabara et al. 2006). Regarding age, elderly men have been suggested by one study as the most likely to leave suicide notes (Heim and Lester 1990), although a second, older study (Capstick 1960) suggests younger persons are more likely to leave notes. And, those younger than age 25 are more likely to leave notes in places other than their homes or at the suicide locations (Ho et al. 1998). Shioiri et al. (2005) concluded that reasons for committing suicide are largely unrelated to whether a note is left or not. However, those who employ more lethal methods may be more likely to leave suicide notes (Lester 1998; Chavez-Hernandez et al. 2006; Kuwabara et al. 2006). An interesting, but unexplained, finding is that suicides occurring on a Monday are more likely than those on other days of the week to leave a note (Heim and Lester 1990). Overall, most research concludes there are few differences between suicides that do and do not leave notes.[2] This would suggest that the study of suicide notes would provide an accurate view into the reasons for and factors related to suicides—the sample is not skewed in any meaningful manner.

Content of Suicide Notes

Scholars assessing the content of suicide notes have approached notes with an eye toward examining whether the content of notes corresponds with theoretical explanations for suicide (Leenaars and Balance,1981, 1984). Others have focused exclusively on identifying the content of suicide notes, emphasizing stated reasons as well as emotional statements, requests for forgiveness, and statements about the individual's relationships (good or bad) with others.

When considering methods of suicide and whether a note is left or not, Lester and Linn (1998) report that notes from individuals who hang themselves typically contain more statements of anger than notes from persons employing other methods. When focusing on expressed reasons for committing suicide, there are more similarities than differences across age groups (Leenaars et al. 2001), although notes from teens show a greater tendency to focus on rejection (Leenaars et al. 2001), and notes from elderly men are more likely than those from younger men to focus on interpersonal relationship problems (Leenaars 1992).

Emotional statements are also common in suicide notes, with Chavez-Hernandez et al. (2006) reporting that suicide notes in Mexico most often include emotions of hopelessness (40 percent), grieving (37 percent), and forgiveness (32 percent). In Northern Ireland, the most common themes identified in suicide notes were apologies/shame, love for those left behind, life being too much to bear, and instructions for postdeath actions (Foster 2003). O'Donnell et al. (1993) report that among a sample of 42 suicides committed on the London underground rail system, three types of reasons are identified in suicide notes: (1) financial difficulty; (2) an end of a personal, intimate relationship; or (3) significant interpersonal problem and illness.

Ho et al. (1998) report that among those under age 25 in Hong Kong, more than three-quarters (78.6 percent) of suicide notes specifically identify the event as a suicide (explaining that foul play was not involved) and more than one-fifth (21.4 percent) included instructions for repaying one or more of the decedent's debts. Only 7.1 percent of notes included instructions for disposal of any/all of the individuals' possessions and funeral arrangements. In Mexico, 24 percent of suicide notes included instructions regarding finances, possessions, or a funeral, and 22 percent included specific messages for loved ones (Chavez-Hernandez et al. 2006). More than one-third (35.7 percent) of young men's suicide notes refer to job/financial difficulties, and the same number refer to interpersonal problems (Ho et al. 1998). Women are less likely to refer to specific life difficulties, but when they do so in suicide notes, the most common references are to illness/pain (by 20 percent of women under age 25 and 27.6 percent of women aged 25–59) (Ho et al. 1998).

Younger people's suicide notes tend to be longer, rich in emotions, and frequently contain statements of requests for forgiveness (Ho et al. 1998). Younger women are also more likely to leave longer notes (Ho et al. 1998). Teenage females' suicide notes are more than twice as long on average as other suicide notes (Ho et al. 1998). Also, suicide notes from younger persons tend to be more self-critical, harsh, and reflect a lower self-esteem while suggesting the individuals view themselves as an object (Leenaars and Balance 1984). Others (Peck 1989) have demonstrated the content of teens' suicide notes do not lend themselves to identifying exact reasons for their suicides. The content, however, of such notes does offer insights into the thinking and reasoning of teens as they make (and act upon) their decisions to end their lives.

Durkheim and Suicide

The scientific study of motivations for suicide has long been structured around the typology of suicides originally proposed by Durkheim in 1897. Although his original theory has been explored and expanded in the twentieth century (Selvin 1958; Dohrenwend 1959; Johnson 1965; Miley and Micklin 1972; Pope 1976; Stark, Doyle, and Rushing 1983; Breault 1986; Day 1987; Pescosolido and Georgianna 1989; van Poppel and Day 1996), the central issues of regulation (the amount of social control and social bonds binding the individual to society) and integration (the extent to which individuals accept the moral demands placed on them by society) remain critical to any taxonomies of reasons for suicide. If and when one or the other of these issues in an individual's life becomes either too strong or too weak, the outcome may be suicide. As proposed by Durkheim (1951[1897]), the ways in which too strong or too weak regulation and integration can interact yields four categories of suicides: anomic, altruistic, egoistic, and fatalistic.

Anomic suicide can be the result of major social or cultural changes, leading to social instability and individual perceptions of a lack of meaning in one's life. When society as a whole or what the individual perceives as society lacks regulation and there is high integration present, the individual may feel unable to cope with the drastic changes and feel overwhelmed. These feelings of uncertainty may push individuals into taking their own lives as a way to resolve this feeling of a lack of meaning. Anomic suicide results from an individual perceiving his or her desires to be blocked, and therefore yielding frustration. When the norms in one's life are significantly altered, an inability to effectively cope with such changes may lead to a feeling of hopelessness and a sense that life is unmanageable and not worth continuing.

Altruistic suicide occurs when both an individual's integration and regulation into society are too strong. In such a case, one tends to lose a sense of individuality and ability to prioritize life above the collective goals of society. Pursuit of a greater goal, one that would require sacrificing one's own life so as to move toward a goal for all of society, is the motivation for such suicides. Altruistic suicides are exemplified through military or terrorist suicide missions or the taking of one's life so as to fulfill a religious calling.

Egoistic suicide occurs when a person becomes overwhelmed by seemingly inescapable problems. Individuals who commit suicide for egoistic reasons do so to end what is perceived as insufferable levels of pain, sorrow, or loss. The egoistic suicide results from too little regulation and integration.

Finally, fatalistic suicides are the result of low levels of integration and too-high levels of regulation. The fatalistic suicide is committed because the individual lacks social bonds and abilities to fulfill a future that he or she desires.

Utilizing these social environment typologies that may predispose individuals to suicide, properly classified suicide notes can provide additional insight into the motivations of suicidal individuals. Exposing the incentives for suicide may also subsequently encourage the development of social remedies. Moreover, appropriate cataloging of suicide notes allows society to identify sources of psychological stress. In turn, solutions can be established to address these stressors.

The Present Study

The present study explores the motivations (e.g., typological categories) of youth suicides as expressed and explained in suicide notes. Through a review of the content of suicide notes, analytic focus is on expressed reasons for the suicide, and identification of if and how the content of the suicide note corresponds with the typological categories of reasons for suicide explained by Durkheim (1897). The focus of the analysis is on identifying the Durkheimian reason for suicides among youth, as well as specific issues and experiences offered by suicidal teens within each category.

Methods

Data for the present study were drawn from suicide notes left by 65 teenagers and young adults (all age 21 or younger) who committed suicide between 1965 and 2009 in one Midwestern city. All suicide notes were drawn from the coroner's office case file for the case.

After the suicide notes were obtained, each was reviewed by two independent coders who read each note multiple times. Each note was assigned to a category—anomic, altruistic, egoistic, or fatalistic—based on the predominant content. After each coder assigned each note to a conceptual category, conceptual assignments were reviewed. Sixty-two (95 percent) of all notes were similarly categorized by the two independent coders. The three (5 percent) notes for which different initial conceptual categories were assigned were reviewed by the two independent coders and a third coder for final conceptual assignment. In the following section, all presentations of suicide note contents are present exactly as written by the suicidal teens and young adults.

Findings

Examination of the sample of suicide notes shows that of the 65 notes examined 34 percent (n = 22) indicated an anomic suicide, 12 percent (n = 8) were indicative of egoistic suicide, 42 percent (n = 27) suggested a fatalistic suicide, and no notes exemplified an altruistic suicide. Additionally, 12 percent (n = 8) of suicide notes did not reflect any of Durkheim's classifications, instead either simply stating that the individual was committing suicide or including either unintelligible or unrelated statements.

It is interesting to note that in the sample studied, 83 percent (n = 54) of suicide notes are from teenage males. When examining the sex distribution of notes within each category, we see that males account for 86 percent of the anomic suicide notes, 63 percent of the egoistic suicide notes, and 85 percent of the fatalistic suicide notes.

Anomic Suicide Notes

Notes from teens who killed themselves for anomic reasons are those that emphasize some significant change in the individual's life, which is perceived as too difficult to bear. As evidenced in the following neatly handwritten note from an 18-year-old male in 1968, the change from adolescent to wartime soldier serving in the Army was perceived as simply too overwhelming for the young man to manage.

Dear Mom & Dad,

I guess by now you have found out what I've done. I can't explain just what is on my mind but I know that the Army has the effects on me.

I know that I should be proud to serve my country through the Armed Forces but I can't adjust to the fact of the Army and I don't want to go back to that place.

Maybe someday, I really don't know but maybe God will find a place in his heart to forgive me for this thing I've done and maybe Mom you and Dad can forgive me.

I know as long as I have a mind to think with I'll remember all the fun times we have had together and all the wonderful memories that I will always cherish for you and Mom are the best people in the world and you'll always be a big image in my soul and mind.

I do hope you can find it in your heart to forgive me for my wrong.

You Loving Son
Signature

Within the category of anomic suicide notes, several specific issues are emphasized by suicidal teens. These issues—family matters, romantic relationships, and personal life issues—appear to be presented by the teens as areas of life in which changes occur that push the teen into territories where life is perceived to lose meaning and means for coping with and managing changes are unidentifiable. As a result of these perceived changes, these teens express frustrations and disappointments with their lives and a feeling of inability to successfully deal with the changes in ways that are not overly painful or destructive to their lives.

In regard to family matters, three of the notes (5 percent of all, and 14 percent of the anomic suicide notes) included a focus on family conflicts being the reason for the teen's suicide. Interestingly, this issue was expressed only by young women, all of whom wrote that difficulties with their parents were experienced as so highly conflictual that they were unable to see any viable ways to resolve the problem, other than simply permanently removing themselves from the family. A 14-year-old girl left the following handwritten note.

Mom,

Sorry you hate me so. The boys were not for me so that I would have a date. I was not trying to make a fool of (name) because he treated me like a real father. I was not trying to be grown. I did not ask to be the way I was. My mind was not like a fourteen year olds'. I was not trying to flirt with (name) as you said I was. I committed suicide because you turned on me and hated me so. I did not do it as a sign of weakness. (Name) good luck on your wedding day. Now, momma, you won't have to feed me or send me to school. Goodbye (name), momma, and (name). I did the best I could with the cleaning of the house this summer.

Signature

Romantic relationship issues were presented as the central conflictual issue in 13 teens' suicide notes (20 percent of all notes and 59 percent of the anomic classified suicide notes). Here, perhaps contrary to popular assumptions, all notes centering on the loss of, or a deeply troubled, romantic relationship were authored by males. These males expressed in their notes such deep and profound emotional losses that they do not believe they are able to continue living, because of the depth of their loss and despair. The deep personal loss and feeling of being unable to see his way through the loss are reflected in the following handwritten note from a 20-year-old man.

Dear (name),

I am Sorry for what happened yesterday really I am! It's just that I been through so much for you. I just can't live without you. so if I die, call my mom and Dad and tell them I Love them. I Sorry (name) I didn't mean to hurt you so I going to show you the Greatest way to show I Love you—death! You think I treated you bad. Well (name) I don't. we made had had a few bad times. But, think about all the good times. (Name) if I do this and don't die don't let your mom or the cab co. but if I do don't be mad at me. Cause (names) I doing this because I Love you and if you ever Love me like you use to then you meet me in heaven! Just Rember one thing I Love you and I be waiting in heaven for ever if it takes that Long. But I think they if you Love me you meet me There and we can be together for ever.

I LOVE YOU

(Signature)

Issues centering on personal life issues, such as loss of a significant person in one's life, poor academic performance, and substance use/abuse issues, are a third specific type that suicidal teens express as pushing them to the point of killing themselves. When explaining these issues in their suicide notes, youth always express the issue as one for which they see no possible resolution, other than death. Six notes (9 percent of all and 27 percent of notes classified as anomic in nature) have personal life issues as their central focus. The loss of meaning and inescapable nature of his problems are evident in the following note left by a 17-year-old who also wrote and left a will allocating his belongings to his family members and friends.

Dear (name),

I hoped we did the right thing tell (name) I love her she is the best stepmother any one can have.

I committed suside cause life has ran out on me all my hope and Dreams ran away Just like my Friends did They turned me away I was hurting in side and no one helped me. I did not do this cause I wanted to punish (name) or (name). I did it because I needed to be set free and this is the only that it could happened so cry you need to cry. Don't pretend to cry. Do it. Let it all out.

Don't leave (name) or (name) now they will need you more than ever. Tell (name) that he is the best friend that I ever had and tell him to grow up. Don't hang around (name) or (name) cause they are to young. Tell (name) that Deep Down in side me there is a love for god but it would not come out. I love you as a Friend hope we stale can be friends

(Name) can me and you when I am well work out an agreement the both of us.

You would be proud of me I am passing all my classes and that I may be picked for (name) singer next year.

(Name), (name) (name) I love you so much.

Signature

Egoistic Suicide Notes

Egoistic suicides are the outcomes for individuals who perceive their own importance as above and beyond the value and importance of the world around them. In many instances, egoistic suicides are committed by individuals who exhibit delusional thought patterns or who demonstrate difficulties distinguishing fantasy from reality. The following type-written note, from a 21-year-old male who was well known to be a very devoted fan of the television series *Star Trek*, shows how a sense of self-importance and a blending of reality and fantasy combine to yield a feeling of being greater in importance and perhaps more powerful and influential than others.

To whom it may concern (hopefully someone),

If you are reading this, than I am dead by my own hand. Do not grieve long, for this is the way it was meant to be for me. I could not accomplish in this life what I was destined to do, to make history and benefit mankind with my knowledge. All that I know is not lost however, because I have shared some of my wisdom with those who know me well. Use these insights and remember me. I am going to Sto-vo-kor to take my place with the honored dead. I have known about this day for along time, since was younger than (name) is now. I had a vision which told me of my future. I tried to tell this, but no one believed me. Well, believe me now when I say I am proud to have ended life on my terms, and no one else's. Please cremate my remains, for I no longer need this crude flesh. My spirit will always be watching over (name), to protect her and guide her. In fact, I hope that I will be able to do more to help her now than I ever could in life. She will carry on and achieve the greatness that I could not. Enough rambling.

As for my possessions, my truck is to be sold and used to pay off my debts. The remaining money shall go to Mom to do with as she sees fit. I wish (name) to have my State championship ring. I wish (name) to have my football jersey. (Name) may have any of my Star Trek cards he needs for his collection. (Name) may have any action figures he would like to keep in remembrance of me. Every other possession is to go to (name), when she is 18. Mom will be entrusted with holding that stuff in the meantime.

I hope you will remember me with good memories and use them as inspiration, not deadweight. To my professors in college, I learned a great deal from you and appreciate your guidance. To my friends, thanks for the good times, especially (name). To my family (names), I love you. Farewell. I hope you all die well.

QAPLA!!

(Signature)[3]

As with anomic suicide notes, so too can a set of specific themes be identified in egoistic suicide notes. As an individual who perceives him self or herself as of central and primary importance in either the world or the environment in which he or she lives, the egoistic suicide youth will typically express one of three types of views in his or her suicide notes. These include self-hatred, pessimistic, and negative outlooks toward the world in general, and delusional thoughts.

A total of four suicide notes (50 percent of the egoistic notes and 6 percent of all suicide notes examined) focus on the suicidal individual's negative perception of self and feelings of disdain for themselves. These notes are clear in their revelation of the suicidal writers' extremely negative self-concept and the fact that some event or series of events in their life lead to severe damage to their self-esteem. The following two-page handwritten note from a 21-year-old mother who killed herself with a drug overdose exemplifies this variety of suicide note.

To my love ones:

I know you all are mad at me for this. I know the question on everyone's mind is how can I do this to my kids! The truth is when I was alive I asked myself the same thing. I know that this was a very selfish thing to do. But, if I didn't do it now my life just would have got worse. I couldn't handle that. I had lots of hopes and dreams but they just seem to impossible to handle. (Name) and (name) you all was all my friends and my sister's as well. I never had any other friends but you all and I love you alot. Moma I thank you for raising me and I love you a lot more than you ever know. Mom, I love you a lot and I wish we could have had a better relationship. I just couldn't handle if you was to relapse again. I prayed for 10 years of my life to get you clean and through the grace of god it happen. It was the best thing that could have happen. I thank god every time I think of it. To my nephew I love you like you was my own, an watch for your cousins. To (name) and (name) I know you probly hate me for this and I don't blame you. But please remember I love you more than anything in this world!! Please grow up to be men, and If you can find it in your heart Please forgive me. I love you both!!!

I know people are thinking that if I love the people that I wrote than I wouldn't have done this. But the truth is I just didn't love my self. And belive it are not it is possible to love other people and not your self.

PS: I don't want anybody to think that (name) cause this because He didn't. Not at all. (Name) I know you probly don't belive this but I did love you.

Everybody please make me happy and smile by putting a moving on please. (smiley face)

Signature

Three egoistic suicide notes (38 percent of the group and 5 percent of all) reflected beliefs by the writer that the individual attributed his or her insurmountable problems to the environment in which he or she lived. These externally imposed problems are perceived as of such magnitude that successful coping is inconceivable for the individual. These individuals expressed feelings of being victims of circumstances, not instigators of their own problems. A type-written suicide note from a 17-year-old male shows these feelings:

To the World,

You really have been stupid place to live, so hollow, there's nothing to exist for, because nothing worth a damn.

To my Parents and bother

I do care about people, but only people who care about, and so far I have't found any.

To (name)

All I wanted was for people to think about be interested, I thought you were the kind of girl who could be at least like me and think about me, but you couldn't even remember what cat I work in Carnival. (Name) please tell the senior class I've committed suicide. If I can't be remembered in life, I'll be remembered through my death.

To the religious world,

I'll find out what's on the other side. "For Sure."

Delusional notes are the rarest of the suicide notes. Only one youth suicide note was classified as such. As seen earlier in the note from the 21-year-old *Star Trek* fan, the delusional note displays a confusion of reality and fantasy, with an obvious sense of perceiving oneself as possessing superior powers and abilities, although opportunities for expressing and displaying superiority may be blocked in life.

Fatalistic Suicide Notes

Fatalistic suicides are those that are based on an individual perceiving no escape from a seemingly unbearable, overwhelming situation. Typical in expressions from fatalistic suicides are feelings of meaninglessness and hopelessness. In nearly all of the notes that were classified as indicative of fatalistic suicide, there are explicit statements that life has no meaning to the individual. Expressions of a perceived need to fulfill social expectations, but also a lack of means or ability to do so, are common in notes from fatalistic suicides. The following handwritten note from an 18-year-old woman shows these issues clearly.

> *I cannot go on living as I am. Life has no meaning.*
>
> *People give me too much hassle.*
>
> *I love everyone for what they have done for me and I am sorry that it had to end this way.*
>
> *All my love,*
> *Signature*

Or, as shown in the following handwritten note from an 18-year-old male who shot himself in the head, the sense of one's inability to live up to social standards can be so strong that killing oneself may be perceived as the only option.

I am a failure. I am a complete and total failure. There is no good in me. I am a slob. I am lazy, I am rude, and I am stupid. I have no good talents. I am ugly, fat, and unathletic. I bring nothing good to this world, I only mess it up. People tell me I have potential, but it's all lies. I know that I am destined for failure. I mean look at me, I can't even keep my room strait much less make good grades. I have nothing to look forward to in life. Mom and Dad, I'm sorry you had to have such a shitty son in having me, I never ment to hurt you but I did anyways. You were great parents and I thank you, but it is my problem. To (name)—thanks for being a great friend, you are the greatest friend anyone could have, I will miss you. (Name) you are a great guy, You have always been good to me, and I thank you. All I can say is I'm not ment for the world and the world isn't meant for me. Dying is my punishment for such a loser.

Clearly this young man lacked self-esteem and perceived himself as unable to live up to what he believed society expected of him. This note was written just before he killed himself in the front seat of his car in his school's parking lot on the day he was suspended from school.

Within the category of fatalistic suicides there are three clusters of notes that reflect feelings of unbearable circumstances attributed to mental illness, isolation, or undefined/unenumerated reasons.

The subgroup of suicide notes attributing one's fatalistic view to mental illness is fairly small. Only two youth suicide notes (7 percent of the fatalistic suicide notes and 3 percent of the total sample of youth suicide notes) contain references to mental illness as the factor instigating one's suicide. By far the most common theme in youth's fatalistic suicide notes is the theme of isolation. Eighty-one percent ($n = 22$) of the fatalistic suicide notes (39 percent of all youth suicide notes) focus on some sense of personal or social isolation experienced by the individual. These notes emphasize that the individual feels completely alone or alienated and does not believe that any efforts in life would be able to lead him or her out of his or her painful, lonely place in life. The following handwritten note from a 17-year-old boy shows his sense of isolation and loneliness, although he also acknowledges having a loving, supportive family and being "very happy with what I had here."

Dear Family,

I want you all to know that this is something that I have been considering for very long time. I have been thinking about things very much and I have come to this decision out of my own free will. I knew that I have hurt all of you very much, and I hope you don't ever feel like I did it on purpose. I love you all very much, even though I never told you as much as I should of. Please don't ever feel like you let me down in any way. You all have never been anything but the perfect parents. God truely blessed me when he gave me this family. God gave me a gift one time and since then I have done nothing to repay him. I have let him and you all down so many times. So now I am taking this moment to apologize for it all. I know that this is very painful and confusing to you, but always remember this was my choice. At this time in my life, I am so homesick for a country which I've never been. I am just one step closer there now. I'm resting now and I will see all of you again one day. I'd like to thank you for giving me life and allowing me into your hearts. Mom, I understand everything you said to me now. You have always been right. I know I could never pay you back but I want you to know that I understand. Please, please don't feel sad because of me. I am very happy with what I had here and what I've got waiting for me. I need you guys to be strong now, just like I know you are. You all will get through this together. Please always remember that this was my choice and the reason I did this is very simple. I'm tired of life. I'm tired of this place. I just don't want to grow any older. Dad, thank you for always being there, and trying to teach me to be a man. You two hug (name) for me. I love you three more than anything, and this goodbye won't be forever, just a for a little while. Mom, please tell (name) that I love him. (Name) is a good man with a good heart. He is just a little rough around the edges, that's all. He is a good friend. Thank you all very much. I love you and always will.

Your son and brother
(Signature)

Finally, three youth suicide notes (11 percent of the fatalistic notes and 5 percent of all notes) did not reference any specific issue and are classified as undefined/unenumerated reasons for a fatalistic view. In these notes the individual essentially states that he or she is killing himself or herself, and hints at a sense of loss and sadness, but does not give any reasons for his or her actions or feelings. This is shown in the following short handwritten note from an 18-year-old boy.

I love you mom and dad

I'm sorry it turned out this way.

Please forgive me

Suicide Notes That Do Not Provide Intelligible or Relevant Information

Although it may be commonly believed that suicide notes include information to explain why an individual elects to end his or her life, this in fact is not always the case. Twelve percent (n = 8) of the suicide notes left by youth in this sample indicate that the individual is killing himself or herself, but the note provides no statement or hint of the reason for doing so. The function of these notes appears to be to simply make clear that the individual's death is self-inflicted. The lack of information provided in these types of suicide notes is evidenced by the following handwritten suicide note from an 18-year-old boy in which he tells his survivors that he has killed himself, but also includes seemingly unrelated information.

If the Colts win the Super bowl I'll see you in Heaven.

I'm sooooooo sorry.

Please forgive me it's nothing you did!!!!

Love,

(Signature)

Conclusion

The purpose of this study was to identify the Durkheimian reason for suicides among teenagers and young adults. Through the examination and classification of suicide notes, this research attempted to gain insight into the motivations of teenagers seeking their own death. The results of this study largely support the literature concerning suicide notes, as well as suggest directions for future research.

Evidence from examined suicide notes most commonly revealed fatalistic suicides. Feeling forlorn and alone, the authors of these notes often mentioned an inability to break away from seemingly futile situations. Hopelessness and anguish are often described by suicidal writers, and emotional reports of this despondency are compatible with prior research (Chavez-Hernandez et al. 2006). Apparently, these individuals do not ascribe meaning to their lives and do not anticipate successfully meeting social expectations. In this way, a lack of personal purpose and self-esteem can be equated with their suicides. Without a doubt, Durkheim's fatalistic typology comprises a significant portion of teenage suicides.

Anomic suicides represented the second most significant category of suicide notes. Encompassing slightly more than one-third of all suicide notes, these writings depicted significant life changes for individuals were so overwhelming that management of such circumstances was deemed impossible. Congruous with previous research (Leenaars et al. 2001) concerning teenage suicide notes and their focus on rejection, this lack of acceptance was found to be signified through family matters, romantic relationships, and personal issues within notes describing anomic suicide.

Perhaps the most bizarre correspondence emanates from egoistic suicide notes. Coupled with notes that had no definitive Durkheimian classification, these suicide notes followed behind fatalistic and anomic suicide notes in prevalence. However, egoistic suicide notes often indicated delusional mentalities, suggesting that some suicidal individuals are truly out of touch with reality. Consistent with earlier research that finds that individuals with psychiatric disorders often do not write suicide notes (Kuwabara et al. 2006), delusional notes were extremely infrequent in this study, as only one teenage suicide note was classified as delusional.

There were no suicide notes in this study that epitomized an altruistic suicide. Because these suicides often entail quests for the betterment of society, rather than for the individual, perhaps self-discovery inherent in adolescence explains this departure from collective society. The complete absence of altruistic suicides may also support the fact that younger people seem to be more focused on themselves in suicide notes (Leenaars and Balance 1984). Regardless of the self-centeredness of teenagers, from this study, it can be concluded that altruistic suicides are not the Durkheimian reason for suicides among youth.

It is recognized that this research has its limitations. Sample selectivity is the first concern. The sample is limited in size (n = 65) and represents suicide notes only from one Midwestern city. Despite the fact that most of these suicide notes can be classified into one of the four suicide typologies defined by Durkheim, these findings may or may not apply for notes recovered at suicides in other communities. Although prior research on authors of suicide notes discusses teenage females and their propensities toward leaving verbose commentary (Ho et al. 1998), the sample in this study predominately consists of suicide notes from teenage males. Further research may need to consider a stratified sampling design to account for the differences in representations of the sexes. Furthermore, in order to adequately address suicidal motivations, it should be acknowledged that the analysis of suicide notes is only one method of examining suicidal tendencies. Upon further research of suicide notes, as well as different approaches to general suicide research, implications for suicide prevention can be successfully developed.

Suicide notes potentially capture motivations for seeking death, providing essential glimpses into the minds of society's suicidal members. Although each adolescent or young adult author is markedly different, by cataloging suicide notes into Durkheim's four dominant suicide categories, the thought patterns of teenagers and young adults can be clarified. Utilizing these social environment typologies that may predispose youth to suicide, properly classified suicide notes can indeed provide insights into the motivations of suicidal individuals. Exposing the incentives for youth suicide should subsequently encourage community efforts to further identify sources of psychological stress, particularly stressors with anomic, altruistic, egoistic, and fatalistic explanations. In turn, solutions can be established to remedy these distinguished stressors. Evidence of fatalistic suicides among teenagers and young adults should promote the development of social integration programs and the exposure of healthy leisure activities. Anomic suicides demonstrate that some young adults cannot properly adjust to life situations without appropriate adult influence or psychological counseling. Compelling evidence for mental health services is also seen in suicide notes representing egoistic suicides. More research should be conducted regarding the inspection of suicide notes, as collective examinations of these notes will assist in the identification of sound risk factors for suicide.

Notes

1. However, it is interesting that suicide notes left by alcoholics do not show any significant differences in content from those left by nonalcoholics (Leenaars, Lester, and Wenckstern 1999).

2. This finding has also been consistently shown in international research drawing on suicide notes in Mexico, Australia, England, Ireland, Turkey, India, Japan, Canada, and Germany (O'Donnell et al. 1993; Leenaars et al. 1999, 2003; Girdhar et al. 2004; O'Connor and Leenaars 2004; Chavez-Hernandez et al. 2006; Demirel et al. 2008).

3. This note also had a *Star Trek* Klingon symbol drawn at the bottom, with a note explaining that it was such. Also, handwritten were definitions of "Sto-vo-kor" and "QAPLA.")

Discussion Questions

1. If suicide is viewed as deviant, do you feel individuals who commit suicide are worried about being stigmatized? Why or why not?
2. What intervention strategies would you suggest to minimize the risk of teenagers committing suicide?

References

Beck, Roy W., Jeffrey Morris, and David Lester. 1974. "Suicide Notes and Risk of Future Suicide." *Journal of the American Medical Association* 228(4):495–96.

Breault, K. D. 1986. "Suicide in America: A Test of Durkheim's Theory of Religious and Family Integration, 1933–1980." *American Journal of Sociology* 92(3):628–56.

Capstick, Alan. 1960. "Recognition of Emotional Disturbance and the Prevention of Suicide." *British Medical Journal* 1:1179–82.

Chavez-Hernandez, Ana-Maria, Daniel Paramo, Antoon Leenaars, and Lindsey Leenaars. 2006. "Suicide Notes in Mexico: What Do They Tell Us?" *Suicide and Life-Threatening Behavior* 36(6):709–15.

Centers for Disease Control and Prevention. 2009. *Suicide: Facts at a Glance.* Retrieved December 1, 2010 (http://www.cdc.gov/violenceprevention/pdf/Suicide_DataSheet-a.pdf).

Centers for Disease Control and Prevention. 2010. *Understanding Suicide: Fact Sheet.* Retrieved December 1, 2010 (http://www.cdc.gov/violenceprevention/pdf/Suicide-FactSheet-a.pdf).

Day, Lincoln H. 1987. "Durkheim on Religion and Suicide—A Demographic Critique." *Sociology* 21: 449–61.

Demirel, Birol, Taner Akar, Aslihan Sayın, Selcuk Candansayar, and Antoon A. Leenaars. 2008. "Farewell to the World: Suicide Notes from Turkey." *Suicide and Life-Threatening Behavior* 38(1):122–27.

Dohrenwend, Bruce P. 1959. "Egoism, Altruism, Anomie, and Fatalism: A Conceptual Analysis of Durkheim's Types." *American Sociological Review* 24(4):466–73.

Durkheim, Emile [1897] 1951. *Suicide.* New York: Free Press.

Foster, Tom. 2003. "Suicide Note Themes and Suicide Prevention." *International Journal of Psychiatry in Medicine* 33(4):323–31.

Girdhar, Shalina, Antoon A. Leenaars, T. D. Dogra, Lindsey Leenaars, and Guresh Kumar. 2004.

"Suicide Notes in India: What Do They Tell Us?" *Archives of Suicide Research* 8(2):179–85.

Heim, Nikolaus and David Lester. 1990. "Do Suicides Who Write Notes Differ from Those Who Do Not? A Study of Suicides in West Berlin." *Acta Psychiatrica Scandinavica* 82:372–73.

Ho, T. P., P. S. F. Yip, C. W. F. Chiu, and P. Halliday. 1998. "Suicide Notes: What Do They Tell Us?" *Acta Psychiatrica Scandinavica* 98:467–73.

Holmes, Ronald M. and Stephen T. Holmes. 2005. *Suicide: Theory, Practice, and Investigation*. Thousand Oaks, CA: Sage Publications, Inc.

Johnson, Barclay D. 1965. "Durkheim's One Cause of Suicide." *American Sociological Review* 30(6): 875–86.

Kuwabara, Hideki, Toshiki Shioiri, Akiyoshi Nishimura, Ryo Abe, Hideyuki Nushida, Yasuhiro Ueno, Kohei Akazawa, and Toshiyuki Someya. 2006. "Differences in Characteristics between Suicide Victims Who Left Notes or Not." *Journal of Affective Disorders* 94:145–49.

Leenaars, Antoon A. 1992. "Suicide Notes of the Older Adult." *Suicide and Life-Threatening Behavior* 22(1):62–79.

Leenaars, Antoon A. and W. D. G. Balance. 1981. "A Predictive Approach to the Study of Manifest Content in Suicide Notes." *Journal of Clinical Psychology* 37(1):50–52.

Leenaars, Antoon A. and William D. G. Balance. 1984. "A Predictive Approach to Suicide Notes of Young and Old people from Freud's Formulations with Regard to Suicide." *Journal of Clinical Psychology* 40(6):1362–64.

Leenaars, Antoon A., Erik Jan De Wilde, Susanne Wenckstern, and Michael Kral. 2001. "Suicide Notes of Adolescents: A Life-Span Comparison." *Canadian Journal of Behavioural Science* 33(1):47–57.

Leenaars, Antoon A., David Lester, and Susanne Wenckstern. 1999. "Suicide Notes in Alcoholism." *Psychological Reports* 85(2):363–64.

Leenaars, Antoon A., Janet Haines, Susanne Wenckstern, Christopher L. Williams, and David Lester. 2003. "Suicide Notes from Australia and the United States." *Perceptual and Motor Skills* 96(3):1281–82.

Lester, David 1998. "Differences in Content of Suicide Notes by Age and Method." *Perceptual and Motor Skills* 87(2):530.

Lester, David and Marge Linn. 1998. "The Content of Suicide Notes Written by Those Using Different Methods for Suicide." *Perceptual and Motor Skills* 87(2):722.

Miley, James D. and Michael Micklin. 1972. "Structural Change and the Durkheimian Legacy: A Macrosocial Analysis of Suicide Rates." *American Journal of Sociology* 78(3):657–73.

O'Connor, Rory C. and Antoon A. Leenaars. 2004. "A Thematic Comparison of Suicide Notes Drawn from Northern Ireland and the United States." *Current Psychology* 22(4):339–47.

O'Donnell, Ian, Richard Farmer, and Jose Catalan. 1993. "Suicide Notes." *British Journal of Psychiatry* 163:45–48.

Peck, Dennis L. 1989. "Teenage Suicide Expressions: Echoes from the Past." *International Quarterly of Community Health Education* 10(1):53–64.

Pescosolido, Bernice A. and Sharon Georgianna. 1989. "Durkheim, Suicide, and Religion: Toward a Network Theory of Suicide." *American Sociological Review* 54(1):33–48.

Pope, Whitney. (1976). *Durkheim's Suicide: A Classic Analyzed*. Chicago, IL: University of Chicago Press.

van Poppel, Frans. and Lincoln H. Day. 1996. "A Test of Durkheim's Theory of Suicide—Without Committing the 'ecological fallacy.'" *American Sociological Review* 61(3):500–07.

Selvin, Hanan C. 1958. "Durkheim's Suicide and Problems of Empirical Research." *American Journal of Sociology* 63(6):607–19.

Shioiri, Toshiki, Akiyoshi Nishimura, Kohei Akazawa, Ryo Abe, Hideyuki Nushida, Yasuhiro Ueno, Maki Kojika-Maruyama, and Toshiyuki Someya. 2005. "Incidence of Note-Leaving Remains Constant Despite Increasing Suicide Rates." *Psychiatry and Clinical Neurosciences* 59:226–28.

Stark, Rodney, Daniel P. Doyle, and Jesse Lynn Rushing. 1983. "Beyond Durkheim: Religion and Suicide." *Journal for the Scientific Study of Religion* 11:120–31.

PART SEVEN

Elite Deviance

As the boss of the worldwide conglomerate Tyco, Dennis Kozlowski made tons of money for his corporation and himself. In the 1990s, he went on a frenzied shopping spree, spending more than $60 billion to buy 200 major corporations and hundreds of smaller ones. As a result, Tyco, once a relatively small industrial-parts manufacturer with $3 billion in yearly sales, turned into a global colossus that annually pulled in $36 billion, selling practically everything from diapers to fire alarms. For that feat, Kozlowski rewarded himself with more than $300 million in total compensation for the three years before the good times ended. He further acquired for himself, among other things, three Harley-Davidson motorcycles, a 130-foot sailing yacht, a private place, and lavish homes in four states. Unfortunately, for him, in the summer of 2002 he was charged first with failing to pay $1 million in sales tax on art purchases and then with stealing $150 million from Tyco. In 2005, he was convicted for systematically looting the company and sentenced to serve 8 to 25 years in prison.[1]

Kozlowski's crime may be called elite deviance, deviance that characteristically involves privileged people—the relatively wealthy, powerful, or well educated. In this part we take a look at elite deviance. This part begins with Mandeep K. Dhami's article entitled "White-Collar Crime." The title of this article is also a concept defined by Edwin Sutherland. Dhami explores the social reaction to white-collar crime and presents research on offenders' perceptions of others' reactions. Paul Klenowski and colleagues examine how white-collar criminals neutralize their crimes in "How Men and Women Avoid the Stigma of White-Collar Crime." This part concludes with an article by Anson Shupe entitled "Clergy Misconduct as Elite Deviance: Assessing the Problem." Shupe discusses topics such as economic violations and sexual misconduct in organized religious institutions.

Note

1. *Wall Street Journal*, "Tyco Convictions Upheld," November 16, 2007, p. C2; Daniel Eisenberg, "Dennis the Menace." *Time*, June 17, 2002, pp. 46–49; Andrew Hill, "Ex-Tyco Chairman Free on $10m Bail." *FT.com*, September 27, 2002.

ARTICLE 17

Mandeep K. Dhami
University of Surrey, UK

White-Collar Crime

In 2009, multimillionaire Bernard L. Madoff pleaded guilty to the largest fraud and money-laundering operation ever committed by an individual, which resulted in his clients losing approximately $65 billion. The victims of this giant Ponzi scheme included individual investors who lost their life savings and charities that went bankrupt. Madoff was sentenced to 150 years in prison with restitution of $170 billion. His friends and family deserted him, the sentencing judge called him "evil," and Madoff himself apologized and expressed shame. In this article, we show that this reaction to white-collar crime was as spectacular as the crime itself.

White-Collar Crime

White-collar crime was originally defined by Sutherland in 1949 as "a crime committed by a person of respectability and high social status in the course of his occupation" (1983:7). This definition combines characteristics of the offender and the offence. Although it is clear that white-collar crimes may be committed by people from a broad spectrum of society, many theorists still find the focus on offenders of high social status, income, or power within the organization to be useful (Weisburd et al. 1991). Indeed, white-collar offenders tend to differ from conventional offenders in many respects. Sutherland (1940, 1945) also pointed out that society does not view white-collar crime as "real" crime. Indeed, crimes such as antitrust violations, bankruptcy fraud, tax evasion, insider trading, and embezzlement are often defined and explained in ways that are incompatible with our notion of conventional crime, and consequently, societal reaction to white-collar crime has tended to be unlike the punitive reaction to conventional crime.

Sutherland (1983) asserted that social reaction to white-collar crime was characterized by acceptance and support at best, and by ambivalence at worst. He argued that this enables white-collar offenders to escape stigmatization and maintain a noncriminal self-concept. Indeed, white-collar crimes have tended to fall under the jurisdiction of private laws, such as civil law and regulatory law, and so are dealt with by special regulatory agencies or are self-regulated. Regulation has been primarily through administrative means, and has been reactive. Prosecution has tended to be infrequent as trials are characteristically long, expensive, and complex, and the efficacy of the criminal law is limited by the difficulties inherent in defining behaviors as illegal, the need to keep up to date with technological advances, and the existence of loopholes. Moreover, offenders have sometimes controlled information that indicates blameworthiness, intent, or responsibility. Evidence suggests that the police may be reluctant to pursue white-collar offenders (Mitchell, Sikka, and Willmot 1998), and that judges respond with leniency toward such offenders, who are rarely imprisoned, and if so, only for short terms (Tillman and Pontell 1988; Levi 1989). A common legal sanction against white-collar crimes has been a financial penalty.

Social reaction to crime is influenced by the prevailing norms (Quinney 1970). Thus, there are cultural, spatial, and temporal variations in the social response to crime, and tolerance for particular crimes may change. Since the 1970s, there appears to have been a societal-level change in perceptions of, and reactions to, white-collar crime, prompted by the Watergate scandal (Katz 1980). This movement is reflected by both formal and informal shifts (Pontell, Rosoff, and Goode 1994). The formal response to white-collar crime appears to be changing. First, governments have constructed special teams and programs to detect, investigate, and record white-collar crime (e.g., new serious fraud units and more regulatory agencies). Second, legislation has been constructed to deal with white-collar crimes (e.g., securities fraud laws). Third, the likelihood of prosecuting white-collar crime has increased (Benson, Cullen, and Maakestad 1990). Fourth, evidence suggests that white-collar offenders are more likely to face punitive sanctions than they were in the past (Hagan and Palloni 1986; Breyer 1988; Higgins 1999), and that these sentences are longer (Reason 2000).

In addition, there appears to be a shift in the informal response to white-collar crime (Schrager and Short 1980). This is reflected in a general public intolerance for white-collar crime (Cullen, Hartman, and Jonson 2009), which is a departure from the indifference of the 1970s (Rossi et al. 1974). The public perceives white-collar crimes as more serious than street crimes (Piquero, Carmichael, and Piquero 2008). A survey conducted by the National White Collar Crime Center (2006) indicates that the public perceives fraud and embezzlement to be more serious than burglary and robbery. In addition, crimes committed by high-status offenders are seen as more serious than those committed by nonstatus offenders. Over half of the public believes that not enough resources are devoted to combating white-collar crime. Police chiefs also view white-collar crime as more serious than conventional crime (Pontell et al. 1985).

According to labeling theorists, one of the consequences of being labeled a criminal (i.e., conviction) or experiencing negative audience reaction and exclusion from participation in conventional social roles (i.e., prison sentence) is the increased likelihood that the individual will develop a criminal self-image (Lemert 1951; Becker 1963; Schur 1971). The development of a criminal self-image constitutes one step in the process of developing a criminal career. Thus, according to this perspective, criminal behavior is constructed through the interaction between the offender and those who react toward him or her (Erikson 1962; Kitsuse 1962; Becker 1963). The audience may include agents of formal control, such as the police and judiciary, the offender's significant others, society in general (Schur 1971), and the offender himself or herself (Becker 1963). The nature of the reaction may range from permissiveness through indifference to condemnation (Lemert 1951). However, the individual is not passive to the effects of labeling or negative audience reaction, and may in fact negotiate the label that is applied through various techniques, including "fighting back" (Rogers and Buffalo 1974) and "neutralization" (Sykes and Matza 1957).

A Study of Audience Reaction to White-Collar Prisoners

This article presents a study (Dhami 2007) that explores (1) how white-collar offenders who have been convicted and sentenced to imprisonment perceive the reaction of others, such as the judiciary, media, significant others, prison staff, and prison inmates toward them; (2) how these offenders perceive their own criminal behavior; and (3) the mechanisms that may shape these perceptions.

For the present purposes, white-collar crime is defined as an economic crime committed through the use of fraud and/or deception by a person occupying a senior position in an organization. This definition incorporates the main elements of Sutherland's (1983) original conception of white-collar crime and a recent focus on white-collar offenders as high in socioeconomic status, income, or power within the organization, and abusing trust (Wheeler and Rothman 1982; Coleman 1987; Shapiro 1990; Croall

2001). Furthermore, this definition refers to the types of offenders against whom the criminal justice system, the public, and media appear to be reacting in more recent years.

The categories of audience who may react to white-collar crime include those identified by Schur (1971) and Becker (1963): judiciary, media, significant others, prison staff, prison inmates, and self. The judiciary (involved in the white-collar offender's conviction) and prison staff (where the white-collar offender is based) represent agents of formal control. Agents of informal control include the media, significant others (i.e., the white-collar offender's relatives and business associates), and prison inmates. Finally, Becker (1963) pointed out that the individual is also audience to his or her own behavior.

White-collar offenders in the study were selected using a two-stage purposive sampling procedure. First, one minimum-security prison in England was selected because it accommodated a large group of white-collar offenders. Second, inmates serving sentences for crimes of fraud or deception and who fit the aforementioned definition of a white-collar criminal were selected. Fourteen (out of 19) adult male white-collar prisoners volunteered to participate in this study. All could be described as Caucasian. Ten had received a one- to three-year sentence and four were serving sentences over three years. At the time of the study, half of the sample had served less than six months, six offenders had served from six to twelve months, and one had served over twelve months. Thus, demographically, the sample of white-collar offenders in the study differs from the stereotype of a conventional offender by virtue of their offences, their older age, being employed prior to conviction, being educated, having few or no previous convictions, and serving their sentence in a minimum-security prison.

The white-collar offenders were asked about their perceptions of the reaction of the judiciary, the media, significant others, prison staff, and prison inmates, and perceptions of their own behavior. In each section of the individual interview (e.g., judiciary section), open-ended questions established the reaction an offender experienced, followed by whether he expected that reaction, and whether he perceived it to be more positive or negative than he had expected. Probes requiring offenders to provide reasons for their responses were also included. Analysis of the interview data focused on categories and commonalties of responses (the frequency of responses is presented in parentheses).

White-Collar Offenders' Perceptions of Others' Reactions

The formal response to the white-collar crimes committed by offenders in the study was punitive (Erikson 1962). A majority of white-collar offenders (11) perceived the reaction of the judiciary as negative and punitive. This perception was because they had not expected the conviction, prison sentence, or the length of sentence. These expectations in turn appeared to be based on their conceptions of white-collar crime as not being "real" crime. Typical responses were:

> The barrister didn't think I'd be sent to prison. The nature of the offence is complex and white-collar crime isn't easily defined. I didn't commit a crime in the normal sense of the word (Offender 13).
>
> I didn't expect to be convicted because the trial was so complex, so I expected an acquittal. The investigations took over four years. . . . The judge was negative and extremely harsh considering that only a small amount of money was involved (Offender 14).
>
> After reading about other similar cases in the media I thought I'd receive a short sentence. I was shocked with the judge's negative attitude. . . . Sending a white-collar criminal to prison is a waste of time and money. . . . White-collar criminals are not a danger to other human beings (Offender 4).

Nine of the eleven white-collar offenders who were aware of media attention to their case perceived the reaction of the media as negative and biased. Indeed, they viewed the media coverage as fictional. They had, however, expected media attention, often because the organization was well known or because a substantial sum of money was involved. Typical responses were:

> [I expected media attention] because of the large amount of money involved. . . . My case was reported mainly in the local papers when I first got caught, before the trial. The coverage was negative because the media did not report the facts but just the "news" (Offender 2).
>
> The local and national press were negative . . . they stereotyped me as a Walter Mitty character. It was slanderous (Offender 3).
>
> The local press were negative. The case was badly reported, sensational and biased against me, despite the fact that the reporters weren't in the court to collect information for most of the hearing (Offender 10).

All but one of the white-collar offenders perceived the reaction of some or all of his significant others as positive and supportive. These offenders believed that their significant others did not regard them as criminals, but concurred that they had been harshly treated by the criminal justice system. Typical responses were:

> My wife's bitter towards the system but she's supportive towards me. . . . She feels that I've been hard done by. . . . The twins are supportive. They don't agree that I should be in prison because I didn't hurt anyone or take anything (Offender 3).
>
> My son has coped well. He's 17 and he's very angry about what he perceives to be very unfair. . . . My daughter was worried for "daddy" (Offender 13).

In fact, most of the white-collar offenders (nine) did not expect the reaction of their significant others to change. Typical reasons for this were because they had not committed a conventional crime and because significant others had been supportive in the past. Seven of the eleven offenders who said that the reaction of significant others had changed since being convicted and sentenced to imprisonment perceived the change as positive in that it strengthened relations.

Most of the white-collar offenders (nine) claimed to have daily contact with prison staff, largely in work situations. All of them perceived the reaction of staff in the current prison as positive and respectful. They believed that staff treated them as individuals rather than "criminals." This was contrasted with their perceptions of staff reactions in the higher security prisons in which offenders were located presentence. Typical responses were:

> The staff have been fine, generally very fair, not judgmental. They take you as the person you are, not the crime you've committed. They're very professional. . . . I'm treated with respect here . . . [In the higher security prison] every officer's interpretation of an inmate is that they're arse-holes—scum of the earth. . . . They lacked respect and insisted that everyone call them "boss" (Offender 3).
>
> Staff are fine. Everyone is treated as human, rather than a convict . . . [In the higher security prison] the officers treated everyone like a criminal from day one (Offender 8).

Furthermore, all but one of the white-collar offenders expected staff to treat them the same as other inmates. Typical reasons for this were because staff do not necessarily know what crimes individual inmates have committed, and all inmates in the current prison were deemed to be at the same level of risk. However, some of the offenders (four) believed that they had been treated differently and more positively by prison staff than other inmates convicted of conventional crimes, largely because they believed staff knew that they had not committed a violent crime and that they had money (on the outside).

All offenders in the sample claimed to have daily contact with other inmates in both work and social situations. All perceived the reaction of other inmates in the current prison as positive, friendly, and accepting. This was contrasted with their perceptions of inmate reactions in the higher-security prisons in which they were located presentence. Furthermore, the positive reaction appeared partly to be by virtue of the situation that the white-collar offender was in. Typical responses were:

> The other inmates are sympathetic. There's a lot more support between inmates in this prison. . . . I was expecting a lot of antagonism (Offender 7).
>
> The other inmates have been positive because I expected there to be an inmate hierarchy like in closed prisons (Offender 5).
>
> The other inmates see me as someone they can talk to if they have a problem because I work in the Chaplaincy and in my career I've worked with the general public. . . . I expected to be ridiculed because I've been to school. And I expected to be bullied, but I haven't been (Offender 10).
>
> I get on really well with everyone, from the lifers to the rogues. Everyone's been fine generally. A lot depends on where you live. On my landing there's a fair amount of mixing. I'm very accepted (Offender 11).

Most of the white-collar offenders (nine) said that they did not expect other inmates to treat them differently from those convicted of conventional crimes because they thought all people are considered equal in prison. Nevertheless, a majority (12) believed that they had been treated differently, namely, more positively by other inmates. Typical reasons for this were that inmates treated them with more respect, inmates did not "bother" or bully them, and inmates offered them "stuff." Offenders appeared to believe that this differential reaction from other inmates was partly due to white-collar offenders' better financial status, and fascination with their type of crime.

As Lemert (1951) noted, audience reaction may be characterized as negative in terms of rejection, withdrawal, and condemnation or as positive in terms of acceptance and support. Indifference and tolerance represent a middle position. White-collar offenders' *perceptions* of audience reactions as positive can be characterized as supportive, respectful, friendly, and accepting. By contrast, their perceptions of audience reactions as negative referred to being punitive and biased.

From one perspective, the categories of audience represented earlier can be divided into agents of formal control (i.e., judiciary and prison staff) and agents of informal control (i.e., media, significant others, prison inmates, and self). Alternatively, these categories of audience can be divided into those who have a greater opportunity to interact directly with the individual offender (i.e., significant others, prison inmates, prison staff, and self) and those who do not (i.e., judiciary and media). From the first perspective, it was found that white-collar offenders in the present study had a mixed perception of the reactions of both agents of formal control and informal control. These offenders tended to perceive the reaction of the judiciary as negative, but the reaction of prison staff as positive. They tended to perceive the reaction of significant others and prison inmates as positive, and their own behavior as noncriminal, but the reaction of media as negative. However, from the second perspective it was found that the offenders perceived the reaction of groups with whom they had an opportunity to have direct, personal interaction as positive and the reaction of groups with whom they did not have such an opportunity as negative.

An implication of these findings is that white-collar offenders' positive perceptions of the reactions of audiences with whom they have had an opportunity for direct interaction suggests that audience reaction may be moderated by the individual offender's ability to portray himself or herself as more than an "offender" and so the audience may react not only to his or her behavior but also to his or her personal attributes.

White-Collar Offenders' Reactions to Their Own Behavior

Becker (1963) stated that an individual may perceive his or her own behavior as either criminal or noncriminal. All but one of the white-collar offenders perceived their own offending behavior as noncriminal because they had not harmed anyone, or because their offence differed from conventional crimes, and was in fact legal in other countries. Typical responses were:

> There's no victim in white-collar crime, only the organization. White-collar crime isn't a danger to society. . . . There was no visual damage, no physical damage, no-one was hurt. It was mostly a financial matter (Offender 1).
>
> What I was accused of doing wasn't a crime until the 1985 Company's Act and it's still not a crime in other countries. The public's harsher on white-collar crime since Maxwell (Offender 11).
>
> With a business fraud there's a very fine line between right and wrong. The judge directed the jury to perceive it as a crime. I don't agree that I was breaking the law, so I may do it again (Offender 3).

Therefore, white-collar offenders' reactions to their own behavior may be characterized as positive. Indeed, these offenders, like other offenders, displayed a specific mode of adaptation to the criminal label. The specific "fighting back" phenomenon referred to as "redefinition" by Rogers and Buffalo (1974) displayed by white-collar offenders was that they disagreed with the label thus canceling it out. They also neutralized their behavior using techniques similar to those described by Sykes and Matza (1957). For example, offenders denied responsibility by claiming they were influenced by market forces beyond their control. They denied injury by arguing that no one was hurt, or there was little harm done. Offenders denied the existence of a victim by arguing that the victim was absent or unknown, or transforming the victim (e.g., bank) into the "wrong-doer" while seeing themselves as the "avenger." In expressing condemnation for the condemners, offenders shifted the focus of attention from themselves to the motives and behavior of those who disapproved of their behavior. Finally, offenders' appeal to higher loyalties suggested they had to forfeit the needs of wider society to fulfill the needs of a smaller group of businessmen to which they belonged. Other studies have also shown that white-collar offenders often use neutralization techniques to legitimize their behavior (Benson 1985; Hollinger 1991; McBarnet 1991; Dabney 1995; Gauthier 2001; Willott, Griffin, and Torrance, 2001).

It is interesting to consider why white-collar offenders exhibit self-serving attitudes toward their criminal behavior given the growing societal-level intolerance toward white-collar crime. One possible explanation may be that these self-serving attitudes help them to maintain a positive self-concept (i.e., noncriminal/deviant self-image, high self-esteem, and positive ideal self).

One implication of these findings is that the mechanism explaining why convicted and imprisoned white-collar offenders may re-offend upon release is different to that offered by some theorists (Lemert 1951; Becker 1963; Schur 1971) who argue that being labeled a criminal and/or experiencing exclusion from participation in conventional social roles increases the likelihood of developing a criminal self-image and engaging in criminal behavior. According to this study, potential re-offending may be explained by the offender's denial of the criminality of his or her behavior and/or the counterbalance provided by informal agents, such as significant others to the criminal label attached by formal agents of control, such as the judiciary.

Factors Shaping Perceptions of Audience Reaction

White-collar offenders' perceptions of audience reaction were shaped by their expectations of how others would react, and by their conceptions of crime. Expectations were informed by offenders' knowledge of how white-collar offenders are often dealt with by the criminal justice system; how crimes are reported in the media; by the nature of offenders' relations with significant others prior to conviction; and by their experience of being in a higher-security prison presentence. Specifically, white-collar offenders did not expect the judiciary, media, significant others, prison staff, and other prison inmates to treat them like "criminals" or change their reactions toward them in accordance with the criminal label. Thus, the judiciary's decision to convict and sentence them to prison was perceived as punitive and the media coverage, which pointed to the offenders' criminality, was also perceived as biased. White-collar offenders were aware that in comparison to conventional crime, white-collar crime constitutes a small proportion of criminal convictions, that prison sentences are relatively rare for white-collar offenders, and that crimes reported in the media tend to be sensationalized. By contrast, the support provided by significant others and the favorable experiences of prison staff and other inmates in the minimum-security prison were perceived as positive by white-collar offenders. This may partly be explained by the fact that they tended to have stable personal relationships prior to conviction, and they were able to successfully justify and neutralize their offending behavior to significant others. Finally, white-collar offenders were sent to high-security prisons presentence where they had negative experiences of staff and inmates, and in the current minimum-security prison they found themselves at the top of a criminal hierarchy. Thus, white-collar offenders' perceptions of audience reaction were shaped by their expectations, which in turn were derived from their past experiences and knowledge.

White-collar offenders' perceptions of audience reaction were also shaped by their own conceptions of crime. These offenders did not view white-collar crimes as criminal. Rather, they typically distinguished white-collar crimes from conventional crimes. Offenders viewed white-collar crimes as noncriminal partly because there were no visible victims or violence, and because some white-collar crimes were legal in the past or currently so in other jurisdictions. They believed that it was both acceptable and common to overcome financial difficulties to succeed or to make a profit by resorting to illegal means, especially if the victim is an organization rather than an identifiable individual. Thus, white-collar offenders' perceptions of audience reaction were shaped by their conceptions of crime, which in turn were derived from a distinction between white-collar and conventional crimes.

In sum, like other groups of offenders, white-collar offenders were not passive recipients of the criminal label. They did not perceive themselves as criminal. Offenders interpreted audience reaction by drawing on their past experiences and knowledge, and their conceptions of crime. This can have implications for our theoretical understanding of the effects of labeling. Offenders' perceptions of audience reaction may or may not coincide with the audiences' intended reaction. To the extent that there is a discrepancy between these two perspectives, there may be misunderstanding and misprediction in how offenders ought to be affected by the criminal label.

Beyond the implications that have already been highlighted, it may be important for white-collar offenders while in prison to maintain contact with others, such as significant others who can negate the criminal label. Furthermore, as Payne (2003:chapter 3) points out, the use of neutralization techniques has several implications for how white-collar offenders should be treated in prison. As for conventional offenders, for instance, programs need to aid offenders in taking responsibility, realizing the consequences of their behavior, and showing remorse. The fact that societal reaction is influenced by the seriousness of the crime and the blameworthiness of the offender necessitates efforts to encourage white-collar offenders to acknowledge the harm caused and their role in the crime.

Discussion Questions

1. What would be the typical audience reaction to white-collar offenders who have been released from prison?
2. Given the reaction to white-collar crime, what are the chances that such offenders would re-offend?
3. What would be the self-image of white-collar offenders who have been convicted and sentenced to imprisonment?

References

Becker, Howard, S. 1963. *Outsiders: Studies in the Sociology of Deviance*. London: Free Press of Glencoe Collier-Macmillan.

Benson, Michael, L. 1985. "Denying the Guilty Mind: Accounting for Involvement in a White-Collar Crime." *Criminology* 23:583–607.

Benson, Michael, L., Francis T. Cullen, and William J. Maakestad. 1990. "Local Prosecutors and Corporate Crime." *Crime and Delinquency* 36: 356–72.

Breyer, Stephen, 1988. "The Federal Sentencing Guidelines and the Key Compromises Upon Which They Rest." *Hofstra Law Review* 17:1–50.

Coleman, James. W. 1987. "Toward an Integrated Theory of White-Collar Crime." *American Journal of Sociology* 93:406–39.

Croall, Hazel. 2001. *Understanding White Collar Crime*. Buckingham, England: Open University Press.

Cullen, Francis, Jennifer Hartman, and Cheryl Jonson. 2009. "Bad Guys: Why the Public Supports Punishing White-Collar Offenders." *Crime, Law and Social Change* 51:31–44.

Dabney, Dean. 1995. "Neutralization and Deviance in the Workplace." *Deviant Behavior* 16:313–33.

Dhami, Mandeep K. 2007. "White-Collar Prisoners' Perceptions of Audience Reaction: Findings from a Small-Scale Interview Study."*Deviant Behavior* 28:57–77.

Erikson, Kai T. 1962. "Notes on the Sociology of Deviance." *Social Problems* 9:307–14.

Gauthier, Deann K. 2001. "Professional Lapses: Occupational Deviance and Neutralization Techniques in Veterinary Medical Practice." *Deviant Behavior* 22:467–90.

Hagan, John and Alberto Palloni. 1986. "Club Fed and the Sentencing of White-Collar Offenders Before and After Watergate." *Criminology* 24:603–22.

Higgins, Michael. 1999. "Sizing up Sentences." *ABA Journal* 85:42–47.

Hollinger, Richard C. 1991. "Neutralizing in the Workplace." *Deviant Behavior* 12:169–202.

Katz, Jack. 1980. "The Social Movement Against White-Collar Crime." Pp.161–181 in *Criminology Review Yearbook*, vol. 2, edited by E. Bittner and S. L. Messinger. Beverly Hills, CA: Sage.

Kitsuse, John I. 1962. "Societal Reaction to Deviant Behavior: Problems of Theory and Method." *Social Problems* 9:247–56.

Lemert, Edwin M. 1951. *Social Pathology*. New York: McGraw-Hill.

Levi, Michael. 1989. "Fraudulent Justice? Sentencing the Business Criminal." Pp. 86–109 in *Paying for Crime*, edited by P. Carlen and D. Cook. Milton Keynes, England: Open University Press.

McBarnet, Doreen. 1991. "Whiter Than White Collar Crime: Tax, Fraud Insurance and the Management of Stigma." *British Journal of Sociology* 42:323–44.

Mitchell, Austin, Prem Sikka, and Hugh Willmot. 1998. "Sweeping It Under the Carpet: The Role of Accountancy Firms in Moneylaundering." *Accounting Organizations and Society* 23:589–607.

National White Collar Crime Center. 2006. *The 2005 National Public Survey on White Collar Crime*. Fairmont, VW: National White Collar Crime Center.

Payne, Brian K. 2003. *Incarcerating White-Collar Offenders: The Prison Experience and Beyond*. Springfield, IL: Charles C. Thomas Publisher.

Piquero, Nicole L., Stephanie Carmichael, and Alex R. Piquero. 2008. "Assessing the Perceived Seriousness of White-Collar and Street Crimes." *Crime and Delinquency* 54:291–312.

Pontell, Henry, N., Daniel Granite, Constance Keenan, and Gilbert Geis. 1985. "Seriousness of Crimes: A Survey of the Nation's Chiefs of Police." *Journal of Criminal Justice* 13:1–13.

Pontell, Henry, N., Stephen M. Rosoff, and Erich Goode. 1994. "White-Collar Crime." Pp. 345–371 in *Deviant Behavior*, edited by E. Goode. New Jersey, NY: Prentice Hall.

Quinney, Richard. 1970. *The Social Reality of Crime.* Boston, MA: Little, Brown and Company.

Reason, Tim. 2000. "Jailhouse Shock." *The Magazine for Senior Financial Executives* 16:111–18.

Rogers, Joseph W. and M. D. Buffalo. 1974. "Fighting Back: Nine Modes of Adaptation to a Deviant Label." *Social Problems* 22:101–18.

Rossi, P. H., E. Waite, C. E. Rose, and Richard, E. Berk. 1974. "The Seriousness of Crimes: Normative Structure and Individual Differences." *American Sociological Review* 39:224–37.

Schrager, L. S. and J. F. Short. 1980. "How Serious a Crime? Perceptions of Organizational and Common Crimes." Pp. 14–31 in *White-Collar Crime: Theory and Research*, G. Geis and E. Stotland. London: Sage.

Schur, Edwin M. 1971. *Labeling Deviant Behavior: Its Sociological Implications.* New York: Harper and Row.

Shapiro, Susan. 1990. "Collaring the Crime, Not the Criminal: Reconsidering the Concept of White-Collar Crime." *American Sociological Review* 55:346–65.

Sutherland, Edwin H. 1940. "White-Collar Criminality." *American Sociological Review* 5:1–12.

Sutherland, Edwin H. 1945. "Is 'White Collar Crime' Crime?" *American Sociological Review* 10:132–39.

Sutherland, Edwin H. 1983. *White-Collar Crime: The Uncut Version*. New Haven, MA: Yale University Press.

Sykes, Gresham M. and David Matza. 1957. "Techniques of Neutralization: A Theory of Delinquency." *American Sociological Review* 22:664–70.

Tillman, Robert and Henry Pontell. 1988. "Is Justice 'Collar-Blind'?: Punishing Medicaid Provider Fraud." *Criminology* 53:294–302.

Weisburd, Davis, Stanton Wheeler, Elin Waring, and Nancy Bode. 1991. *Crimes of the Middle Classes: White-Collar Offenders in the Federal Courts*. New Haven, MA: Yale University Press.

Wheeler, Stanton and Mitchell L. Rothman. 1982. "The Organization as Weapon in White-Collar Crime." *Michigan Law Review* 80:1403–26.

Willott, Sara, Christine Griffin, and Mark Torrance. 2001. "Snakes and Ladders: Upper-Middle Class Male Offenders Talk about Economic Crime." *Criminology* 39:441–66.

ARTICLE 18

Paul M. Klenowski
Clarion University of Pennsylvania

Heith Copes
University of Alabama at Birmingham

Christopher Mullins
Southern Illinois University Carbondale

Lynne Vieraitis
University of Texas at Dallas

How Men and Women Avoid the Stigma of White-Collar Crime

Qualitative research on criminal decision making gives offenders a voice in explaining their actions by asking directly why they choose to participate in criminal behavior. Whether using surveys, case studies, or semistructured interviews, the responses to questions about motivation are often interpreted literally. However, when individuals violate social norms, they often try to defend their behavior so they can maintain a positive sense of self and avoid being stigmatized by others. Perhaps one of the most well-known explanations of this process is the theory of accounts, which maintains that when individuals are questioned about their criminal behavior they justify or excuse their actions (Scott and Lyman 1968). In short, deviants of all types describe their behaviors to present their actions in the best possible light to make themselves appear acceptable to others (Sykes and Matza 1957; Scott and Lyman 1968). The definition of "acceptable" behavior, however, is partially defined by one's gender. Thus, when discussing norm violations, it is not uncommon for people to frame their actions in terms of gendered normative expectations, attitudes, and conceptions. Having to explain one's actions, criminal or legitimate, in a way that is consistent with one's own self-identity will be an innately gendered process.

In this article, we analyze data from semistructured interviews with men and women convicted of white-collar crimes. Our goal is to find out how white-collar offenders account for their crimes and to determine if gender is an important constraint on how they do so. To accomplish this goal we rely on two sources of data. The first source comes from 40 semistructured interviews with individuals federally convicted for white-collar crimes (20 men and 20 women). These individuals were convicted of a white-collar crime while in the position of fiduciary responsibility and trust. The types of crimes committed include embezzlement, false corporate reporting, false bank or credit loans, securities and exchange violations, and tax fraud. The second source of data comes from semistructured interviews with 59 federally convicted identity thieves (23 men and 36 women). By combining these two data sets we are better able to discuss the many ways that men and women account for their criminal indiscretions.

Accounting for White-Collar Crime

Analysis of the offenders' descriptions reveals that they used various accounts to make sense of and justify their crimes. Both male and female participants justified or excused their crimes in one or more of the following ways: appeal to higher loyalties, denial of injury, claim of normality, claim of entitlement, condemnation of the condemners, and the denial of responsibility. We discuss the various ways that white-collar crime offenders presented their crimes to us, with an emphasis on how their gender contributed to differences in the frequency and style of the accounts.

Appeal to Higher Loyalties

The most commonly used technique for all offenders was the appeal to higher loyalties. Those using this technique neutralized the stigma of their illegal behavior by stating they committed their crimes for the betterment of others. This neutralization was most frequently connected to assisting the respondent's family and friends. As one identity thief (Betty) explained:

> It's like I tell the judge, I regret what I had put my family through, but I don't regret at all what I did because everything that I did was for the safety of my kids. And I don't regret it. As a mother, I think you do whatever needs to [be done] to keep your kids safe.

Similarly, Abbey, another identity thief, said:

> I did it for my son. I thought if I had money and I was able to live, have a nice place to live, and not have to worry about a car payment, I could just start a new life and that life is for him. . . . I just wanted my son to be happy and loved.

Xavier, who was incarcerated for his wrongdoings in the investment industry, also exemplified this technique and provided the following explanation for his crimes:

> My parents never really supported me. They never came to any of my athletic events or school functions. I think part of me never forgot that. So, I guess when I was committing my acts, I believed that maybe I was doing some of this for my family. I wanted to have the time and the financial security to be around my family to make sure I would be there for my children, so I guess family also subconsciously played into why I did what I did. It all boils down to power and greed and decisions you make in life, in my case, my family was part of my decision making for why I did what I did.

Finally, Anissa was faced with a self-defined desperate situation due to financial, family, and health issues. Thus, she tried to hide assets from federal bankruptcy officials so that she and her husband would not lose their businesses or home. She explained that her efforts to "support" her husband were a natural and compassionate attempt to save everything he had created. When asked what her motivation was, she replied:

> I would say survival. I would say that my part in it was just being supportive of my husband. . . . I wanted to walk beside him . . . to me it is true commitment. It is showing the unity that we have.

While most claimed that their actions were to support their families, others said that they were merely trying to help support the larger community. Iris attributed her illegal activities to her desire both to succeed in business and, more importantly, to "help" those members of her community who needed her company's services. When explaining her story, she proclaimed that it was both her need to provide for her terminally ill husband and her desire to do "God's Will" that led her to her current, and in her mind unjustifiable, incarceration.

> I helped a church with a real estate issue. You know there were churches that were behind in their mortgage and they were facing foreclosure and I would help negotiate with the mortgage lender. I was doing a whole host

> of things but the more I helped one church, the more churches called. But then I realized they couldn't afford to pay me so it was very difficult to work with these churches. I took a sabbatical from working for them and began developing a business model because I felt as though this was something that God wanted me to do, use my skills to help the church.

It seems that committing crime to support families, friends, and the larger community is a common, believable excuse regardless of gender. For example, for both men and women, taking care of one's family and friends is a key aspect of gender identity, whether it is as a provider (men) or as a caregiver (women). This fact likely explains why appealing to higher loyalties was the most common technique for both men and women. Yet, while both men and women emphasized the desire to protect their families, the content of their accounts reflected their gendered roles as provider or caregiver. For example, when women used this excuse, they made it clear that the men in their family were unable to provide support and this necessitated their participation in crime. It was common for the women to introduce their primary gendered positions—motherhood—to account for their behaviors. In addition, women pointed to the lack of capable others to support them, which necessitated that they assume the responsibility to take care of the family. While men also used this technique, they did not mention why others failed in their task. Instead, they focused their accounts on themselves.

Denial of Injury

The denial of injury technique was the second most frequently offered accounts by male participants, but one of the least common used by women. When using this technique, individuals justify their actions by arguing that "nobody is getting hurt," "it's only money," or "I am only borrowing it." Bruce, who had a long history of identity theft, "borrowed" the identity of a friend. In his words:

> Sonny was a friend of mine and I was in a bind at that time. I wasn't going to steal his identity of course, I was just going to use his identity to filter some of my clean cash into a fund at that time and then I was going to take it out and go on about my business. . . . I was going to borrow [his identity] for a little while and then get the corporation going. He's going to benefit, I'm going to benefit. I'm going to get a perfect identity and then live from there.

Similarly, Isaac, the owner and operator of a construction company, was serving time for providing construction services and gifts to superintendents, school board members, and other politically connected individuals in his home state. In return, he received multimillion dollar contracts from various school districts. When asked why he did it, he replied:

> Why did I do it? I always looked at it to the point in the beginning, you know, I wasn't stealing from anybody. I didn't take that money. It wasn't for me. You gave me an 8 percent fee. Come on what you are talking about 8 percent fee on 70 million is 5.6 million dollars.

Sheila claimed that she did not feel bad about her crimes at the time because she "needed the money as bad as these people did and besides they had it sitting in their account for so long earning interest." She thought, "I'm just gonna borrow it for a minute and [I'm] gonna pay you back. I just can't do it right now so. . . . I didn't think it was really bad." White-collar offenders, like Bruce, Isaac, and Sheila, framed their actions as anything but theft. By using phrases like "I wasn't stealing" or "I was only borrowing the money," they claimed that they did not intend to cause any real harm and if given more time they would have paid their victims back in full.

Men used the denial of injury technique more frequently than women. One explanation for the variation in its frequency is that femininity in the Western world directs women to be attentive to the consequences of their behaviors on the lives and experiences of others. Maintaining networks of emotional and social support has been frequently identified as a quintessentially feminine pursuit. It is likely that denying injury has less cultural credibility when done by someone who is expected to be hyperattuned to injuries. Although male offenders used the denial of injury at a much higher frequency than did women, the nature of the stories and excuses was quite similar. That is, everyone using this account emphasized the mutual trust between themselves and their victims and the intent of paying the "borrowed" money back when they were able.

Claim of Normality

Offenders who relied on the claim of normality argued that others engaged in the same activity and that it was common business practice. These respondents claimed their crimes were justifiable because others in their respective industries were committing the same types of behaviors with impunity. A noteworthy illustration of this technique was offered by Alex who was incarcerated for creating and distributing counterfeit products.

> We had to stay up with the competition. The competition was doing it, why couldn't we? Why can't we all do it? I've been to conventions where 30 other distributors were doing it, all companies based here in the U.S. . . . We had to stay up with competition; they were doing it, why couldn't we? Tell me, why?"

Purvis echoed this sentiment about how everybody in sales deceives and steals to remain viable and successful in the industry, "This whole industry is based on lies. Manipulation of buyers is the name of the game. . . . Everybody does it." The most noteworthy example of the claim of normality from a female offender was given by Rachel who was convicted of multiple counts of bank fraud for falsifying loan applications for her husband's business and for the mortgage on their home. She stated that since everybody at some time or another fails to provide the full truth on applications, what she did was not wrong. In her words, "I mean a lot of people lie on their application for their work, for a phone, for credit cards, if they want new credit cards. I mean, it's not my fault. . . . Everybody does this, not just me."

We found that more men than women provided dialogue to support the claim of normality. Men's accounts were distinctly tied to the nature of competition in modern capitalism and often invoked images of a "dog eat dog" world where if one loses the slightest competitive edge, failure is imminent. This capitalizes on the central role that competition plays in contemporary Western masculinities. Thus, these men are asserting that they are not only engaged in behavior that is normal in their line of work, but is normal for men in general. The women who used this technique typically pointed to more generalized claims about this being normal behavior. That is, they claimed that all people, not just in their specific industry, cut corners or bend rules to get ahead.

Denial of Responsibility

Many participants claimed that they should not be held responsible for the commission of their acts because they were acting due to either social conditions or bad advice from others (i.e., boss, spouse, family) whom they trusted. Consequently, these offenders blamed the social conditions of their environment or, in some cases, people for their decision to engage in their trust-violating behavior. In one of the most notable examples of this technique, Terri, a real estate paralegal, stated that it was the actions of her corrupt boss that led to both the demise of the company and her current incarceration. She explained:

> Basically, as far as I know what I was doing was legitimate. I was putting closing packages together for somebody to do closings. . . . I had

> no clue that disbursements were being made late or that checks were bouncing. I had no clue that any of that was going on. Unfortunately the employees that did know that was going on decided that I did and they decided to tell the FBI that I knew about it. I had nothing to do with money.

All the men who used this technique referred to either their impoverished upbringing or an unhealthy and/or abusive relationship with a parent. For example, Kent referenced familial money problems growing up as a catalyst for the commission of his criminal acts.

> I always had some guilt in feeling as though that I did not get the proper upbringing at a primary level, that I did not have the proper parental guidance that I know other children had. I always had to try to make more, to work harder. No matter what I did growing up, I wanted to be number one at what I did. . . . You just have to take a close look at yourself. I see a lot of the inmates here are attention deficit, a lot of them and they need therapy, they need pills, they don't need prison. These are hyper individuals. They were hyper children, out of control. They became hyper adults, out of control. And I know I was ADD as a child and never diagnosed. I could not sit still, I couldn't sit still. I couldn't concentrate but I had a high intellect and it was all over the place. There was no focus. It was a shotgun effect rather than a rifle effect.

While the women and men denied responsibility for their crimes at comparable levels, they did so in rhetorically different ways. Men who denied their responsibility were at risk of jeopardizing masculine capital. Not being in control of their actions runs distinctly counter to a central tenet of hegemonic masculinity: being in control of yourself and the environment around you. The men presented accounts rooted in psychological-medical ways that allowed them to invoke the sick role. The active nature of masculinity presents an interpretive problem for men who want to claim they were not responsible for their actions. Traditional masculinity in the United States emphasizes being in control, if not outright dominating the environment. Drawing upon the sick role is one of the few acceptable ways for men attempting a traditional presentation of self to deny responsibility. Women, however, were culturally situated where they could safely rely upon denial of responsibility without having their gender identity challenged because they are not expected to wield large amounts of control in either their daily lives or their occupational settings.

Condemning the Condemners

It was not uncommon for the offenders to redirect the focus of their own actions toward those who condemned or judged them. The men who used this technique typically pointed out hypocrisy within the federal government as being the vehicle that allowed them to carry out their illicit activities. When asked why he chose to commit fraud, Quinton replied:

> The laws are too strict. Federal and state governments force people in this field to be criminal. Let's face it, we have to make money too—to earn a living. I would say five percent of this is my fault, 95 percent is my partner's fault, but the government acts like it plays no part, when in fact, it motivates us to do what we do. Why should we follow regulations that the government itself does not follow?

Similarly, in what came as an afterthought of his explanation as to why he engaged in his crimes, Martin expressed his view of the government and how this view contributed to his decisions.

> Oh yeah, and the thing about the Government because I said I never paid taxes on any of that money and what went through my mind quite a bit was "Fuck the Government." If we can do something under the table, let's do it. I mean that was it more so than anything else was the Government, that's how it started, that's what caused this all to start.

We found that condemnation of condemners was common among the men but rare for the women. When women did use this technique, they typically pointed out that the crooked or dishonest behaviors of state or federal agents justified their actions and allowed them to carry out their crimes with a sense of righteousness. When asked what happened to land her in prison, Carrie replied bluntly, "I believe the government is the mafia." It is likely that differences in social expectations and socialization generate different motivational patterns for men and women. For example, a study of moral reasoning showed that women are more likely to see "moral issues in terms of a network of interconnecting responsibilities," while men are more prone to see concerns in terms of "individual rights based on formal rules and guidelines" (Gilligan 1982:47). The stronger emphasis on pointing out flaws in those who are assigned the task of controlling white-collar crime by men is consistent with this idea. Also, the centrality of autonomy within hegemonic masculinity is perfectly positioned to question authority, which is why men are far likelier than women to condemn the condemners. Men are expected to challenge hierarchies to advance within them. Women have historically been expected to comply with authority, legitimate or not.

Claim of Entitlement

An equal number of men and women claimed that they were entitled to the spoils of their crimes. All thought that through the commission of their illicit acts, they were ultimately and justly receiving what was owed to them. Jason thought that both he and his father had been wronged by their country, a country that they had both admirably served through their careers in the military.

> Once again, the fact that I had served my country admirably and when I had gotten injured due to a service connected disability, they kind of pushed me out of the military and I was no longer good enough for the Federal Government. . . . I felt entitled somewhat, you know, giving my life, putting my life on the line every day for the military and then you know, having them treat my Father the way that they did. . . . I felt like I was entitled to a better lifestyle than what I had so I just started, I mean at the time it really looked like an opportunity you know, in my mind, I thought it was, it was an opportunity to do something good.

When participants were asked what had allowed them to psychologically cross that moral and legal boundary to commit their individual acts, all of those using this technique indicated that their legitimate efforts were not meeting their financial expectations. Thus, they were entitled to the extra benefits that they obtained.

When claiming they were entitled to the money, it was common for men to discuss the victims or condemners in broad, general terms. They used phrases like they "put the time in" or "I've worked hard all my life." Some men even referenced entities like the government or the military as being deserving victims or for why they were entitled to better lives. Women, on the other hand, made references to specific events when they claimed to be entitled to their spoils. They mentioned incidences where they were not given a raise or were not compensated for an increase in job duties. Felicia stated that she felt deserving of better compensation for her work as an officer manager. Because she never received what she thought she was owed, she began to steal the financial information of her boss's clients to increase her salary. When asked if she ever thought that she shouldn't do this, Felicia replied, "I would justify it and say, 'Well he didn't give me the raise that I was supposed to get, so you know I can keep it.' You know you justify it and before, like I said you wouldn't even think about it." Thus, instead of saying the "government" deserved being defrauded, they would blame their employers for mistreating them. In this sense the women in the sample justified their crimes on a more personal level than did the men.

Denial of Victim

Men and women were equally likely to lay blame for their crimes onto the victims. When framing their crimes this way, offenders must present their actions as excusable because their victims were deserving of victimization. Each participant admitted that they thought they were the real victim and that the person they were stealing from "had it coming" for the way they had treated others. In effect, they claimed that corporations and banks should not be given victim status because of their prior actions of preying on individuals. When asked if he felt guilty for his crimes, Danny explained confidently:

> I mean, like real identity theft, man I can't do that. Intentionally screw someone over—it's not right to me. So I couldn't do it. But corporations, banks, police departments, the government? Oh, yeah, let's go get 'em. Because that's the way they treat you, you know what I'm saying. If they done screwed me over, screw them! That's just the way I feel about it. I'm the eye for an eye type person. You poke out my eye, I'm going to poke out both of yours. That's just the type of person I am.

Purvis mentioned on numerous occasions how he despised and disagreed with the federal government.

> I did not want to pay taxes plain and simple. I do not believe in a Government that forces individuals to pay taxes. The downfall for me in regards to the Federal Government is when they legalized abortion. I lost all faith in our Government when they proceeded with this particular item and allowed it become legal. The Federal Government calls me a tax protestor, I agree. The tax rates are way too high. The Federal Government legalized abortion, screw the Government. I hate the IRS. I will tell you that. I had two brothers in Vietnam. When they came back they were not treated with respect. So tell me, why should I respect the Government? Tell me.

Whereas the men who used this technique pointed to generalized victims (e.g., the government), the women more often pointed to specific individuals who wronged them (e.g., employers); however, this may be because the only men who used this technique defrauded the government and not specific individuals. Those using this technique claimed that they were merely seeking a justifiable reprisal for the wrong that had been committed against them. Exemplifying this technique was Quinn, who admitted that she believed it was the lack of appreciation for her efforts as the administrative assistant that justified the commission of her devious acts.

> The family that I was working for was a close family friend. . . . They had a whole lot of money and they were not paying me a whole lot of money and I had no health insurance, I had no vacation time, I couldn't afford car insurance, they didn't hold out taxes so every April I'm getting this $5,000 tax bill and I guess I feel like I kind of snapped. At the same time I was expected to run with their crowd socially, I couldn't afford to. . . . I was shopping and doing her personal errands and being sent to these ritzy boutiques to buy $600 lampshades whereas I couldn't even afford to fix my car when the radiator broke and basically I just started using the credit cards for my own purposes and shopping and buying things that I wanted that I couldn't afford.

The demands of emphasized femininity in the Western world direct women to be attentive to the consequences of their behaviors on the lives and experiences of others. Further, there are other, more gender-legitimate, accounts that women can draw upon, like denial of responsibility or appeal to higher loyalties.

Defense of Necessity

The other technique with the greatest variation between men and women was the defense of necessity. Women were much more likely to mention this account than men. Those using this account claimed to be in a desperate situation and that their crimes were borne out of this necessity. Due to a feeling of exigency, they invoked this technique to pacify their conscience to carry out their crimes. In describing the events that led up to her getting involved in fraud, Jeannette highlighted the overwhelming pressure she was feeling from an abusive husband, mounting debt, and dependent family members. Jeannette felt as if she had no one to help dig her out of this situation.

> My parents were totally reliant on me for their transportation and stuff to doctors and I just felt like they were asking too much of me. . . . [I felt] financial pressure and just, you know, time pressure. . . . I just felt that I couldn't talk to them. . . . [My husband] was a wife abuser. He was physically abusing me along with mentally so I was trying to prove to him that I have some worth that I can do this. . . . One time when I had an overdrawn account and I was asking him to help me balance my checkbook he went ballistic. So it was a matter that you couldn't tell him anything. If you were a penny short on your checking account he would just be livid. You can't do this right, it was always I couldn't do it right. . . . Right, and my parents were dependent upon me for everything, for transportation and medical needs and stuff like that, so there was like a lot of time constraints and that contributed a lot to my marriage disintegration. I had to be there for my parents so I wasn't there for my husband so it was like a major balancing act.

Offenders using the defense of necessity technique often coupled them with the fulfilling of the caregiver role (i.e., appeal to higher loyalties). They claimed that the necessity of their crimes was heightened because of their desire to protect or shield their family from harm. Again, when describing their self-defined desperation, they almost always made mention of why others around them (usually men) were not around to offer help. There is a social burden to explain why they were in an active position about their crimes instead of a more gender-typical passive one. This differed significantly from men's descriptions of their offense as this technique was almost never mentioned by men.

Conclusion

We could take at face value the offenders' claims about what motivated them to engage in crime; however, doing so ignores the fact that the way offenders describe their motives for crime is designed to present a desired identity to others. By looking deeper we can see that by framing their crimes as a means to overcome self-defined desperate situations or to support their families, offenders can show how they were not irrational actors who are under the control of drug addiction or who lack a moral compass. Instead, given such situational demands they were merely practical actors who made reasonable, if not rational, decisions. When they tell stories about succumbing to external pressures or being faced with desperate financial situations to explain their frauds, they are painting their actions as out of character, but still consistent with expectations of others like them.

It is clear from the interviews with white-collar offenders that both men and women account for their actions, but they do so in different ways. This raises the question, why is it that women and men differ in their linguistic strategies to excuse participation in various forms of fraud? We argue that gendered expectations and the subsequent interactional construction of gendered identity play a large role in making these accounts available to some but not others. For accounts to be effective at minimizing guilt, maintaining a positive self-image, and removing stigma, they must be honored by the social audience. That is, these excuses must be believable to all parties of the interaction. It is doubtful that an excuse will be used if audiences will not identify with the excuse giver. This implies that it is more believable for women to place blame on the necessity of their crimes than it is for men. Similarly, it implies that it is easier for men to get away with denying injury, condemning the condemners, and claim the behavior is normal than it is for women.

As shown here, and elsewhere, when people engage in wrongdoings, it is common for them to justify their behavior in a way that constructs themselves as decent people, more specifically as decent women and decent men. The acceptable criteria of "decency" lie within situated, gendered expectations. In addition to these individual-level benefits, excuse making seems to have numerous social benefits for the excuse maker. Excuse making is understood by social psychologists as a way to align one's actions with social expectations. When doing so, expectations pertaining to their social positions (including gender) impact heavily how they tell their stories.

While the use of accounts to make sense of their crimes is unique neither to men nor to women, the linguistic subtleties of how and which accounts are used is gendered. Among the middle classes (from where all of the participants hailed), masculinity is associated with provision, economic success, and authority. Thus, when excusing their crimes, men often drew on themes that not only justified their actions but also reinforced, or at least not threatened, their identities as respectable men. This identity-construction feature of accounts likely explains their variable use between the sexes. Gender differences in the defense of necessity exemplified this idea. If part of what it means to be man (at least among the middle classes) is that men are competent and can succeed in the business world, then claiming that they "had" to commit the crime out of necessity would threaten their masculine identity. It signifies that they could not compete with any degree of success with others. This heavy emphasis on self-reliance is not a defining feature of femininity. Perhaps women's blocked access to advanced positions in the corporate world makes their self-described sense of desperation and necessity to commit crime more believable than men, who are presumed to have more opportunities to overcome financial troubles. This position also facilitates the use of denial of responsibility. Thus, these self presentations are less damaging to women's gender identity.

Those in the corporate world, especially men, are expected to present themselves as rational, decisive, and focused on their careers (Messerschmidt 1997; Connell 2005). Here masculinity is measured in the ability to accomplish goals, even at the expense of all else. By focusing on the goals of the business (making money and providing services) the men in the sample could justify their crimes and still maintain an image of themselves as respectable business men. By excusing their actions on the fact that what they did was common business practices among the successful in their field (e.g., claim of normality) they could frame their actions as being common and appropriate. Further, the intensely competitive nature of masculinity further validates these presentations, as by emphasizing that "everyone else" engages in such actions, *not* "keeping up" becomes a failure of masculinity in a corporate environment.

In short, our findings suggest that when discussing their illegal behaviors both male and female white-collar offenders employed rhetorical and linguistic constructions that made their indiscretions seem inoffensive, reasonable, routine, and sometimes even acceptable. By referring to various excuses and justifications, offenders attempted to construct identities as being decent, respectable people regardless of their actions. Most importantly, these accounts drew on themes that framed their actions as consistent, or at least not completely in contradiction, to gendered expectations. That is, it appears that participants were "doing gender" when accounting for their crimes (Messerschmidt 1997). Despite using many of the same accounts, they did so in subtly differing ways that were consistent with cultural expectations of their respective gender.

Discussion Questions

1. One of the central arguments of this article is that the type of account white-collar offenders use is partly determined by their position in the social structure. That is, women use different accounts than do men because of cultural assumptions about gender. What other factors might shape the types of accounts deviants use when explaining their behaviors? How do you think age or race influences the types of accounts people provide?
2. Think about a deviant act that you have engaged in. If someone asked you why you did it what would you say? What accounts (e.g., justifications and excuses) would you give to avoid being seen as a "bad" person?

References

Connell, R. W. 2005. *Masculinities.* Cambridge, UK: Polity Press.

Gilligan, Carol. 1982. *In a Different Voice: Psychological Theory and Women's Development.* Cambridge, MA: Harvard University Press.

Messerschmidt, James W. 1997. *Crime as Structured Action: Gender, Race, Class and Crime in the Making.* Thousand Oaks, CA: Sage.

Scott, Marvin B. and Stanford Lyman. 1968. "Accounts." *American Sociological Review* 33:46–62.

Sykes, Gresham and David Matza. 1957. "Techniques of Neutralization: A Theory of Delinquency." *American Sociological Review* 22:664–70.

ARTICLE 19

Anson Shupe
Indiana University-Purdue Fort Wayne

Clergy Misconduct as Elite Deviance: Assessing the Problem

The scandal of an exploitive clergyperson, or as I term the phenomenon *clergy malfeasance*, is a specific form of elite deviance. A clergyperson is a *fiduciary*, just like a physician, a therapist, an accountant, or an attorney. Fiduciaries are the professionals who have special expert knowledge to help (biblically "to minister") other less expert persons and are responsible for looking out for their best interests. Clerical fiduciaries can also be seen as *brokers* or intermediate agents between the average layperson or parishioner and the supernatural. They are especially trusted when they occupy that role. As such, when clergy elites betray the trust—the unique confidence placed in them by persons in the pews—we have a particularly painful, damaging, and egregious form of deviance.

Here I want to present a brief assessment of the clergy misconduct problem: how widespread it is, how recent our awareness of it is, and as a social problem how this deviance both transcends religious denominations and faith traditions as well as national boundaries. To anticipate the balloons or myths to be punctured, clergy malfeasance is neither exclusively Roman Catholic/Christian nor North American nor by any means strictly "modern." These conclusions are based on several decades of scholarship conducted by me and others, including therapists, journalists, and historians, using a variety of methods and sources.

The Domain of Clergy Malfeasance

Much of clergy malfeasance involves not primary deviance (i.e., one-time or rare lapses of fiduciary responsibility) but rather secondary deviance (i.e., recidivism or repeat offenses where the clergyperson must reconcile his or her actions with his or her self-concept and outward propriety (Lemert 1958). A useful sociological (*not* psychological) typology covering all such actions is that of sexual, economic, and authoritative malfeasance. Some would argue that all clergy misconduct involves a misuse of authority. True, but there are some exploitive behaviors that are strictly sexual; others purely involve deception and money; and still others involve neither sex nor money but rather authoritative pastoral abuse reaching into other areas of congregants' personal lives.

Sexual violations as a category entail the religious leaders groping, fondling, and touching intimate bodily areas of the victim; oral, vaginal, and anal penetration by the perpetrator; sexual harassment by letters, telephone calls, fax, Internet, or face-to-face; exhibiting lewd and pornographic images to parishioners; and adultery. The last may not technically be against the civil law, though it is normatively out of bounds for a pastor and thus may be considered abuse of office. (For reasons of brevity no distinction here is made among pedophilia [sex with a pre-adolescent], ephebophilia [sex with an adolescent or young teen], or sexual acts with adults.)

This defining list is blunt, which is not always how perpetrators and their defenders want it stated. For example, two grand juries over a 40-month period beginning in 2002 read through more than 30,000 pages of records from the Philadelphia Archdiocese, which was accused of repeatedly harboring abusive priests. The juries listened to over 100 witnesses (including the archbishop, Cardinal Anthony J. Bevilacqua, who testified at least 10 times). The archdiocese repeatedly referred to the sexual misconduct of priests as "inappropriate touching." The juries, exposed to such an exhaustive list of the types of sexual abuse listed earlier, did not buy such tepid euphemisms, rejecting them as transparent attempts to minimize or deny the gross, horrific damage to victims (Walsh 2006). Face-saving attempts by perpetrators to "neutralize" or downplay the harm from such scandals are legion, ranging from the darkly creative to the ludicrous. (See, for some particularly lame attempts, Shupe 2008:107–112.)

It is the sexual misconduct committed by clerics that has dominated the reports in mainstream media and undoubtedly established the stereotype in most people's minds of a philandering priest or pastor as the typical malfeasant leader in churches. Early in the breaking national Catholic scandal in the United States during the 1980s and early 1990s, a few academics, such as Jenkins (1996:67), tried to dismiss the whole uproar in symbolic interactionist terms as a "moral panic" or overblown hysterically "constructed" crisis, the result of the mass media focusing their scrutiny on only (at most) a few hundred "bad apples" or rogues in the Roman Catholic priesthood. However, this claim was quickly disproved and abandoned as that church's priest abuse scandals continued into the twenty-first century and reached epidemic proportions both in the United States and elsewhere.

Economic violations by clerics, compared to more sensational sexual deviance, in reality probably have hurt more individuals and more churches: local and regional, Protestant and Catholic, Christian and non-Christian, white and black. Violations in this economic category closely resemble aspects of both *white-collar crime* (when an individual schemes to enrich himself or herself at the expense of an organization) and *corporate crime* (where commission and/or cover-up of deviant acts enriches the individual and/or the organization as *operating policy* at the expense of duped rank-and-file members). These acts of economic misconduct include embezzlement; selling church members phony insurance policies/investment stocks/bogus funeral arrangements; pyramid scheme investments; pilfering the Sunday collection plates; secretly remortgaging church property; and collecting contributions for nonexistent missions. The perpetrators range from local pastors (some being merely greedy, others desperate to pay off gambling debts or defray the expenses of drug habits) to denominational treasurers and foreign missions administrators, steering tithes and contributions into their private savings accounts or high-living televangelists unaccountable to their viewers. (See, for example, Hadden and Shupe 1988; Shupe 2007:27–36). They often present clear examples of what criminologists term *affinity crimes*, wherein the perpetrator (if not a pastor, then a person within the same community of faith, often in an ecclesiastically high position and with leadership endorsements) uses "one's personal religious familiarity or purported background in a particular faith community to lull victims into confidence and trust" (Shupe 2007:30).

Authoritative violations include ministerial authority excessively used (often, it is suspected, for personal psychological reasons, though these are beyond the purview of this article) to enhance and demonstrate the pastor's power over his or her congregation. Some authoritarian abuse can be violent, such as enacting corporal punishment and beatings or involuntary confinement of followers, or less dramatic, such as claiming divine calling as justification to micromanage aspects of group members' lives. Examples of the latter, which are plentiful particularly in independent (nondenominational) evangelical Protestant churches (both black and white) and conservative denominations, include members needing the pastor's explicit permission to date/engage/marry or to change jobs or vote for particular political candidates; what books to read or movies to see; even whether to grow beards or cut one's hair. Part of this type of excessive use of pastoral authority has occurred in the practice called "shepherding" or "discipling," when the belief is established that a less mature Christian (definitions of *that* status vary) requires a (lay or pastoral) leader more mature in faith to guide him or her in life's decision making. The principle is not inherently deviant; religious orders often use it. But many persons —given their own lack of maturity or inexperience in power-imbalanced relationships—take it to extremes, and things get out of hand.

Parenthetically, it appears that the majority of perpetrators seem to restrict themselves to one type of abuse or another (i.e., sexual or economic) though there is also a trend for authoritatively abusive pastors occasionally to commit acts in one or more of the other categories as well.

Something Old, Something New

In 2002 many North Americans suddenly became aware that the Archdiocese of Boston, at that time the fourth largest Roman Catholic diocese in North America, was immersed in a sexual abuse scandal of tremendous scale involving a priest. Thanks to relentless reporting by news outlets, such as the *Boston Globe* (which won a Pulitzer Prize for its coverage) and numerous lawsuits brought against the archdiocese and its leader, Cardinal Bernard Law, it was learned that the Cardinal and various bishops under him had, over a period of years, hushed up laypersons' accusations against priests with money or intimidation. Meanwhile, Law and others with his knowledge had systematically reassigned those priests from parish to parish without the next parish knowing what the abusive cleric had done in his previous assignment (in Catholic circles known as "the geographic cure"). While the scandal continued to mount, Cardinal Law was deposed under oath by plaintiffs' lawyers multiple times and then suddenly recalled by the Vatican to Vatican City and appointed to a relatively symbolic position (thus escaping the very real and serious likelihood of criminal prosecution (see Shupe 2007: 1–4).

By the time the scandal was in full swing in early 2002, there were already 84 lawsuits filed against *just one* of the several dozens of accused priests and 118 suits filed against Cardinal Law. Over 275 persons claimed they had been abused over the years. Then one lawyer announced that he was representing 250 *new* clients, claiming victimization on top of many others. Estimates of the portended damages sought ran into hundreds of millions of dollars.

Much of the mass media, with an acute historical myopia, kept asking the questions "Why has this wave of scandal seemingly surfaced now?" or "Why is this type of abuse suddenly happening?" Both were essentially questions born of ignorance about pastoral abuse in this country and elsewhere.

The truth is, just to use the Roman Catholic Church (the largest religious body in the United States) as an example, such scandals are nothing new. Before 2002, when what I have referred to elsewhere as the Second Wave of post–World War II pastoral scandals in the Unites States occurred, there was an earlier wave starting the mid-1980s and continuing into the early 1990s (Shupe 2008:174–78). Historians have found a lengthy record of sexual exploitation of nuns, sisters, and male novitiates (young aspirants to holy orders and the priesthood) by older priests and church superiors stretching back over 900 years into medieval times in Europe (e.g., Ladurie 1978; Boswell 1981; Daichman 1990), both heterosexual and homosexual. Indeed, three Catholic scholars, in an extensive review of literature on the medieval Catholic Church's repeated attempts to outlaw clerical sexual immorality and exploitation, concluded that

> It is clear that the bishops were not as preoccupied with secrecy as they are today. Clergy sexual abuse of all kinds was apparently well known by the public, the clergy, and secular law enforcement authorities. There was a constant stream of disciplinary legislation from the

church but none of it was successful in changing clergy behavior. (Doyle, Sipe, and Wall, 2006:27)

We can also say with confidence, on the basis of numerous historical studies, including lengthy case analyses (such as those by Johnson and Wilentz 1994; Jenkins 2002), that half a millennium later in North America, both in the United States and Canada, there has been a steady parade of hustlers, con-men, charlatans, and lecherous clergy persons, most of them Protestant, during the eighteenth, nineteenth, and twentieth centuries. We have evidence of pastoral chicanery in modern Jewish congregations (Schwab 2002) as well as (from my own research) similar sexual/financial abuses in modern American Zen Buddhism (Shupe and Bradley 2010:161–163), television preachers (with their nonstop appeals for money), and the Church of Jesus Christ of Latter-day Saints (Shupe 2008). I have even discovered historians' notations about the abbots of Zen Buddhist monasteries in eleventh and twelfth-century Song Dynasty China notoriously enriching themselves at the expense of the organizations they managed (Schuttler 2009:40–41). (Now we call it embezzlement.)

Thus, there is nothing new about clergy malfeasance, only our periodic rediscovery of it.

How We Know What We Know

In the United States there are no "official" statistics on clergy malfeasance collected by any law enforcement agency at federal, state, or local levels. This is because the various sorts of deviance committed by clergy (battery, sexual assault, rape, embezzlement, fraud, and so forth) are not recorded in any special "religious" category but rather are folded in with secular cases. And the American Constitutional separation of church and state means that clergy have to be prosecuted in the same way as nonclergy. We have no Ministry of Religious Affairs to monitor or record clergy deviance.

Therefore, our sources of the extent of clergy malfeasance are "unofficial": journalistic reports (by far now the largest), scholarly anecdotal case investigations of individual ministries and pastors, clinical studies of client samples, denominational surveys, victim-instigated investigations, and regional surveys. Elsewhere (Shupe 2007, 2008), I have provided detailed references on each type of source. Here I offer just a few examples.

A. W. Richard Sipe, an ordained Roman Catholic priest and for 40 years a psychotherapist specializing in Catholic clergy sexual problems, performed a longitudinal analysis of his clients (with over 1,500 cases by 1990, with data continuously added into the twenty-first century). Sipe (1990, 1995, 2003) found that one-third of his priest patients were sexually active; another third had been witnesses to clergy sexual abuse; and a final third had been sexual partners, lovers, or victims with priests, nuns, seminarians, and ex-priests. Twenty percent of the active priests were engaged in heterosexual relationships and 8–10 percent were at some stage of intimacy with others. About 20 percent have been involved in homosexual relationships. About 2 percent were pedophiles; another 4 percent were practicing or inactive ephebophiles. Given that there are around 49,000 to 50,000 active priests in the United States, Sipe estimates that about 6 percent of priests are attracted to young persons.

A 2004 study of *all* Roman Catholic dioceses in the United States by the John Jay College of Criminal Justice in New York City (commissioned by the U.S. Catholic Conference of Bishops) studied 110,00 priests who had served between 1950 and 2000 and found a figure slightly lower than Sipes's estimate for sexually abusive priests. John Jay's figure was 4 percent (though higher than the Catholic Church's own earlier guesstimate of 1 percent). Noted Catholic priest-sociologist Andrew M. Greeley also estimated independently the same figure (Shupe 2008:31).

Among Protestants (from Southern Baptists to United Methodists to Pentecostals) there exist a number of smaller studies, some commissioned by denominations themselves and others conducted by independent academics, that find as little as 1 in 10 or as many as 1 in 3 Protestant pastors "crossing the line" sexually with persons in the pews (Shupe 2008:32–33).

Surprisingly no national survey by any major survey institute (such as the National Opinion Research Center) or pollster (such as George Gallup, Jr.) has yet been conducted on prevalence of victims of clergy abuses. The largest regional survey to date was conducted by the University of Texas at Arlington's Center for Social Research in 1996 (six years before the 2002 Boston mega scandal). The Dallas-Fort Worth Metroplex provided a multistage random sample of 1,067 single-dwelling householders narrating their own abuse experience or about the experiences of persons close to them (family members, friends, coworkers) concerning pastoral abuse of any kind. Five percent of the respondents reported knowing someone firsthand who had been abused (sexually, financially, or otherwise) and another 3 percent reported having personally experienced mental, economic, or physical abuse. Stacey, Shupe, and Darnell (2000) relate that respondents were given the opportunity to provide details, and they did—graphically.

In the 1990s, one landmark government investigation occurred in Canada, demanded by victims who are *aboriginals* (the Canadian term) or *Native North Americans* or (in their own term) *First Nations people*. In 1820 Canadian federal authorities, in partnership with four Christian denominations (the Roman Catholic Church, the Presbyterian Church of Canada, the Anglican Church of Canada, and a consortium of conservative Protestant groups called the United Church of Canada), created "Indian residential schools" for First Nation youths to (purportedly) "assimilate" them into white society. During the nineteenth and twentieth centuries, over one hundred thousand First Nations children were forcibly removed from their homes by state authorities and forbidden to contact their families. They were placed in institutions variously described as "homes," "schools," "dormitories," and "campuses" run exclusively by white sectarians. The schools were blatant attempts at cultural genocide, seeking to expunge native languages and cultures, and in many cases the schools became virtual prison campuses that provided minimal education but plenty of forced labor, harsh discipline bordering on torture, and sexual and physical abuse by clergy, all colored with the objective of "Christianizing" the children.

The last residential school was not closed until 1996. During the past two decades, such residential schools and the Canadian government have received almost ten thousands complaints and lawsuits claiming abuse. Some years ago, some experts believed it could cost $1.26 billion overall to settle the lawsuits by 2002, but that was optimistic thinking a decade ago—the figures have jumped dramatically since (Shupe 2007:19–22).

Finally, the problem of exploitation of parishioners by clergy extends far beyond the borders of the North American continent. There are a variety of sources to inform us of this fact, such as associated news services worldwide and local/regional newspaper reports (from the *New York Times* and *Boston Globe* to the more modest *Fort Wayne Journal Gazette*) and television news magazine reports (such as *60 Minutes, 20/20,* and *Prime Time*, not to mention numerous cable news outlets). Other excellent sources are the various Web sites (and publications) of watchdog victims' advocacy groups, such as SCAR (Survivors of Clergy Abuse Reachout), SNAP (Survivors Network of Those Abused by Priests), Survivors Connection, the Linkup, and Voice of the Faithful. These organizations have become literal clearinghouses of information for self-help, referrals to mental health and legal specialists, and news of upcoming local/

regional/national/international meetings. And (more important for our purposes) these sources catalogue a rich trove of bibliographic materials including city-by-city/state-by-state national and foreign reports of scandals taken from the world's mass media, not only of Roman Catholic and Protestant leaders but also of those from other faiths.

Thus we know of revelations of clergy abuse incidents and prolonged scandals in countries such as Australia (including Adelaide, Brisbane, Melbourne, Perth, and Sidney), Austria, Canada, England, France, Germany, Iceland, India, Israel, Italy, Mexico, Nepal, the Netherlands, Northern Ireland, the Philippines, Poland, Scandinavian countries, most nations in South America, Switzerland, Taiwan, Trinidad, the United Kingdom and Scotland, even Vatican City as well as Rome.

As a result, the world knew that when Pope Benedict XVI visited the United Kingdom in 2010 he was greeted not only by warm throngs of Catholics but also by protesters from London to Glasgow to Edinburgh crying with placards and shouts condemning that he had not acted decisively to remove priests who molested children. In London alone 20,000 protesters rallied to decry the pope's stances on AIDS, homosexuality, and most of all clergy pedophilia (Winfield and Simpson 2010). In Dublin, Ireland, the government was investigating the Catholic Church's apparent decade-long policy of sheltering and covering up child-abusing priests, demanding more than 60,000 previously secret Church files (Pogatchnik 2010) including those of 18 religious orders implicated in as many as 14,000 cases of victimization. Almost 4 percent of Dublin's priests (a figure similar to that of the John Jay College of Criminal Justice's study in the United States) were suspected of abusing children in that city's earlier 2005 scandals (Pogatchnik 2006). And an earlier wave of Irish priest sex abuse scandals in the 1990s even brought down the government administration (Sipe 1998).

Thus the domain of clergy malfeasance in time and geographic space is immense, sparing no continent, few countries, and virtually no major religious tradition. The basic question is "Why?", given that most religions teach love, compassion, and support of the weak, all within a family model of trust.

How Churches Can Become Criminogenic

In order to make sense of the undeniable fact that clergy misconduct is actually a constant, not a variable, in the lives of some church members, we have to rethink what the institution is. The following is a simple syllogism, or axiomatic *power* model, of churches that may run contrary to how most persons, particularly devout believers, like to think of them. But it offers a helpful approach, I believe, to understanding how so many churches can become criminogenic. The notion of criminogenesis does not try to absolve organizations that at times promote harm by simply waving away predatory deviant leaders as "a few bad apples in the barrel." Rather, it seeks the seeds of deviance in the very power structure and set-up of these organizations. It is a supremely sociological idea, for sociology does not really explain causes but only clarifies facilitating conditions that increase probabilities.

First, and most important to this model, religious groups and sacred institutions can be understood as *hierarchies of unequal power*.

Second and as a consequence of the first assumption, those in elite positions in churches possess a greater power of moral persuasion (at a minimum) and in some institutions even the theological authority (at a maximum) to deny laity access to privileges of membership (such as sacraments), including the ultimate spiritual trump card of withholding the hope of salvation (however defined).

Third, churches represent a unique type of hierarchy, unlike many secular counterparts, in that those occupying lower statuses in religious organizations are encouraged and perhaps even taught *to trust* or believe in the benevolent intentions, fiduciary reliability, selfless motives, and spiritual insights and wisdom of their leaders, *sometimes without reservation,* thus increasing vulnerability. Churches are trusted hierarchies.

Fourth, and the most significant axiom for victims, specially trusted hierarchies, provide special "opportunity structures" for potential exploitation, abuse, and mismanagement of church organization resources (particularly finances and members) by leaders for their own purposes.

Fifth, the nature of trusted hierarchies systematically (i.e., in predictable, even inevitable ways) provides opportunities and rationales for such deviance by their leaders.

Therefore, the religious institution, which provides a wide array of opportunities for leader deviance more so than do other hierarchical institutions in society, is so often thoroughly trusted by rank-and-file members, thus rendering them emotionally and spiritually at risk. Like this fact or not, think it cynical if you will, unless congregants bring a certain wariness to any relationship with elites within a church as they would in the secular world outside, they will perpetuate the criminogenic potential of clergy. That is the lesson underlying the current scandals.

Discussion Questions

1. It has been reliably established that sexual, economic, and other abuses by clergy are not restricted to any one faith or country. What they seem to have in common, as people experienced in having been betrayed concur, is the degree of trust misplaced in overbearing leaders by followers/believers. Is this *inherently* a problem in religion?
2. Is power (the ability to influence people) admittedly a tragic phenomenon? That means you cannot trust your clergyman anymore than you can trust your banker or accountant. Is this cynical or realistic?

References

Boswell, John. 1981. *Christianity, Social Tolerance, and Homosexuality*. Chicago: IL: University of Chicago Press.

Daichman, Graciela. 1990. "Misconduct in the Medieval Nunnery: Fact, Not Fiction." Pp. 97–117 in *That Gentle Strength: Historical Perspectives on Women in Christianity*, edited by Lynda L. Coon, Katherine J. Haldine, and Elisabeth W. Sommer. Charlottesville, VA: University of Virginia Press.

Doyle, Thomas P., A. W. R. Sipe, and Patrick J. Wall. 2006. *Sex, Priests, and Secret Codes*. Los Angeles: Volt Press.

Hadden, Jeffrey K. and Anson Shupe. 1988. *Televanglism: Power and Politics on God's Frontier*. New York: Henry Holt.

Jenkins, Philip. 1996. *Pedophiles and Priests: Anatomy of a Contemporary Crisis*. New York: Oxford University Press.

Jenkins, Philip. 2002. *Mystics and Messiahs: Cults and New Religions in American History*. New York: Cambridge University Press.

Johnson, Paul E. and Sean Wilentz. 1994. *The Kingdom of Mattias*. New York: Oxford University Press.

Ladurie, Emmanuel Leroy, 1978. *Montaillou: The Promised Land of Error*. Translated by Barbara Bray. New York: Braziller.

Lemert, Edwin A. 1958. "The Behavior of the Systematic Check Forger." *Social Problems* 6 (Fall):141–49.

Pogatchnik, Shawn. 2006. "102 Dublin Priests Suspected of Abuse!" *Associated Press*, March 11, 2006.

Pogatchnik, Shawn. 2010. "Irish Priest Abuse Is Called Systemic." *Associated Press*, April 27, 2009.

Schlutter, Merton. 2009. *How Zen Became Zen*. Honalulu, HI: University of Hawaii Press, Kuroda Institute.

Schwab, Charlotte Rolnick. 2002. *Sex, Lies, and Rabbis: Breaking a Sacred Trust*. Bloomington, IN: 1st Books Library.

Shupe, Anson. ed. 1998. *Wolves within the Fold: Religious Leadership and Abuses of Power*. New Brunswick, NJ: Rutgers University Press.

Shupe, Anson. 2007. *Spoils of the Kingdom: Clergy Misconduct and Social Exchange in American Religion*. Champaign, IL: University of Illinois Press.

Shupe, Anson. 2008. *Rogue Clerics: The Social Problem of Clergy Deviance.* New Brunswick, NJ: Transaction.

Shupe, Anson, and Christopher S. Bradley. 2010. *Self, Attitudes and Emotion Work: Western Social Psychology and Eastern Zen Buddhism Confront Each Other.* New Brunswick, NJ: Transaction.

Sipe, A. W. Richard. 1990. *A Secret World: Sexuality and the Search for Celibacy.* New York: Brunner/Mazel.

Sipe, A. W. Richard. 1995. *Sex, Priests, and Power: Anatomy of a Crisis.* New York: Brunner/Mazel.

Sipe, A. W. Richard. 1998. "Clergy Abuse in Ireland." Pp. 133–51 in *Wolves within the Fold: Religious Leadership and Abuses of Power*, edited by Anson Shupe. New Brunswick, NJ: Rutgers University Press.

Sipe, A. W. Richard. 2003. *Celibacy in Crisis: A Secret World Revisited.* New York: Brunner-Routledge.

Stacey, William A., Anson Shupe, and Susan E. Darnell. 2000. "How Much Clergy Malfeasance Is Really Out There? A Victimization Survey of Prevalence and Perception." Pp. 187–213 in *Bad Pastors: Clergy Misconduct in Modern America*, edited by Anson Shupe, William A. Stacey, and Susan E. Darnell. New York: New York University Press.

Walsh, Andrew. 2006. "No Peace for the Church." *Religion in the News* 8(3):17–19, 24.

Winfield, Nicole and Victor L. Simpson. 2010. "Thousands Protest Pope as He Talks to Victims of Abuse." *Associated Press*, September 18, 2010.

PART EIGHT

Medical Deviance

Can you imagine being penalized for being overweight? This is what airline companies do when they charge obese passengers for two seats if they cannot fit into one seat. Some argue that this act is punitive. It is estimated that over one-third of Americans are obese, which makes this condition not uncommon. Should airline companies adjust to "growing" America? Or should Americans pay the price for a condition that has been medically diagnosed? When one is different, even with medical justification, it does not guarantee protection from the stigmatizing attitudes of society.[1]

In the first article, "Diagnosis as Stigma Management: The Case of Highly Stigmatized Gastrointestinal Symptoms of Celiac Disease," Denise Copleton discusses individuals who live with Celiac disease. They are stigmatized due to the symptoms associated with the disease such as chronic diarrhea, urgent bowel movements, loose and floating stool, undigested food in the stool, and foul-smelling gas. In the second article, "Care Giving without the Care: The Deviant Treatment of Residents in Nursing Homes," Jason Ulsperger and J. David Knottnerus discuss the different types of mistreatment the elderly experience in nursing homes. This part concludes with "The Stigma of Obesity," by Erich Goode who explains why the obese are stigmatized. He discusses how they are stereotyped by members of the public and medical profession.

Note

1. *CBS News*. 2009. "Airlines Put Squeeze on Fat Fliers." May 27. Retrieved June 17, 2011 (http://www.cbsnews.com/stories/2009/04/17/earlyshow/living/travel/main4952134.shtml).

Denise A. Copelton
The College at Brockport, State University of New York

Diagnosis as Stigma Management: The Case of Highly Stigmatized Gastrointestinal Symptoms of Celiac Disease

Introduction

Celiac disease (CD) is an autoimmune disorder triggered by gluten, a protein in wheat, barley, and rye. When persons with CD consume gluten, the autoimmune response damages villi in the small intestine, preventing proper absorption of vitamins and minerals and increasing the risk for nutritional disorders (e.g., malnutrition, osteoporosis, iron-deficiency anemia), gastrointestinal (GI) cancers, and other autoimmune diseases. "Classic" symptoms are gastrointestinal and include chronic diarrhea, flatulence, and loose or floating stool (Green and Jabri 2006). Because the autoimmune reaction can affect any bodily system, symptoms are highly variable and some never develop classic GI distress (Green and Jabri 2006). CD is genetic, so it often runs in families (Green and Jones 2006).

Because of symptom variability, lack of knowledge about the disease, and a misperception that CD is a rare childhood disorder, physicians often misdiagnose CD as psychosomatic illness or irritable bowel syndrome (IBS), especially among adults (Green and Jabri 2006). Consequently, only 10 percent of the estimated 1 percent of the U.S. population with CD is medically diagnosed (Fasano et al. 2003).

The only treatment is lifelong adherence to a gluten-free (GF) diet, which entails eliminating obvious glutenous foods like bread, cereal, and pasta, and foods with hidden gluten, including many processed foods (e.g., soups, sauces, and salad dressings). Strict dietary adherence is necessary because even miniscule amounts of gluten can trigger an autoimmune response (Green and Jones 2006).

This article investigates the role of stigma in medical diagnosis. For highly stigmatized illnesses like sexually transmitted diseases (Brandt 1987; Weitz 1990; Herek 1999; Nack 2008), mental health disorders (Link, Mirotznik, and Cullen 1991; Karp 1996; Barney et al. 2006), and GI and urinary problems (Madoff et al. 2004; Sheldon and Caldwell 2004; Aitola et al. 2010), stigma is often a barrier to medical diagnosis and treatment adherence. However, the experience of stigmatizing symptoms may also encourage persons to seek treatment to relieve symptoms and manage symptom stigma. Drawing on interviews and field work with four CD support groups, I explore how highly stigmatized GI symptoms facilitate medical diagnosis.

Stigma, Stigmatized Illnesses, and Gastrointestinal Stigma

Stigma is "an attribute that is deeply discrediting" that spoils the identity of its bearer (Goffman 1963:3). Stigma results when others impute negative qualities to those with some differentiating trait. Goffman (1963) identified three characteristics that tend to be stigmatizing: blemishes of individual character, abominations of the body, and tribal stigmas signifying membership in particular social groups. Blemishes of individual character lead others to question one's moral fiber. Because people tend to "impute a wide range of imperfections on the basis of the original one," abominations of the body, such as a scar or physical disability, may lead others to question the competence or character of the stigmatized (Goffman 1963:5). Tribal stigmas such as membership in a minority group, a subculture, or an illness or disease group lead to negative stereotyping based on the group affiliation (Tewksbury and McGaughey 1997; Nack 2008). Illnesses most likely to elicit stigma are those for which the sufferer is believed to be partly responsible; are degenerative and/or incurable; are contagious; and are readily apparent to others, thereby disturbing normal social interaction (Weitz 1990; Herek 1999).

The *perception* of stigma is an especially salient issue even in the absence of discriminatory treatment, a point captured by the distinction between enacted and felt stigma. *Enacted stigma* refers to actual instances of differential treatment based on stereotypic negative associations, while *felt stigma* includes "fear of enacted stigma" and shameful feelings resulting from it (Scambler and Hopkins 1986:33). Felt stigma can occur independent of enacted stigma and may precede it. Persons with epilepsy, for example, often define the condition as stigmatizing despite never having experienced discriminatory treatment (Schneider and Conrad 1980; Scambler and Hopkins 1986).

Given the strong societal norms governing bodily outputs, especially fecal matters, illnesses with GI symptoms are highly stigmatized. Weinberg and Williams (2005) examined societal norms regulating fecal matters and the strategies people employ to uphold these norms. Norms of proximity require that people create distance between themselves and their fecal outputs. Embarrassment results when norms are breached, as when fecal matter does not flush completely down the toilet, adheres to one's clothing, or is heard or smelled by others. When an individual cannot control bodily emissions, others may question his or her status "as a mature and poised adult" (Weinberg and Williams 2005:320), leading to felt stigma in the form of embarrassment and shame and enacted stigma in the form of discriminatory treatment.

Stigma Management

Individuals with stigmatizing characteristics use a variety of tactics to lessen stigma or avoid it altogether. The discredited, which includes those with readily apparent and visible forms of stigma, attempt to carefully manage the impressions that others form of them. The discreditable, which includes persons with invisible forms of stigma, attempt to manage information about themselves and their stigmatizing traits (Goffman 1963; Scambler 2009). Strategies for managing disease-related stigma include restricting activities or socially withdrawing (Åsbring and Närvänen 2002; Madoff et al. 2004; Aitola et al. 2010); concealing the illness and its symptoms (Weitz 1990; Åsbring and Närvänen 2002); controlling information about their illness by informing some, but withholding information from others (Weitz 1990; Åsbring and Närvänen 2002); educating people about the disease (Weitz 1990; Link et al. 1991; Åsbring and Närvänen 2002; Taub, McLorg, and Fanflik 2004; Heijnders and Van Der Meij 2006); attempting to deflect stigma through kindness and humor (Taub et al. 2004); demonstrating competence in other endeavors to prove that the condition is not limiting (Weitz 1990; Taub et al. 2004), and using disidentifiers, statements or behaviors that contradict negative stereotypical associations with the stigmatizing condition (Goffman 1963; Broom and Whittaker 2004; Taub et al. 2004). Finally, though claiming a disability status might actually call attention to and heighten the stigmatizing condition, it also excuses or explains the stigmatizing attribute (Taub et al. 2004).

While some GI symptoms are visible (i.e., stool that will not flush, or bowel "accidents"), others, though not visible, are potentially detectable through sound or smell (e.g., belching, flatulence, diarrhea) (Weinberg and Williams 2005). Thus, those with GI disorders must manage impressions (in the case of detected symptoms) and information (in the case of undetected ones). However, effectively managing symptoms by obtaining a medical diagnosis and following prescribed treatments may enable people to avoid GI stigma altogether.

Stigma and Medical Diagnosis

Whether an individual seeks medical care depends on the severity, visibility, frequency, and perceived seriousness of symptoms, the extent to which they disrupt normal activities, and how the individual experiencing symptoms evaluates them (Mechanic 1968). If symptoms are frequent, worrisome, and intrusive of everyday activities, and are perceived to be an indication of disease, the individual is likely to initiate medical care to seek a diagnosis and treatment. Diagnosis socially constructs medical complaints as real, thereby legitimizing symptoms, explaining physical suffering, and excusing departure from normal social roles. Moreover, diagnosis is often a gateway to medical treatment and effective symptom management (Brown 1995).

Most research on stigmatized illnesses examines the stigma *resulting from* rather than *preceding* diagnosis (Schneider and Conrad 1980; Weitz 1990; Herek 1999; Nack 2008; Olsson et al. 2009). Research on adolescents with CD focuses on postdiagnostic stigma resulting from the GFD, while virtually ignoring symptom stigma (Olsson et al. 2009). Other scholars examine stigma as a barrier to effective medical treatment and follow-up (Madoff et al. 2004; Sheldon and Caldwell 2004; Barney et al. 2006; Aitola et al. 2010). However, it is reasonable to expect that individuals experiencing highly stigmatizing GI symptoms such as fecal incontinence, chronic diarrhea, and flatulence would both want and need to control symptoms to maintain a normal, unrestricted lifestyle and avoid embarrassment and stigma. Thus, symptomatic persons may be highly motivated to seek a medical diagnosis as a gateway to effective treatment.

I examine how stigmatizing symptoms *facilitate* diagnosis of CD by motivating respondents to initiate medical care. Given the high rates of misdiagnosis, respondents with severe GI symptoms used a variety of stigma management strategies to manage symptoms while seeking a medical diagnosis and effective treatment. Unlike those with non-GI symptoms, respondents with severe GI symptoms were more likely to welcome the diagnosis and the strict dietary treatment it entailed, which they saw as a gateway to a normal life. Symptom stigma therefore played a primary role in both facilitating diagnosis and motivating persons to comply with diet.

Methods

This article is based on a large ethnographic study of the social experience of living with CD. To ensure confidentiality, I assign pseudonyms to all respondents and organizations. I conducted field research with four celiac support groups in the Northeastern United States, attending monthly meetings, taking detailed notes before, during, and after gatherings, and speaking informally with members. I participated in education seminars, attended regional lectures, and participated in four annual education conferences of two national celiac support groups, speaking informally with celiac experts and persons with CD in attendance.

I also conducted 80 in-depth interviews (face-to-face and phone) with persons with CD and non-celiac gluten intolerance or NCGI (n = 71), their spouses (n = 4), and parents of children and young adults with CD (n = 5). Of the respondents with CD or NCGI, 15 were men and 56 were women; 2 identified as Hispanic, while the remainder identified as white. Participants ranged from 19 to 79 years old, while their educational attainment spanned from completing high school to a PhD. Interviews averaged 90 minutes, were recorded, and fully transcribed.

I analyzed the ethnographic data using a grounded theory approach (Strauss and Corbin 1998), paying attention to symptom stigma, motivation for seeking diagnosis, and post-diagnosis stigma. This permitted me to examine in detail the complex role of stigma in the social process of diagnosis. The following sections describe patients' experience of symptoms and the role of stigma in their quest for a diagnosis.

Findings

The stigmatizing nature of GI symptoms (especially diarrhea and gas) and their negative impact on social interactions motivated many interviewees to engage in a variety of stigma management strategies. Generally, respondents with more severe GI symptoms were more likely to report symptom stigma than those with less severe or non-GI symptoms. Respondents with less severe or non-GI symptoms were more likely to be distressed by the diagnosis due to the strict dietary change it required, while those with severe GI symptoms were relieved that an effective treatment existed.

Symptom Stigma

Gastrointestinal symptoms were both inconvenient and highly stigmatizing. Some of the severe GI symptoms respondents reported included urgent bowel movements, uncontrollable diarrhea, persistent foul-smelling gas, undigested food in the stool, loose and floating stool, belching, vomiting, and abdominal pain. Virginia's GI problems were so severe that she developed diarrhea within 20 minutes every time she ate. Yvonne recalled, "I was moving my bowels regularly, but would not digest whole pieces of food. So after you flush, things would remain in the toilet."

Classic GI symptoms were especially inconvenient because they often intruded on normal activities. Leslie found her commute to work problematic given her chronic diarrhea and severe stomach pains, which necessitated stopping frequently to use a restroom: "There is nothing like trying to get off the Beltway in time to use the bathroom. It was just very inconvenient." Yvonne recalled long car trips with her family and needing quickly to find a public bathroom given the urgency of her bowel movements: "I had to go to the bathroom urgently and told my husband, 'Pull over, pull over,' but we couldn't find a place for me to go, so I went to a gas station. It was horrible."

Even when a bathroom was readily accessible, it did not always afford the privacy needed to deal with symptoms in a socially approved manner. Audrey, a teacher, describes her difficulty finding privacy at work: "I was in a school where there were 150 teachers and just a handful of males, a typical public school situation. And we had two women's teacher's bathrooms so it was, you know, not a very comfortable thing to deal with. There wasn't much privacy." As Weinberg and Williams (2005) note, stigma results from violations of defecation norms, including proximity norms that dictate that others should not see, smell, or hear one's fecal matters. In a crowded women's bathroom, upholding proximity norms becomes challenging and may require multiple flushes to dispense with stool completely, use of air fresheners, and other techniques to cover gas sounds and odors and thereby avoid stigma.

Greg reported experiencing multiple stigmatizing GI symptoms related to his undiagnosed CD and believed other people thought he burped and passed gas on purpose "just to annoy them." He found belching in public "preferable to breaking wind," since most "view gas as a product of evil behavior, not a neutral symptom." Most respondents agreed that when GI symptoms occurred in social settings, others questioned their moral character and judgment, sometimes imparting willfulness to their norm violations and assigning blame.

Stigma Management

Because symptoms intrude on normal activities and cause stigma, respondents with severe GI symptoms attempted to manage symptoms and thereby manage symptom stigma. Many tried to restructure their activities around access to a bathroom or eating times. Audrey recalled,

> I always made sure I was someplace where I knew there was a bathroom, and I would try and schedule appointments for later in the morning. I was always cautious about social things, like I didn't like to go out on boats or anywhere you were away from the bathroom, that type of thing. I was just always unsure of what was going to happen, because [the diarrhea] could just hit.

Greg tried to manage his symptoms through "scheduled eating," which entailed eating only when he could socially isolate himself for one to two hours afterward, when his flatulence would be the worst. Because it was an enclosed space, riding the subway was "a problem" so Greg elected to ride his bicycle whenever possible. He also adjusted shopping times to avoid long lines and the ire of store employees so he "wouldn't be perceived by management as a problem for that store and its customers."

However, respondents were not always able to restructure activities, especially work activities, to limit the visibility, odor, and intrusiveness of their GI symptoms. Virginia tried to manage her gas and felt powerless when symptoms persisted. When she had to pass gas in social settings, she would "run off in a different direction" to avoid being discovered. Similarly, Greg explained, "I try to pull off interactions without being detected and there's all sorts of techniques including mixing in with crowds so people don't know who's doing it (laughs)." Virginia and Greg attempted to manage both information and impressions by concealing the act of passing gas in social settings. In effect, passing gas required passing as normal so others would not suspect that they were responsible for the foul odor. This might entail quickly leaving the scene, as Virginia did, or blending into the crowd, as Greg did.

When symptoms could not be managed effectively and social interactions could not be rescheduled to avoid symptoms, respondents isolated themselves physically and socially. Virginia's strategy was common:

> I'd make up an excuse, you know. I just could not go because I never knew when I would pass gas. . . . And I ate as little as possible, just trying to participate, but it was absolutely horrible so, you know, you just, you pull back. You're embarrassed up to your eyebrows all the time. I just felt like oh god, you know, what can I do? I was doing everything I could prior to the diagnosis.

Virginia's frustration is plainly evident. She describes social avoidance as a strategy of last resort, noting that she "was doing everything [she] could," including not eating. It was only when other symptom management techniques did not work that she turned reluctantly to social isolation and withdrawal to minimize stigma and feelings of shame.

Negative Consequences of Symptom Stigma

When GI symptoms could not be avoided, isolation or avoidance was not possible, and attempts to avoid detection failed, both felt and enacted stigma resulted. Jessica's chronic foul-smelling gas affected her work as a lab technician in a bloodmobile, a small van used for mobile blood collections. "The flatulence was so bad that I used to step outside the truck and inhale because I was so foul smelling." Jessica felt guilty for exposing two coworkers, who shared her confined workspace, to her noxious gas, especially because they were "too polite to object." Though Jessica's coworkers spared her from enacted stigma, her internalization of societal norms against passing gas in public led her to feel stigmatized nonetheless.

Virginia described a similar incident when friends were helping paint her house:

> I couldn't stay in the house with anybody because I would pass gas. And it wasn't that I had *a lot* of gas. It was just a little gas, but the odor was so bad that—I mean, it was so

> embarrassing and everybody around me almost died. I just couldn't stay in the house with them. I mean, it was horrible, and I didn't blame anybody. I understood totally what was going on.

Virginia was mortified that her gas was so malodorous. Given that her friends were helping her with a large and burdensome household chore, she felt especially guilty for making this work even more difficult by contaminating the work environment with her offensive gas. That her friends "almost died" from the stench led her to give up on the work of painting the house so her friends could finish in relative comfort. She both understands their reaction and attempts to accommodate them.

Greg reported suffering harassment at work because of his symptoms and believes he was passed over for promotions as a result of his chronic flatulence. However, he found himself in a no-win situation: "I couldn't get angry because that would have been reason for being dismissed." Instead, he tried to deflect stigma by responding with humor and attempting "to make friends as much as possible and be alert to people around me." Like Virginia, Greg justified negative and stigmatizing treatment from others, noting, "I was stinking up the office and it's perfectly legitimate for management to try to get that problem out." Greg also recalled "rough treatment with the razor" from a barber who presumably did not appreciate his uncontrollable gas, which was "stinking up" the barbershop.

Virginia spoke for many when she explained, "You're a social outcast when you have all these horrible GI things going on and it's like you're, you're just plain ignorant that you don't know any better, and I had no control over it. It's very demoralizing." Attributions of ignorance, moral turpitude, and poor manners abounded in respondents' recollections of social interactions with nonstigmatized others. Stigma, negative stereotypes, and discriminatory treatment motivated those with severe GI symptoms to initiate medical care in search of a diagnosis and effective cure.

Symptom Stigma as Motivation for Medical Diagnosis

Respondents with classic GI symptoms were highly motivated to seek medical care in search of a diagnosis and treatment. While the severity, frequency, and intrusiveness of symptoms factored heavily in their rationale for consulting a doctor, the stigma associated with symptoms was also a major factor. While the very nature of some symptoms made them intrusive (e.g., diarrhea, urgency of bowel movements, vomiting, abdominal pain), other symptoms intruded on normal activities solely because they were so highly stigmatizing (e.g., flatulence, belching). Greg explained, "I couldn't really function as a member of society unless I could control what was going on inside my gut." While Greg's doctor described his symptoms as "medically trivial," Greg found them "socially and financially catastrophic." Similarly, Virginia recalled: "I knew that I had to get rid of the symptoms just so I could go out and live."

As a result, respondents spent much time and effort (sometimes over 20 years) consulting a variety of doctors in search of a concrete diagnosis and effective treatment and undergoing a multitude of tests. The majority of respondents with classic GI symptoms were diagnosed with other conditions prior to receiving a diagnosis of CD. The most common diagnoses were IBS, gastroesophageal reflux disease (GERD or "acid reflux"), Crohn's disease, and "sour stomach," but sometimes doctors attributed symptoms to stress or other psychological issues. Ruth was initially diagnosed with IBS and not tested for CD, though CD was known to run in her family. Gwen had been diagnosed with IBS long before her doctor tested her for celiac. However, the IBS diagnosis and standard treatments did not alleviate her symptoms and she continued to search for a more definitive diagnosis and effective treatment: "After everything is ruled out, I may be content with [the IBS] diagnosis, but usually it's just a name when they don't know the real diagnosis. . . . Something is wrong and they just can't pinpoint it and so they just treat the symptoms instead of the disease." Others called IBS a "throw away" diagnosis, one that doctors applied when no other diagnosis seemed appropriate, and most agreed that doctors preferred to treat the symptoms instead of locating and treating the underlying cause.

Given that the diagnosis was often incorrect, it is not surprising that the prescribed treatments did not alleviate respondents' suffering. Most were prescribed anti-diarrheal medications, directed to take over-the-counter remedies for their symptoms (Imodium, Mylanta, Pepto-Bismal, etc.), or instructed to increase their intake of dietary fiber. Ironically, eating more fiber often entailed consuming more gluten through whole wheat foods, which tended to exacerbate GI symptoms. Charles recalled, "Wanting to help, my wife started baking me these bran muffins, and the more of the bran muffins I ate, the sicker I got."

Respondents found the persistence of symptoms frustrating, in part because they were desperate to control symptoms and believed medical practitioners should be able to provide solutions. Virginia had previously been diagnosed with GERD and pernicious anemia, but none of the prescribed treatments alleviated her symptoms:

> The first time I went to a GI person I was having a lot of bloating and gas, huge floating stools, and flatulence—obnoxious flatulence, terrible odor! And the doctor's words were, 'I can't do anything about the gas.' All these doctors can't understand why you're so upset with them that they just think you're whacky.

Virginia is exasperated and upset that her doctor cannot give her the solutions she seeks. Given the difficulty of managing symptoms and symptom stigma, and the persistence of unsuccessful remedies even after preliminary diagnoses, respondents with severe GI symptoms were happy to finally receive a diagnosis of CD and, with it, the ability to manage symptoms and symptom stigma.

Responses to CD Diagnosis

Until now we have focused on respondents with classic GI symptoms. However, not all persons with CD experience the classic GI distress. Some have non-GI symptoms, which is not to say that they were totally asymptomatic. Common non-GI symptoms included anemia, chronic fatigue, osteopenia/osteoporosis (especially in premenopausal women), joint problems, unexplained weight loss, and vitamin and mineral deficiencies, among others. For these respondents, diagnosis might result from a routine checkup, or it might be the unexpected result of medical care for what seemed initially to be a completely unrelated problem. A few were diagnosed following the diagnosis of a family member. These respondents were more likely than those with classic GI symptoms to be distressed at diagnosis. Lacking classic symptoms, they expected a different diagnosis and resented the dietary changes CD necessitated.

Amy, whose mother had been diagnosed with CD a few weeks before she was tested, was completely surprised by her own diagnosis: "It was really bizarre because they had no idea about it being an issue with me at all. I was probably last on the list actually of the family suspects of celiac disease." Her sister, by contrast, who doctors suspected would have CD, tested negative. Amy recalled, "It was kind of ridiculous because they had thought that my sister would have it if either of us, because she's very petite and she just had a lot of the same traits that my mom had."

Marie described her diagnosis as "accidental." Upon turning 40, she decided it was time to "get a good, full physical with blood work and everything." When her blood work showed signs of iron-deficiency anemia, her general practitioner pursued additional testing to determine the source. "Finally he wanted to do a full endoscopy and colonoscopy, which I tried to talk him out of only because I felt fine. I wasn't sickly. I felt fine." When the results of her endoscopy with biopsy revealed that she had CD, Marie was shocked. She had never heard of CD prior to being diagnosed with it. She immediately began researching it on the Internet: "I'm reading about it and I'm going oh, god. Never going to have a cookie again. Never going to have cake again. No pancakes, no pizza (sighs)." Marie's reaction was typical of those with non-GI symptoms. She was dismayed at the thought of forever changing her diet because of an unfamiliar disease for which she exhibited no obvious outward symptoms.

By contrast, respondents with classic GI symptoms welcomed the diagnosis of CD and willingly embraced the GF diet as their long-sought solution to stigmatizing symptoms and ticket to normality. Jessica's chronic foul-smelling gas, undigested food in her stool, and loose stool eluded doctors for years. When her new gastroenterologist finally diagnosed her with celiac, Jessica was "tickled" to finally have "something concrete to latch onto." The diagnosis confirmed her physical distress, offered a rational explanation for it, and provided an acceptable excuse for prior breaches of fecal norms. Moreover, it reassured her that her foul-smelling gas was not her fault.

Nell, whose symptoms included chronic diarrhea, recalled, "After spending all that time in the bathroom I was really excited and absolutely thrilled [when I was diagnosed]. . . . Now I can actually eat a meal. . . . It used to be I'd eat and I'd have to stop halfway through because I'd just get so uncomfortable." Nell finally had a rational explanation for her persistent symptoms and a promising treatment that, although it would entail changing her diet, would, nonetheless, enable her to finally enjoy a full meal. She exclaimed, "I was thrilled at the fact that it was a diet and I didn't have to take any medications!" Virginia described the typical reaction of respondents with classic GI symptoms upon being given the diagnosis of CD: "I was relieved to think that now that we know what I have, I can do something to make it get better." While the GF diet was not easy to master, those with GI symptoms undertook the task willingly.

Conclusion

Classic GI symptoms of CD, including chronic diarrhea, urgent bowel movements, loose and floating stool, undigested food in the stool, and foul-smelling gas, are highly stigmatizing and therefore distressing. Respondents with classic GI symptoms used a variety of stigma management strategies including concealment and passing, social isolation and withdrawal, and reorienting activities and eating times to avoid stigma. When these strategies failed, they experienced both felt and enacted stigma for breaching widely held social norms. As a consequence, they sought medical diagnosis and treatment in the hopes of eliminating or, at the very least, effectively controlling symptoms. For these respondents, the desire to avoid stigmatizing symptoms like gas and flatulence facilitated diagnosis. They toiled for years to discover the true cause of their symptoms, consulting specialists, undergoing multiple tests, and changing doctors, and welcomed the diagnosis when it was finally offered. They also willingly changed their diet to avoid gluten, which, in most cases, eliminated symptoms and enabled them to live a normal life. However, for respondents with non-GI symptoms, being diagnosed with CD was an unwelcome shock that disrupted their sense of normality, particularly with respect to enjoying a normal diet. While it is clear that GI symptoms are stigmatizing, adopting a GF diet may be equally stigmatizing for those without GI symptoms, as it isolates individuals from friends, family, and coworkers for whom wheat is often a staple food (Olsson et al. 2009). More research is needed to identify the social conditions under which stigma facilitates diagnosis and/or hinders compliance with medical and dietary regimens. It is clear from this study that stigma plays a complex role in the social experience of CD.

Discussion Questions

1. Which of the stigma management strategies employed by those with highly stigmatizing GI symptoms do you think are the most effective, and why? What other strategies not discussed in this article might be useful?
2. Compared to those with GI symptoms, why did those with non-GI symptoms react so differently to their diagnosis of CD? How might you react to being diagnosed with a disease that necessitates a major lifelong dietary change and for which you had no noticeable symptoms?

References

Aitola, P., K. Lehto, R. Fonsell, and H. Huhtala. 2010. "Prevalence of Faecal Incontinence in Adults Aged 30 Years or More in General Population." *Colorectal Disease* 12:687–91.

Åsbring, Pia and Anna-Liisa Närvänen. 2002. "Women's Experiences of Stigma in Relation to Chronic Fatigue Syndrome and Fibromyalgia." *Qualitative Health Research* 12:148–60.

Barney, Lisa J., Kathleen M. Griffiths, Anthony F. Jorm, and Helen Christensen. 2006. "Stigma about Depression and its Impact on Help-Seeking Intentions." *Australian and New Zealand Journal of Psychiatry* 40:51–54.

Brandt, Allan. 1987. *No Magic Bullet: A Social History of Venereal Disease in the United States Since 1880,* 2nd ed. New York: Oxford University.

Broom, Dorothy and Andrea Whittaker. 2004. "Controlling Diabetes, Controlling Diabetics: Moral Language in the Management of Diabetes Type 2." *Social Science and Medicine* 58:2371–82.

Brown, Phil. 1995. "Naming and Framing: The Social Construction of Diagnosis and Illness." *Journal of Health and Social Behavior* 35:34–52.

Fasano, Alessio, Irene Berti, Tania Gerarduzzi, Tarcisio Not, Richard Colletti, Sandro Drago, Yoram Elitsur, Peter Green, Stefano Guandalini, Ivor D. Hill, Michelle Pietzak, Alessandro Ventura, Mary Thorpe, Debbie Kryszak, Fabiola Fornaroli, Steven S. Wasserman, Joseph A. Murray, and Karoly Horvath. 2003. "Prevalence of Celiac Disease in At-Risk and Not-At-Risk Groups in the United States: A Large Multicenter Study." *Archives of Internal Medicine* 163:286–92.

Goffman, Erving. 1963. *Stigma: Notes on the Management of Spoiled Identity.* Englewood Cliffs, NJ: Prentice Hall.

Green, Peter and Bana Jabri. 2006. "Celiac Disease." *Annual Review of Medicine* 57:207–21.

Green, Peter and Rory Jones. 2006. *Celiac Disease: A Hidden Epidemic.* New York: HarperCollins.

Herek, Gregory M. 1999. "AIDS and Stigma." *American Behavioral Scientist* 42(7):1106–16.

Karp, David. 1996. *Speaking of Sadness: Depression, Disconnection, and the Meanings of Illness.* New York: Oxford University Press.

Link, Bruce G., Jerrold Mirotznik, and Francis T. Cullen. 1991. "The Effectiveness of Stigma Coping Orientations: Can Negative Consequences of Mental Illness Labeling Be Avoided?" *Journal of Health and Social Behavior* 32:302–20.

Madoff, Robert D., Susan C. Parker, Madhulika G. Varma, and Ann C. Lowry. 2004. "Fecal Incontinence in Adults." *Lancet* 364:621–32.

Mechanic, David. 1968. *Medical Sociology.* New York: The Free Press.

Nack, Adina. 2008. *Damaged Goods? Women Living with Incurable Sexually Transmitted Diseases.* Philadelphia, PA: Temple University Press.

Olsson, Cecilia, Phil Lyon, Agneta Hörnell, Anneli Ivarsson, and Ylva Mattsson Sydner. 2009. "Food That Makes You Different: The Stigma Experienced by Adolescents with Celiac Disease." *Qualitative Health Research* 19:976–84.

Scambler, Graham. 2009. "Health-Related Stigma." *Sociology of Health and Illness* 31:441–55.

Scambler, Graham and Anthony Hopkins. 1986. "Being Epileptic: Coming to Terms with Stigma." *Sociology of Health and Illness* 8:26–43.

Schneider, Joseph and Peter Conrad. 1983. *Having Epilepsy: The Experience and Control of Illness.* Philadelphia, PA: Temple University Press.

Sheldon, Kathleen and Linda Caldwell. 2004. "Urinary Incontinence in Women: Implications for Therapeutic Recreation." *Therapeutic Recreation Journal* 4:203–12.

Strauss, Anselm and Juliet Corbin. 1998. *Basics of Qualitative Research,* 2nd ed. Thousand Oaks, CA: Sage.

Taub, Diane E., Penelope A. McLorg, and Patricia L Fanflik. 2004. "Stigma Management Strategies among Women with Physical Disabilities: Contrasting Approaches of Downplaying or Claiming a Disability Status." *Deviant Behavior* 25:169–90.

Tewksbury, Richard and Deanna McGaughey. 1997. "Stigmatization of Persons with HIV Disease: Perceptions, Management, and Consequences of AIDS." *Sociological Spectrum* 17:49–70.

Weinberg, Martin S. and Colin J. Williams. 2005. "Fecal Matters: Habitus, Embodiments, and Deviance." *Social Problems* 52:315–36.

Weitz, Rose. 1990. "Living with the Stigma of AIDS." *Qualitative Sociology* 13:23–38.

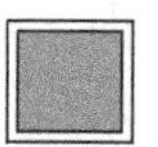 ARTICLE 21

Jason S. Ulsperger
Arkansas Tech University

J. David Knottnerus
Oklahoma State University

Care Giving without the Care: The Deviant Treatment of Residents in Nursing Homes

The United States will soon have its largest elderly population ever. This is partly due to the increase in life expectancy created by advances in medical care. However, not everyone who lives into old age has the ability to live independently. If an older person cannot take care of his or her basic daily needs, a stay in a nursing home might be necessary (Quadagno 2008). Society needs to start focusing on issues involving elder care more than it has before, especially issues involving deviant care provided to older people in nursing homes.

Consider the case of Mary Knight. A nursing home bus crushed her to death. According to the bus driver, something felt like it was keeping her from backing up. It was Mary's body. Mary was arriving at a vocational program affiliated with her long-term care facility when the incident took place. Psychiatrists previously diagnosed her with bipolar disorder and alcohol dependence issues. Some people speculated the death was a suicide. However, Mary's ex-husband thought differently and sued. Mary's death was one in a long line of mysterious deaths at Arkansas Health Center. In a period of one year, five deaths associated with employee mistakes occurred at the institution (Managed Care Weekly 2004; Smith 2005).

Unfortunately, incidents such as Mary's happen in U.S. nursing homes every day, but often employees in nursing homes do not intend for them to happen. They do not show up to work in the morning thinking of ways to abuse and neglect nursing home residents. Instead, they provide care the best they can within the constraints of their work setting—an organizational culture dominated by bureaucratic demands. Over a century ago, sociologist Max Weber (1946) warned us that organizations would become disturbingly obsessed with bureaucratic concerns, such as hierarchical rigidity, rules for the sake of having rules, an overbearing focus on efficiency, and demands to document everything.

With a focus on these bureaucratic characteristics, employees in nursing homes lose sight of what their original goal is supposed to be—providing quality, compassionate care. For many employees, nursing home residents turn into objects of labor. They end up ritualistically "care giving" without "care." With these points in mind, this article uses samples from ethnographic research on nursing home life to review emotional, physical, and verbal dimensions of mistreatment of residents within the medical context of nursing homes (our focus on ritualized behaviors and bureaucratic rituals is grounded in "structural ritualization theory"—Knottnerus 2011).

Emotional Mistreatment

On the premise that employees ritualistically view residents as work products and not people, four types of emotional neglect and abuse exist in nursing homes. They are objectification, inadequate compassion, spiritual neglect, and ridicule.

Objectification

Objectification is any situation where nursing home employees treat residents as impersonal, material items. This involves, for example, nursing home employees referring to residents by room number or ailment instead of by their names (Ulsperger and Knottnerus 2011). Sociologists discuss the process of objectification in a variety of ways. Issues related to it often concern people in power having the ability to label and control others. Consider the objectification that takes place when someone enters prison, a total institution that much of the nursing home literature ironically references when describing resident experiences.

In prison, people provided power by organizational employment strip you down, search your orifices for contraband, tell you what to wear and how to wear it, tell you what you can eat, when to wake up, when to sleep, and what your identification number will be. You are no longer a name, but an object lost in a maze of rules and regulations with little command over your life (Ross and Richards 2002). That sounds a lot like what happens when you enter a nursing home. Joan Retsinas' mother lived in a nursing home. She explains how objectification plays out by way of nurse aides. Retsinas (1986:90) states:

> Whatever the route, however, the individual becomes a "resident" . . . that identity overshadows, even eclipses, any prior identity. In nursing homes, people are identified by disability, by nursing needs, by room number, perhaps even by physician. Mrs. Smith becomes "the self care patient on Unit 3," or "the woman with MS," or "one of Dr. Jones' patients." Mr. Morgan becomes the "terminal case in Room 26."

Facilities do attempt to hold on to some aspects of residents' personal identity. It is not as if all nursing homes have room numbers with signs below that simply say "cancer" or "bed sores." Many put the name of residents on the door for identification purposes along with a photograph of the person. However, it is often just the last name, and the photographs tend to be ones from the person's earlier years. Nursing home aides sometimes indicate that keeping a level of emotional distance from residents is a defense mechanism. They do not want to get close to residents they know will eventually leave or pass away; however, some facilities have explicit policies in place that require aides to keep their emotional distance from residents (Lopez 2006). Consider the practice of color-coding, used for enhancing efficiency of providing medical care. Nursing home staff put colored sticker dots on the outside of resident doors to act as visual keys allowing them to recall a resident's health status (Ulsperger and Knottnerus 2011). It is interesting that serial killers find it easier to victimize people who they view as less human. The same sort of objectified logic might inadvertently facilitate similar attitudes in nursing homes.

Inadequate Compassion

Inadequate compassion is an extension of objectification. It involves staff failing to exhibit emotional awareness of and desire to relieve resident suffering. This includes employees who do not help residents with personal items, although they acknowledge their requests, do not provide food when residents are hungry, and discuss residents' physical conditions without any semblance of pity (Ulsperger and Knottnerus 2011). Kayser-Jones (1981:49) provides an interesting example:

Ninety-nine-year-old Mr. White, a bachelor, is alone in the world. His only visitor is a woman who has been appointed by the court to be his guardian. . . . "Pull up a chair and sit down," he immediately suggested as I entered the room. . . . As I started to offer him a glass of water, I found the pitcher empty. I filled it with ice water and gave him some. "Thank you, that was wonderful," he said. . . . "One boy used to come and give me water, but nobody comes any more. They are all so cruel to me. I asked a nurse for a towel to clean my glasses and she handed me a wet one. I said, this towel is wet and she said it's good enough for you. . . . Some of the boys who mop the floor are nice to me, but the nurses don't talk to me. They walk by the door, but nobody stops to talk with me . . ."

To many people, getting a fresh cup of water is a taken-for-granted task. For the institutionalized, it can be a treat creating an emotional spark. However, with inadequate compassion, more is at play than a cup of water. Nursing home staff will sometimes even comment on how they want problematic residents to die. Vesperi (1983:236) gives an account where workers discussed the possibility of a resident's suffocation and one commented, "What difference does it make? That's much less for us to do."

Spiritual Negligence

Spiritual negligence is the failure to acknowledge and maintain a resident's sacred beliefs or moral feelings. Spirituality is limited to the participation in, and practice of, religion. It concerns any intangible aspect of emotional well-being, including factors associated with personal loss and death. This includes failing to acknowledge resident grief after death or handling a resident death in an unforgiving manner (Ulsperger and Knottnerus 2011). Howsden's (1981:61) research provides us with an example of staff attitudes toward resident spirituality:

> Is that minister still preaching? It's sure getting close to medication time and people should be getting back to their rooms. [The aide replied] . . . this happened last week, too. They are such a long-winded bunch. . . . Maybe someone should mention to them that their service lasts too long. [The nurse said] . . . These people don't need that much religion.

Nurses and aides may have disdain for religious practices because they throw a kink into the work routine. Downplaying the importance of religion takes away from the spiritual side of residents' lives. Ignoring death issues for residents does the same. Outside of nursing home walls, sociologists indicate that circles of death notification exist. With the typical scenario, death news follows a specific path. Hospital personnel are the first to know, then the coroner, immediate family, other relatives, and then friends. Finally, acquaintances and the community members hear about the death (DeSpelder and Strickland 2009). Death news works differently behind nursing home walls. This is, perhaps, due to two factors—bureaucratic divisions and a lack of desire to acknowledge death. As for rigid bureaucratic divisions, multiple pockets of people at various levels of the organization hinder the information flow. In one piece of nursing home research, one analyst went to a facility to visit a resident he befriended only to find her room empty. He asked a resident walking by what happened to her. The resident said, "She's dead." Attempting to confirm this, he turned to staff. He asked an aide. She said, "I think she went to the hospital for a few days." Not believing her statement, which came across with a tone of uncertainty, he asked the director of nursing on duty. She implied nothing was wrong with her and she was in her room as usual. The aide ended up being the one with accurate information (Ulsperger and Knottnerus 2011).

With the lack of desire to acknowledge death, employees, perhaps due to the normalization of dealing with mortality issues, fail to recognize someone passing or its effects on others. This could have positive benefits. In terms of emotional well-being, you do not want a large number of elderly people housed together to be bombarded with death scenes and information. On the other hand, it seems odd to just ignore death issues or treat them in a callous way. When someone dies, employees sometimes act as if the person never lived. Savishinsky (1991:210) indicates, "You see them one week and then, within a few days. . . . It's almost like they did not exist." When it comes to death in nursing homes, it is often just bureaucratic based, business as usual. Hale (2005) was walking around a nursing home she was considering placing her mother in when the administrator quickly threw two odd questions at her. One was, whether or not she had a problem with employees using physical restraints to tie her mother down. The other was what funeral home she preferred. She said she almost left when she heard the second question since she did not plan on her mom dying anytime soon.

Ridiculing Residents

Ridicule involves situations where nursing home employees openly poke fun at residents and their conditions. Sometimes ridicule concerns situations involving general matters where employees engage in laughter that not everyone would interpret as funny (Ulsperger and Knottnerus 2011). Gass (2004:127) details an instance involving a resident taking a shower:

> On my very first day of work here I helped to give Walter a shower. The maneuver required three people—one to wash him and two to restrain him by gripping a towel twisted around both wrists. . . . Deep-purple bruises from a bad fall and two black eyes had transformed his face into a primitive war mask. He was cursing and fighting with all his might. Aides were laughing and dodging....

Vesperi (2003:98–99) reveals her cousin's attitude on staff name calling in a conversation pertaining to his opinion of aides:

> They can't stand to look at me. I'm ridiculed as "Santa Clause" or "Adams." They made a picture of some guy by the name of Adams. He was supposed to be a man of the country, a hill man . . . T.D. was clearly unfamiliar with the television program *Grizzly Adams*. . . . "That's not good, to ridicule anybody," T.D. continued. "That breaks your spirit."

Two prominent areas of ridicule concern incontinence and sexuality. Kayser-Jones (1981:47) discusses how one nurse found humor in a volunteer's reaction to a resident's inability to control urination:

> Mr. Thomas, always sat in a particular location in the hallway. One evening I saw him struggling to get out of his wheelchair. Sensing he needed a urinal, I called the nurse. "Oh, that's all right," she assured me. "Don't worry about him; he has two spots right here in the hallway where he urinates every day." The expression on my face was one of shock and disbelief. . . . "What's the matter," laughed the nurse, "is it too much for you?"

Public urination is a major violation of cultural norms. One thing that classifies people as adult, if not human, is the ability to control bodily fluids (Mitteness and Barker 1995). Nursing home staff making fun of incontinence further dehumanizes residents. In terms of sexual humiliation, Fontana (1978:128) describes a situation observed in one nursing home noting that "big John" walked around with his pants undone pleasuring himself while "aides [just] laughed at him." He further noted that big John once had another resident to perform fellatio on him. When staff caught them, they laughed and never even asked the other resident whether she was a willing participant.

Physical Mistreatment

Physical maltreatment of nursing home residents involves medical, personal, and environmental issues. Of specific concern are aspects of medical dereliction, personal and environmental negligence, and bodily harm.

Medical Dereliction

Medical dereliction involves situations where nursing home employees fail to deliver medicine and services that have the capacity to help or heal resident ailments. This includes doctors failing to provide care and nursing staff using pharmaceutical drugs, such as Thorazine, for the sole purpose of controlling a resident's behavior. In these situations, residents do not require medication, but staff will still use it to keep annoying patients from disrupting the bureaucratic necessities of work (Ulsperger and Knottnerus 2011).

Physicians sometimes refuse to provide medical care for residents, believing that it is pointless due to their age. Kayser-Jones (1981:76) recalls, "The nurse in charge of Unit B said that on some occasions when she had suggested glasses or a hearing aid for a patient, the doctor had rejected this suggestion with, 'Oh well, she's old anyhow.'" There are also situations where doctors request forms of care and nursing home employees simply do not comply. It may be because they are uncomfortable with a resident's condition. In one study of nursing homes, a former aide told researchers that she worked in a facility that had a resident with AIDS. Some of the workers did not like to provide the resident care or even feed him. Aides who were more compassionate picked up the unwilling aides' slack and even snuck in burgers for the resident from time to time to lift his spirits (Ulsperger and Knottnerus 2011).

The lack of medical attention in nursing homes sometimes just revolves around money. Diamond reports that when working in a nursing home he would tell residents "it costs a lot to take care of sick people these days" (1992:151). However, he did not believe the administrator in his facility was always appropriately spending on the medical needs of residents. When this happens, it puts employees, specifically aides, in a pinch. It is more common than most people would think for aides to bring medical supplies from home to use on residents. A better aide complained to Diamond (1992:151) one day stating, "Damn... I forgot to bring those Epsom salts. Now Violet is not going to be able to soak her foot."

Regardless of subpar levels of medical care, sometimes employees provide an overabundance of it. As mentioned, nursing home workers overmedicate residents that cause disruptions to the bureaucratic flow of the workday. Workers label residents "disrupting deviants" even when medications to control them cause the initial problem. Fontana (1978:128) explains:

> The center exhibited many forms of deviance, which were perpetrated by individual members of the organization but were really done for and normalized in the name of the organization. The goal of the center, a typical one in this respect, was to provide a smooth-running schedule and flow of work, minimizing disturbances and avoiding trouble. What constituted disturbances and trouble was defined by the staff. Hence many deviant acts perpetrated by patients on other patients or by staff members were handled to minimize their hindrance to the running of the organization. Often these acts were normalized in order to avoid stopping the center's smoothly flowing machine. Therefore if Maria, a wiry old patient, fell heavily to the ground after having been pumped full of Thorazine, the incident was dismissed as the result of an obfuscated mind and deteriorated body.

Sometimes aides even blackmail nurses by refusing to provide care on their wings until the drugging of annoyingly disruptive residents takes place. Nurses in a crunch do not have a problem complying. In his classic study on nursing home life, Gubrium (1975:148) describes the feelings of one nurse after being pressured to administer medications to subdue residents, "As one floor nurse stated to several aides just before leaving for her break, 'Well, I guess I can take my break now. Everyone's sedated.'"

Along with medication issues, medical dereliction also involves staff failing to turn the bodies of bedridden residents. When medical conditions confine older people with frail skin to their beds, there is a high possibility that a decubitus ulcer, better known as a bedsore, can form. If these painful, open wounds become infected, they can lead to serious cases of gangrene and even amputation (Ulsperger and Knottnerus 2011).

Personal Negligence

Personal negligence involves staff failing to provide sufficient upkeep of tangible features of residents. This includes clothing and personal hygiene. Accounts show busy aides often fail to properly clean or clothe residents. In one piece of research on nursing home culture, a former aide reported (Ulsperger and Knottnerus 2011:105–106):

> [The clothing and hygiene issue] was the most noticeable problem with staff efficiency. We rarely had the staff needed to spend time with each resident in the morning. There was always tension between the third shift and the morning shift regarding how many residents were up and ready for the day. I was lectured on several occasions about being too slow and leaving too many residents for the first shift to get ready. . . . I would often see residents without their hair combed or their face washed properly.

As a former activity director, Poxon (2004) explains her frustrations of having residents attend recreational events with large amounts of feces accumulated under their nails. Deutschman (2005) tells of residents wearing the same clothes from Monday to Friday. Laird (1979:99) elaborates on the clothing issue stating, "Florence had a daffodil-yellow dress which didn't entirely satisfy her. One day she said, 'I believe I'll give this to Annie. The color will be becoming to her . . . ' Annie wore it. But to our disappointment, the aide had put it on her backwards." It would be easy to assume that putting on a dress backward is a mistake and not intentional ritualistic personal negligence. However, putting clothes on the wrong way is often an unfortunate case of intentional bureaucratic backwardness. Kayser-Jones (1981:46) explains:

> Many residents at Pacific Manor do not have personal clothing, and what is provided for them is ill-fitting, un-pressed, and inappropriate. . . . Mrs. White, an attractive 78-year-old woman who normally sat in a wheelchair clad in a sweater and slip, had to wear a bathrobe tied backwards around her waist to simulate a skirt when the therapist came to help her walk. To lack underclothes or to have clothes put on backwards is also dehumanizing for the elderly. Robes often are put on this way, staff informed me, to decrease the amount of work involved in changing an incontinent patient and to decrease the amount of laundry. If robes are put on backwards and not tucked under, they are not soiled when patients are incontinent.

With so much to do, the emphasis on hygienic care is not what it should be either. Employees view levels of hygiene people outside of nursing home walls might find repugnant as normal. With hygienic care carrying a prime value, aides have the ability to withhold it as punishment when residents upset them. Shield (1988:159) states, "Staff retribution can result when residents are too demanding. In subtle and not so subtle ways, staff members neglect or delay doing things."

Environmental Negligence

Environmental negligence involves nursing home employees failing to maintain domains of interaction such as living areas, recreational rooms, kitchens, and grounds outside of the facility. This includes aspects of cleanliness that have the potential to put nursing home residents in health-related danger (Ulsperger and Knottnerus 2011).

Gubrium (1993:170) details one account provided by a former nursing home surveyor turned resident recalling the man stating, "We are having a roach war here." The issue is not that nursing homes directly cause physical harm to residents by not maintaining a clean environment, but their ecological oversight has the potential to increase the likelihood that disease-related germs, which can have a physical impact, spread among residents. In one piece of nursing home research, a resident family member elaborates on his concerns with this issue (Ulsperger and Knottnerus 2011:108):

> When my Mom had an infection, she was moved to the nursing home's isolation wing.

> When isolation wing aides cleaned Mom after she defecated, they would then toss the feces-covered rags into an open box in Mom's room and leave them there all day. Often when I came in the evening, flies would be buzzing about the opened box, and the stench was overwhelming.

In his seminal research on nursing homes in the 1960s, Henry (1963) argues employees ignore potential health risks when not adequately cleaning standard items in resident rooms, such as bedpans left dirty and dried with feces at bedsides. Over 40 years later, the comments from a family member as seen earlier confirm that not much has changed.

Bodily Harm

Bodily harm involves any physical abuse by nursing home employees directed toward residents. This includes anything from the misuse of physical restraints to acts akin to assault and battery (Ulsperger and Knottnerus 2011).

Stannard (1973) suggests nursing home employees sometimes give scalding hot baths to residents as a type of punishment for behaving in ways staff members do not like. Here, the bureaucratic demand of worker efficiency is important to discuss. As another form of punishment, employees sometimes improperly use physical restraints on residents who disrupt workflow. Paterniti (2000:106) provides an account:

> Out of frustration and a perceived need to keep Scott restrained, aides frequently tied a square knot in the nylon vest restraint that secured Scott in a reclining Gerry chair. . . . Some even remarked, "If you're a mechanic, let's see you get yourself out of this one!" On one occasion, an aide locked Scott, tied to a chair, in the janitors' closet. The aide entertained himself by keeping records of how long it took Scott to work his way out of the restraints and to the door of the closet. Ironically, additional work to this staff member's schedule, generated under his own control, seemed to present no obstacle to his work timetable.

The misuse of restraints is also an employee response to understaffing. Diamond (1992:182) explains:

> Mary Ryan, like many others, spent all day in the dayroom, secured to her chair with a restraining vest. . . . I passed the question on to Beulah Feders, the LPN in charge. "Beulah, why does she have to wear that thing all the time?" Beulah accompanied her quick comeback with a chuckle. "That's so they don't have to hire any more of you."

Sometimes residents act out violently against staff and the nursing home has to restrain them to protect themselves and other residents. In one source, the executive director was showing a researcher around a facility when she displayed her lack of knowledge on the condition of a resident. In an attempt to show how close she was to her residents, she leaned down to a sweet-looking old woman and yelled in her ear to ask how she was doing. The resident, who the executive director did not know had a history of violence, pulled her arm back like a major league baseball pitcher and swung an opened hand to the director's face. After the fierce impact, it was clear the director was not pleased. She did mumble a few orders to the nurse aide standing nearby (Ulsperger and Knottnerus 2011). Restraints were surely in the unruly resident's future. Unfortunately, some employees do not resort to restraints when assaulted, but simply carry out the same action against the resident. Tisdale's conversation with a staff member explains one worker's opinion on bodily harm, "Some are kind, some are cruel. . . . They kick me, I kick them" (1987:109).

Verbal Mistreatment

The links between bureaucracy in nursing homes and the verbal abuse and neglect of nursing home residents are just as interesting as the ones with emotional and physical mistreatment. They involve infantilization, spoken aggression, and the ignoring of residents.

Infantilization

Infantilization involves nursing home residents speaking to residents in a condescending way that reduces the status of a resident to that of a young child (Ulsperger and Knottnerus 2011). Kayser-Jones (1981:39) provides a vivid representation:

> At Pacific Manor there were innumerable incidents of staff treating the residents like children. Authoritarian scoldings of the aged by staff were common. For example, one day a nurse aide walked into the lounge and, seeing a puddle of water on the floor, asked loudly, "Who wet the floor?" Pointing her finger at one woman, she inquired in an accusing voice, "Did you wet the floor?" Very embarrassed at being singled out as the culprit, the patient replied, "Why, no it wasn't me." Staff frequently command patients in a parental voice: "Shut up," "Stay in your chair!"; "Go to your place for lunch"; "I want you to go in and put on a dress, now get dressed!" and "Sit down, Grace."

Staff members do not always intend to be outright malicious with infantilizing comments. Diamond (1992:138) points out:

> She was using the term "baby" to ridicule the rule, which many residents made fun of as well, that bibs had to be tied on to each resident for each meal. "Baby" was often used, and in more than one way. In some contexts it was used to create fictive family roles. Dorothy Tomason put her arm around Joanne Macon when she cried. "C'mere, my baby, now what's the trouble."... "Baby" was also used more broadly as a designation of the impersonal, referring to infants who were incompetent and unaware. "Oh, you work up there on the baby floor," observed a first-floor nursing assistant.

Sometimes nursing home employees unintentionally use infantilization as a form of cognitive resonance. They are providing the type of parental care given to infants, such as bathing and feeding, but doing it for an adult. Reliant on previous relationship structures such as parent–child relationships, it makes sense to nursing home employees to refer to residents in a child-like fashion. In other words, it is likely that it eases subconscious confusion (Ulsperger and Knottnerus 2011).

The spoken word is not the only thing that produces infantilization in nursing homes. Other infantilizing actions exist. Some are required, such as the use of "adult diapers" for incontinent residents. However, many are not. Consider having Santa Claus come to give out presents on Christmas (Metz 1999), or various aspects of television viewing. Employees put on cartoons for residents to watch on television and borrow kid movies from local daycares to show residents. When mix-ups happen and children's shows are not on the viewing menu, staff become disturbed since many do not see adult television as appropriate, even if it is adults who will be watching. Poxon (2004:66–67) notes:

> Barry volunteered to tape movies for us from HBO for our movie matinee. ... He fell asleep during the taping and the next morning he rewound the video and brought it with him to work. When it was time for the movie, my assistant Geneva put in the movie and went to the nurses' station to do some charting. After an hour or so she was approached by one of the nurses who asked her what type of movie she was showing the residents. . . . So she went into the TV room to find several nurses and residents watching an adult X-rated movie. Geneva immediately stopped the video. One of our residents who was engrossed in what was on the screen hollered, "Why did you turn that off? I was enjoying that." What had happened was after Barry went to sleep an adult movie came on. Since he didn't have the time to view it before bringing it in he was totally unaware of all he had taped.

In relation to power issues, the inability to control your own television viewing is quite demoralizing. Kidder (1993:203–204) illustrates this situation with the story of Earl, who liked to watch shows knowing his wife was at home watching the same thing:

> Sometimes Earl's roommate got confused, and the man was prey to those abrupt fits of weeping that strokes often induce. Once, over a month ago, he had been parked out by the nurses' station and had started weeping saying he couldn't watch what he wanted on TV. But that had all been straightened out, Earl thought ... Earl had asked his roommate, "Mind if I watch this show?" His roommate had said he didn't mind. . . . As always, he had reminded Jean to be sure and watch this show at home tonight. . . . Suddenly, two young women entered. One of them picked up the remote control from Earl's bedside table. She put it down on his roommate's table and said, "Mr. Duncan, you can't have this." But Earl's roommate himself had given Earl the control to handle. . . . "*Mister* Duncan," said the other young woman, "you *cannot* have that." When the social worker visited him the next morning . . . Earl told her that he felt as though he'd been treated like a five-year-old.

Spoken Aggression

Spoken aggression involves hostile vocal attacks by staff directed against a resident (Ulsperger and Knottnerus 2010). Ethnographies on nursing home life indicate that nursing home employees use spoken aggression to deter residents from annoying staff. Howsden (1981:76) explains:

> A typical encounter includes a complaint of a headache, stomach ache or another patient who has caused them distress. The patient is not ignored, but merely put off with the typical response, "Oh, go sit down and you will feel better," . . . The tactic is one of diversion which if unsuccessful is followed by threats, such as "If you don't leave me alone, I'll send you to your room."

Administrative staff also sometimes show favor to nurses and aides who use spoken aggression because it speeds up the completion of work tasks. Speaking to residents in an intimidating tone cuts back on their resistance and demands for service. Verbal assaults can also lead to very threatening language. In one study, a resident's son stated to researchers, "Mom has reported to me an instance in which one of the aides yelled at her for pressing her call button twice in succession . . . [soon after] another aide said she was going to beat [her] up." (Ulsperger and Knottnerus 2011:124).

Ignoring

Ignoring concerns times when nursing home employees refuse to take notice of communication initiated by residents. This includes ignoring attempts at conversation or disregarding audible requests for personal and medical assistance. With ignoring, employees are not actively engaging in verbal abuse, but passively engaging in it by refusing to communicate at all. In other words, failing to respond is a conscious decision-based response to people in need. This is distinct from personal negligence and medical dereliction. With those deviant forms of nursing home care, employees recognize personal and medical issues, but fail to do anything about them. With ignoring, residents make personal or medical requests without staff acknowledgement (Ulsperger and Knottnerus 2011).

In relation to bureaucratic constraints with ignoring, another maltreatment pattern based on residents disrupting goals of efficiency in a workday exists. Paterniti (2000:106) explains that nursing home employees tend to disregard residents whom they identify as disruptive or incompetent when they feel like it because most residents requesting assistance do not have pressing needs. Nursing staff have to ignore them for the sake of completing important work, even if the nursing home limits the opportunities for residents to engage in activities to keep pain off their minds. Reflecting patterns of ignoring, one resident told Gubrium (1993:144), "You ask them to do something and they ignore you like dirty shit." Mollette (2001:58) observed aides shutting doors so they would not have to "hear what they are being asked to do" by residents.

Conclusion

Policymakers have tried fixing the problems discussed in this article many times before. New nursing home laws pop up when enough horror stories and citizen complaints emerge, but concerns soon subside only to emerge again when citizen rights groups garner enough support to make nursing home abuse and neglect important again (Ulsperger 2002). Unfortunately, this cycle adds to the problem of unintentional mistreatment facilitated by a bureaucratic work culture. Demands for nursing home reform led to an array of more regulations every time the government acts to lessen elder care problems. The result is more bureaucracy. However, there is some hope. A movement known as "culture change" is currently occurring in the nursing home industry.

The movement toward culture change in nursing homes involves a shift away from the bureaucratic nursing home model. It pushes for the enhancement of personal relationships between residents and employees, acknowledges the importance of spirituality, downplays the traditional medical themes of elder care, and encourages the presence of plants, pets, and children into nursing home environments to create a more humane habitat for residents (for elaboration see Ulsperger and Knottnerus 2011). The movement has the potential to lower current rates of deviant practices in facilities for the aged. If successful, it could put the "care" back in "care giving," and take some of the bureaucracy out.

Discussion Questions

1. Which form of mistreatment is the most harmful? Why?
2. Whose responsibility is it to handle cases when persons are mistreated? How should the "mistreaters" be handled?

References

DeSpelder, Lynne Ann, and Albert Lee Strickland. 2009. *The Last Dance: Encountering Death and Dying*. Boston, MA: McGraw Hill.

Deutschman, Marian T. 2005. "An Ethnographic Study of Nursing Home Culture to Define Organizational Realities of Culture Change." *Journal of Health and Human Services Administration* 28(2):246–81.

Diamond, Timothy. 1992. *Making Gray Gold: Narratives of Nursing Home Care*. Chicago, IL: University of Chicago Press.

Fontana, Andrea. 1978. "Ripping Off the Elderly: Inside the Nursing Home." Pp.125–32 in *Crime at the Top: Deviance in Business and the Professions,* edited by John M. Johnson and Jack D. Douglas. Philadelphia, PA: J.B. Lippincott Company.

Gass, Thomas Edward. 2004. *Nobody's Home: Candid Reflections of a Nursing Home Aide*. Ithaca, NY: Cornell University Press.

Gubrium, Jaber F. 1975. *Living and Dying at Murray Manor*. New York: St. Martin's Press.

Gubrium, Jaber F. 1993. *Speaking of Life: Horizons of Meaning for Nursing Home Residents*. New York: Aldine de Gruyter.

Hale, Sue A. 2005. *Nursing Home Diary: A Lesson in Survival*. Mustang, OK: Tate Publishing.

Henry, Jules. 1963. *Culture Against Man*. New York: Random House.

Howsden, Jackie L. 1981. *Work and the Helpless Self: The Social Organization of the Nursing Home. Lanham,* MD: University Press of America.

Kayser-Jones, Jeanie. 1981. *Old, Alone, and Neglected: Care of the Aged in Scotland and the U.S.* Berkley, CA: University of California Press.

Kidder, Tracy. 1993. *Old Friends*. Boston, MA: Houghton Mifflin.

Knottnerus, J. David. 2011. *Ritual as a Missing Link: Sociology, Structural Ritualization Theory and Research*. Boulder, CO: Paradigm Publishers.

Laird, Carobeth. 1979. Limbo: *A Memoir about Life in a Nursing Home by a Survivor*. Novato, CA: Chandler and Sharp.

Lopez, Steven. 2006. "Emotional Labor and Organized Emotional Care: Conceptualizing Nursing Home Care Work." *Work and Occupations* 33(2):133–60.

Managed Care Weekly. 2004. "Nursing Home Bus Kills Mental Patient." *Managed Care Weekly*, May 10.

Metz, Ricca. 1999. *Maudie: A Positive Nursing Home Experience.* Hanover, MA: Christopher Publishing House.

Mitteness, Linda S. and Judith C. Barker. 1995. "Stigmatizing a 'Normal' Condition: Urinary Incontinence in Later Life." *Medial Anthropology Quarterly* 9:188–210.

Mollette, Glenn. 2001. *Nursing Home Nightmares: America's Disgrace.* New York: Milo House.

Paterniti, Debora A. 2000. "The Micropolitics of Identity in Adverse Circumstance: A Study of Identity Making in a Total Institution." *Journal of Contemporary Ethnography* 29:93–119.

Poxon, Joyce M. 2004. *Nursing Homes, Heaven or Hell?: A True Story of What Nursing Home Living Could Be Like for You or a Loved One.* Bloomington, IN: 1st Books Library.

Quadagno, Jill. 2008. *Aging and the Life Course,* 4th ed. New York: McGraw-Hill.

Retsinas, Joan. 1986. *It's OK, Mom: The Nursing Home from a Sociological Perspective.* New York: The Tiresias Press, Inc.

Ross, Jeffrey and Stephen Richards. 2002. *Behind Bars: Surviving Prison.* Indianapolis, In: Alpha Books.

Savishinsky, Joel S. 1991. *The Ends of Time: Life and Work in a Nursing Home*. New York: Bergen and Garvey.

Shield, Renee R. 1988. *Uneasy Endings: Daily Life in an American Nursing Home.* Ithaca, NY: Cornell University Press.

Smith, Nell. 2005. "Nursing Home Litigation: Patient Died at Hands of Pathfinder, Suit by Ex-Husband Points Finger at Health Center Too." *Arkansas Democrat Gazette*, March 5, p. 1B.

Stannard, Charles. 1973. "Old Folks and Dirty Work: The Social Conditions for Patient Abuse in a Nursing Home." *Social Problems* 20:329–42.

Tisdale, Sallie. 1987. *Harvest Moon: Portrait of a Nursing Home.* New York: Henry Holt and Company.

Ulsperger, Jason S. 2002. "Geezers, Greed, Grief, and Grammar: Frame Transformation in the Nursing Home Reform Movement." *Sociological Spectrum* 22(4):385–406.

Ulsperger, Jason S. and J. David Knottnerus. 2011. *Elder Care Catastrophe: Rituals of Abuse in Nursing Homes—and What You Can Do about It.* Boulder, CO: Paradigm Publishers.

Vesperi, Maria. 1983. "The Reluctant Consumer: Nursing Home Residents in the Post-Bergman Era." Pp. 225–237 in *Growing Old in Different Societies: Cross-Cultural Perspectives*, edited by Jay Sokolovsky. Belmont, CA: Wadsworth Publishing Company.

Vesperi, Maria. 2003. "The Use of Irony in Contemporary Ethnographic Narrative." Pp. 69–102 in *Gray Areas: Ethnographic Encounters with Nursing Home Culture*, edited by Philip B. Stafford. Santa Fe, NM: School of American Research Press.

Weber, Max. 1946. *From Max Weber: Essays in Sociology,* translated, edited and with an introduction by Hans Gerth and C. Wright Mills. New York: Oxford University Press.

ARTICLE 22

Erich Goode

Professor Emeritus at Stony Brook University

The Stigma of Obesity

I walk into a restaurant or a store and people come to a standstill. They nudge one another and stare at me as if to say, "Get a load of that one! I wonder how much she weighs?" Or, "Gee, the circus must be in town." Or they come up to me and actually say, "Why did you let yourself get this way?" I've heard lots of similar cracks. People in public feel as if they have the right to say these things to a fat person. I'm looked at as if I'm some sort of animal, some subhuman creature. You wouldn't do the same thing to a handicapped person—it would be cruel. But somehow it's OK [to do it] with us because that will encourage us to lose weight. It's almost as if cruelty and self-righteousness are acts of kindness and charity.

Obesity[1] is widely regarded as an undesirable physical trait—and a stigma—as this 300-pound woman who I interviewed told me. Stigma is a mark of disgrace, an attribute, based on shared cultural understandings, that clings to a person. Stigmatized individuals are considered inferior, discredited, and contaminated. In his classic discussion, *Stigma*, Erving Goffman distinguishes three types of stigma: *abominations of the body*, such as paralysis, blindness, extreme ugliness, being a hunchback, being facially disfigured, missing one or more limbs, and having cerebral palsy; *blemishes of individual character*, "perceived as weak will, domineering or unnatural passions, treacherous and rigid beliefs, and dishonesty," exemplified by "mental disorder, imprisonment, addiction, alcoholism, homosexuality, unemployment, suicidal attempts, and radical political behavior"; and *tribal stigma of race, nation, ethnicity, and religion*, those that can be "transmitted through lineages and equally contaminate all members of a family" (1963:4). Goffman uses the term *normal* to refer to persons who do not share the stigmatizing trait or characteristic in question, that is, people who do not possess the requisite bodily abominations, blemishes of individual character, or tribal stigma. He does not imply that stigmatized persons are not "normal" in the psychiatric or medical sense of the word, only that stigma places relational and interactional barriers between stigmatized and nonstigmatized persons. The so-called normal person *thinks* and *talks about*, and *interacts with* stigmatized persons *as if* they were not normal, as if they were "not quite human" (p. 5). Hence, the term, *normal.*

In *Stigma,* Goffman (1963) mentions obesity only twice (pp. 22, 142), first with respect to whether stigmatized persons form clubs whose members "huddle together" to interact with and help one another, and second, to indicate that the "fraternity fat boy" often serves as a "mascot" for his group, much like the "village idiot, the small-town drunk, and the platoon clown"—in other words, *the ingroup deviant.* Clearly we need to know much more about the stigma of obesity than Goffman, with all his insight, tells us.

Edward Jones and his colleagues (Jones et al. 1984) delineate six dimensions of the "mark" of stigma: *concealability,* that is, how detectible or visible a condition, trait, or characteristic is to observers; *course,* or whether and to what extent the mark changes over time—whether it is temporary, episodic, or chronic; *disruptiveness*, whether the mark interrupts or puts a strain on social interactions between its bearer and others; *esthetics*, or how unpleasant the mark is or appears to be to the observer's or bystander's senses and sensibilities; *origin*, whether it is "controllable," that is, perceived as an act of will, or "uncontrollable," or based on inherited, congenital physical characteristics; and *peril*, or perceived dangerousness, that is, whether the condition places others in harm's way.

Visually, obesity is not easily concealable, especially at its more extreme range. Though weight can change over time, the obese usually find it difficult to change their condition and hence, obesity tends to be more often chronic than temporary. Its disruptiveness is typically socially caused and situation specific in that it is often relevant and important to others and so, to that extent, it impedes interaction between the obese and others. As to whether it violates esthetic standards is in the eye of the beholder, though many non-obese observers do regard fat people as "disgusting." With regard to its origin, medical researchers continue to debate the relative weight of "nature" and "nurture," having reached something of a consensus that both factors play a prominent role in its etiology (Weinsier 1998; Vögele 2005)—although, regardless of its objective cause, most of the public considers obesity to be the *fault* of the obese and hence, it is stigmatizing. It is difficult to imagine what danger obesity places others in the path of, though many physicians and epidemiologists believe that obesity is medically harmful to the obese themselves (Behan 2010).

In contemporary America, obesity is stigmatized. Fat people are considered less worthy human beings than average-sized or thin people. They receive less and fewer of the good things that life has to offer, and more of the bad. Men and women of average weight look down on the obese, feel superior to them, reward them less, punish them more, and often make fun of them. The obese are often an object of derision and harassment because of their weight. What is more, as we saw in our opening quote, thin people will feel that this treatment is just, that the obese deserve it, indeed, that such derision is something of a humanitarian gesture, since such humiliation will supposedly inspire the overweight to lose that excess poundage. The stigma of obesity is so intense and pervasive that eventually the obese will frequently come to see themselves as deserving of it, too.

The obese, in the words of one observer, "are a genuine minority, with all the attributes that a corrosive social atmosphere lends to such groups: poor self-image, heightened sensitivity, passivity, and withdrawal, a sense of isolation and rejection" (Louderback 1970:v). They are subject to relentless discrimination, the butt of denigrating jokes, and objects of persecution. It would not be an exaggeration to say that they attract cruelty from the average-sized or thin majority. Moreover, their friends and family rarely give the kind of support and understanding they need to deal with this cruelty. In fact, it is often friends and family who are themselves meting out the cruelest treatment. The social climate has become "so completely permeated with anti-fat prejudice that the fat themselves have been infected with it. They hate other fat people, hate themselves when they are fat, and will risk anything—even their lives—in an attempt to get thin. . . . Anti-fat bigotry . . . is a psychic net in which the overweight are entangled every moment of their lives" (Louderback 1970:vi, vii). The obese typically accept the denigration that thin society dishes out to them because they feel, for the most part, that they deserve it. And they do not defend other fat people who are being criticized because they mirror their own defects—the very defects that are so repugnant to themselves. Unlike the members of most other minorities, they don't fight back; in fact, they feel they *can't* fight back. Racial, ethnic, and religious minorities can isolate themselves to a degree from majority prejudices; the obese, intermingled as they are with the thin majority, cannot. The chances are, most of the people they meet are of average size, and they live in a world built for individuals with much smaller bodies.

During the past generation, the proportion of the population in the United States who are categorized as obese has increased; we are now, in the words of some experts, in the midst of an "obesity crisis" (Brownell and Horgen 2003). The degree of overweight is measured by physicians by Body Mass Index (BMI), which is related to, but not identical with, adiposity or percentage of fat tissue in one's body. In the United States today, one-third of the population has a BMI over 30; taking fat tissue into consideration, medical researchers consider a quarter of the population to be obese. Although on a year-by-year basis the increase has not been steady, this percentage is higher today than it was a decade ago (Flegal et al. 2010).

The Stigma of Obesity

In Goffman's framework, persons who possess an "abomination of the body" are stigmatized, regardless of whether they are responsible for their condition. They receive the same or similar treatment from "normals" as persons who chose to engage in morally stigmatizing behavior. But are these persons *deviant?* Goffman was ambivalent about the matter, arguing that "shameful differentness" (1963:140) is not exactly the same thing as deviance, whose enactors are "considered to be engaged in some kind of collective denial of the social order" (p. 144). In a similar but more extreme vein, Polsky argues that people who suffer from stigmatizing physical "abominations" but are not responsible for their condition should be *excluded* from the sociologist's definition of deviance and from our courses and books on the sociology of deviance. The unusually ugly, the physically handicapped, the blind, and the deformed might indeed be stigmatized (e.g., by being avoided socially, humiliated and joked about, and discriminated against in employment) but their condition is "not their fault" and hence are not forms of deviance since it is not motivated and cannot be accounted for by the usual "theories" of deviance (1998:202–203). According to Polsky, deviance is defined by and should be regarded as a form of behavior that is voluntary, whose enactment can be explained sociologically, behavior that *is* the actor's "fault" and *does* reflect on his or her character. Polsky also insists that while sectors of the public disagree about what actions or conditions should be regarded as morally tainting or discrediting, physical conditions that were imposed on someone as a result of accident, circumstance, or a genetic roll of the dice should not be regarded as a form of deviance

Most contemporary sociologists disagree. In *The Stigma of Obesity*, Werner Cahnman provides the bridge between stigma and deviance. Obesity is widely considered "detrimental to health, a blemish to appearance, and a social disgrace." Moreover, though less obviously—and perhaps most importantly—obesity "is held to be morally reprehensible" (1968:283). Over the years, the moral dimension has remained with obesity; it contaminates and *inferiorizes* persons with the attribute, makes them less than human, narrows their life-chances, spoils their identity, taints their relations with persons of average size, pollutes the image that "normals" have of overweight people, and reinforces self-hate and self-derogation among the latter. "Normals" or people of average weight attribute the obese "with a wide range of imperfections on the basis of the original one." The stigma that radiates from an attribute as serious as obesity tends to "spread from the stigmatized individual to his close connections," which "provides a reason why such relations tend either to be avoided or terminated" (Goffman 1963:5, 7, 30).

Nutritionists, says Cahnman, "tend to be crusaders, trying to convert sinners into saints." Obesity, they claim, is a manifestation of self-indulgence and overindulgence, which implies "the depravity of the overweight person." The "condescending solicitude" extended to the obese "serves chiefly to confirm the superiority of virtue over vice" (1968:287). In contemporary, urban, industrialized society, we observe an inverse relationship between socioeconomic status (SES) and obesity: the lower the education, income, and social class, the higher the incidence of obesity (Sobal and Stunkard 1989). "It remains a moot question," says Cahnman, "whether the lower socioeconomic strata are held in low esteem because they tend to be obese or whether obese individuals that are held in low esteem are relegated to these strata" (1968:289). Especially among girls, obesity "is not so much a mark of low SES as a condemnation to it" (p. 290).

Cahnman argues that the SES-obesity connection constitutes a major source of its stigma. Underlying the definition of obesity as both a health hazard and a sign of lower status "is the notion of the depravity of the obese person" (p. 291). Gluttony is related to a need for oral gratification, which is related to low impulse control and is related to obesity. The obese person "is looked upon as an individually pathological case, possibly an object of pity, and not infrequently as an instance of mental disturbance" (pp. 292–93). Stigmatization is central to the process by which the obese are labeled. "In stigmatization, deviance, rather than being an attribute of the deviant, becomes a label attached to a person by others." The obese person suffers from rejection and disgrace, regarded as possessing a "physical deformity and a behavioral aberration." Eventually, the person so labeled comes to accept the validity of the label. This "vicious circle is completed when the victim agrees with his [or her] detractor and considers the discriminatory treatment which is meted out to him [or her] deserved and the prejudicial attitude which underlies it justified" (p. 293).

According to Cahnman, obesity straddles two of the primary types of stigmatic attributes: it is both an "abomination of the body" and a "blemish of individual character." Obesity is not only regarded as unsightly, unaesthetic, and unappealing—and hence, a bodily "abomination"—but a moral failing as well, a personal and individual flaw of character. The obese, the reasoning goes, "are presumed to hold their fate in their own hands." If only they were "a little less greedy or lazy or yielding to impulse or oblivious of advice, they would restrict excessive food intake, resort to strenuous exercise, and as a consequence of such deliberate action, they would reduce" (p. 294). While being blind, deaf, or physically handicapped are considered misfortunes, "obesity is branded as a defect." The physically disabled will be helped by their peers; the obese will be "derided." The ill-treatment by persons of average weight which is meted out to the obese "will not elicit sympathy from onlookers, but a sense of gratification." To the contrary, onlookers will feel "they have got what was coming to them" (p. 294). The general public is indifferent to the fact that experts regard obesity as largely a neurological, physiological, and genetically caused condition (Friedman 2004) rather than a "personal choice," and will continue to stigmatize and "deviantize" the obese.

Finally, Cahnman tells us, socializing with the obese contaminates the "normal" who does so, along with any and all groups or social circles into which the obese are introduced. Young males confirm that the reason why they avoid dating heavy women is the "fear of ridicule." Obese adolescents are "deprived of their right to be judged according to their personalities" and very possibly permanently frozen into a rigid role and a narrow opportunity structure (p. 297). According to Goffman's formulation, persons who possess potentially discrediting attributes that are not immediately evident can avoid being stigmatized by controlling access to information that would discredit them (1963:48). But since being fat is not only visible but obtrusive, the obese "cannot resort to very much in the way of stigma management." The obese "must either retreat or stand exposed" (Cahnman 1968:297).

Prejudice and Discrimination against the Obese

Researchers have documented behavioral bias against persons who are considered overweight or obese in a wide range of settings, including interpersonal relationships with friends and family members, their representation in the media, employment and education, and health care. What have the findings of behavioral and attitudinal studies taught us about how the obese are thought about and treated by "normals"? As we saw, the prevalence of weight discrimination has increased significantly over the past decade, and "is comparable to rates of racial discrimination, especially among women." Widespread stereotypes hold that the obese "are lazy, unmotivated, lacking in self-discipline, less competent, non-compliant, and sloppy." These stereotypes are widespread and leave the overweight "vulnerable to social injustice, unfair treatment, and impaired quality of life as a result of substantial disadvantages and stigma" (Puhl and Heuer 2009:941). Such stereotypes, attitudes, and behavioral biases manifest themselves in a wide range of social, economic, and educational spheres.

A team of researchers (Puhl, Andreyeva, and Brownell 2008) asked questions about lifetime and "experiences on a day-to-day basis." The everyday question was asked in the following wording: "How often on a day-to-day basis do you experience each of the following types of discrimination?" The experiences were broken into eight categories: "you are treated with less courtesy than other people," "you are treated with less respect than other people," "you receive poorer service than other people at restaurants or stores," "people act as if they are afraid of you," "people act as if you are dishonest," "people act as if they think you are not as good as they are," "you are called names or insulted," and "you are threatened or harassed." Far from weakening, the stigma of obesity—or at least, *perceived* discrimination—has strengthened over time. Between the 1990s and the 2000s, the proportion of overweight children and adults in a nationally representative sample of 3,500 respondents was one-and-one-half times more likely to report that they suffered from discrimination in their daily lives, in work-related settings, and from medical personnel, as a result of their weight. In the 2000s, only 1 percent of thin respondents (those with a BMI of under 27) reported such discrimination, while 63 percent of the obese, or those with a BMI of over 45, did so (Andreyeva, Puhl, and Brownell 2008). Clearly, prejudice and discrimination of the obese will not go away any time soon.

Representation of overweight people in the media portrays, and can influence, how real-life fat people are regarded and treated by others. One research team examined the characteristics of over a thousand characters on 10 top-rated prime-time television programs. Overweight and obese females were less likely to be considered attractive, less likely to be depicted as having a relationship with a romantic partner, less likely to express affection with others, less likely to have a friend, less likely to talk about dating, and more likely to be shown eating. The conclusions of this study were that overweight and obese television characters are significantly more likely to be shown to have stereotypically "fat" negative characteristics and engaged in stereotypically "fat" social behavior. There are three strikes against fat characters on television dramas: they are less likely than is true in real life to be present and depicted in broadcast dramas; they are more likely to be represented, when they are, as outside the mainstream; and they are more likely to be depicted as passive or inactive; that is, they had fewer interactions with friends or romantic partners, and were involved with fewer instrumental roles, such as leadership; less likely to help with specific tasks, less likely to demonstrate physical affection, date, and to have sex; and more likely to be shown eating and to be the butt of jokes and derision (Greenberg et al. 2003; Greenberg and Worrell 2005).

As I pointed out, a substantial volume of research indicates that, statistically speaking, the obese stand lower on the socioeconomic ladder than the national norm; they tend to be less well educated, tend to be less likely to hold professional or executive positions, earn a lower income, and are more likely to be unemployed (Fikkan and Rothblum 2005). One European study (Brunello and D'Hombres 2007) found that males with a 10 percent higher BMI than the norm earn 3.27 percent less than the national average, while for females, the figure was 1.86 percent. In the American workplace, a difference in weight of two standard deviations from the mean (roughly 65 pounds higher than average) is associated with a 9 percent lower income (Cawley 2004). Another study conducted in the United States found that wages for obese males were 3.4 percent lower than for non-obese males, while they were 6.1 percent lower for obese females than non-obese females (Baum and Ford 2004). A study in an English setting revealed exactly the same relationship there between obesity and employment (Morris 2007). In a study of the relationship between obesity and education in Sweden it was found that among a sample of nearly 100,000 males who were born in 1972 and 1973, those who were obese at the age of 18 (BMI of 30 or higher) had lower high school grades and a lower level of educational attainment than was true of the non-obese (Karnehed et al. 2006).

The issue of lower educational and occupational attainment by the obese is incontrovertible; virtually no researcher has found otherwise. What *is* controversial is whether and to what extent this pattern is a result of prejudice and discrimination against fat people or factors having to do with the inability or unwillingness of the obese to perform in the economic and educational spheres at the same level as their peers of average weight. A team of sociologists (Glass, Haas, and Reither 2010) examined the relationship between obesity and occupational standing, considered three possible explanations for the lower achievement levels of heavier men and women: discrimination; educational attainment, independent of discrimination; and a factor not previously empirically explored—marriage market processes. After controlling for factors such as social background, age of forming a family, and academic ability and achievement, these researchers concluded that direct discrimination against the obese does not account for their relatively low economic achievement. They also argued that because fat women are considered relatively less desirable on the marriage marketplace, they are less likely to get married, they tend to marry later, and they more often marry economically less desirable partners when they do marry—factors that negatively influence their socioeconomic success.

Of all the complaints that fat people lodge about the stigma, bias, prejudice, and discrimination they experience from average-sized society, none is more vociferous and poignant than their treatment at the hands of medical professionals. Foundational studies conducted decades ago demonstrated that physicians and other medical professionals tend to hold negative attitudes toward the obese, usually have less optimistic expectations about improvement in their health as a result of treatment, and commonly accept widespread stereotypes about their characteristics (that they are slothful, lazy, and gluttonous, and have poor hygiene). Many physicians are "repulsed" and "disgusted" with their fat patients, preferring not to touch or even treat them. Medical students link obesity with a number of "derogatory adjectives, including worthless, unpleasant, bad, ugly, awkward, unsuccessful, and lacking in self-control" (Fabricatore, Wadden, and Foster 2005:31). Recent research has come to virtually the same conclusions as was reached by investigators decades ago (Harvey and Hill 2001; Foster et al. 2003). "Health care professionals' anti-obesity attitudes, originally reported nearly 40 years ago, appear to persist today" (Fabricatore et al. 2005:38). A team of researchers submitted a thematic attitude measure to a sample of obesity specialists and found that the respondents more often categorized fat people with negative attributes such as "bad," "lazy," "stupid," and "worthless" than with positive attributes such as "good," "motivated," "smart," and "valuable" (Schwartz et al. 2003). Hypothetical vignettes submitted to physicians asking what they would recommend for their obese as opposed to their average-sized patients revealed that these doctors would refer the obese to a psychologist significantly more, and reported that they would themselves spend significantly less time with their obese patients (Hebl and Xu 2001). In short, the complaints of fat people about how they are treated by members of the medical profession seem to have a substantial basis in fact.

Conclusion

In *Stigma*, Erving Goffman delineated three sources of stigma—blemishes of character; abominations of the body; and stigma of tribe, nation, ethnicity, and religion. Obesity shares in the first two of these sources in that it is widely regarded as a physical abomination that is the outward manifestation of a characterological defect or moral flaw. The obese are stigmatized, commonly stereotyped as gluttonous, weak-willed, lazy, and sloppy, and are looked down upon by people of average size—regarded, in Goffman's words, as "not quite human." Obesity is a readily visible, obtrusive trait that often draws denigrating public comment. The fact that experts regard obesity as largely neurological and genetic in origin plays little role in moderating the public's expression of contempt for the obese. In the view of most contemporary sociologists, obesity is not only stigmatizing, it is a form of deviance. And the ill-treatment of the obese is not only widespread, but it seems to be increasing over time. The media portray the obese in a condescending, stereotypical fashion, depicting them less often than is reflected in real life, emphasizing their overeating, portraying them as having fewer friends or romantic relationships, and all-too-often making them the butt of derision. The obese earn less on the job and in the marketplace than the national average, though some researchers argue that this is due to objective factors such as a lower level of education rather than discrimination per se. Obese women are less likely to get married, to get married later, and more often marry—when they do marry—men who earn less than women of average size. A common complaint of the obese is that they are often mistreated and stereotyped by members of the medical profession, and research, conducted both in the past and more contemporaneously, bears out this charge.

Note

1. There is political import in naming a phenomenon. Fat "activists" (Wann 2009) argue that the use of the words *obese* and *obesity* medicalizes fatness and fat people, making the assumption that being fat is undesirable and medically harmful. These fat spokespersons prefer the neutral, nonpejorative term, *fat*. In my opinion, in most social circles *fat* is regarded as equally as pejorative as *obese*. In any case, my use of the word *obese* comes down to my answer to the question: which audiences do I want to communicate with—a tiny cadre of fat activists, or a substantially larger number of academics, researchers, students, sociologists, psychologists, physicians, and the general public? In any case, "The Stigma of Fat" sounds clumsy and inelegant, which is another reason why I use the word *obesity*. Perhaps it is futile to plead that I intend no denigration by using the word, but that is what I am saying.

Discussion Questions

1. What can be done to change societal views on the obese?
2. Which term is more stigmatizing: *fat, obese,* or *overweight?* Why?

References

Andreyeva, Tatiana, Rebecca M. Puhl, and Kelly D. Brownell. 2008. "Changes in Perceived Weight Discrimination among Americans, 1995–1996 Through 2004–2006." *Obesity* 16 (May): 1129–34.

Baum, Charles L. and William F. Ford. 2004. "The Wage Effects of Obesity: A Longitudinal Study." *Health Economics* 13(9):885–99.

Behan, Donald F., Samuel H. Cox, Yijia Lin, Jeffrey Pai, Hal W. Pedersen, and Ming Yi. 2010. *Obesity and Its Relation to Mortality and Morbidity Costs*. Schaumberg, IL: Society of Actuaries.

Brownell, Kelly D. and Katherine Battle Horgen. 2003. *Food Fight: The Inside Story of the Food Industry, America's Obesity Crisis, and What We Can Do about It*. New York: McGraw-Hill.

Brunello, Giorgio and Béatrice D'Hombres. 2007. "Does Body Weight Affect Wages? Evidence from Europe." *Economics and Human Biology* 5(1):1–19.

Cahnman, Werner J. 1968. "The Stigma of Obesity." *The Sociological Quarterly* 9 (Summer):283–99.

Cawley, John. 2004. "The Impact of Obesity on Wages." *The Journal of Human Resources* 39 (Spring):451–74.

Fabricatore, Anthony N., Thomas A. Wadden, and Gary D. Foster. 2005. "Bias in Health Care Settings.", pp. 29–41 in *Weight Bias: Nature, Consequences, and Remedies*, edited by Kelly D. Brownell, Rebecca M. Puhl, Marlene B. Schwartz, and Leslie Rudd. New York: Guilford Press.

Fikkan, Janna and Esther Rothblum. 2005. "Weight Bias in Employment." pp. 15–28 in *Weight Bias: Nature, Consequences, Remedies*, edited by Kelly D. Brownell, Rebecca M. Puhl, Marlene B. Schwartz, and Leslie Rudd. New York: Guilford Press.

Flegal, Katherine M., Margaret D. Carroll, Cynthia L. Ogden, and Lester R. Curtin. 2010. "Prevalence and Trends in Obesity among US Adults, 1999–2008." *JAMA: Journal of the American Medical Association* 303 (January 20):235–41.

Foster, Gary D., Thomas A. Wadden, Angela P. Makris, Duncan Davidson, Rebecca Swain Sanderson, David B. Allison, and Amy Kessler. 2003. "Primary Care Physicians' Attitudes about Obesity and Its Treatment." *Obesity Research* 11(10):1168–77.

Friedman, Jeffrey M. 2004. "Modern Science versus the Stigma of Obesity." *Nature Medicine* 10(June):563–69.

Glass, Christy M., Steven A. Haas, and Eric N. Reither. 2010. "The Skinny on Success: Body Mass, Gender, and Occupational Standing across the Life Course." *Social Forces* 88(June):1777–1806.

Goffman, Erving. 1963. *Stigma: Notes on the Management of Spoiled Identity*. Englewood Cliffs, NJ: Prentice-Hall/Spectrum.

Greenberg, Bradley S., Matthew Eastin, Linda Hofschire, Ken Lachlan, and Kelly D. Brownell. 2003. "Portrayals of Overweight and Obese Individuals on Commercial Television." *American Journal of Public Health* 93(August):1342–48.

Greenberg, Bradley S. and Tracy R. Worrell. 2005. "The Portrayal of Weight in the Media and Its Social Impact." Pp. 42–53 in *Weight Bias: Nature, Consequences, and Remedies*, edited by Kelly D. Brownell, Rebecca M. Puhl, Marlene B. Schwartz, and Leslie Rudd. New York: Guilford Press.

Harvey, E. L. and A. J. Hill. 2001. "Health Professionals' Views of Overweight People and Smokers." *International Journal of Obesity* 25 (August):1253–61.

Hebl, Michelle R. and J. Xu. 2001. "Weighing the Care: Physicians' Reactions to the Size of a Patient." *International Journal of Obesity* 25 (August):1246–52.

Jones, Edward E.Amerigo Farina, Albert H. Hastorf, Hazel Markus, Dale T. Miller, and Robert A. Scott. 1984. *Social Stigma: The Psychology of Marked Relationships*. New York: Freeman.

Karnehed, Nina, Finn Rasmussen, Thomas Hemmingsson, and Per Tynelius. 2006. "Obesity and Attained Education: Cohort Study of More Than 700,000 Swedish Men." *Obesity* 14 (August):1421–28.

Louderback, Llewellyn. 1970. *Fat Power: Whatever You Weigh Is Right*. New York: Hawthorn Books.

Morris, Stephen. 2007. "The Impact of Obesity on Employment." *Labour Economics* 14 (3):413–33.

Polsky, Ned. 1998. *Hustlers, Beats, and Others*, exp. ed. New York: Lyons Press.

Puhl, Rebecca M., Tatiana Andreyeva, and Kelly Brownell. 2008. "Perceptions of Weight Discrimination: Prevalence and Comparison to

Race and Gender Discrimination in America." *International Journal of Obesity* 32(June):992–1000.

Puhl, Rebecca M. and Chelsea A. Heuer. 2009. "The Stigma of Obesity: A Review and Update." *Obesity* 17(May):941–64.

Schwartz, Marlene B., Heather O. Neal Chambliss, Kelly D. Brownell, Steven N. Blain, and Charles Billington. 2003. "Weight Bias among Health Professionals Specializing in Obesity." *Obesity Research* 11(September):1033–39.

Sobal, Jeffrey and Albert J. Stunkard. 1989. "Socioeconomic Status and Obesity: A Review of the Literature." *Psychological Bulletin* 105(2):260–75.

Vögele, Claus. 2005. "Etiology of Obesity." Pp. 62–71 in *Obesity and Binge Eating Disorder* edited by Simone Munsch and Christoph Beglinger. Basel, Switzerland: Karger.

Wann, Marilyn. 2009. "Foreword: Fat Studies: An Invitation to Revolution." Pp. xi–xxv in *The Fat Studies Reader*, edited by Esther Rothblum and Sondra Solovay. New York: New York University Press.

Weinsier, Roland L., Gary R. Hunter, Adrian F. Heini Michael I. Goran, and Susan M. Sell. 1998. "The Etiology of Obesity." *American Journal of Medicine* 105(August): 145–50.

PART NINE

Deviant Communities

A community is commonly viewed as a group who lives in the same area or share common characteristics and interests. A community serves multiple purposes including, but not limited to, comfort, camaraderie, support, togetherness, and protection. After a long hard day, nothing compares to being around people who can understand and provide comfort. This sense of belonging is magnified when you are marginalized from everyday society due to stigmatization.

In this part of the reader we examine the communities of the marginalized—deviant communities.

Part Nine begins by delving into the world of furries. Jackie Eller and her colleagues take us to a community where people have strong personal connections with animals and commonly display an animal identity. Sexual identity is commonly a hot topic in the furry community, and the authors take us there head first. Melissa Powell-Williams's "Are You 'Deaf Enough?'" examines the deaf community, where deafness as a condition is ascribed, but culturally powered deafness is achieved. The difference between the pathological deaf and culturally empowered deaf has a significant influence on one being accepted in the deaf community. This part concludes with Corrie Hammers investigating the lesbian/queer bathhouse where opportunities are available for impersonal homosexual sex. She discusses this community through in-depth analysis on the setting, organization, and gendered patterns of bathhouses.

 ARTICLE 23

Jackie Eller
Middle Tennessee State University

A. R. Eller
University of Oregon

Zachary Santoni-Sanchez
Middle Tennessee State University

Furries and Their Communities

Some weeks ago Dr. Eller received an e-mail from a student who was doing research on taboo subjects and wanted to research the furries. In his experience, it seems that these two were coincident—furries are deviants and the subject of their interactions led him to conclude that being a furry is taboo. Unfortunately, this young man was a high school student and not where we could have a conversation about the error of his assumptions, so I can only surmise how he came to that conclusion. In his defense and relevant to the current article, there has been no serious sociological study of the people involved with and in a furry community, so it is no surprise that erroneous and prejudicial assumptions exist. His inquiry does point to what we have found to be a common assumption held by those outside the furry community—furries are participating in deviance, most likely sexual deviance, and should therefore be sanctioned and/ or condemned.

For our purposes in this article this student's inquiry serves as segue into an important discussion of what we mean by deviance. At the simplest level, deviance could be defined as a violation of agreed-upon social norms or actions that might be perceived to challenge existing folkways, mores, or laws (Sumner 2010 [1906]). Adler and Adler (2011) argue that although behavior is the most common category of deviance, we must also include the consideration of attitudes and conditions, the ABC's of deviance, for a fuller understanding. Along with Adler and Adler, others, such as Goode (2010), are more relativist or constructionist in their views and argue that deviance, paraphrasing Becker (1963), is not the ABC per se but that which people so label. Hence deviance, less a thing and more a process, is created within social interaction, but why would any particular ABC be labeled as deviant? Again, for our purposes, deviance is that which an audience (tied to a situation and time) perceives by its very existence as threatening, which leads that audience to act on that threat. This threat might be to norms of appropriate behavior or discourse, values that support and extend a way of life, or to one's person or personal space. The key component in this definition is the perception of the threat. In responding to this threat and in order to maintain a boundary of cultural and personal integrity (Erikson 2004 [1966]), persons will label the offender as an outsider (Becker 1963) deserving of social discredit (Kitsuse 1962; Kitsuse and Spector 1975). Aspects of this discredit include attempts at social control—informal or formal sanctions, such as ostracism, censure, derogatory labeling and name calling, avoidance, fines, imprisonment, and even capital punishment. The question for this article on furries, then, is might furries be considered a threat and if so, what do they threaten and what is done to discredit and "control" them? We will return to this discussion at the end of this article.

This article is primarily an investigation of furries and the furry community—how it is divided, defined within itself and by others, made deviant by others, and how members have strategized toward social legitimization. We are drawing from an analysis of Web sites designed and visited by furries, newspaper articles on the furries, as well as a series of 11 online interviews from members within one particular large online community. It is our contention that, like other marginalized groups striving for general social acceptance and freedoms of social interaction, furries attempt to avoid stigma and construct group identity, legitimacy of behaviors, and lifestyles.

Who Are the Furries?

Perhaps you have watched the *CSI* episode (2003) of furries "scritching" (affectionately scratching or rubbing the back, neck or between the ears—http://www.wikifur.com) and "yiffing" (sexual activity and interaction—http://www.wikifur.com) or read "Pleasures of the Fur," a *Vanity Fair* article by George Gurley (2001) in which the sexualities of furries were made prominent. Although these portrayals of furrydom have some legitimacy, as we will address later in this article, the assumption that furries are only persons dressed in fursuits and engaged in sexual interactions is hotly debated within the community.

In reality, though a common and agreed-upon definition is elusive, a furry is a person who has strong personal connections or associations with animals/animal characters and/or asserts a particular animal identity. One community member we interviewed referred to furries having "a kindred association" with animals. These associations or identities encompass an expansive range of activities from playful dress-up and chatter, spiritual or sexual identities to claims of "species dysmorphia": a neologism that puns on body dysmorphic disorder (http://www.therianthropes.com/furries.htm). Nast (2006:317) also refers to this phenomenon as "species dystopia" or the belief that one is "an animal trapped in a human body." Like many other group memberships, meaning may be found in a level of casual to significant involvement and/or to one's primary/important identity. And it is commonly accepted that the depth of involvement and what then constitutes the meaning of being a furry is individual yet includes a sense of community as well. As attested to by all of our interviewees, community is important. The average time they have been in the community is 9.2 years, with the longest membership/identification being 22 years.

Why an Elusive Definition?

Those who identify or are identified as being a furry are divided into many cohesive but also competing groups: goth, dragons, cubs (erotica, some pornographic), baby furs, Old Guard (20+ years of membership), monsters, hipsters, furzi, and plushies, to name a few. We should also note that furries can and often do belong to more than one group or type, again depending on individual choices. One of the largest group memberships, but not the one we will concentrate on in this article, is one whose members participate in furry-centered cartoons or art, either as artists or as fans. According to http://www.anthrocon.org, Anthrocon, a Pennsylvania-based organization, sponsors what is now the largest furry convention in the world. In its brochure, furry fandom (an artistic and literary genre) is defined as the "devotees of anthropomorphic animals" in which *anthropomorphic* "refers to animals or objects given human characteristics . . . everything from the gods of ancient Egypt with their dog, cat, and crocodile heads, to the tool-using characters of the Sonic the Hedgehog video games, to the talking sea creatures of the SpongeBob Squarepants television series."

Others argue that furries are part of a larger community called Cosplay—short for costume play—that originated in Japan (Fron et al. 2007) where people dress up in costumes that represent or approximate favored characters. This may be true, but fursuits, in particular, are very expensive to purchase or make, are limiting in terms of workplace attire, and are extremely hot to wear, for example. One interviewee emphasized this point, "I always liked the idea of wearing a cat suit and got my chance at a fancy dress ball. Unfortunately it was a once in a lifetime experience. It was so baking hot in that blasted suit that I nearly passed out. Now I restrict fur wearing to gloves, it gives me a superb tactile feeling when I put them on." Another furry commented that:

> I currently own approximately 10 suits that range from cheap Chinese ripoff suits which sell for less than $200 on eBay to a custom made fully realistic quadrapedal black bear which cost several thousand dollars. Since suits are expensive and people are afraid they might not be able to wear one for an extended period of time, I give them the opportunity to try it out. Usually the person ends up buying their own suit within a year. I guess I should insert the disclaimer here that wearing a fursuit does not make a person a furry. Only around 10–20 percent of the fandom owns a fursuit. This is probably one of the biggest misconceptions facilitated by the media.

Consequently due to cost, complications, and temperature, being a "fursuiter" represents a relatively small number of those who claim to be furries. Another interviewee estimated that at the last conference she attended there were perhaps 700 fursuiters among the 4,200 attendees. Being a furry, then, may include aspects of, but less than a full body presentation of the revered animal. Others, such as noted in the following post and however erroneous the assumption may be, are adamant that there is a distinct difference that centers primarily on the sexual implications between those who participate in Cosplay and those who claim to be furries. "Mascot costumes/fursuits are not the issue. People dressing as animal-shaped characters wear them. Those people are cosplayers, not furries. Furries are another thing entirely and there's a sexual aspect that a lot of people, myself included, want to push away with a very sharp stick" (http://www.cosplay.com).

There are others who role-play in Second Life or other similar fantasy games, while still others may do that as well but view themselves as animals in human form such as the following furry explains.

> I am a black short-haird [*sic*] domestic feline, stuck in a human body (re-incarnation can have a twisted sense of humour at times!). Loves to curl up and sleep in warm places, especially after a nice meal. Purrs, groals [*sic*], scratches and bites, but never on demand! The human is a Goff and we are often seen with "Eye of Ra" make-up on our left eye and sporting tails and ears, while bouncing around on the dance floor of clubs across the UK, tail a swishing. (http://www.darkfurr.org)

One might also argue that persons like Erik "The Lizardman" Sprague (http://www.thelizardman.com) and Stalking Cat (http://www.stalkingcat.net/) who have made significant "flesh journeys" (Atkinson and Young 2001) are also furries. Sprague though, in an e-mail exchange, did not claim to be a furry and writes on his FAQ that his journey is an artistic transformation that explores "what it means to be human from a linguistic standpoint." Stalking Cat writes that his transformation "in following a very old Huron tradition" is transforming himself into a tiger, his proclaimed totem. Similarities abound between these two particular individuals and the neoprimitives Atkinson and Young interviewed, but among those who claim to be furries, the comparisons are less significant in terms of physical transformation. Atkinson and Young did note that subcultural membership, status passages, creativity and individuality, physical endurance and pain, beauty, art and spirituality are meaningful aspects in becoming a neoprimitive, which is often the case for membership in a furry community as well. Despite differences in identity claims, furries and persons such as those who through tattooing make claim to historical connections (neoprimitives), those involved with traditions such as Stalking Cat, and those involved with artistic transformations such as Lizardman share common meaning constructions with furries. Consequently, the definition of who is a furry or what being a furry means depends on what group and what individuals are being asked.

Demographics

As mentioned before, to date, there have been no serious *sociological* studies of the furry subculture or community, but there is some ongoing research from which a preliminary sketch can be determined. Gerbasi et al. (2008) surveyed some 217 self-identified furry conference goers whose ages were mostly in their 20s. Based on our examinations of Web sites and interviewees we think this is a somewhat accurate estimation. In our small group of 11 interviewees, the median age was 26 but with 2 over 50 years old. As much as can be identified, Web site owners over all groups tended to be in their 30s, so it is important to keep in mind that although younger, perhaps more savvy Internet users may predominate the groups, particularly the furry art groups, the age range is broad. Again, starting with the Gerbasi et al. study, adding our own information and then a nonrandom, nonscientific online poll ($N = 1{,}745$) conducted by Osaki (2011), furries are more likely to be male than female, a 3:1 ratio or even higher, and most (maybe as high as 90 percent) are self-identified as white.

Furries are likely to be more sexually open—homosexual, heterosexual, bisexual, pansexual, and others, than is generally found in a comparable population of same-aged males and females. One of our interviewees described herself as a "heteroflexible, polyamorous, non participating pagan." The Osaki (2011) survey reported that only 21 percent of the respondents self-identified as completely heterosexual and approximately 14 percent as completely homosexual. All of this is to suggest that those who participate in the furry fandom report being less constrained by conventional binaries in their furry or nonfurry personal lives. It could also mean that for some, sexual preference is not so clearly delineated when in fursuit, sexually involved with plushies (stuffed animals) or nonhuman animals (zoophilia): a suggestion we have found some support for through examinations of the Web sites. Although not particularly common among the fandom or among any other group, for that matter, sexual preferences are complicated because of species dysmorphia/dystopia (not feeling completely human). How does one accurately capture a sexual preference when a female fox feels that she is trapped in an adult male body, for example? We also want to note that those we interviewed were adamant that sexual preference openness and love of animals does not lead to bestiality/zoophilia (perhaps a choice among a really small percentage—Osaki found approximately 14 percent would describe themselves as zoophiles). One furry we interviewed said simply, "we don't go that way." This sexual openness and "public assumed" preoccupation with sex may be the grounds for others who both overgeneralize and claim the fandom to be deviant; we will return to this point later in this article.

Nonhuman Animal Selves and Identities

A central argument of the furry community in all of its diversity is that the sharp dichotomy between human and nonhuman animal is a false, socially constructed one. Although this is a consistent theme, it seems there is some temptation to draw on this very dichotomy when claiming "I am a fox inside a human form," for example, but it seems likely that the structure of this claim is hampered by the structure of language per se. The point to be made is that to a great extent, those within the furry community do not view themselves as separate and distinct from the animals that are their avatars, artistic creations, or personal presentations. This leads us, then, to an examination of the nonhuman animal "choices."

By far the most common of nonhuman animal choices made are canines (especially wolves, huskies, and foxes), felines (domestic as well as the big cats), and mystical dragon species. Rodents (rabbits and mice), cervines (deer) of various types, and other mystical creatures like unicorns or werefurries (human by day, nonhuman by night) are also likely to be seen. Of course, there are also choices that are less common, but recognizable, such as raptors, raccoons, and goats, to name a few. Some of the most rarely represented nonhuman animals and insects are cockroaches, ducks, sharks, and whales. The emergence and popularity of anthropomorphic avatars or cartoon characters often lead to creative choices that reflect a blending of animals for their assumed qualities or interests. One of our interviewees noted, with some disdain, that this blending has sometimes reached a level of "silliness" when people create such creatures as a deer/zebra/dolphin.

As Berry (2008:79) argues, ". . . nonhuman animals, in their relationship to humans, serve as reflection of human needs for positive attributes." They are a social aesthetic or prop, as Goffman (1959) would say, that reflects status, prestige, personality, power, attractiveness, or specialness. If we consider her point here, we could argue that "choice" of nonhuman animal identity may reflect a similar symbolic or spiritual existence, such as *Otherkin*[1] represents. It is also important to note that *choice* is in quotes because many emphasized that one may not, and indeed often does not, consciously *choose* a nonhuman animal fursona from a list of alternatives. One of our respondents said, "They're not chosen . . . it's kind of like sexuality. You don't choose to be gay, bisexual or straight. You just are who you are." Dark Wolf said of his wolf "choice,"

> I've always found them to be a strong and compassionate and loyal creature, which is what I'm a lot like. So I guess it's just a natural fit for me. I guess it's kind of always been a natural connection that I've never questioned.

Specifically chosen are canines (wolves and foxes in particular) who are viewed as powerful, swift, or cunning, therefore the person *is* also powerful, swift, or cunning. (Note that we write *is* versus *seen* because when in the animal form, the person may not be readily identifiable.) As several of our interviewees said, wolves are noble loners who live in complex hierarchies, while foxes are also sexy and cute. Dogs are protectors and companions, but also easily and understandably mimicked. Big cats (most often tigers and cheetahs) are also powerful, in control of their world, and/or swift. Despite the community's affinity to "The Lion King," no one in our analysis mentioned being a lion. Is the lion too wrought with symbolism and a hierarchy of control, or is the lion too cliché? No one has addressed this point, only that other big cats are the chosen fursona. Small cats are cuddly, lovable, yet independent. Deer are graceful and tender, yet our popular culture history has constructed them as fierce defenders of home and family. One interviewee said his choice of deer was in appreciative homage to their grace and beauty. Raccoons, beavers, mice, and even dragons all represent a set of desirable and identifiable characteristics. For many furries the nonhuman animal may portray more clearly an aspect of his or her character, which is of particular value if that aspect is not obviously visible or attainable in person. One interviewee said that animal "choice" is to create an image and "oftentimes this image is uniquely different than self." This is particularly relevant if we consider gendered expectations. Nonhuman animals may be presented in fursuit, adornments, dress, avatar, cartoon, or art that displays gendered appearances or norms that are not so easily embraced in everyday life.

Nonhuman animal choices are further understood through an examination of what is *not* frequently chosen—for example, cows, buffalo. Few snakes are chosen, although lizards are not uncommon, horses sometimes but more often unicorns or Pegasus, or birds. Why is there less affinity with these creatures? Is it because it is difficult to appear as a cow or snake if possessing a human body? This would not be so limiting in cartoon or avatar format. Is it the traits or assumed characteristics of the nonhuman animal that are attractive? The resistance to presenting oneself as a snake, given the negative reptilian imagery is understandable, but why not a bird of prey? We find birds of prey as religious or spiritual totems, so why are these not common choices? Again, the answer lies in the reasons for one's affinity: a presentation of the "wished for" self; a presentation of the actual self; or the self that is spiritually connected to nonhuman animals or *otherkin*.

It is interesting that nowhere in the Gerbasi et al. (2008) study, in our Web site examination, or in our interviews has anyone claimed a nonhuman primate identity. Again, we ask why this is so? Regarding pet ownership, for example, Berry (2008:79) offers a relevant explanation. "We possess special animals as a way of impression management." Perhaps the breakdown of the human/nonhuman animal dichotomy is not sufficiently addressed with primates. They are too close already and might be viewed as subhuman rather than having their own unique and positive characteristics. Nonhuman primates symbolically carry the weight of evolution and evolutionary critique for many people. This has a potentiality that detracts from the desired claim about one's identity. In other words, the primates may not give off the desired impression.

Others may choose their nonhuman animal selves for the reasons stated earlier as well as for political or environmental reasons. Sabot L'our suggests, in an e-mail exchange:

> In 1985 I rented a mascot-style raccoon suit which I wore to a Halloween street party. It was such a thrill to actually become a furry critter. Had the Internet been in existence as we know it today, I would have been completely hooked into the fandom right then and there. As it was, I kept my strange fantasy of a human wanting to be an animal or at least have animal characteristics to myself. At this point in my life I was also developing a strong environmentalist bent.
>
> I developed the character "Sabot" as an ideal anthropomorphic version of myself. In a lot of ways he is simply a reflection of me in bear form. The name Sabot came to me one night as I was developing his character's backstory (which once again reflected my own). He was a large brown black bear who was threatened by the encroach[ment] of Man and waged a guerrilla war to keep them in their place. After many years of seemingly fruitless fight he gave up to simply live in the woods with his fellow creatures. He opened a bar/cantina where his friends could get together for a friendly drink. Cheers in the woods, so to speak. I also developed a secondary character who is perhaps my alter ego. Abbey Raccoon was [a] fellow fighter who never gave up the fight. He is still out there fighting for the cause, but his actions are mainly harmless and ineffective. He retains that hippie ideal.

In summary, there are many reasons for the "choices" made concerning one's nonhuman fursona. Ideological assumptions about masculinity and femininity guide some. Wishing to use the furry identity in order to give voice to the animal or to use the particular animal fursona as a different voice guides others. Some spoke of being a nonhuman animal as a "return to innocence" and as "an escape from the evil world." Yet another of our interviewees said, "I share a lot of the traits that people generally assign to foxes, but it's mostly an entertainment thing." Several on Web sites and in the interviews stressed this entertainment aspect, along with having a particular economic or artistic motive as well. Some even spoke of feeling vulnerable in human form but strong and less a victim in their fursona. Nast (2006:320) argued that whatever the animal figure, furries are in essence rendering "the 'wild' rather harmless or at least subject to an animating will." She goes on to claim that their "activities make all animals into pets" possibly including the humans as well. Finally, although Gerbasi et al. (2008) found that nearly 66 percent of the 209 conference goers reported some degree of not feeling 100 percent human or wanting to be 0 percent human, while 24 percent reported a persistent feeling of discomfort or inappropriateness concerning their human body, this does not seem to be a primary motivation for those we interviewed or who talked about their fursonas on Web sites or in chat groups. We do think that as the societal movement toward acceptance of being a furry continues, so will the diversity of animal "choices." And with that diversity come those whose fursonas challenge the norms as they are for sexual and often considered deviant reasons: baby furs or pedophiles, zoophiles or bestiality, Nazifurs (those who create furry characters or are furries who wear Nazi uniforms)[2], predator/prey scenarios, or for plushie love (sexual intimacy with stuffed animals).

"Deviant" Fursonas

If we return for a moment to consider the meaning of deviance, you are reminded that deviance represents a threat connected to a perceived violation of normative attitudes, behaviors, and/or conditions. The perceived threat brings attempts to discredit and efforts at social control. Zoophilia or bestiality, although practiced by those outside the furry community as well, is one such discrediting and "threatening" behavior often associated with the furry community. Wisch (2008) states that "zoophilia is broadly defined as the affinity or sexual attraction by a human to a non-human animal," and is often used interchangeably with bestiality. "Zoos," as they are often called, are viewed, by some, as the undesirable element that misrepresents the rest of the community. To love animals is one thing, but to want to sexually love animals is another thing entirely. As one interviewee emphasized, "most of us don't go that way." Echoing the dominant cultural values, tolerance for or acceptance of this kind of diversity is often too much. If we are to believe the validity of Osaki's 2011 nonscientific survey, a relatively small percentage of the community claims this affinity, but for some this small percentage is just too much as it becomes fodder for sensationalism by the media. One of our interviewees told us he left the community after many years of interaction because of what he considered to be these "deviant aspects" and how they were discrediting him as well as the community. Another female furry pointed out that the community image suffers because the media has exploited the more outrageous members. Such is a similar case for the "plushies."

Plushies are collectors of large numbers of stuffed animals, who find great pleasure in cuddling or snuggling stuffed animals, and/or who extend intimacy with stuffed animals into sexual, romantic, or spiritual realms.[3] As sexual intimacy with stuffed animals falls outside of most people's definitions of "normal"—as do many fetishes—this particular furry choice is often seen as the "fringe of the fringe" and hence, sensationalized. One day in class when I started a discussion of the furries and the furry community, one student spoke up and said, "Oh those are the people who have sex with stuffed animals. That's really sick." Although I corrected the overgeneralization and suggested a reconsideration of such a value-specific statement, I think the student's comment to be most indicative of the tendency to align the "strange and weird" that is somewhat known as representative of the whole, which is often unknown.

Furries who are plushies with sexual interests or plushophiles "love" stuffed animals in conventional and unconventional ways. Fox Wolfie Galen writes of his fondness for his stuffed animal Meeko and several others whose bodies are attractive, feel good when caressed, never complain when you work late, and are constructed such that it allows for "strategically placed holes" conducive to sexual relations. Those who identify as plushophiles (all are male that we have encountered) have constructed Web sites and chatgroups where they compare and show off collections, their designs and constructions, their furry families, and their love interests. These interests are harmless if we consider that no living creature is hurt, but as you might imagine, may be deemed harmful and deviant if one is concerned about the maintenance of conventional sexuality as *the* sexuality standard.

The final group that also potentially pushes the boundaries of a "hyper-accepting" community is the babyfurs. As Quinn and Forsyth (2005:193–194) note, normal sexual deviance "is sexual behavior that is widespread and occurs with low visibility, partly because of its sexual nature and partly as a result of the fact that it is felt to offend the normative standards of most people in a community." Pathological sexual deviance, on the other hand, "describes behaviors that are severely proscribed by rigorously enforced law and mores ... considered harmful by most . . . and few people actually engage in them." Babyfurs, the final group we will discuss who at least potentially push the boundaries of a "hyper-accepting" community, fit their latter definition. Babyfurs like to act like or become a young anthropomorphic animal such as a puppy, kit, and so on or perhaps a babyfur just enjoys diaper play. The concern that makes these furries potentially deviant is the small step or as one interviewee said, eventual regression, to pedophilia. The furry community is no more accepting of the "child lover" than are conventional communities.

Deviance and the Struggle for Community Legitimacy

Parrish (2002:261) states that a community

> . . . is a group of people who, by virtue of a natural longing for interaction, and shared goals, interest, and fears, feel a sustained bond of connection, cooperation, and support with one another.

He goes on to note that

> . . . virtual communities exist in a virtual, constructed, agreed upon geography with (1) a minimum level of interactivity; (2) a variety of communicators; (3) a minimum level of sustained membership; and (4) a virtual common public space where a significant portion of interaction occurs (265).

Although this is but one definition, it seems an appropriate one to apply. Our interviewees unanimously mentioned the importance of community, particularly the Internet community, to living as a furry. The Internet, as an agreed-upon space for interaction, allows furry fans to meet, exchange their passions and art, get to know one another, and it allows a forum that may lead to meeting in "real" life. To this extent, the furry fandom comprises a very general and diverse community as well as many specific ones predicated on particular interests and location: those who interact through chat groups, Second Life, attending "confurences," or by creating safe spaces for interaction in local areas. Sabout L'our, mentioned earlier, turned his home into a meeting place for like-minded others in the Santa Fe area.

Like any large community of diverse others and like any other at least potentially marginalized community (lesbian, bisexual, gay, transgendered, queer, and intersexed, for example) there is a struggle in terms of desired goals and means to achieve those goals. Is the community to be recognized, legitimized, accepted, or merely tolerated? And is the appropriate strategy to achieve these goals, however defined, to align with the dominant culture or to reject the dominant culture in favor of a more inclusive one? In reviewing Web sites and listening to our interviewees, we believe the furry community as a whole both aligns with and rejects aspects of the dominant culture. Like other communities there are levels of acceptability—the furries are open and so are not too critical of diversity in appearances, sexual experimentation, sexual orientations, and so on. But they wish to protect the community and their identities from the fringes that, because they are exotic, tend to be the ones that get the most press and form peoples' opinions about being a furry in general. Furries indeed may be on the "suburbs of normalcy" or may be stigmatized because of their personal associations with animals and animal characters, but they are, after all, simply working, creating their art, their friendships, and their communities like everyone else. They also appreciate the importance of not recreating the intolerance evident in the media that, from their perspective, unfairly and negatively define the whole community by the actions of a few. To this end, the community appears to be "hyper-accepting" as one interviewee stressed, but yet attempts to be more socially palatable by defining those on the boundaries of what is acceptable as deviant, for example, the plushies.

In essence, the furry community, challenging the social norms, drawing criticism from nonfurry others, and threatening others through their acceptance of many different lifestyles, also considers those who push their own boundaries as deviant. Few among the furries accept the zoos, plushies, or "piles of yiffing fursuiters" as those who define all, yet an important characteristic of the furry community and communities is that joining together brings support against those who do not understand and condemn their work, choices, and lifestyles. The "God hates furries website"—a fair, unbiased, factual resource, or so it claims—is dedicated to demeaning the "dark, crazy side" of the furry Internet community. Although we are not allowed to directly quote his Web site, Buddy "laughs at" and demonizes those he thinks are devoid of decency or morality. Of course, he is overgeneralizing the choices and behaviors of some to the whole, but he is also bringing up what many in the community also find threatening and hence deviant: ". . . all kinds of pedo shit, babyfurs (who may not be pedos, they just like adult baby roleplay), balloon/inflation fetishists, all sort of stuff . . ." Mirroring other communities thought of as deviant, the members struggle with their place, identities, and legitimacy. In conclusion, we ask, "Are they deviant?" The answer is yours to explain and defend.

Notes

1. *Otherkin*—A descriptive noun for those people who perceive themselves to be something other than human. For detailed information and discussion see http://www.otherkin.net/articles/what.html.

2. For more information on plushies and the furries who share their lives with stuffed animals, see Fox Wolfie Galen's plushie page at http://www.velocity.net/~galen/.

3. For more information about the debate within the community concerning this group often defined as anti-Semitic, see the Jewish Defense League of Second Life at http://jdlsl.wordpress.com/2008/10/26/victory-over-the-nazi-furs/.

Discussion Questions

1. Drawing on points made in this article, are furries deviant? In what ways and from whose perspective? In other words, defend/support your decision. Do you think it would be stigmatizing or embarrassing to tell your parents or friends that you are a furry? Why or why not?
2. Thinking about all the different groups of people who are labeled as deviants or deviant subcultures, what makes the furries both the same and different? How is the idea of community like that of other deviant groups? Or is it?

References

Adler, Patricia A. and Peter Adler. 2011. *Constructions of Deviance: Social Power, Context, and Interaction*, 7th ed. Belmont, CA: Wadsworth, Cengage Learning.

Anthrocon. 2011. Retrieved February 1, 2011 (http://www.anthrocon.org/about-furry).

Atkinson, Michael and Kevin Young. 2001. "Flesh Journeys: The Radical Body Modification of Neoprimitives." *Deviant Behavior* 22, 2:117–46.

Avner, Dennis. 2011. "Stalking Cat." Retrieved February 7, 2011 (http://www.stalkingcat.net).

Becker, Howard S. 1963. *Outsiders: Studies in the Sociology of Deviance*. New York: Free Press.

Berry, Bonnie. 2008. "Interactionism and Animal Aesthetics: A Theory of Reflected Social Power." *Society and Animals* 16:75–89.

Erikson, Kai T. 2004 [1966]. *Wayward Puritans: A Study in the Sociology of Deviance*, Classic Edition. Boston, MA: Allyn & Bacon.

Fron, Janie, Tracy Fullerton, J. F. Morie, and Celia Pearce. 2007. "Playing Dress-Up: Costumes, Roleplay and Imagination." Paper presented at the First Philosophy of Computer Games Conference (Modena, January 2007).

"Fur and Loathing." *CSI: Crime Scene Investigation*. CBS. 2003-10-30. No. 5, season 4.

Gerbasi, Kathleen, Nicholas Paolone, Justin Higner, Laura Scaletta, Penny L. Bernstein,Samuel Conway, and Adam Privitera. 2008. "Furries from A to Z (Anthropomorphism to Zoomorphism)." *Society & Animals* 16:197–222.

"God hates furries" Retrieved April 24, 2011 (http://www.godhatesfurries.com/).

Goffman, Erving. 1959. *Presentation of Self in Everyday Life*. Garden City, NY: Doubleday.

Goode, Erich. 2010. *Deviant Behavior*, 9th ed. Upper Saddle River, NJ: Prentice Hall.

Gurley, George. 2001. "Pleasures of the Fur." *Vanity Fair*.

Kitsuse, John I. 1962. "Societal Reaction to Deviant Behavior: Problems of Theory and Method." *Social Problems* 9:247–56.

Kitsuse, John I. 1980. "Coming Out All Over: Deviants and the Politics of Social Problems" *Social Problems*. 28(1):1–13.

Kitsuse, John I. and Malcom Spector. 1975. "Social Problems and Deviance: Some Parallel Issues." *Social Problems* 22(5):584–94.

Meyers, Olin E. Jr. 2003. "No Longer the Lonely Species: A Post-Mead Perspective on Animals and Sociology." *International Journal of Sociology and Social Policy* 23(3):46–68.

Nast, Heidi J. 2006. "Loving. . . .Whatever: Alienation, Neoliberalism and Pet-Love in the Twenty-First Century" *ACME: An International E-Journal for Critical Geographies* 5(2):300–27.NatasiaSoftpaw at www.babyfur.com. Retrieved April 24, 2011 (www.babyfur.com).

Osaki, Alex. 2011. "Furry Survey v. 5.0.0." Retrieved March 13, 2011 (http://www.klisoura.com/furrypoll.php).

Parrish, Rick. 2002. "The Changing Nature of Community." *Strategies* 15(2):259–84.

Quinn, James F. and Craig J. Forsyth. 2005. "Describing Sexual Behavior in the Era of the Internet: A Typology for Empirical Research." *Deviant Behavior* 26:191–207.

Rust, David. 2002. "The Sociology of Furry Fandom." Retrieved February 1, 2011 (http://www.visi.com/~phantos/furrysoc.html).

Sprague, Erik. "The Lizardman." Retrieved February 7, 2011 (http://www.thelizardman.com).

Sumner, William Graham. 2010 [1906]. *Folkways: A Study of the Sociological Importance of Usages, Manners, Customs, Mores and Morals*. Ithaca, NY: Cornell University Library.

Thread. 2007. Retrieved February 7, 2011 (www.cosplay.com).

Winterman, Denise. 2009. "Who Are the Furries?" Retrieved February 1, 2011 (http://news.bbc.co.uk/2/hi/uk_news/magazine/8355287.stm).

Wisch, Rebecca F. 2008. "Overview of State Bestiality Laws." Animal Legal and Historical Center, Michigan State University College of Law. Retrieved April 25, 2011 (http://www.animallaw.info/articles/ovuszoophilia.htm).

Retrieved February 9, 2011 (http://www.therianthropes.com/furries.htm).

ARTICLE 24

Melissa Powell-Williams
Augusta State University

Are You "Deaf Enough?"

The first day I was introduced to American Sign Language and the deaf community, I was informed that I would never be able to understand deafness and that the deaf world did not belong to me. The first deaf person that I met was a culturally empowered deaf[1] instructor who pointed to me and signed, "Do you think you're better than me? You're not. Do you think I want to be like you, to hear, I don't. Do you think you're here to 'help' me? You can leave!" During break (when we hearing students snuck off to talk and "hear" freely) we fervently protested the audacity and arrogance of his assumptions. Though no one admitted to this for years, we had been forced to face our own ethnocentrism and "hearist" biases, and we resented it—we resented him. I felt particularly offended; since I had recently concluded nearly three full semesters as a sociology major and arrogantly imagined that I had learned my way out of such bigoted notions. Five years later, when I asked this instructor to serve on my dissertation committee, he promised to continue to remind me of my arrogance, hearism, and ethnocentrism. For this I am eternally grateful.

I pursued my love for the language and interest in the community by conducting interviews with 22 deaf individuals, (primarily face-to-face in American Sign Language (ASL) and through a video relay service), and observed and participated in over 150 hours of various deaf-related events. As I was conducting this research, I quickly learned that while hearing status served as an initial barrier preventing entrance into the culturally deaf community, it is by far not the only one. Though linked with the common experiences associated with lacking the ability to hear in a predominately hearing world, a great deal separates the culturally *D*eaf from the pathologically *d*eaf—and the *D*eaf community is a well-guarded space. When I asked Carol, who identifies as biculturally deaf with equal footing in both hearing and deaf worlds, about her experiences with the deaf community she aptly asked:

> Which one? What does the deaf community mean? Many, many, things, deaf people are varied. But with the culturally deaf world is very specific to the deaf culture, go to all-deaf schools, know ASL, and you cluster with each other. Now the [larger] deaf community varies a lot from old semi-communication to ASL. (Carol)

According to Carol, the community is flexible, varied. At its core resides a minority of culturally empowered deaf who maintain clearly identifiable behavioral and ideological boundaries within which they "cluster with each other." Carol explained to me that the culturally deaf are understood as part of the larger deaf community but not all deaf are necessarily part of the culturally deaf community. Pathological deafness is ascribed whereas culturally empowered deafness is achieved.

For some time, deaf scholars have reported that possessing group knowledge and shared deaf experiences is a commonality shared among the members of the culturally deaf community; (Padden 1996; Wrigley 1996; Groch 2001; Padden and Humphries 2005). Thus, I was not surprised to find that group knowledge in its relation to an "authentic" deaf identity was a common theme shared in interviews, presented in meetings, addressed in workshops, captured in artistic displays, and reified in the interactions I observed. Further, authenticity in any subcultural context is an interactional accomplishment—something that we must "do" and "do" consistently (Gubrium and Holstein 2000; 2009). For the deaf, proficiency in group knowledge is accomplished when one presents himself or herself as adhering to convention, mastering of cultural history, and/or possessing a culturally deaf attitude.

I began to dig a bit deeper into both the form and content of these criteria as they were experienced regardless of where those interviewed found themselves on the pathologically deaf-culturally deaf continuum. Specifically, I wanted to determine in what context and in what manner the concept of knowledge is intertwined with articulations of self and community membership not just for the culturally deaf but also for those who report feelings of exclusion. Most interviewed candidly discussed the successes and failures—of others and their own—as manifested in momentary glitches within interaction, defects in one's biography, or a possession of an essence that is either responsible for or indicative of their variable mastery of group knowledge. As will be addressed later, this mastery of both substance and delivery of "how to be deaf" or "deaf enough" is vital for inclusion into the culturally deaf community.

The Gatekeepers

Group members continuously create and sustain the boundaries needed to effectively separate the insiders from outsiders, (Taylor and Whittier 1992; Berbrier 2002 Benford 2002). Boundary markers in the culturally deaf community separating the hearing and the pathological deaf from the empowered deaf are maintained by a relatively small group of culturally deaf leaders (Padden 1996; Berbrier 2001). Groch (2001) explains that empowered deaf individuals must 1) believe that the deaf share a collective identity, (2) recognize that the deaf are oppressed and thus are treated unfairly by the hearing majority, (3) realize the need for unity in fighting injustices, (4) place appropriate blame of this oppression on the hearing majority, and (5) recognize that acting collectively is the best way to overcome this oppression. Additional criteria distinguishing those who are culturally deaf from other deaf individuals include the recognition of ASL as the primary form of communication, acceptance rather than renouncement of deafness, shared deaf experiences and grievances, and participation in culturally deaf activities (Higgins 1981). The construction and production of group boundaries was easily observable in the interactions at the weekend camps, various social gatherings, and meetings I attended. For the culturally deaf I met and interviewed, acquisition of group knowledge is key to accomplishing authenticity, perhaps because such acquisition is an observable expression of the commitment to "self-values" thought to be necessary for subcultural authenticity (Erickson 1995).

At times, those interviewed described this knowledge as a product that can be obtained with the willingness of members to learn conventions or through socialization within the community at an early age. At other times, possession of this knowledge is expressed as a more deterministic designation that is intrinsically linked to an essence that one simply does or does not possess. Gary, a Gallaudet University[2] alumni, former administrator in state school for the deaf, and self described fully authenticated member of the culturally deaf community, is an example of the former in that he conceptualizes his and others' group knowledge as something that is or is not obtained. When describing the deaf community, he designates himself and others as full members based on the knowledge gained through shared deaf experience that links all deaf historically:

> We have the same interests, same activities. We have a history that we all know, the deaf history. Mainstreamed kids, they don't know who Thomas Hopkins Gallaudet is. They don't know their history or other deaf things or

> culture. They need to be exposed especially at the college level. Gallaudet is big in Washington, DC many, many students sign and they know their history. I thank my lucky stars that I had that experience.

Gary uses the term *we* in reference to those who were not mainstreamed or are not alumni from Gallaudet in contrast to *they* in reference to the "mainstreamed" or "pathologically" deaf. According to Gary, knowing the deaf history legitimizes this history and is a necessary component for inclusion. Throughout our discussion Gary emphasized this knowledge over language skills or level of (auditory) deafness as a greater determinant for inclusion and definitive of the "type of deaf" one was. As will be discussed in the following section, this connection between inclusion and the acquisition of practical knowledge regarding (cultural) deafness was pervasive in the stories shared by not only the culturally deaf but also the biculturally deaf, and even the "hearized" deaf.

Others depict this knowledge in essentialist terms by suggesting that some simply "have it" when others do not. This characterization assumes that group knowledge is reflected in one's ownership of an identifiable essence that surfaces within interaction. In other words, to some, one is or is not "deaf enough[3] for full membership. But what does "deaf enough" mean to the deaf I met? I asked Alice, who was a member of the board of directors at Gallaudet at the time of "Tent City." For Alice, being deaf enough transcends beyond what can be actively obtained into something one simply "is." This essence is brought to life and made observable within the community itself and if you are deaf enough, like her, others will "know" it:

> Not "deaf enough" maybe is not socializing with the deaf community or interacting with the deaf community or having deafness strongly in your heart. It is not connected with sign language skills but rather how you feel and interact with the community. We can read it in their interactions. We can tell, we can watch someone interact and we just know—we know if they have a deaf-heart and we can watch someone interact and know that deafness is not in their heart . . . it is something that we connect with and see a connection within the interactions You know other groups like women and ethnic groups that kind of see eye to eye. You know if you're accepted in their community or not."

For Alice, membership is not necessarily contingent upon one'sign skills; rather it is determined by whether his or her actions demonstrate the possession of a "deaf-heart." She compares the culturally deaf to other minority group members, in that if you are not part of it—despite sharing the inability to hear—then you are incapable of understanding it. Alice, like Gary, uses the term *we* to describe members who are capable of evaluating the behaviors, interactions, and density of deafness in the heart of others through critical interactional examinations. Later in our conversation, Alice repeats her assertion that the connective nature of this group knowledge—as validated through her own possession of a deaf heart—allows her the ability to observe its possession by others. Those whose interactional performances fail in some regard are disqualified from full membership, and they too will *know* this exclusion. These deaf, who claim to be ineligible for entry into the culturally deaf community, discuss this process in the following section.

The Kept

The relationship between being deaf enough and community acceptance was perhaps most vividly addressed by those on the receiving end of full-member evaluations. Several deaf that I met were fully aware of their either temporary or persistent disqualification from complete authentic membership and their stories carried comparable assumptions regarding the dualistic (agentic and deterministic) nature of full inclusion. While maintaining superior sign skills, knowledge, and competency as a biculturally deaf woman, Carol discussed the mixed reactions she receives from fully authenticated members:

> It depends on the attitude; some deaf would look down on me for not coming from a state school growing up, and judge me. Other deaf look at me and say "wow, you didn't go to a state school. But wow, you can sign really well that's great!"

Since Carol did not come from a state-school, she is met by those who either anticipate her shame or who assume her pride in her ability to overcome her discrediting past. In either case, Carol's background is understood as a vulnerability to her full inclusion.

In another example, Vivian, who today identifies as an empowered deaf community member possessing a strong deaf identity, shares that on her quest for community authenticity she suffered considerable setbacks. She attributes these obstructions to her ignorance of how to be a deaf person, that surfaced within her interactions with the culturally deaf community. She claims to have eventually overcome these interactional failings through her decreased association with hearing and pathologically deaf individuals and her increased involvement with the culturally deaf community. When asked whether she felt accepted within the culturally deaf community, she comments:

> Not at first, when I started meeting [culturally] deaf people I couldn't even fingerspell my name. I was slow and awkward . . . The people within the community are not the same. It really depended on the individual; they were exposed to their experiences. Many deaf are just like me, they are from the same background, and they know. They may have tried to teach me sign and they were more kind. Other deaf would look at me differently. Maybe they grew up profoundly deaf, their whole life so they had a negative view of voicing and talking but most were very welcoming to me. They wanted to see me involved. There were some that judged me based on my skills at that time I did not know very much about the culture or their expectations or really know how to act like a deaf person.

To Vivian, inclusion initially was out of her control because it was determined by the reactions she received from those around her. Resembling Carol's experience with signing skills, for Vivian the consequences experienced from not acting like a deaf person were contingent upon the experiences, biography, and perspectives of those she met, not her own. Others who were previous "outsiders," shared her experience and possessed the knowledge to properly interact with her as she became acclimated to the group. Those who never lived as outsiders did not. Despite this recognition, Vivian clearly internalized the culturally deaf standard of normality and "grew" as a deaf woman through her adherence to this normality.

In another example, Candice directly incorporates the phrase *deaf enough* within her own quest for inclusion within the community. Candice's story is perhaps the most problematic in terms of formulating a cohesive identity narrative that I have come across. To summarize, Candice had the rare fate to be born hard-of-hearing in an all culturally deaf family. At the time of our meeting she was profoundly deaf but prefers to identify herself as a hard-of-hearing. She states that this identification stems from her early childhood in which her initial, residual hearing served as a barrier to full inclusion into her fully culturally deaf family. Her narrative is one of discrimination, exclusion, and isolation not only from the hearing world but also from her own culturally deaf family and the broader deaf community. As an adult, she attributes her persistent inability to be included within the deaf community explicitly to her failure to be deaf enough.

> I will never—if you're going to be a part of the deaf world, you go to Gallaudet, you have to go to a residential school in order to understand, and I will never understand I am not "deaf enough."

Candice uses nearly the same evaluative criteria as Gary in her connection of educational experiences and inclusion, and is fully aware of her inability to ever make the cut. Rather than stating that her disconnection from the community is based on knowledge, as an outsider Candice describes her inability to *understand* what it means to be deaf enough—or lack of possession of its essence—as a barrier to full inclusion. Interestingly, as an adult Candice now works in a deaf-related agency, is married to a hearing man who was raised by deaf parents, and has two sons—one is deaf and the other hearing.

Katie, who shares the identical educational and language background as the authenticated member Alice—works at a deaf school and attended all-deaf schools—speaks of community inclusion through the perspective of an outsider. When asked to explain how she viewed the deaf community, her response directly addressed this notion of acceptance or rejection.

> It's kind of hard to explain because it's so abstract, but . . . it's pretty much whether you are accepted or not. And you will feel it . . . a lot of it depends on whether they know if you're a true native ASL person or if you are a deaf person with a capital D. It's almost like a club so-to-speak, and either you are accepted or rejected. They have their own beliefs their own system, certain identifiable traits, and it's just I would say that I'm not part of their culture, because I have a cochlear implant.

Unlike Alice, Katie refers to the community members as *they*, explicitly acknowledging her exclusion from the community because she is not one of the "true ASL people" or "Deaf with a capital D." She has been evaluated by others and thus she does not *know* what it means to be "truly" culturally deaf herself but can identify it in others.

For Katie, group authenticity is accomplished by knowing that it is best to refute the assumed advantages of cochlear implants by either refusing the treatment or removing the device after it has been implanted. She identifies that her decision to be implanted epitomizes her lack of possession of the essence or deaf heart and is one of the "certain identifiable traits" that routinely reaffirms her outsider status.

> I know for a fact that I am not part of their culture, and that's okay. Everyone's entitled to their opinions and their differences, but I mean when I got the cochlear implant, I was shunned. I was condemned, you know, "you don't do that. That is not right. You should be proud of your deafness.". . .It's a choice I made the decision. You make the decision you do what you want and you have to put up with the consequences, because after all, no one lives your life. You have to live it and I don't regret it.

According to those interviewed, the cochlear implant is perhaps the most referenced visual stigma marker (Goffman 1963) in need of management (removal, covering, etc.) when in the company of culturally deaf individuals. Having an implant is deemed a recognizable deformation that separates possessors from full inclusion into the culturally deaf world for some. It also is understood as a "blemish of one's character" since it signifies an individual's choice to either be implanted or refuse to remove it. According to Katie and the others interviewed, these choices have been met with hostility by others who claim that those with implants lack pride in their deafness. The clear visibility of these stigma symbols may lead to its possessor being considered "unfit" members of the deaf community (Kent and Smith 2006). In fact, several culturally deaf I interviewed refer to the willful removal of their implant as a "transformational" act that transitioned them into a more empowered and authentic deaf identity. Similar to Hutson's (2010) research on the "coming-out" process of gays and lesbians, such forms of visual representation serve to "align their outer appearances with their own self-values," which ultimately strengthens their claims of authenticity (p. 229).

Jim, for example shares that "in mainstream schools, deaf with cochlear implants were accepted by others, but not at deaf schools," and today he often does not wear his implant when in an all-deaf context. Interestingly, when I met Jim at a local picnic, he wore his implant for part of the day but eventually removed it due to anticipated and observed contingencies it created with the other picnic goers. He shared that his implant needed continued adjustment because he could "hear what the hearing couldn't hear," like heartbeats, bugs crawling, and leaves dropping. While he was explaining this to me, his aids admitted a piercing sound that he only became aware of only after his hearing companion quickly pointed it out to him. Once he was informed of the sound, his face turned red and he abruptly removed himself from the table to adjust his settings. Due to their overt stares and gestures, it was clear that his frustrating attempts to adjust his device added to its visibility and his vulnerability to scrutiny by deaf peers.

Conclusion

Though no one who was interviewed reported asking or being asked, "Are you 'deaf enough?'" directly, the interviews reveal that the level of adherence to and adoption of appropriate behavior and worldview is embedded in deaf—deaf, deaf—Deaf, and Deaf—Deaf interactions for the deaf in my research. The embattled history of the deaf community demonstrates that it has been the strong guard maintained by the culturally empowered deaf community that has progressed the lives of all deaf individuals and is essential to the continued pursuit of equal rights and communicative access. According to those interviewed, the effectiveness of one's performance and knowledge of convention reveals a great deal regarding his or her commitment to the deaf community, and by proxy this rich deaf history. In short, this commitment to community and the deaf essence are deemed vital for its continued strength, progress, and survival.

This research also reports a latent consequence associated with safeguarding the community: the exclusion of many (most) deaf who, for a number of reasons, do not feel accepted within the culturally deaf community. Signifying effective presentation of group knowledge and community commitment as markers of authenticity is not unique to the deaf experience; however, given the relative marginalization the population shares within a predominately hearing world, the implications of exclusion may exacerbate this burden for many. Candice exemplifies this concern when she shares, "I don't feel connected with the deaf world. I do not feel I have connections with the hearing world. So my identity is very imbalanced, what do you do?"

Notes

1. Though not used in this brief article, it is convention for researchers and activists within the deaf community to differentiate those who align themselves with the deaf experience as the standard for "normalcy" with a capital *D*, from those who align themselves with the hearing experience as a standard for normalcy with a lower-case *d*.

2. Gallaudet University is the only university in the world that serves primarily deaf students.

3. "Tent City" is the name of the protest that occurred on the grounds of Gallaudet University in 2006. Protesters primarily included students who were opposed to the board's selection of a new president of the university, Jane K. Fernandez. During this protest, the phrase *deaf enough* was directed toward the protestors as a means to undermine their concerns regarding the lack of fairness and transparency in the selection of a new president. Its use triggered a strong reaction from the culturally deaf who claimed to be misrepresented and also those who felt excluded from the community.

Discussion Questions

1. What is the difference between the culturally deaf from other deaf individuals? How does this distinction relate broader understandings of deviance and deviant groups?

2. What does being deaf enough mean? How can individuals tell who is deaf enough or who is not?
3. What do you think are some consequences for individuals who are not considered deaf enough?

References

Benford, Robert D. 2002. "Controlling Narratives and Narratives as Control within Social Movements." Pp. 53–75 in *Stories of Change: Narrative and Social Movements*, edited by Joseph E. Davis. Albany, NY: SUNY Press.

Berbrier, Mitch. 2002. "Making Minorities: Cultural Space, Stigma Transformation Frames, and the Categorical Status Claims of Deaf, Gay, and White Supremacist Activists in Late Twentieth Century America." *Sociological Forum* 17:553–91.

Erickson, Rebecca J. 1995. "The Importance of Authenticity for Self and Society." *Symbolic Interaction* 18(2):121–44.

Goffman, Eriving. 1963. *Stigma: Notes on the Management of Spoiled Identity*. New York: Simon and Schuster.

Groch, Sharon. 2001. "Free Spaces: Creating Oppositional Consciousness in the Disability Rights Movement." Pp. 65–98 in *Oppositional Consciousness: The Subjective Roots of Protest*. Chicago, IL: University of Chicago Press.

Gubrium, Jaber F. and James A. Holstein. 2000. "The Self in a World of Going Concerns." Pp. 420–32 in *Inside Social Life*, edited by S.E. Cahill. Los Angeles, CA: Oxford University Press.

Higgins, Paul C. 1981. *Outsiders in a Hearing World: A Sociology of Deafness*. Beverly Hills, CA: Sage.

Hutson, David J. 2010. "Standing OUT/Fitting IN: Identity, Appearance, and Authenticity in Gay and Lesbian Communities." *Symbolic Interaction* 33(2):213–33.

Kent Bruce, and Sandra Smith. 2006. "They Only See It When the Sun Shines in My Ears: Perceptions of Adolescent Hearing Aid Users." *Journal of Deaf Studies and Deaf Education* 11(4): 461–76.

Padden, Carol. 1996. "From the Cultural to the Bicultural: The Modern Deaf Community." Pp. 79–98 in *Cultural and Language Diversity and the Deaf Experience*, edited by Ila Parasnis. Cambridge, UK: Cambridge University Press.

Padden, Carol and Tom Humphries. 2005. *Inside Deaf Culture*. Cambridge, MA: Harvard University Press.

Taylor, Verta and Nancy E. Whittier. 1992. "Collective Identity in Social Movement Communities: Lesbian Feminist Mobilization." Pp. 505–19 in *Social Movements: Perspectives and Issues*, edited by Steven M. Buechler and F. Kurt Cylke, Jr. Mountain View, CA: Mayfield Publishing.

Wrigley, Owen. 1996. *The Politics of Deafness*. Washington, DC: Gallaudet University Press.

ARTICLE 25

Corie Hammers
Macalester College

Lesbian/Queer Bathhouse Culture and the Organization of (Im)Personal Sex

Introduction to Bathhouses

With urbanization came a rise in "highly specialized sexual subcultures" (Green 2008), such that in urban centers today one can find a plethora of spaces and subcultures catering "to a plurality of desires, practices and bodies" (p. 25). The bathhouse is merely one type of erotic space whose primary function is to offer opportunities for impersonal homosexual sex (certainly heterosexually identified men can and do seek sex in such venues). Bathhouses are licensed "health" clubs where individuals pay an entry fee (Weinberg and Williams 1975), and usually contain a steam room, sauna, and sometimes an outdoor swimming pool. Baths are typically found in larger cities and tend to be unremarkable in appearance—often located in unmarked buildings in order to maintain a low profile, which is an important strategy for longevity and protection from police. Because baths operate in a zone of legal ambiguity, owners put a variety of measures in place to protect clientele. In addition to security personnel, there are often multiple locked doors and rooms one has to navigate before entering the interior. These barriers function to "delay intrusion and allow patrons to stop sexual activity" (Weinberg and Williams 1975:128) in case of police raids, since individuals "caught in the act" can be arrested under indecency charges (or under bawdy house laws in Canada).

Providing an almost instantaneous sense of security and anonymity is crucial for bathhouse business. Customers will not return if they feel unsafe or believe the bathhouse is too conspicuous. Additionally, there is a strong stigma attached to this activity within the gay male community, which makes bathhouse sex off-limits as a topic of discussion (Tewksbury 2003). Shame and embarrassment are tied to such activity, since the perception is that only a certain type—the unattractive, old(er), and heavier set man—utilizes the space (although this is far from true). Consequently, if using a bathhouse is purportedly proof of one's failure in "getting sex," maintaining an anonymous and safe environment becomes that much more important. These elements—safety, secrecy, and anonymity—will resurface repeatedly in this discussion, for these components take on qualitatively different dimensions when it comes to the lesbian/queer bathhouse culture. Before delving further into the bathhouse literature, I introduce the two lesbian/queer bathhouses—Pussy Palace and SheDogs—that inform this article.

Pussy Palace and SheDogs

Pussy Palace and SheDogs are not bathhouses per se, but the organizations/committees that put on lesbian/queer bathhouse events by taking over men's baths every few months. Although these are irregular and episodic events, the organizations—Pussy Palace and SheDogs—are permanent, ongoing entities. Pussy Palace began holding events in 1998, while SheDogs held its first bathhouse event in 2004. Each organization has between six and eight committee members. These members are responsible for myriad tasks from staffing to maintaining

Web sites to providing security. Of all these duties, the most important is ensuring that patrons adhere to the bathhouse's three cardinal rules: consent, respect, and confidentiality. Creating a safe(er) space is a top priority, for if the space is not safe or does not *feel* safe, then the members' very objective—fostering conditions for sexual exploration—is undermined. While "safety" for male bathhouse users is one *primarily* yoked to anonymity, the overriding concern here is that of sexual safety and acceptance (in terms of body type, gender/sexual identities, and race).

Besides their permanency, these lesbian/queer baths stand apart for the particular brand of feminist politics they embrace. This comes through most tellingly in their admission policy. Pussy Palace and SheDogs stress in their advertising that these are neither "women-only" events nor events confined to those who identify as lesbian or queer. Rather, all individuals (in theory) are welcome regardless of sexual persuasion/orientation, as well as individuals whose gender falls outside the bounds of "woman." Thus, gender variant, transgender, and transsexual men and women are welcome. One organizer put it this way: "We don't care who you are. This is for all those who at some point were, have been, are going to be, or consider themselves now to be female-bodied." This "non-negotiable" (as per Pussy Palace's Web site) policy, initially somewhat controversial, sees gender self-determination and sexual freedom as equally important to Pussy Palace's main mission. Operating from a pro-sex feminist and queer framework, these bathhouses seek the eradication of phobia in all of its permutations (bi-phobia, trans-phobia, racism). In short, to not include transmen and transwomen—and those in-between—is oppressive and antifeminist. In addition to countering the societal denigration of women's sexuality, these lesbian/queer bathhouses are cast as a resistance to the feminist sexual policing of the past where carnality and desire were deemed to be objectionable and predatory behaviors (Roy 1993).

Bathhouse Setting

Pussy Palace takes over a men's bathhouse located in the heart of Toronto's "gay village." The bathhouse itself is quite large with four floors, each of which has its own set of private rooms on either side of long, narrow hallways. Hallways and stairwells are so constricted that two bodies moving in opposite directions have to adjust in order to move past each other. The numerous floors and hallways, coupled with dim lighting, make for a confusing space. The labyrinth style is a purposive architectural maneuver to induce a mood-altering effect. As Richters (2007) notes, sex venues are "constructed to create space 'out of time' " (p. 282). There is an indoor sauna, showers, and restrooms adjacent to the outdoor space, which has a swimming pool and lounge area. Like Pussy Palace, SheDogs takes over a men's bath once every few months. The bathhouse is in a working-class neighborhood with several other queer establishments in proximity. This bath has just one floor and is, spatially speaking, quite small. Upon entry there is a lounge area, which immediately opens up to the central portion, on either side of which are private rooms. Showers, restrooms, and a sauna are located at the back.

Space, Sex, and the Social Organization of Impersonal Sex

The physical features of space shape the sexual encounters therein. Through both written and unwritten rules—the codes of conduct—and the physical features of space, the built environment facilitates certain behaviors while inhibiting others. The field of sexuality studies has increasingly attuned us to the ways in which space informs sexual sociality (Knopp 1992). All spaces have their own norms and styles of relating. Owners of sex venues arrange space in ways that work to promote sexual interaction and elicit certain behaviors. As you will see, there is a particular way of doing bathhouse sex—that is, there are norms attached to this sexual performance. That there is an etiquette and organization to bathhouse behavior belies the assumption that sexual venues are unruly, no-holds-barred places. Tattelman describes this orderliness in the following manner:

> Sexual opportunities, which are embedded in the rituals of the baths, are often formalized and silent. Behavior and meaning are coded by location, posture and dress with sufficient distinctions between one and another. These standing rules, symbols, and expressions are generally followed, understood and respected. They create a common understanding, giving coherence and clarity to the activities. (1999:82)

Besides rituals and codes, the architectural style is one deliberately structured "to make sex easy" (Richters 2007). This includes things such as tight vertical spaces, private rooms or nooks, and darkrooms (where group sex and/or multiple, consecutive sexual exchanges occur). I elaborate next on these codes and physical features, and the kind of sexual performance that emerges in the bathhouse. Baths offer, in short, a "road map" for sex (Weinberg and Williams 1975).

The Bounding of the Sexual Exchange

The organization of sex in male baths has been characterized as one of bounding (Weinberg and Williams 1975) in that there is an abrupt beginning and end to the sexual encounter. This bounding ensures an impersonal, efficient, and quick exchange, enabling patrons to maximize their time and pleasure by interacting with a variety of individuals. Weinberg and Williams describe this bounding as:

> a desirable condition for impersonal sex. It is facilitated by interactional rules and territories that clearly define sex as an outcome, that limit socializing, and that sustain the expectation of closed horizons regarding the future of the relationship. (1975:31)

This bounding depends on "asocial sexual behavior" (Flowers et al. 2000), wherein silence, a de-emphasis on identity, and being discreet pervade the sexual exchange (Tattelman 1999). As a result, the atmosphere in men's baths is one of an overarching silence, where verbal communication is severely restricted and frowned upon. While talking does take place, particularly in the nonsexual or open facilities (outdoor areas, lounges), it is "almost always short, succinct and direct" and "very rarely reveals personal information" (Tewksbury 2003:224). As Richters (2006) and Elwood et al. (2003) have reported, the pressure to be silent is so intense that it alone contributes to risky sexual behaviors—curtailing as it does sexual negotiation, including condom use. As a result of such expectations, "the demeanor inside the venue is serious" (Richters 2006:288).

Dim lighting, loud music, nooks and crannies, orgy rooms, and darkrooms foster a sense of privacy, in turn reinforcing feelings of anonymity and silence. Moreover and importantly, this spatial layout is one that prioritizes bodily communication. As the name implies, darkrooms are just that, dark, wherein any and all identity markers are suspended. Navigation of the space is a sensory, corporeal, and tactile pursuit. It is in the bathhouse where one learns to communicate through and with the body via gestures, touch, and codes—such as the placement of one's towel, eye contact, or the rubbing of one's genitals. Male bathhouse users understand that body language is the primary mode of communicating sexual interest, as noted by Tewksbury who states, "The way a man presents himself and how he emphasizes his body (and the parts of his body he emphasizes in presentation) are the ways to suggest one's sexual interests and availability" (2003:226). I now turn to the methods section.

Methods

Data collection for this project began in the fall of 2004 and ended in June of 2007. The present analysis is based on 27 interviews

(20 face-to-face and 7 phone interviews) and participant observation at bathhouse events. The approach to data collection and the research process was one of an inductive method of analysis, wherein themes/categories/patterns emerged from the data (Patton 1980). My first initial step for this project was getting permission from bathhouse organizers to gain access to their bathhouse events, making it clear from the beginning that I was a researcher interested in examining these spaces and speaking with attendees. I also wanted to establish this line of communication with the organizers for I knew how important it was to get their own perspectives—they were after all the ones who started these committees and thus the bathhouse events. Upon getting permission, I immediately began contacting other members to set up interviews for upcoming visits. I believe my sample closely mirrored the general demographic when it came to attendees. The majority of interviewees were in their mid-20s to late 30s, with most identifying as queer or bisexual. Approximately 30 percent identified as lesbian. The majority of attendees were white, with persons of color making up approximately 10 percent of bathhouse patrons. Three participants identified as transgender and two as transwomen. Over half identified as nonmonogamous or polyamorous.

Interviews were done using snowball and convenience sampling techniques, with my target population being those who patronize the bathhouse. Interviews were conducted either at the bathhouse (in a quieter area of the bath), the person's place of work, or at a neutral location (a nearby restaurant/coffee shop). Interview data were transcribed, coded, and analyzed using NVivo, a qualitative software program. Field notes stem from visits I made to four bathhouse events. During events, I disclosed my researcher role to potential interviewees, for I did not set out to be a covert researcher. Certainly, my own stance as researcher, who while not directly engaging in sexual activities but nonetheless participating through observation, casual conversation, and interviews, impacts my own understanding of lesbian/queer public sexual culture. Having set myself apart by choosing not to directly engage in the scene—that is, engage in sexual activities—had I overlooked certain subtleties and cues (of negotiation, body language) that can be accessed only through sexual participation? Due to the concise nature of this article, there is not an in-depth discussion on these ethnographic issues and the ways "degrees of involvement" impact the research process (for a helpful discussion on types of field roles see Davidson and Layder 1994). I now turn back to men's bathhouse culture in order to situate this environment in relation to these lesbian/queer bathhouses, where I hope to show a different logic is operating.

The Social Organization of Personal Sex

The Boundlessness of the Sexual Exchange

The "known and shared intent" (Weinberg and Williams 1975) of the bathhouse means that participants are "on the same page" as it relates to bathhouse language, motivation, and sexual satiation. As mentioned earlier, sexual encounters between men are depersonalized, bounded experiences. Describing an encounter as stranger sex denotes two things: prior to the sexual exchange the individuals involved have no degree of affiliation, and no attempts are made to get to know one another either during or after sex—that is, a "getting to know you" rapport is irrelevant to sexual satiation and undesirable. Additionally, personalizing sex takes time away from other interactions, and ruptures feelings of anonymity and "the wish to compartmentalize the activity" (Weinberg and Williams 1975:131). Again, this is not to say that all interactions within men's baths fulfill the criteria of stranger/impersonal sex. Certainly, men do establish more permanent ties and/or have more personalized encounters. But bath norms limit socializing and "sustain the expectation of closed horizons" (1975:131) such that intimate encounters are the exception to the rule.

The closed horizon that overhangs these encounters diverges from that found among Pussy Palace and SheDogs participants. Of those lesbian/queer/trans participants who had had sexual experiences at the bathhouse, for the vast majority, an abrupt halt or bounding to the sexual encounter rarely, if ever occurred, was not an expected aspect of the sexual exchange, and if anything, would be considered awkward and rude behavior. When it came to participants' narratives, sex involved a more fluid quality in that encounters took on an amorphous shape, with no real beginning or end. These encounters, given their fluidity and lack of compartmentalization, have what I characterize as an "open horizon." One interviewee, who had had sex earlier that night, in elaborating on this sexual encounter remarked, "You know, we talk, tell each other what we want, how we want to play. We do a lot of touching, kissing, rubbing before sex. It's playful. We're having sex, but having fun while doing it."

One of the qualities sustaining this open horizon is the verbal component within the sexual exchange. Whereas encounters among men contain little or no verbal communication, in all of the sexual exchanges I observed and of those transactions discussed in interviews, verbal communication played a central role. Not only did participants see talking as critical to the negotiation process, but verbal communication heightened the encounter's erotic appeal and made for more satisfying sex. During the three Pussy Palace bathhouse events I attended, there was always some degree of public sex going on. I define public sex in this instance as sex which took place in the open areas—such as a stairwell or the outdoor area. These public sex scenes were always quite loud in that the individuals involved not only communicated their signs of pleasure verbally (e.g., moaning, noises) but speaking to one another throughout the encounter was part of the display. One woman, who I had just interviewed and was seated next to me when a public sex scene unfolded in the outdoor lounge area, remarked on this auditory element of pleasure, asserting "This is one of the most exciting parts of the bathhouse, hearing those noises, listening to that. Isn't this fabulous!" Christie, a Pussy Palace organizer, in comparing Pussy Palace to men's baths where it is "quiet and discreet and there's no talking," characterizes this atmosphere as one both demonstrative and noisy, stating "I want to party, I want to have a good time, I want to be loud about having sex. Women are a lot louder than men. . . . I want to celebrate this so we are sort of doing a bit of a different culture."

Unlike men's baths where stranger sex is the primary type of encounter, at these bathhouses sexual exchanges contained some degree of affiliation or acquaintanceship. Individuals either already knew one another on some level or a personalized rapport occurred before the sexual transaction ensued. Many of those I observed engaging in sex were often found at later points in the evening talking or hanging out together. The most commonly cited reason given as to the rarity of stranger sex had to do with what one respondent described as the "safety factor." Although bathhouses are considered to be "safe spaces"—security is provided, and others are present and thus could intervene at any time—it nonetheless might be the case that lesbian/queer individuals are more likely to view stranger sex as just too risky. Twice I observed encounters in which the two individuals involved were strangers. Yet, these encounters quickly morphed into personalized interactions that entailed a "getting to know one another" dialogue. These verbal exchanges continued for several minutes, whereupon couples headed off to a private room. Trish, a Pussy Palace participant, began our interview by explaining enthusiastically how she had just had "great and hot sex with a complete stranger." Trish described how they "talked a bit before doing it . . . and what we wanted to do." When I asked her about how long they talked before going into one of the rooms, Trish stated, "about 5 minutes. . . . We introduced each other, talked about . . . what we did, you know the basic kind of get-to-know-you stuff." After their sexual engagement, phone numbers and e-mail addresses were exchanged.

Here again, contrary to the depersonalization and bounding found in men's baths, sexual exchanges among lesbian/queer women entailed *some* degree of connection. Where prior to the encounter, lesbian/queer participants might be strangers, a personalization process took place before sexual activities commenced. Again, I am not at all arguing that stranger or impersonal sex does not take place. I believe it does. What I am saying is that, given my observations and respondents' descriptions of their own experiences, impersonal exchanges were few and far between—the opposite of that found in men's baths where depersonalization itself generates sex. As can be gleaned from the preceding, the milieus at Pussy Palace and She Dogs were simultaneously social, playful, and sexual—elements of which are not found (certainly not endorsed) in men's baths where, to reiterate, a solemn, formal affect prevails wherein men's "interaction is focused" (Tewksbury 2003:223), to the point, and asocial. In these lesbian/queer baths the interactional style is one of social sexual behavior.

Finally, this sociality lends the lesbian/queer baths an air of *openness* that, given the taboo surrounding bathhouses and the patriarchal resistances to women's sexual agency, is somewhat paradoxical. That is, while men are compelled to remain secretive and furtive when it comes to bathhouse sex, patrons of the lesbian/queer baths were neither furtive nor felt ashamed. That many saw this event as political and resistive—to societal messages regarding queer women's sexuality as well as sexual and bodily shame—could I believe explain this openness that permeated the space. This is also I believe why participants felt so comfortable talking rather unabashedly about their experiences. A quite vivid example of this openness occurred before each of the Pussy Palace events I attended. Ironically, while bathhouses are zones of sexual transgression in a land of legal ambiguity, concealed from the outside world and thus hidden from public view, before each event long queues had formed outside the venue. The line of participants spilled out into the street, at times wrapping around a street corner, which is a fairly busy intersection in Toronto. This public visibility and lack of ambivalence sits in stark contrast to male bathhouse users, where furtiveness and invisibility hold sway. Tewksbury, in his own fieldwork on male baths, has observed the haste with which men exit the bathhouse, and how patrons plan their entrances to avoid having to wait in line (personal communication February, 2008). Tewksbury also notes that upon entering, there is little eye contact, palpable discomfort, and minimal conversation in the lobby area. I examine in the following section how organizers arranged the bathhouse setting in specific ways—ways the organizers hoped would foster conditions for sexual exploration.

Inciting the Verbal

Because Pussy Palace and SheDogs use men's bathhouses, modifying the space is obviously somewhat limited. In several of the interviews, respondents brought up their dislike of "having to use a men's bathhouse," and thought that if they had their own venue, "the space would be entirely different." Many also believed more individuals would come if they had a venue of their own, since the mere thought of utilizing men's baths was for some "off-putting." Shawn, a SheDogs member, sees the spatial layout as itself problematic since it is set up for men's anatomical and physical needs:

> This is one of the ways that the bathhouse structurally, architecturally was not designed for us. There is not enough horizontal play space, cause boys don't need it as much. There aren't enough big spaces where a crowd of people could gather . . . we like to do things communally. . . .

Besides the "institutional barriers, legal barriers and cultural barriers," women have thus to contend with a built environment specifically equipped for those whose anatomy is biologically "male."

Nonetheless, such settings can be altered in various ways so as to facilitate particular practices, interactions, and sexual activities. Many organizers saw it their duty to arrange the bathhouse in ways that would "induce desire." Moreover, running throughout organizers' interviews was this casting of the bathhouse as "a place of possibility." Organizers attempted to induce desire through an offering of services, which, according to Christie, a Pussy Palace organizer, are "free sexual rides" that provide a "warming up process that is safe." These sexual rides are themed rooms where sexual services are provided by volunteers. When I was there (services changed with each event), the following services were available: the g-spot room; massage room; lap dance room; fuck/fisting room—volunteers, wearing gloves, penetrate and/or stimulate clients; butt plug room; chick-with-a-dick room—a volunteer, wearing a strap-on, is at the ready to service people; porn room; S/M room; and the Temple Priestess room—wherein clients tell the "Temple Priestess" what they want who in turn services them. The sundry of services offered, as one organizer put it, "a variety of risk levels" that "maximize pleasure." Another organizer stated that such services "help get women in the mood," which it is thought will generate sexual activity outside the rooms. SheDogs also had activities available, such as a kissing (kissing and touching are allowed from the waist up) and massage room. There were also demonstrations at each event, such as fisting, strap-on, and female ejaculation demos. These demos were mainly for educational purposes, where volunteers dispense tips and advice throughout.

There were at both venues continuous lines to these rooms, which at times were quite long—depending on the service, from 5 to 15 individuals were waiting their turn. Tewksbury notes that within men's baths the most common form of sexual interaction is manual stimulation, while "'more exotic' forms of male-male sexual interaction (fisting, watersports, sadomasochistic scenes) and displays of intimacy (kissing, holding hands) are relatively rare, if present at all" (2003: 220). Yet, the more "exotic" sexual activities at Pussy Palace (and to a lesser extent SheDogs) attracted the most attendees. At Pussy Palace, the Temple Priestess, g-spot, and fuck/fisting rooms were *by far* the most popular services. Interestingly, although stranger sex was uncommon, participants getting serviced in these rooms almost never knew the volunteer who was, for all practical purposes, fucking them. Not only was it here that I observed some of the longest lines, but moreover, these activities always generated a bevy of onlookers. Because doors to these rooms were often completely open or ajar (or there were no doors), it was at these intersections where much commotion, whispering, and voyeurism took place.

What was it about these particular activities that caused such raucousness, curiosity, and amusement? A prominent theme among interviewees, when asked this question, revolved around shame at it relates to women's bodies and sexuality. According to almost every individual I spoke with, this "deep-seated shame" inhibits women from getting to know their bodies and what they desire. One long-time Pussy Palace committee member put it this way:

> I continue to be appalled at the amount of shame women have when it comes to their sexuality and desire. The bathhouse is a place where people can come to counter that negative social conditioning. We, as women and queers, carry that baggage, that social engineering whether we like it or not. We are not supposed to be sexual and ask for what we want. . . . I guess it [the bathhouse] is just trying to break that down [shame] naturally.

According to organizers, making such services available was a tactical maneuver for the following reasons: it gave patrons an opportunity to explore without having to seek it out, thus minimizing risk of rejection; volunteers understood the rules of bathhouse etiquette—thus, it was safe; it gave participants an opportunity to "practice their [negotiating] skills"; individuals could get to know their bodies; and finally, these services imbued the scene with sensuality and desire, thus fostering a sense that the bathhouse was indeed a "place of possibility" where "anything goes." In reference to the specific activities that were on offer at the bathhouse, one Pussy Palace volunteer and organizer stated, "It just creates all sorts of options, whatever kind of sex you are into. . . . So then that changes their sexuality in a way that wouldn't have happened, or it would have taken a lot longer." That the bathhouse enabled participants to "get to know their bodies" was a common refrain echoed by organizers and participants alike, implying thus the continued societal repudiation when it comes to women's sexuality. One Pussy Palace organizer, an owner of a popular sex shop, remarked:

> Women simply do not have the information, or they get it in the wrong places. There are still so many myths . . . when it comes to the g-spot, or fisting, or S/M. We are attempting to provide accurate information, allow queer women to know their bodies in a way that is genuine . . .

Such sentiment is only too familiar, for this is what the women's movement was asserting over 30 years ago. Part of the women's health movement was just that: dispensing medical and sexual information about women's bodies from a feminist perspective (Morgen 2002). Organizers thus see these services as facilitation devices for sexual experimentation, which are also, as one member put it, teaching "women that their bodies and desires are okay and should be celebrated."

How do we make sense of the fact that, taking into consideration patriarchal society's treatment of women's and queer (sex)ualities/bodies, it is in these lesbian/queer bathhouses, as opposed to men's baths, where we find individuals openly engaging in the more "taboo" and "transgressive" sexual activities? As I have argued elsewhere (Hammers 2008), I believe that, besides providing participants sexual satiation without having to seek out sex, it gives participants a feeling of *entitlement* to sexual pleasure. While a variety of sexual venues and products are available to men (pornography, strip clubs, cabarets, bathhouses, massage parlors), there has never been a sexual entertainment infrastructure *for* women. Thus, feeling entitled to sexual pleasure, while being *active in the decision-making process*, is for many individuals a new and empowering experience. Moreover, this agency and the sexual articulation, which develops out of agential desire, is about knowledge *and* language production. Frye, in her article "Lesbian 'Sex,'" sees society's androcentric and heteronormative language as failing to grasp and account for queer women's experiential knowledge—a prime example being how society conceives of "sex." Frye asserts:

> Gay male sex, I realized then, is *articulate*. . . . Lesbian "sex" as I have known it, most of the time I have known it, is utterly *in* articulate. . . . I have, in effect, no linguistic community, no language, and therefore in one important sense, no knowledge. . . . Men's meanings, and no women's meanings, are encoded in what is presumed to be the whole population's language . . . (1990:311)

These demos and services were in part about the dissemination of corporeal information. Frye criticizes any attempt at incorporation, an enfolding of women's sexual experiences into phallocentric language—a language which starts with "a point in the life of a body unlike our own," and instead imagines starting with "a wide field of our passions and bodily pleasures . . . that weave a web across it" (1990:313).

Finally, I want to briefly expand upon this notion of being *active* within the decision-making process. There is by now a large body of feminist scholarship—almost all of which is in reference to heterosexual encounters—documenting the silence and passivity surrounding women's sexuality within sexual encounters. Qualitative investigations into young women's sexuality and women's negotiation of sex with men are disturbing in what they do *not* find (Phillips 2000; Tolman 2005). That is, an overriding uncertainty pervades these young women's sexual narratives, reflecting in turn a lack of bodily ownership and confusion with regard to their own desires. In essence, in reflecting upon their experiences, respondents' *own* desires were almost always "missing," and/or deemed to be of less relevance. Rather, it was their male partner's sexual "needs," which were given top priority. Relating this work back to the bathhouse, a pervading sense of shame, albeit a shame that was recognized and contested, surfaced in many of the interviews. Every interviewee in this project saw the bathhouse as that which could, as one SheDogs participant put it, "conquer" the shame individuals felt regarding their bodies and sexuality. This shame could be addressed, according to organizers, through opportunities wherein patrons were actively involved in the sexual negotiation process—that is, they had to voice their own desires. This of course is what transpired in the service rooms, wherein participants determined what was to take place. Individuals are, in essence, honing their skills when it comes to negotiating sex—a negotiation that is forthright and, above all, verbal. A SheDogs organizer eloquently connected the relevance of these services to counteracting women's "inability to communicate":

> Most people I know . . . lack two basic words in their vocabulary. One of them is "no." People will give all kinds of excuses rather than say "thanks, I am not interested." The other missing word is "yes." In the absence of these two words it's impossible to communicate honestly. . . . These services encourage people to talk more, not less. This is so critical because verbal boundaries not only lessen the stigma and shame around sex and desire, but empower individuals . . .

I began this section by noting the differences in men's and women's bathhouse experiences, wherein within male baths, the sexual encounter is bounded and focused. In such encounters it is the expectation that verbal communication be kept to an absolute minimum. As one can see in the earlier narratives, within these sexual encounters great emphasis is placed on just the opposite—that of verbal communication. Yet, a type of bounding did occur in the service rooms due to the conditions therein. That is, it was on the participants' terms, there was always a time-limit (5 or 10 minutes depending on the service)—a definitive end which gave the encounter a degree of levity, participants knew that volunteers were there *for them*, and related to this, rejection did not factor into the equation. In sum, while the primary form of interaction involved open-ended encounters, the safety and unambiguous design (these rooms were about sex) enabled a certain degree of bounding in the service rooms.

Conclusion

Although bathhouses shape sexual practice and attempt to install a place "out of time" or a "place of possibility" where "anything goes," they are nonetheless a product of the wider sociocultural milieu (Green 2008). That is, bathhouse behavior and the logic of desire found in baths cannot be delinked from dominant society's structuring of desire. In this article I have attempted to illuminate men's and women's public sexual bathhouse cultures, and the different gendered patterns that emerge when it comes to communication patterns, participant expectations, and modifications of space. Venue owners, and in this case, the organizers of Pussy Palace and SheDogs, influence the physical features of space so as to create their desired objectives. This is not to say venue owners or organizers control and/or determine behavior; rather, they set the tone and provide parameters for what they consider to be proper bathhouse etiquette. Within men's baths, anonymity is the overriding concern such that sexual encounters are one of silence and discretion. The taboo on conversing is so strong that talking, even after having had sexual contact and even if only momentary, can be seen as intrusive behavior (Richters 2007). Richters (2007), in her study on men's baths, found that this emphasis on silence and depersonalization was for some patrons troubling in that they "found venues chilly and unsociable" (p. 289). Thus, although attendees know the unwritten rules of bathhouse behavior, not all participants enjoy the limits put on socializing. In addition to this "asocial sexual behavior," the spatial layout and its physical features, such as dim lighting and darkrooms, create a highly charged atmosphere that positions the body as the primary signifier and mode of communication. Since verbal communication jeopardizes feelings of anonymity, body language is the main form of communicating sexual interest.

In my ethnographic study of Pussy Palace and SheDogs, a different set of norms, communication styles, and objectives are operating here. Contrary to the bounding found in men's sexual encounters, a much more fluid and open-ended sexual exchange emerged, where identities and the personalization of the exchange were part and parcel of sexual satiation. While the majority of encounters in male baths involve stranger sex, sexual interactions at Pussy Palace and SheDogs almost always involved some degree of personal connection. However, a degree of bounding and elements of stranger sex were noted in the themed rooms. In these spaces, the tightly concealed parameters, explicit rules (e.g., time limits, "no touch zones"), feelings of safety, and lack of rejection obviated the necessity of personalizing service room encounters. Finally, unlike male bathhouse owners, Pussy Palace and SheDogs organizers desire an environment that is simultaneously sexual *and* social. At these sites it is a "celebratory" ethos, which involves "being loud" about sex. Besides witnessing a large portion of individuals chatting and mingling, sexual encounters were verbal, auditory affairs. Although bodily language is no doubt part of the sexual language in lesbian/queer baths, it was the stimulation of speech and sounds that made encounters particularly powerful and arousing.

In exploring the divergent gendered patterns that occur within these sexual spaces I did not fully delve into the structural supports that might underpin these differences. I briefly posit on some possible factors that might help explain these variations. Geographers see place and space as two different entities, with place being a location that has yet to take hold of any one particular meaning, while space "emerges when practices are imposed on place, when forms of human activity impose meanings on a given location" (Leap 1999:7). Public sites for sex (parks, public restrooms) and commercial venues like bathhouses are, using this distinction, loaded with human meaning. Men's sexual language is borne out of a sexual infrastructure, wherein a substantial transfiguring over time of place into space has occurred. Men's sexual economies are institutionalized, and thus form part of the fabric of society. Women do not have any such public sexual economy. This might partially explain some of these differences I found, wherein institutionalization and an entitlement to desire enable a privileging of bodies, wherein bodies become the main signifier in signaling sexual interest. I can think of many reasons as to why speech is given such a prominent place in lesbian/queer bathhouse encounters (and beyond). To begin, it is often only through saying something *out loud* that we discern and feel its message, that we fully acknowledge what we want (becoming an *embodied* desire), and of course, by communicating verbally, we can reduce the ambiguity of a situation. In sum, by saying something through speech we protect and empower ourselves. This becomes even more important when sex, bodies, and desire are involved, which is why bath organizers put so much emphasis on "sexual articulation." This ability to be forthright about sex is a "skill" rooted in a vocabulary that is easily accessible. Something is deeply amiss in society when even adults have great difficulty traversing the sexual terrain and articulating what they want. It should be something women do, and do with ease. Considering its embryonic nature, this study is merely an initial assessment of lesbian/queer public sex. Thus, it is an "open" field for future engagement and interrogation. The emerging and evolving norms and codes that flow out of these spaces over time will certainly provoke new lines of inquiry. Will the proliferation of lesbian/queer public sexual spaces bring about an *articulate* sexual vocabulary that Frye saw as being so crucial to lesbian/queer sexual agency? This of course remains to be seen.

Discussion Questions

1. Given this sketch of lesbian/queer public sexual economies and how they compare in relation to gay men's sexual subcultures, in what ways might gender and gender expectations influence and underpin these public sex environments?
2. Why is (semi)public sex viewed as deviant in our society? How do you feel about these sexual practices and these sexual spaces? How are our perceptions and feelings shaped by our own sociocultural values and belief systems?

References

Davidson, Julia O'Connell and Derek Layder. 1994. *Methods, Sex and Madness*. New York: Routledge.

Elwood, William N., Kathryn Greene, and Karen K. Carter. 2003. "Gentlemen Don't Speak." *Journal of Applied Communication Research* 31(4): 277–97.

Flowers, Paul, Claire Marriott, and Graham Hart. 2000. "The Bars, the Bogs and the Bushes." *Culture, Health & Sexuality* 2(1):69–86.

Frye, Marilyn. 1990. "Lesbian 'Sex.'" Pp. 63–88 in *Lesbian Philosophies and Cultures*, edited by Jeffner Allen. New York: State University of New York Press.

Green, Adam. 2008. "The Social Organization of Desire: The Sexual Fields Approach." *Sociological Theory* 26: 25-50.

Hammers, Corie. 2008. "Bodies That Speak and the Promises of Queer." *Journal of Gender Studies* 17(2):147–64.

Knopp, Lawrence. 1992. "Sexuality and the Spatial Dynamics of Capitalism." *Environment and Planning D: Society and Space* 10(6):651–69.

Leap, William. 1999. *Public Sex/Gay Space*. New York: Columbia University Press.

Morgen, Sandra. 2002. *Into Our Own Hands*. New York: Rutgers University Press.

Phillips, Lynn M. 2000. *Flirting with Danger*. New York: New York University Press.

Patton, M. Q. 1980. *Qualitative Evaluation Methods*. Beverly Hills, CA: Sage.

Richters, Juliet. 2007. "Through a Hole in the Wall." *Sexualities* 10(3):275–98.

Roy, Camille. 1993. "Speaking in Tongues." Pp. 6–12 in *Sisters, Sexperts, Queers: Beyond the Lesbian Nation,* edited by Arlene Stein. New York: Penguin Books.

Tattelman, Ira. 1999. "Speaking to the Gay Bathhouse: Communicating in Sexually Charged Spaces." Pp. 71–94 in *Public Sex/Gay Space*, edited by William Leap. New York: Columbia.

Tewksbury, Richard. 2003. "Bathhouse Intercourse." Pp. 203–32 in *Sexual Deviance: A Reader*, edited by Christopher Hensley and Richard Tewksbury. Boulder, CO: Lynne Rienner Publishers.

Tolman, Deborah. 2005. *Dilemmas of* Desire. New York: Harvard.

Weinberg, Martin S. and Colin J. Williams. 1975. "Gay Baths and the Social Organization of Impersonal Sex." *Social Problems* 23(2):124–36.

PART TEN

Emergent Deviance

On May 2, 2011, President Barack Obama announced to the United States that Osama bin Laden, the leader of al-Qaeda, has been killed. If we rewind almost 10 years earlier, some can recall the images of hijacked planes crashing into the World Trade Center. The United States of America began the "war on terror," by sending tens of thousands of troops to the Middle East in search of the deviant mind they felt masterminded that terrorist act, Osama Bin Laden. Nearly 10 years later, after the deaths of thousands of U.S. soldiers, America's forces find and kill Osama Bin Laden. The deviant act of terrorism has existed for thousands of years, but after 9/11 it *emerged* to be one of the most feared and talked about deviant acts in the world.[1]

The conclusion of the reader discusses emergent deviance; deviance which has come into view and arisen in a public spotlight. The first article in this part, Durkin's "Dawn of a New Era," examines deviance during the Internet age. He discusses the Internet as an opportunity for deviant behavior, a social consolidation mechanism, and a learning environment for deviant behavior. Erich Goode, in "Paranormal Beliefs as Deviance," takes us into the world of paranormals. He examines the social construction of paranormals and why they are viewed as deviant. In the last article of this part, "Conceptualizing the Criminological Problem of Terrorism," James Ross discusses the conceptualization of terrorism. He provides definitions of terrorism, the basic typologies, and attempts to distinguish terrorism from crime and war.

Note

1. Philips, Macon. 2011. "Osama Bin Laden Dead." *The White House Blog*, May 2. Retrieved June 17, 2011 (http://www.whitehouse.gov/blog/2011/05/02/osama-bin-laden-dead).

 ARTICLE 26

Keith F. Durkin
Ohio Northern University

The Dawn of a New Era: Renewed Prospects for the Sociology of Deviance in the Internet Age

The sociology of deviance has a rich legacy in the discipline, dating back to the work of pioneering sociologists such as Emile Durkheim (Best 2004). However, this area of inquiry has generated a remarkable amount of criticism, especially over the course of the last 40 years. The most vociferous of these criticisms have been based on political grounds. Essentially, critics have attempted to declare the sociological study of deviance politically and morally bankrupt (Konty 2006). In the frequently cited article, "The Poverty of the Sociology of Deviance: Nuts, Sluts, and Preverts," Liazos (1972:111) attacked the subfield based on his claim that bias is "rooted in the very conception and definition of the field." He asserted that deviance specialists were focusing on the behavior of the powerless members of society, while ignoring the more detrimental misconduct of corporate and governmental criminals. More recently, Colin Sumner (1994) went even further in his book *The Sociology of Deviance: An Obituary*. He advanced a rather convoluted argument claiming that the specialty area "died" in 1975. Summer opined that the field of inquiry was "a corpse rather than a corpus of knowledge" (p. ix). In his estimation, the subdiscipline had been killed by the critiques of radical scholars on the left such as himself. Not only is this death of the sociology of deviance argument based on disingenuous characterizations of this subfield, it is relatively devoid of empirical merit (Goode 2003; Konty 2007).

Although this area of sociological inquiry is by no means dead, or even terminally ill for that matter, deviance specialists acknowledge that it has become somewhat stagnant conceptually and theoretically, and is by no means as vibrant as it could be (Best 2004). In recent decades, many of the substantive contributions of the sociology of deviance have been to its remarkably successful and highly visible offspring criminology (Goode 2003). Similarly, some of the specialty area's traditional terrain has been incorporated into some of the various newer interdisciplinary fields such as victimology, criminal justice, and gay/lesbian studies (Durkin, Forsyth, and Quinn 2006). There is no reason to abandon hope, however. Advances in computer and communication technologies have revolutionized social life, creating a so-called virtual world with novel patterns of behavior, interaction, and identity (Durkin 2009). The rise of the Internet creates seemingly endless possibilities for research on deviants and deviance. At the most basic level, online environments are socially constructed (Waskul and Douglass 1997). As such, there will be "new forms of deviance emerging, the formation of new rules, the discovery of new harms, and new responses (as well as resistance) to these forms" (Konty 2006:626). Accordingly, the sociological examination of this type of deviance should provide us with unprecedented insights into contemporary life (Adler and Adler 2006).

Admittedly, many of the current research opportunities are for ethnographic and other types of qualitative investigations. However, approximately 100 years ago many of the pioneering studies of deviance conducted by members of the Chicago school used such an approach (Bryant 1990). This type of research on deviance is essential since it helps to illustrate "the dynamics of processes that transcend the particulars of the local situation" (Goode 2002:115). Drawing heavily on the results of these qualitative studies of Internet deviance, I would like to make four observations regarding deviance in cyberspace. First, the Internet represents an unprecedented opportunity structure for deviance. Second, the Internet serves as a social consolidation mechanism by bringing like-minded groups of deviant actors together. Third, the Internet can serve as a learning environment for deviance. Fourth, deviance on the Internet seems to epitomize the postmodern condition.

Internet and Opportunity

Technological innovations create new opportunity structures for the pursuit and commission of deviant activities. The Internet provides all types of unprecedented opportunities for many people to engage in many types of deviance that would not have been available previously. For instance, this technology has opened up access to illicit markets in gambling, pornography, illegal drugs, and pirated music and computer software. There is an extensive black market on the Internet for the buying and selling of stolen credit card numbers and other financial information (Choo and Smith 2008). Online classified ads are creating a new marketplace for stolen goods and illicit sexual services (Adler and Adler 2006). On the Internet a person can find the opportunity to engage in any type of sexual deviance, no matter how esoteric or even pathological (Durkin et al. 2006). It takes very little skill or technological sophistication to discover these deviant opportunities. For instance, in one recent study a Google search for terms related to male escorts resulted in approximately 2 million results (Lee-Gonyea, Castle, and Gonyea 2009).

The Internet provides the opportunity for anonymous communication and interaction. This felt anonymity can encourage antinormative behavior and may be a contributory factor in deviant behaviors, such as cyber harassment, cyber stalking, and cyber bullying (Durkin and Patterson 2011). This anonymity gives extremists the chance to operate in a relatively open fashion and still avoid apprehension (Cilluffo, Cardash, and Whitehead 2007). The use of proxy servers and anonymous e-mails allows con artists to visibly conduct scams with relative impunity (Durkin and Brinkman 2009). Furthermore, it is relatively easy for people to distance themselves from the social ramifications of their online activities. For example, on the Internet one can explore all types of sexual topics without concern of public stigmatization (Durkin et al. 2006).

The Internet also offers a variety of appealing targets for all sorts of predatory offenders. There is the widely publicized problem of adult men using online services to attempt to locate children to victimize. Nigerian 419 fraud, which is now a $3 billion a year industry, illustrates just how relatively simple it is for motivated offenders to reach a seemingly infinite pool of potential victims. More recently, the popular online advertisement system craigslist has served as a source of predatory targets. Phillip Markoff, better known as the craigslist killer, targeted women who advertised erotic massage services online (Goodnough and O'Connor 2010). More recently, a gang of criminals fatally wounded a father in a home invasion robbery that targeted his family after they had advertised a television for sale online (Holtz 2010). The popular routine activities theory (Felson 2001) appears to be exceptionally helpful for understanding these types of predatory offenses. This perspective views crime to be a function of people's everyday life. On a basic level, the Internet is putting motivated offenders in proximity to attractive targets in the relative absence of capable guardians on a daily basis (Holt and Bossler 2009).

Internet as a Social Consolidation Mechanism

The Internet also serves as an important vehicle for deviant subcultures in contemporary society. Prior to the Internet, all types of subcultures were naturally limited by geographical boundaries (Durkin and Bryant 1995). Moreover, some practices, behaviors, and beliefs are so objectively deviant or rare that it is practically impossible that a subculture would ever form in physical space (Jenkins and Thomas 2004). Yet cyber communities provide a mechanism and space for deviant behavior to grow and even thrive in a manner that simply would not have been possible 20 years ago (Adler and Adler 2006). Indeed, deviant organizations were quick to utilize the new communicative capacities of computers. Since its inception, the Internet has been used by radical groups for the recruitment of new members and the dissemination of propaganda. More than 15 years ago, the UFO doomsday cult Heaven's Gate was using the Internet for recruitment and propaganda. As early as 1995, a Ku Klux Klan leader boasted that his group was getting their message out to tens of thousands of people who would not have been exposed to it otherwise (Durkin and Bryant 1999). In recent years, jihadists have been exceptionally effective in their use of the Internet. Many make use of videos that can be instantaneously distributed to a global audience over the Internet. Groups such as al-Qaeda can remain relatively decentralized and fluid while conducting nearly 100 percent of its communication and fund-raising online (Gray and Head 2009). The Internet has also proven to be an effective tool for the radicalization and recruitment of Westerners to the jihadist cause (Cilluffo et al. 2007).

The Internet is a social consolidation mechanism, which brings together people with similar interests "seeking a social context for their deviant inclinations" (Durkin and Bryant 1995:195). An excellent example of this would be the so-called pathologically deviant (see Quinn and Forsyth 2005) sexual subcultures found on the Internet. The term *pathological deviance* is used to refer to behaviors that are "so far beyond normative boundaries" that they are considered "sick" by most members of the general public (Durkin et al. 2006:569). Two examples would be bestiality and pedophilia. Pro-pedophilia groups such as NAMBLA (the North American Man Boy Love Association) are remarkably active on the Web, using this medium not only for recruitment and organizational purposes, but to also propagandize their ideology (Durkin and Bryant 1999). Pedophiles have recently launched a project called BoyWiki modeled after the online encyclopedia Wikipedia (Durkin and Hundersmarck 2008). Also, bestiality is clearly a pathological, not to mention illegal, sexual practice. However, on the Internet there is an active community of bestiality enthusiasts that refers to itself as the "zoo" or "zoophile community" (Jenkins and Thomas 2004). There are also cyber communities for some truly esoteric, albeit legal, sexual interests such as infantilism ("adult babies") and apotemnophilia (a sexual attraction to persons with amputated limbs) (Durkin et al. 2006).

Internet as a Learning Environment for Deviance

The Internet has proven to be a highly effective learning mechanism for deviant behavior. Some Web content actually serves as a blueprint for deviant behavior by elaborating "the methods for actually carrying out specific" acts (D'Ovidio et al. 2009). The Internet is a veritable cornucopia of deviant knowledge, including varied information such as the techniques for shoplifting, making explosive devices, locating street prostitutes in various locales, and evading the detection of drug use during urinalysis. On Web pages, chat rooms, and computer forums, individuals can transmit practical knowledge to others, which actually helps them to perform the deviant act (Adler and Adler 2006). For instance, there are a number of pro-anorexia or "pro-ana" Web sites that feature "tips and tricks" for promoting dangerous weight loss including the use of laxatives, diets pills, and extreme fasting (Norris et al. 2006). There are also a growing number of reports of Internet users engaging in very dangerous practices such as genital self-mutilation after receiving instructions on the Internet (Wise and Kalyanam 2000; Summers 2003). Likewise, there have been cases of children and adolescents taking drug overdoses or having other types of adverse reactions after following information about recreational drugs they obtained from the Internet (Wax 2002).

Additionally, the Internet can facilitate learning the mindset involved in deviance. Although deviants are confronted with a variety of difficult issues, protecting their self-image and identity from possible destruction is a primary consideration (Kelly 1996). Internet subcultures are an excellent venue by which people can learn various ways to rationalize or justify the deviant acts (Holt 2007). Such attitudes are essential, since they can serve to alleviate the moral reprehension that is often associated with deviance (D'Ovidio et al. 2009). The Internet can also serve as a source of information on how to cope with a deviant identity. People can actually learn techniques for dealing with the stigma associated with deviance from the Internet. For example, by their participation in virtual communities, people involved in some of the most pathological forms of sexual deviance, such as bestiality and pedophilia, are exposed to a number of stigma management techniques such as accounts, deviance disavowal, and semantic manipulation of the deviant label (Durkin and Bryant 1999; Durkin 2004).

Accordingly, Akers' (2000) social learning theory may be a useful framework for understanding many types of Internet-related crime and deviance. First, the people that an individual interacts with on the Internet, including other members of deviant cyber communities, may serve as differential associations (Durkin 2007). Not only can they instruct an individual in the respective techniques to perform the deviant act, but they can also teach the individual ways to approve of and justify deviant behavior (Holt 2007). The Internet can also provide differential reinforcement for deviant behavior. On the most basic level, Internet participation may provide validation, since the deviant knows they are no longer alone and that other individuals share a similarly disvalued identity. The mere interaction with others of similar interests, no matter how radical, esoteric, or even pathological, is a powerful reinforcement for deviance (Durkin et al. 2006). Moreover, Internet users can receive reinforcement for sexual deviance by masturbating while viewing pornography. Definitions, or the attitudes and meanings a person attaches to a behavior, are another important component of social learning theory. This would include the aforementioned mindset of criminal and deviant behavior, which can be learned from the Internet.

Internet and the Postmodern Condition

Society has been undergoing a transition into the so-called postmodern age. America has moved from a manufacturing-based society to one based on information technology, a service economy, and the trend toward globalization. Internet technology has transformed the computer from a mere computational deviance to a remarkably effective communication device (Durkin and Bryant 1995). In turn this revolutionized social life by spawning new patterns of activity, association, behavior, and even identity. In postmodern society, we depend heavily on this technology for virtually every aspect of our daily life (Choi 2008). Therefore, a key to understanding Internet-related deviance and crime is a consideration of the context in which it occurs. However, it is essential to realize that some modern concepts (e.g., space) are not very helpful for understanding cyberspace. The Internet has caused a literal implosion of established economic, social, and political boundaries (Berthon, Pitt, and Watson 2000). For example, the Internet has provided terrorists groups such as al-Qaeda a true safe haven that transcends national, geographical, and political boundaries (Gray and Head 2009). Furthermore, Nigerian con artists, a group traditionally located on the fringes of the global economy, can now instantaneously target a seeming infinite number of Westerners with their fraudulent business proposals by e-mail (Durkin and Brinkman 2009).

In postmodern society, the line between reality and unreality is blurred (Dotter 2004). We now live in an era where people are constantly "substituting signs of the real for the real" (Baudrillard 1994:2). The Internet is a type of hyperreality where the signs that we use to signify everyday reality are often foundationless. On the Web, "the physical real is digitized and the digital becomes real" (Berthon et al. 2000:272). For example, criminal syndicates now launder illicit funds via "digital currency" such as e-gold or World of Warcraft credits (Choo and Smith 2008). It is simple to create and misrepresent fraudulent documents in cyberspace, and this is one reason for the remarkable success of Internet fraud (Baker 2002; Durkin and Brinkman 2009). Although cyberspace may be a hyperreal manifestation of the postmodern condition, it is imperative to be mindful of the fact that Internet deviance often has real consequences for real people in the physical world. For instance, radical groups now have the unprecedented ability to incite hatred and violence, and this represents a real threat to the social and economic stability of society (Choo and Smith 2008). Moreover, some victims of online fraud lose their life's savings, and children are abused by sexual predators they meet online.

Discussion

The virtual world offers renewed prospects for the sociology of deviance to remain a lively area of inquiry in the twenty-first century. New forms of deviance are constantly emerging while others are experiencing remarkable transformations. New opportunity structures are being created, and motivated offenders are being brought into proximity to attractive targets on a daily basis in cyberspace. The Internet offers revolutionary prospects for research on deviance. There are unprecedented opportunities for sociologists to describe, explore, and analyze various forms of deviant behavior. In cyberspace, we have practically instantaneous access to a seemingly endless number of people who engage in deviant activities or posses a deviant identity. The findings of these studies should produce valuable insights that can inform other areas of sociology, such as criminology and social theory, as well as other academic disciplines, including anthropology, business, cultural studies, legal studies, and victimiology.

The remarkable growth and diffusion of cell phones have created even more new opportunities for deviant behavior, and new forms and patterns of deviance are emerging as a consequence. One prominent example is sexting, a behavior that involves the transmission of sexually explicit messages or photographs via cell phone (Richards and Calvert 2009). Also, there are new varieties of computer viruses and other forms of malware that exclusively target cell phone users (Lomo-David and Shannon 2009). Advance-fee frauds and other types of scam solicitations are now being sent by text message. Cell phones are also being used to menace and harass others (Durkin and Patterson 2011). These new developments are sure to present a wide variety of research opportunities on deviance well into the twenty-first century.

This is a long overdue opportunity for the sociology of deviance to provide some innovative insights into the nature of social life. Simultaneously, we need to recognize that it is inevitable that the political attacks will be levied against this specialty area. While it is clear that the sociology of deviance has not died because of some leftist critiques, it is also clear that radical attacks will not die anytime soon. Individuals with certain ideological inclinations will predictably take offense to the mere existence of this area of inquiry. They seem convinced that the subfield harbors a politically incorrect agenda of using what they perceive to be value-laden concepts, such as deviants and deviants to stigmatize their powerless research subjects (Goode 2003). There is really no need for deviance specialists to spend any more time engaging in this futile debate, since "the politicization of the sociology of deviance will not produce better sociology" (Konty 2006:629).

Discussion Questions

1. Discuss some of the reasons the Internet has become a safe haven for deviant behavior. What other forms of deviant behavior do you foresee growing from the Internet?
2. If the Internet is the dawn of a new era for deviance, what new social conditions in the future will open up more opportunities for deviant behavior?

References

Adler, Patricia A. and Peter Adler. 2006. "The Deviance Society." *Deviant Behavior* 27: 129–48.

Akers, Ronald L. 2000. *Criminological Theories: Introduction, Evaluation, and Application*, 3rd ed. Los Angeles, CA: Roxbury.

Baker, C. Richard. 2002. "Crime Fraud and Deceit on the Internet: Is There Hyperreality in Cyberspace?" *Critical Perspectives on Accounting* 13:1–15.

Baudrillard, Jean. 1994. *Simulacra and Simulations*. Ann Arbor, MI: University of Michigan Press.

Berthon, Pierre, Leyland Pitt, and Richard T. Watson. 2000. "Postmodernism and the Web: Meta Themes and Discourse." *Technological Forecasting and Social Change* 65:265–79.

Best, Joel. 2004. "Deviance May Be Alive, But Is It Lively? A Reaction to Goode." *Deviant Behavior* 25:483–92.

Bryant, Clifton D. 1990. *Deviant Behavior: Readings in the Sociology of Norm Violations*. New York: Hemisphere.

Choi, Kyung-shick. 2008. "Computer Crime Victimization and Integrated Theory: An Empirical Assessment." *International Journal of Cyber Criminology* 2:308–33.

Choo, Kim-Kwang Raymond and Russell G. Smith. 2008. "Criminal Exploitation of Online Systems by Organized Crime Groups." *Asian Journal of Criminology* 3:37–59.

Cilluffo, Frank J., Sharon L. Cardash, and Andrew J. Whitehead. 2007. "Radicalization behind Bars and Beyond Borders." *Brown Journal of World Affairs* 13:113–22.

D'Ovidio, Rob, Tyson Mitnam, Imanni Jamillah El-Burki, and Wesley Shumar. 2009. "Adult-Child Sex Advocacy Websites as Social Learning Environments." *International Journal of Cyber Criminology* 3:421–40.

Dotter, Daniel. 2004. *Creating Deviance*. New York: Altamir.

Durkin, Keith F. 2004. "The Internet as a Milieu for the Management of a Stigmatized Sexual Identity." Pp. 124–39 in *Net.SeXXX: Sex, Pornography, and the Internet*, edited by Dennis Waskul. New York: Peter Lang.

Durkin, Keith F. and Clifton D. Bryant. 1995. "Log on to Sex: Some Notes on the Carnal Computer and Erotic Cyberspace as an Emerging Research Frontier." *Deviant Behavior* 16:179–200.

Durkin, Keith F. and Clifton D. Bryant. 1999. "Propagandizing Pederasty: A Thematic Analysis of the On-Line Exculpatory Accounts of Unrepentant Pedophiles." *Deviant Behavior* 20:103–28.

Durkin, Keith F. and Denay Patterson. 2011. "Cyber Bullying, Cyber Harassing and Cyber Stalking." Pp.450–55 in *The Handbook of Deviant Behavior*, edited by Clifton D. Bryant. New York: Routledge.

Durkin, Keith F. and Richard Brinkman. 2009. "419 Fraud: A Crime without Borders in a Postmodern World." *International Review of Modern Sociology* 35:271–83.

Durkin, Keith F., Craig J. Forsyth, and James F. Quinn. 2006. "Pathological Internet Communities: A New Direction for Sexual Deviance Research in the Postmodern Era." *Sociological Spectrum* 26:595–606.

Durkin, Keith F. and Steven Hundersmarck. 2008. "Pedophiles and Child Molesters." Pp. 144–150 in *Extreme Deviance*, edited by D. Angus Vail and Erich Goode. Newbury Park, CA: Sage.

Felson, Marcus. 2001. "Routine Activity Theory: The Theorist's Perspective." Pp. 338–39 in *Encyclopedia of Criminology and Deviant Behavior, Volume I: Historical, Conceptual, and Theoretical Issues*, edited by Clifton D. Bryant. Philadelphia, PA: Brunner-Routledge.

Goode, Erich. 2002. "Does the Death of the Sociology Deviance Claim Make Sense?" *The American Sociologist* 33:107–18.

Goode, Erich. 2003. "The MacGuffin That Refuses to Die: An Investigation into the Condition of the Sociology of Deviance." *Deviant Behavior* 24:507–33.

Goodnough, Abby and Anahad O'Connor. 2010. "Boston Craigslist Case: Med Student's Preppy Profile." *Seattle Times.* Retrieved August 22, 2010 (http://seattletimes.nwsource.com).

Gray, David H. and Albon Head. 2009. "The Importance of the Internet to the Post-Modern Terrorist and Its Role as a Form of Safe Haven." *European Journal of Scientific Research* 25:396–404.

Holt, Thomas J. 2007. "Subcultural Evolution? Examining the Influence of On- and Off-Line Experiences of Deviant Subcultures." *Deviant Behavior* 28:171–98.

Holt, Thomas J. and Adam M. Bossler. 2009. "Examining the Applicability of Lifestyle-Routine Activities Theory for Cybercrime Victimization." *Deviant Behavior* 28:1–25.

Holtz, Jackson. 2010. "Craigslist Murder, Robbery Suspects Charged." *HeraldNet.* Retrieved August 22, 2010 (http://www.Heraldnet.com).

Jenkins, Robert E. and Alexander R. Thomas. 2004. *Deviance Online: Portrayals of Bestiality on the Internet*. Oneonta, NY: Center for Social Science Research.

Kelly, Delos H. 1996. *Deviant Behavior: A Text Reader in the Sociology of Deviance*, 5th ed. New York: St. Martin's.

Konty, Mark. 2006. "Of Deviance and Deviants." *Sociological Spectrum* 26:621–31.

Konty, Mark. 2007. "When in Doubt, Tell the Truth: Pragmatism and the Sociology of Deviance." *Deviant Behavior* 28:153–70.

Lee-Gonyea, Jenifer A., Tammy Castle, and Nathan E. Gonyea. 2009. "Laid to Order: Male Escorts Advertising on the Internet." *Deviant Behavior* 30:321–48.

Liazos, Alexander. 1972. "The Poverty of the Sociology of Deviance: Nuts, Sluts, and Perverts." *Social Problems* 20:103–20.

Lomo-David, Ewuuk and Shannon Li-Jen. 2009. "Critical Analysis of Mobile Phone Communication Safety and Security Measures." *Proceedings of ISECON* 29:1–19.

Norris, Mark L., Katherine M. Boydell, Leora Pinhas, and Debra K. Katzman. 2006. "Ana and the Internet: A Review of Pro-Anorexia Websites." *International Journal of Eating Disorders* 39:443–47.

Quinn, James F. and Craig J. Forsyth. 2005. "Describing Sexual Behavior in the Era of the Internet: A Typology for Empirical Research." *Deviant Behavior* 26:191–208.

Richards, Robert D. and Clay Calvert. 2009. "When Sex and Cell Phones Collide: Inside the Prosecution of a Teen Sexting Case." *Hastings Communication and Entertainment Law Journal* 32:1–40.

Summers, Jeffrey A. 2003. "A Complication of an Unusual Sexual Practice." *Southern Medical Journal* 96:716–17.

Sumner, Colin. 1994. *The Sociology of Deviance: An Obituary*. London: Open University Press.

Waskul, Dennis and Mark Douglass. 1997. "Cyberself: The Emergence of Self in On-Line Chat." *Information Society* 13:375–97.

Wax, Paul M. 2002. "Just a Click Away: Recreational Drug Web Sites on the Internet." *Pediatrics* 109:e96–e99.

Wise, Thomas N. and Ram Chandran Kalyanam. 2000. "Amputee Fetishism and Genital Mutilation: Care Report and Literature Review." *Journal of Sex and Marital Therapy* 26:339–44.

 ARTICLE 27

Erich Goode
Professor Emeritus at Stony Brook University

Paranormal Beliefs as Deviance[1]

Sociologists have located three major sources or dimensions of social deviance. These may be referred to as the "ABCs" of deviance—*attitudes, behaviors,* and *conditions* (Adler and Adler 2009:13–15). Deviant beliefs, also referred to as cognitive or intellectual deviance, represent the expression of attitudes that are contrary to the views of specific audiences, and hence, are likely to elicit negative reactions among those audiences. Conceiving of deviance as being defined by the reactions of specific audiences is crucial here. What is regarded as a deviant belief in one social circle or audience is often considered conventional, acceptable, and valid in another. Atheists think of belief in the reality of the Holy Trinity as silly and superstitious; orthodox Catholics see atheists as deluded and, in all likelihood, damned. In contemplating deviance, we have to conceptualize society both horizontally and vertically. Horizontally, every society is a hodge-podge or mosaic of different beliefs, the members of each circle holding views that vary or diverge from what is acceptable in other circles, these divergent opinions only clashing at the micro or interpersonal level. But vertically, the holders of some beliefs have more purchase or influence than others in the society as a whole, and hence, whoever holds a contrary view is generally more likely to be condemned, get into trouble, or be punished. Hence, from a vertical perspective, what is believed in more powerful social circles impinges or impacts on what is held as true in less powerful circles, but the reverse tends not to be true; typically, the powerful may safely ignore the beliefs of the powerless.

Many rationalistic nineteenth-century intellectuals, such as Auguste Comte (1798–1857), Karl Marx (1818–1883), and Herbert Spencer (1820–1903), believed that "superstitious" and "irrational" beliefs, such as theism and paranormalism, would disappear with the advance of industrialism and higher education. Chances are, if they could have seen into the future, they would have been shocked by how persistent such notions remain into the twenty-first century. Paranormal beliefs are enormously popular and extremely widely held in contemporary America. A 2009 Harris Poll found that a majority or a substantial minority said they believe in a supernatural power: three-quarters of the respondents believe in the literal reality of miracles (76 percent) and heaven as a physically real place (75 percent); seven of ten said they had faith in the physical reality of angels (72 percent); six of ten saw hell as a physically real place (62 percent) and believed the virgin birth and the reality of the devil to be literally true (62 and 61 percent, respectively); four of ten (42 percent) believed in ghosts; a third said that unidentified flying objects (UFOs) are "something real" (32 percent); a quarter believed that astrology is valid (26 percent) and that witches are real (23 percent); and a fifth believed in reincarnation (20 percent). Other polling organizations report substantially the same finding, the exact results varying by only a few percentage points. Faith in the paranormal remains strong among much of the public. Given that paranormal beliefs are widespread, it is difficult to consider them a form of deviance. But popularity is not the whole story.

How can beliefs be "deviant"? It might seem that beliefs are qualitatively different from behavior. Does not everyone have the right to believe whatever he or she pleases? Is not what you believe "nobody's business but your own"? Well, ideally—but not in practice. First, in the past, you *could* be arrested for expressing a particular belief. In Europe a few hundred years ago, the air was rank from the burning flesh of supposed heretics and blasphemers. During the first half of the 1950s, Senator Joseph McCarthy launched witch hunts against supposed communists in the government, ruining the careers of men and women who, for the most part, simply expressed liberal or socialist views. Today, many thousands of persons in countries such as China, Iran, Saudi Arabia, Burma, Congo, Rwanda, and Zimbabwe have been arrested for espousing views their government regards as dissident or subversive, and a substantial but untold number of them have been subjected to torture, even execution.

More important for our purposes, now, in the West, *informal* reactions to definitions of right and wrong define what is deviant, and, by this definition, there is no doubt that expressing certain ideas *is* deviant in numerous social circles. Many audiences *do* react negatively to the expression of particular beliefs. Even if people today are not arrested in the Western world for expressing unconventional views, they can be criticized, humiliated, denounced, shunned, and isolated. Almost as many—and in some eras of history, even more—people have been punished, stigmatized, and condemned for verbalizing beliefs as for engaging in specific behavior. One of Erving Goffman's types of stigma is possessing "blemishes of individual character," one variety of which includes "treacherous and rigid beliefs" (1963:4). And, a belief that one person regards as "treacherous and rigid," another sees as just and righteous, and vice versa. So, *of course*, holding beliefs that wander away from the conventional path is a form of deviance. Holding and expressing unorthodox beliefs is an *important* form of deviance. Cognitive deviance may not be an appropriate subject when discussing *criminology*, but it is for the topic of *deviance*.

Cognition refers to knowing—that is, what one believes to be true. When sociologists refer to *knowing*, we do not imply that these views are empirically correct (or that they are wrong). What we mean is that many, or certain, people *think* they are true. Cognition refers to the belief that an assertion or claim is valid. And it is the *expression* of beliefs that gets the believer in trouble. After all, the belief has to be *known* to disapproving audiences.

With respect to the central analytic features of deviance—that is, what *makes* something or someone deviant—in principle, deviant beliefs are identical in all basic respects to deviant acts. The same basic principles apply: someone, or a category of persons, is regarded by the members of one or more audiences as having violated a rule or norm, and the members of those audiences are likely to condemn or punish them. The content of the belief is less important than the fact that the belief is deemed normatively unacceptable. Thus, being an atheist violates a religious principle that says one should believe in God; belief in divine creation violates the principles of scientific reasoning; belief in evolution violates a literal reading of the Bible; belief in alien space ships violates what scientists see as a law of nature that says that objects cannot travel faster than the speed of light; and so on. Because specific audiences hold certain beliefs to be non-normative, unconventional, unacceptable, scandalous, heretical, vulgar, unseemly, improper, and/or just plain wrong, again, audiences tend to isolate, stigmatize, condemn, and/or punish the persons who hold them. Of course, precisely the beliefs that *one* audience finds unconventional *another* accepts as normatively correct. In these respects, holding unconventional beliefs is no different from engaging in unconventional behavior. Both result in stigma and condemnation. In other words, social rules apply to both behavior and what one believes to be true.

What Is a Paranormal Belief?

Dictionaries define the "paranormal" as that which is beyond, surpasses, or violates scientific explanation. Hence, a paranormal belief entails accepting the truth of an assertion about how the world works that is contrary to what scientists believe to be valid. Sociologists understand paranormalism to be a *socially constructed* phenomenon; that is, it is determined by the views of a particular audience: *scientists*, or persons who are studying or who possess expert knowledge and accreditation in one or more of the natural or physical sciences. Members of this category regard certain beliefs as wrong, unscientific, contrary to the workings of nature—and hence, "paranormal." And when prestigious and influential social actors *label* people and beliefs as wrong, this usually has important consequences. Most prior discussions on paranormal claims are dedicated to debunking them—empirically demonstrating that they are false (Gardner 1957; Randi 1995; Hines 2003)—*or* endorsing and verifying them (for instance, Radin 1997; Imbrogno 2008; Lisle 2009). The definition of paranormalism I use here sidesteps the question of whether "paranormal" beliefs are ultimately true. They may be true, they may be false, but scientists *believe* them to be false—and that is a documentable fact, with empirical consequences.

To many people, the term *paranormal* bears a negative connotation. Ask a dozen people on the street what the word means, and most will say it means "kooky," "weird," "far-out," "spooky," "strange," "bizarre." Hence, the believers of any system of thought that is referred to as paranormal are likely to feel that what they take to be true is *tainted, stigmatized,* or *discredited* by—and hence, would emphatically reject—the term *paranormal.* Certainly this is the case with astrology, creationism, parapsychology, and the view that UFOs are "something real," all of which are based on causal mechanisms that scientists regard as unscientific. In contrast to casting aspersion on such beliefs and believers, I define the term *paranormal* in a neutral and nonpejorative way. When I use the term, *paranormal,* I intend it to convey no derogatory implication whatsoever. Following this definition, paranormal beliefs can be regarded as a form of deviance—at the very least, to scientists and their followers. Again, the negative reactions that are elicited in certain audiences as a result of the expression of paranormal beliefs are empirical in nature, documentable with concrete evidence.

When John Mack (1995) published a book asserting that his patients really were abducted by aliens, some of his Harvard colleagues in psychiatry pressured the university administration to have him fired. (The attempt was unsuccessful.) Creationists are virtually absent among the university faculties of the country's most prestigious departments of geology and biology, and the number of articles in the scientific literature affirming the creationist argument is virtually, if not precisely, zero. Teachers who endorse creationism in their courses are told to keep their religious views out of the classroom. None of the largest, most prestigious, and influential museums in the country valorize the truth of paranormal belief systems; this is especially true of creationism. Advocates of astrology are virtually lacking among university faculty; those who take this belief system to be true tend not to make it public. Lawyers who inform clients that they base their cases on astrological principles are not likely to retain their patronage. The nation's most influential newspapers—*The New York Times* and *The Washington Post*—marginalize and "deviantize" paranormalism, so do nearly all the major, high-profile magazines. Political candidates running for president or a seat in the Senate who endorse one or another version of the beliefs discussed here are likely to find their fitness for higher office questioned. An economist basing his or her analyses or predictions on seers, psychics, or astrologers is likely to be derided among peers, colleagues, and the media.

These regularities tell us that paranormalism is deviant to many relevant audiences. Espousing assertions that scientists regard as violating the laws of nature tends to provoke a negative reaction *among* certain parties or social actors, *in* certain social circles or institutions. Again, this does not mean that these assertions are wrong, but it does say that they are unconventional and lacking in legitimacy—*to* those parties, *in* those circles. This is the feature of deviant beliefs that sociologists regard as most crucial and important. In short, paranormal beliefs are not fully institutionalized, firmly established, completely legitimate, or *hegemonic* in this society. We rarely question how someone comes to believe that the earth revolves around the sun. We do, however, wonder how someone came to learn that the sun, the moon, the planets, and the stars rule our destiny, because that represents a departure from widely accepted norms about epistemology and ontology or the truth of the material world that scientists, and hence, most of higher education, accept as true. It is this departure from these norms that makes paranormalists interesting to sociologists. Again, another way to describe a departure from a conventional belief is to label them *deviant*. But by *deviant* I do not mean mentally ill, sick, or pathological. I mean that persons who hold such beliefs are regarded in specific, designated social circles or quarters as unconventional, peculiar, unacceptable, or just plain wrong.

Belief systems that depart from science lie outside the institutionally approved boundaries and as such they are interesting to sociologists, especially sociologists of deviance. Expressing such beliefs elicits interesting responses from much of the society, and that intersection between the expression and the response is worth studying from a sociological perspective. Sociologists are primarily interested in the issue of who holds such unconventional beliefs, why, and with what consequences, and how adherents of each perspective organize and promulgate their views. In our society, currently, paranormalism demands an explanation more than belief in science does. In many dominant social circles, such beliefs also produce reproachful, admonishing reactions by persons who hold the mainstream point of view. Hence, endorsing beliefs that invoke forces that, scientists argue, violate natural law is both paranormal and deviant. Such beliefs are regarded as illegitimate, invalid, and marginalized, in the most influential institutions in the society.

Cognitive Deviance and Mental Disorder

Contrary to what some psychologists and psychiatrists assert (Rabeyron and Watt 2010), sociologists do not argue that paranormalism is a manifestation of mental disorder. In fact, the opposite is true. People who hold paranormal beliefs are as psychologically normal as people who do not, and we can explain the paranormalist enterprise by the ordinary, mundane sociological and individual forces and processes that govern our everyday lives—by means of socialization, differential association, deviance labeling, conformity, social interaction, and persuasion. However, the sociologist *does* insist that in scientific circles, paranormalism is regarded as deviant, but, again, stating that someone holds a deviant belief does *not* imply that that person is mentally disordered.

Let us turn the equation around. Although most cognitive deviants are not mentally disordered, mental disorder is typically accompanied by ideation that is regarded by psychiatrists and clinical psychologists as delusional, bizarre, and empirically wrong—that is, cognitively deviant. Hence, cognitive deviance overlaps, albeit imperfectly, with mental disorder. Mental health professionals regard the expression of certain beliefs as a manifestation or an indicator of a pathological psychic condition. For instance, schizophrenics are said to suffer from *delusions* and *hallucinations*. One man describes a transmitter that has been implanted in his teeth that receives signals from a distant galaxy commanding him to deliver a message to everyone on earth about a coming catastrophe. A woman believes that her thoughts have been sucked out of her mind by a "phrenological vacuum extractor." A woman claims that she is "just a puppet who is manipulated by cosmic strings. When the strings are pulled my body moves and I cannot prevent it." Clearly, people who are diagnosed as having a mental disorder often hold deviant beliefs (Kring et al. 2010).

Just as there are parallels between mental disorder and cognitive deviance, however, there are differences as well. Schizophrenia, a *thought disorder*, is nearly always accompanied by a number of other disturbances in addition to cognitive delusions and hallucinations. Some of these include flat or inappropriate emotions, bizarre motor activity, and the use of jumbled words ("word *salad*"). Clinical depression, too, is often marked by inappropriate beliefs, but it is a *mood* disorder characterized by feelings of sadness, dread, apprehension, worthlessness, guilt, and anhedonia—an inability to take pleasure in life. Hence, it is mainly among sufferers of thought disorders rather than mood disorders who tend to hold unscientific or paranormal beliefs. Again, *most* paranormal beliefs are *not* manifestations of mental disorder, but many patients suffering from thought disorders (or schizophrenics) hold paranormal beliefs.

Deviance and Scientific Truth

Beliefs are not deviant simply because of their content. No belief, however bizarre it might seem to us, is *inherently* or *objectively* deviant. A belief is deviant in two ways—one, normatively, and two, reactively: in other words, one, because it violates the tenets of the dominant belief system, or simply *a* specific belief system, and two, because its adherents are likely to be condemned or punished by the members of the society at large, or specific subgroups within that society, that is, one or more given "audiences." A belief is deviant both because it is *considered* wrong and its believers are *treated* as socially unacceptable—*in* a given society or collectivity.

Many ideas have been regarded as heretical—and therefore *deviant*—at one point in time, yet later *came to be* accepted as true or valid. In 1633, the Catholic Inquisition imposed the penalty of house arrest on Galileo because he argued that the earth revolved around the sun, an assertion that was then contrary to Catholic dogma, which held that the earth was the center of the universe. In 1854, Viennese physicians ridiculed Ignaz Semmelweis for asserting that physicians could transmit disease to patients after they dissected rotting cadavers; in the 1850s, the medical establishment regarded Semmelweis as a deviant. Today, any physician asserting that physicians should *not* wash their hands before thrusting them into patients' bodies would be regarded as the deviant. Beginning in 1915, and, in revisions throughout the 1920s, a German astrophysicist Alfred Wenger proposed the theory that, 300 million years ago, the earth's crust formed one giant continent, Pangaea, that broke apart over time into the continents we know today. Continents are still drifting and will continue to do so for as long as the earth exists. For nearly a half century, Wenger's theory met with scathing derision and almost uniform hostility; it was not until the 1960s that virtually all earth scientists accepted continental drift and plate tectonics as a valid description of geological processes (Ben-Yehuda 1985).

Because of his astronomical statements, *to* the hierarchy of the Catholic Church, *in* the 1600s, Galileo was a cognitive deviant; *because* of his medical claim, *to* physicians *in* the 1800s, Ignaz Semmelweis was a cognitive deviant; *because* of the publication of his books espousing the theory of continental drift, *to* geologists between 1915 and the 1950s, Alfred Wenger was a cognitive deviant (Ben-Yehuda 1985). The fact that these theories were later proven to be, and are now accepted as, valid is *irrelevant* to the fact that *at* one time, *to* a certain audience, they *were* heretical and hence their creator *was* condemned and punished—and hence deviant. Historical processes are as germane to the subject of deviance as current ones.

Deviance makes sense *only* with reference to the beliefs and reactions of certain audiences. Beliefs that are regarded as wrong, unacceptable, and deviant in one social circle may be considered right, good, proper, and true in another. Among political radicals, conservativism is anathema—unacceptable and deviant. Contrarily, among conservatives, radicals are on the hot seat. To the fundamentalist Christian, the atheist is the spawn of Satan, most decidedly a deviant. Turn the picture around. To the atheist, fundamentalist Christians are ignorant, narrow-minded fools. Here, we encounter the process of "mutual deviantization" (Aho 1994:62).

But let us be clear about this. Deviance is never *solely* a matter of the word of the members of one social category's word against the word of another. Yes, we live in a society that is an assemblage of different and mutually antagonistic belief systems. But society is as much a ladder as a mosaic. This means that some beliefs are more *dominant* than others; their adherents have more power and credibility and hence can legitimate their beliefs and discredit those of their opponents. To the extent that a particular belief is taught as true in the educational system, it is dominant, legitimate, and credible; to the extent that, when a belief is expressed in schools, its proponents tend to be *disparaged*, that belief is deviant. To the extent that holding a certain belief is a criterion among a majority of the electorate to vote for a given political candidate, it is a dominant belief. To the extent that a substantial segment of the electorate *refuses* to vote for a political candidate because he or she is known to hold a certain view, that view is deviant. To the extent that a given belief is taken for granted as true in the mainstream media, it is dominant; to the extent that holders of a given belief are scorned, rebuked, and ridiculed—that belief is deviant. In each of society's major institutions, we can locate beliefs that are mainstream, "inside the lines," conventional, dominant, or hegemonic; *and* we can locate those beliefs that are nonmainstream, outside the lines, beyond the pale, unconventional—in a word, from the societal point of view, *deviant*.

Sources of Paranormal Belief Systems

What makes paranormal beliefs—those that contradict what scientists believe to be the laws of nature—a form of cognitive deviance? As with creationism, how can beliefs held by half, or more than half, of the population be regarded as *deviant*? As we saw, polls show that nearly half the American public believes in ghosts, a third in astrology, three-quarters in miracles, and six in ten in the devil. How can beliefs with such widespread support be unconventional or non-normative? It is simple. *In* certain contexts, these beliefs are derided, scorned, not permitted a serious hearing. These beliefs are not valorized in the dominant institutions; they are nonhegemonic, not validated by the dominant educational, media, and religious institutions. The higher we move on the ladder of prestige and power, the less and less acceptable—and the more deviant—they are.

Sociologically, we look at paranormal beliefs by focusing on how they are generated and sustained. The routes through which this takes place are many and varied. Perhaps five are most likely to be interesting to the sociologist. For each, we should ask the basic question: "Who is the paranormalist's social constituency?" And for each belief, the answer is significantly different.

First, there are paranormal beliefs that originate from the mind of a social isolate, a single person with an unusual, highly implausible vision of how nature works. The isolate's message is presumably directed mainly at scientists, although any connection with the scientific community is tenuous or nonexistent. Scientists refer to these people as *cranks*. Here, the social constituency of the crank usually does not extend beyond himself (most cranks are men). It is deceptive to think that cranks address their message to the scientific community, since they do not engage in science-like activities or associate with other scientists; their goal is to *overturn* or *annihilate* conventional science, not contribute to it. Not enough attention has been paid to the crank, but it is a sociologically revealing subject, nonetheless. Donna Kossey (1994) devotes an entire book, entitled *Kooks*, to the topic.

Second, there are paranormal belief systems that begin within a religious tradition that existed long before there was such a thing as a scientist. Such beliefs sustain, and continue to be sustained by, an identifiable religious organization. Creationism is a prime example. The social constituency of the creationist is the like-minded religious community.

Third, there are beliefs that depend on a client–practitioner relationship. In other words, the key fact of certain belief systems is that they are validated by professionals who possess special expertise that is sought by laypersons in need of personal assistance, guidance, an occult interpretation of reality of their lives, or a demonstration of paranormal proficiency. Astrologers and other psychics exemplify this type of paranormalism. The social constituency of the astrologer and the psychic is made up primarily of the client and secondarily of other astrologers and psychics.

Fourth, another form of paranormalism is kept alive by a core of researchers who practice what seems to be the *form* but not the *content* of science. Many adherents are trained as scientists, conduct experiments, publish their findings in professional journals, and maintain something of a scientific community of believers, but most traditional scientists reject their conclusions. Parapsychology offers the best example here (Irwin and Watt 2007). Unlike astrologers and psychics, parapsychologists do not have clients. They are researchers and theorists, not hired for a fee. While a substantial number of laypersons may share the beliefs paranormalists claim to validate in the laboratory, these paranormal scientists or "protoscientists" form the sociological core of this system of thinking. For the *professional* parapsychologist, that is, the parapsychological *researcher*, the social constituency is that tiny band of other professional parapsychologists and, ultimately, the mainstream scientific community.

Fifth, there are paranormal belief systems that can be characterized as "grass roots" in nature. They are sustained less by individual theorists, a religious tradition or organization, a client–practitioner relationship, or a core of researchers, than by a broad-based public. In spite of the fact that it is strongly influenced by media reports and the fact that there are numerous UFO organizations and journals, the belief that UFOs are "something real" has owed its existence primarily to a more-or-less spontaneous feeling among the population at large. The ufologist's social constituency is primarily other ufologists, secondarily the society as a whole.

Conclusion

Is paranormalism a form of deviance? Yes and no. Yes, to the extent that it is not the dominant, established, or hegemonic perspective in Western society. Claims and assertions that scientists regard as contrary to the workings of nature tend not to be valorized in the mainstream educational curricula, the upper rungs of the media ladder, the economic sphere, and the political realm. The higher one moves in a given social institution, the less likely that paranormal beliefs are valorized. Persons expressing belief in creationism, the reality of UFOs, astrology, ghosts, psychic powers, and the like tend be chastised and reproached at the most prestigious educational institutions, by the more highly respected media, as well as the upper reaches of the political and economic realms, and so on. Even in the religious sphere, the most prestigious institutions tend to be ecumenical, secular, and nonfundamentalist, soft-pedaling paranormal phenomena such as miracles, prophecies, cataclysms, apocalypses, angels and the devil, even heaven and hell, while emphasizing real-world phenomena such as good works and ethical proscriptions. In that sense, again, yes, paranormal beliefs do represent a form of deviance.

But in another sense, paranormalism is not deviant: believers can usually find social "spaces" in which paranormal beliefs of one type or another are validated. UFOs clubs abound; Bible colleges instruct the truth of creationism and biblical literalism; charismatic and evangelical churches proliferate, and members satisfy their other worldly impulses by participating in their services and holding to their belief systems; gurus of every stripe attract adherents and preach a gospel that expresses faith in levitation, past lives, immortality, or dematerialization. Paranormal believers can find not only an array of institutions that reinforce their views, but, on the interpersonal level, a substantial number of like-minded adherents as well. In the sense that paranormalists are able to navigate in social circles that are largely free of negative judgments of their views, holding to their convictions does not constitute a form of deviance, indeed, that their unconventional beliefs express the real-world truth. As in all spheres, what is regarded as deviant is not a black-or-white, cut-and-dried affair, varying as it does from one context, social circle, group, or category to another. In this sense, there will never be a final or definitive answer to the question, "What is deviant?" This shifting, situational feature of the phenomenon of deviance makes it of eternal fascination to any interested observer.

Note

1. I have adapted several paragraphs of this essay from Goode (2011, 2012).

Discussion Questions

1. Do you feel paranormalism is deviant? Why or why not? What other types of behavior are in the same realm of paranormalism?
2. How is paranormalism portrayed in the media? How does this influence the public's reaction to the phenomena?

References

Adler, Patricia A., and Peter Adler (eds.). 2009. *Constructions of Deviance: Social Power, Context, and Interaction*, 6th ed. Belmont, CA: Thompson Wadsworth.

Aho, James A. 1994. *This Thing of Darkness: A Sociology of the Enemy*. Seattle, WA: University of Washington Press.

Ben-Yehuda, Nachman. 1985. *Deviance and Moral Boundaries*. Chicago, IL: University of Chicago Press.

Gardner, Martin. 1957. *Fads and Fallacies in the Name of Science*, 2nd rev. ed. New York: Dover.

Goffman, Erving. 1963. *Stigma: Notes on the Management of Spoiled Identity*. Englewood Cliffs, NJ: Prentice-Hall/Spectrum.

Goode, Erich. 2011. *Deviant Behavior*. Englewood Cliffs, NJ: Prentice Hall.

Goode, Erich. 2012. *Paranormal Beliefs: A Sociological Introduction*, 2nd ed. Buffalo, NY: Prometheus Books.

Hines, Terence. 2003. *Pseudoscience and the Paranormal: An Examination of the Evidence*, 2nd ed. Buffalo, NY: Prometheus Books.

Imbrogno, Philip. 2008. *Interdimensional Universe*. Woodbury, MN: Llewellyn Publications.

Irwin, Harvey J. and Carolyn A. Watt. 2007. *An Introduction to Parapsychology*, 5th ed. Jefferson, NC: McFarland.

Kossey, Donna. 1994. *Kooks: Guide to the Outer Limit of Human Belief*. Venice, CA: Feral House.

Kring, Ann, Sheri Johnson, Gerald Davison, and John M. Neale. 2010. *Abnormal Psychology*, 11th ed. New York: John Wiley & Sons.

Lisle, Jason. 2009. *The Ultimate Proof of Creation*. Green Forest, AR: Master Books.

Mack, John. 1995. *Abductions: Human Encounters with Aliens*, rev. ed. New York: Bantam Books.

Rabeyron, Thomas, and Caroline A. Watt. 2010. "Paranormal Experiences, Mental Health and Mental Boundaries, and Psi." *Personality and Individual Differences* 48 (March):487–92.

Radin, Dean. 1997. *The Conscious Universe: The Psychic Truth of Psychic Phenomena*. New York: HarperEdge.

Randi, James. 1995. *An Encyclopedia of Claims, Frauds, and Hoaxes of the Occult and Supernatural*. New York: St. Martin's Press.

 ARTICLE 28

James Ross
College at Brockport, State University of New York

Conceptualizing the Criminological Problem of Terrorism

While nothing is easier than to denounce the evildoer,
Nothing is more difficult than to understand him.
—*Fyodor Mikhailovich Dostoevsky*

First Perspective

Gaza-Ezzedeen Al Qassam Brigades (E.Q.B), the military wing of the Islamic resistance movement Hamas, declared in a military communiqué released on April 7th, 2011 the full responsibility for the operation of targeting Israeli bus traveling in the nearby Israeli settlement of Kfar Sa'ad east of Gaza Strip. The brigades said that E.Q.B.'s fighters targeted an Israeli bus at 15:05 p.m. The operation left two Israeli settlers injured, one of them was in a critical condition and evacuated by the Israeli medical crews to Soroka Medical Center. The E.Q.B. confirmed in its military communiqué that the operation was a primary response to the Israeli occupation crimes, which led recently to the killing of three Qassam leaders Ismail Lubad, Abdullah Lubad, and Mohammed al Dahya in an Israeli air strike in Khan Younis city south of Gaza Strip. (Al-Qassam Web site).

Second Perspective

An antitank missile fired from the Gaza Strip struck a school bus in the Negev, Israel, on April 7, 2011, critically wounding Daniel Viflic, a 16-year-old boy. The missile, which was fired by Hamas, hit the bus moments after most of the children got off, while it was being driven near Kibbutz Saad, about 2.5 km from Gaza. Only two individuals were on the bus when it was hit—the driver who received minor injures to his leg, and the boy on the way to visit his grandmother. Daniel was evacuated to Soroka Medical Center and admitted in critical condition. He was mortally wounded by shrapnel that penetrated his brain and was declared dead 10 days later. This incident set off a fierce round of retaliatory clashes between the Israeli Defense Forces and Hamas (an acronym for *Harakat al-Muqāāwamat al-Islāāmiyyah* meaning "Islamic Resistance Movement"), the Islamist political party that governs the Gaza Strip and its military wing, the Izz ad-Din al-Qassam Brigades.

Under what conditions are acts such as these labeled as terrorism considered deviance or social control? As simplistic as this question may appear, it involves a subsequent complex analysis of culture, social relationships, and politics (Crenshaw 1995).

For many Americans, particularly those in this generation, examples of acts that an observer would label as terrorism are outside our common experience. While America has experienced over the entirety of its history numerous acts committed by individuals of both foreign and domestic origin, its experience has not been akin to that of Europe or the Middle East

(Turk 2002). The defining moment that forced all Americans to reexamine their thoughts and fears on acts so alien to them was the tragic terrorist attacks on September 11, 2001, when over 2,900 individuals lost their lives. The brief timeframe during that day belies the immense need for the sociological study of terrorism is encapsulated from 8:46 a.m. to 10:29 a.m. EST. That brief span of time, fewer than two hours, encompasses the time from when Flight 11 crashed into the north face of North Tower (1 WTC) of the World Trade Center, between floors 93 and 99 and culminated in the collapse of the North Tower following the earlier collapse of the South Tower of the World Trade Center. The then secretary of state, Colin L. Powell, stated in May of 2002:

> In this global campaign against terrorism, no country has the luxury of remaining on the sidelines. There are no sidelines. Terrorists respect no limits, geographic or moral. The frontlines are everywhere, and the stakes are high. Terrorism not only kills people. It also threatens democratic institutions, undermines economies, and destabilizes regions. (State Department 2002:iii)

The Socially Constructed Nature of Definition of Terrorism

When evaluating the assortment of operational descriptions of terrorism, one can sense the intrinsically judgmental nature of those definitions. This, however, is to be contemplated, the lens in which we, as appalled onlookers, contemplate terrorism bestows it meaning. One would expect differences in the view of acts labeled as terrorism from the level it is experienced (Ganor 2002). It would be useful to contemplate the effect and response to an act labeled as terrorism from the perspective of various entities and individuals within society. How does the state responsible for order and peace conceptualize these acts differently from an observer (either one who saw things firsthand or followed the events on radio and television), from that an individual who suffered directly as a result of these actions or family member of such an individual, and, from those performing the act themselves?

- The state must crack down on what it sees as behavior exceeding the limits of protest and convention. As seen with the United States' response to the events of September 11, the state's response will often be prompt and dogmatic to remove a threat to peace, order, and security. This view rarely allows for a protracted analysis of the causes of a terroristic attack.
- Observers innately abhor vicious, lethal, antisocial behavior. Observers are often enflamed by media outlets and narratives that often focus on political protest that surpassed the bounds of the acceptable. This behavior is branded as evil, and the term *terrorism* is conflated to characterize a wide range of political behavior.
- Casualties, both those injured as innocent collateral victims or specifically targeted, must perceive the violence involving them with a sense, a profound sense, of injustice and anger toward the seemingly senseless acts.
- Perpetrators are given the label of vicious fanatics, as evil. Those engaging in "self-help" behavior and resort to political violence habitually repudiate the label of *terrorist*. They repeatedly assert that their only option is employing violence to make their plight or grievance heard by larger society, and are eager to express their self-professed noble objectives.

Seeing the Forest for the Trees and the Problem of Defining Terrorism

When attempting to understand the social phenomenon of terrorism, it is often difficult to arrive at a definitive definition of what is or is not terrorism. There are more than one hundred working definitions of terrorism developed by the academic, legal, and political contributors in circulation. With such a cacophony of definitional noise, it is sometimes difficult to find an undercurrent of consistency in these varied definitions.

That no consensus exists on the proper definition of terrorism is to an extent expected. This definitional conundrum is caused in no small part because *terrorism* is not simply a denotative label but also a label of reprobation (i.e., disapproval, blame, or censure). Definitions of terrorism are reprobative in that they ardently condemn the acts as unworthy, unacceptable or evil. The phenomenon observed is one where adherents of a particular political or ideological affinity will apply it to groups that they disapprove readily, while hesitating to apply it to those groups that they champion, even when the actions being committed by the two groups may be markedly analogous. A secondary issue is that all military or insurgent forces could be said to engage occasionally in activities that may be possibly portrayed as terrorism. There is no clear answer to the question regarding when should combatants cease to be labeled as having broad recognition as legitimation and begin to be labeled as a terrorist group.

The approach used in this article is to regard terrorism as the acts of those groups that will ordinarily attack civilian targets as freely as they military targets. Similarly, their choice of policies reveals whether they discriminate between combatants and noncombatants. To differentiate terrorism from traditional criminal violence, it is not enough to define terrorism as politically motivated violence, as other forms of nonterrorist violence, such as insurgencies and revolution, can have political origins. The particular attribute crucial to identifying terrorism is that it purposefully seeks to produce terror in its victims for a dogmatic purpose, whereas other forms of political violence have as their primary aim exacting loss on assets or personnel, with terror being a derivative. Terrorists foster terror in their targets and witnesses not out of specific malice for the specific victims of their actions but to produce terror in the larger mass of humanity that is the audience of the terrorist incident. Terrorists desire to influence this audience into provoking a response from them in some manner. Cooper (1974) proposed a definition in which, "Terrorism is the use of violence to create terror in others who are not the direct object of violence in order to cause them to act in certain ways."

Domestic versus International

Often, the study of terrorism is bifurcated by the distinction made between domestic terrorism and international terrorism. Domestic terrorism is usually defined as being limited to a given country or region and is customarily part of a domestic insurgence or revolutionary conflict. International terrorism is extranational in that it is not restricted to one particular nation or geographic region. Domestic terrorism and international terrorism often differ in that domestic terrorism is frequently identified in conjunction with an insurgency movement that is attempting to gain formal recognition in the international community. Examples of groups that act in an attempt to seek recognition as legitimate governments or as new nation-states are the Basque separatists in northern Spain and Irish Republican Army (IRA) members in Northern Ireland.

The motivation often differs for groups that engage in acts labeled as international terrorism. They seek to attack the nation-state system for either tactical or ideological reasons. In international terrorism, the perpetrating group often seeks to establish its identity separate from a recognized government. Often, this is for ideological reasons, but occasionally the cause is a "sponsoring" government wishing to maintain a "plausible deniability" of regarding any link with the group, as acts of violence averse to civilians in another sovereign jurisdiction are considered acts of war.

Occasionally there is a blurring of these distinctions just as it is shown by the campaign of bombings in England and Germany, and attempted exploits in Gibraltar enacted by members of the IRA in the 1970s and 1980s. These activities augmented the scope of IRA terrorism from being domestic to having extranational characteristics. The English civilians and British soldiers in Germany who were killed were typically unconnected to the issues motivating the conflict within Northern Ireland. The resulting harm wreaked little direct injury on the IRA's stated adversaries, namely, the British régime, Unionist politicians, or the Ulster Protestant paramilitaries forces. The real purpose of such incidents was to propagate terror and anxiety among the British public to motivate them to pressure the British government to remove its forces from Northern Ireland and to allow the Irish self-determination regarding the northern six counties that the British occupied. These actions bear significant similarity to many Islamic fundamentalist groups, such as al-Qaeda that has utilized similar tactics in crossing international borders. These Islamic fundamentalist groups in their attempts to impose their particular vision of Islamic rule on Muslim nations feel they have strayed from their ideological perspective to inflict injury on nations they consider nemeses of the expansion of Islam, such as the United States and Israel.

Regardless of such acts being labeled as domestic or international terrorism there are several uniform characteristics:

- Terrorism is a practice of conflict carried out for political purposes. Such political conflict is a form of low-intensity combat that manipulates the inconsistency of the Western philosophy toward such forms of conflict falling between the edges of declared conventional warfare and official external and internal diplomatic negotiations. This type of conflict is very cost-effective for the sponsoring group but very costly to the targeted governments or countries, where these governments and businesses are forced to spend much on protecting their executives and whose citizens are frightened sometimes to the point of paralysis.
- Terrorism is propaganda, in that it forces the particular audience it is directed toward to heed the political demands and threats the group is forwarding. The goal is to get people to contemplate the ramifications for ignoring these groups and consider capitulating to certain demands because of the risk of future threats. An example of this is seen in the actions of groups taking hostages. This is exemplified by the case involving Terry Anderson and other hostages held by the Lebanese Hezbollah group. The actions of Hezbollah resulted in an attempt by some of the hostages' relatives to try to bring pressure on the U.S. government to make concessions to Hezbollah to gain their emancipation.
- The actions are intended to create reactions among the terrorist' larger audience, in the form of a moral panic. Terrorists often seek out civilian targets instead of military, as this tends to create maximum terror in the intended audience. Those who are not direct victims of these acts often reflect on the capricious nature of chance and how they might have been victims themselves.
- Terrorism has connotations of law-breaking, but it is not ordinary law-breaking. While the acts, kidnappings, and murders, committed by groups labeled as terrorist, have parallels regarding the actus reus and mens rea to those committed by everyday criminals, it would be an error to contemplate them the same. While motivation is usually not an elemental aspect in the definition of criminal acts, it is an integral part of any act labeled as terrorist. In understanding terrorism, one must realize that the actions of the groups or individuals labeled as terrorists are a means to ends beyond the crimes themselves.

It is this last point, the ambivalence toward terrorism, that tends to create policy ambivalence among victims of terrorism. If these acts are to be considered purely as ordinary criminality, then it is a law enforcement matter, requiring suitable use of force to effect an arrest so that the perpetrators can be tried and, if found guilty, punished. However, if these acts were defined in a military context, then such an attack would invoke a military response, utilizing maximum force to assure successful conclusion of any military campaign. Finally, if these acts were contextualized as a political issue, then the proper course of action would be to negotiate in an attempt to reach compromise. Subsequently, terrorism historically has flourished through the selfsame ambiguity that veils its nature.

Toward a Theoretical Understanding of Terrorism

As attributed earlier a broadly recognized definition of terrorism has not yet been accepted. The lack of a broadly recognized definition of terrorism has serious implications, making the construction of a solid theoretical foundation for the study of the subject problematic at best. Most definitions of terrorism in use are far too broad for the application of any single theory to be capable of elucidating such behavior (Senechal de la Roche 2004). While not proposing a new definition of terrorism, we rely on the uniform characteristic of terrorism as outlined earlier to inform our discussion of the theoretical as it applies to terrorism.

Sociological and criminological development of theories of terrorism has generally not been as extensive as that in other areas, but the events of September 11, 2001, provided a stimulus for reengaging this overlooked area of study. Several academics have recently provided a rich environment in which to cultivate a theoretical discussion of terrorism. Black (2002, 2004) provides one of the more novel explanations of terrorism as a form of self-help, essentially forwarding the view that terrorism is a form of "social control of social control" in response to perceived deviance of the enemy. Black employs a unique definition of terrorism as an idealized form of "self-help by organized civilians who covertly inflict mass violence on other civilians" (Black 2004:6). This definition is in stark contrast to the normatively based definitions often produced by governments that have dominated the conversation about terrorism for years (Martin 2010). Black's theoretical perspective is unique in that it provides a specifically testable definition of terrorism with the distinct lack of characteristic bias that is so prevalent in many current theories of terrorism (Messner and Rosenfield 2004).

Black's theory is focused on "moralistic" violence, which in the eyes of the perpetrator is provoked by the victim, and its purpose is deterrence, retribution, or perceived self-defense (2004). However, terrorism is problematic because it frequently crosses the line between actions, what Rosenfeld (2002) calls justice-oriented violence, and criminal violence through targeting innocents to forward its "moralistic" ideologies. Rosenfeld (2004) would contribute to Black's theory to expand it beyond its narrow focus on only "moralistic" violence.

It is undeniable that terrorism has distinct features of predatory or opportunity-based violence, wherein the victim is innocent of provoking the subsequent violence and simply is an available target. Moralistic justification is distinctly lacking predatory crime. This inclusion of predatory violence can only aid in the understanding of terrorism, rather detract from it. With this in mind, *terrorism can therefore be viewed as deviant as it employs the means of predatory violence to achieve the transmission of the message inherent in the terrorists' moralistic violence.* However, this fundamental contradiction inherent in terrorism has implications for policy responses that have dominated debate whether law enforcement or the military should respond to these threats.

What Gives Rise to Terrorism?

Terrorism arises from "social polarization" between groups denoted by high levels of cultural distance (e.g., differences in religion, values, and language), relational distance (e.g., level of connectedness), and inequality (e.g., discrepancies in wealth and power) (Senechal de la Roche 1996:105–122). Black has constructed a "geometry of terrorism," in which terrorism is a form of social control exercised from below. Terrorism habitually communicates historic accusations of offense, as opposed to solitary incidents. Terrorism arises in an environment of extremely strong partisanship and solidarity (Senechal de la Roche 2001). It is these strong ties among the perpetrators of terrorism, and the lack of ties with those attacked, that give rise to the fermentation of highly moralistic and lethal potential for violence (Cooney 1998). In this manner, as actors in multidimensional space, perpetrators can be conceived of as agents of social control (Black 2002, 2004).

Using this basic structure of the geometry of terrorism as provided by Black, how does one elucidate acts of terrorism between collectives of people based on their distance from one another on this measure of social space? Rosenfeld has proposed that the answer may lie in the institutional arrangements of the collectives involved in the clash (2004). Borrowing concepts from institutional-anomie theory, Rosenfeld posits that recent terrorism may be a result from clashing among societies dominated by contrasting institutional bases of domination. In modern Western societies the balance of institutional power is found in the free-market, a democratic state, and formalized educational systems. The institutions of family and religion tend to be weak by comparison. Societies that have recently given rise to the formation of terrorist groups are contrastingly dominated by the social institutions of family/kinship, ethnicity, and religion. The social distance among such societies seems to have provided ample justification for terrorists to strike out against the West.

In both historic and modern examples, societies dominated by the institutions of family/kin, ethnicity, and religion lead to intense principled vigilance and hypermoralism. Obligations to those with whom individuals share a sense of social identity, based primarily on family/kin, ethnic, or religious distinctiveness, develop intensely. For those within these tightly constructed social groups when who interact with outsiders, social obligations limiting behavior are often absent. When support for general rules of conduct is lacking in a larger society, the social distance between these disparate groups only increases.

Viewing recent terrorism through this lens, terrorists are waging a battle averse to cultural contamination by economic and political ideologies. In attacking those they label as "infidels," they not only attack those ideologies but also serve to reinforce the ideologies they hold traditional to their society. As Barber (1996) states, it is "Jihad vs. McWorld." The perpetrators of terrorism are attempting to maintain and restore to its former prominence a societal order that is based on family/kin, ethnicity, and religion. They feel morally justified in their actions to protect their society from a corrupt and drifting world.

Are Terrorism's Days Numbered?

If acts of terrorism are prompted by social distance, does the historic decline of social distance in an increasingly global world made smaller by technological advances spell the eventual demise of terrorism? Does the view that the world is inexorably moving toward a unified social order built on the free-market, egalitarianism, and forbearance hold true? Does social distance necessarily reduce when cultures clash? This is an encouraging view of historic inevitability. Ignorance of the fact that social distance varies in congruence with historic occurrences makes relying on technology and social contact to reduce social distance and turn enemies into allies optimistic. It has been more than 50 years since the establishment of the nation of Israel, and there has not been significant alleviating of the social distance between the Israelis and Palestinians. However, recent social change in the Middle East may lead to some hope of optimism. Of particular interest is the Egyptian revolution that happened following a popular uprising that began in January 2011, and in Tunisia where the self-immolation of a frustrated 26-year-old man sparked a popular uprising in December 2010, which in large part owed to the role of technology, the Internet, and social networks such as Facebook and Twitter. The use of such technology, particularly social networks such as Facebook and Twitter, may signal new points of communication for groups that feel separated by severe social distances.

However, if terrorism is truly rooted in social distance and fostered by the belief of ethnoreligious superiority and a backlash against modernism, then its demise may be premature. As long as groups feel their traditional and sacred values are threatened by modernity,[1] then terrorism may persist.

Note

1. A shorthand term for modern society, or industrial civilization. Portrayed in more detail, it is associated with (1) a certain set of attitudes toward the world, the idea of the world as open to transformation, by human intervention; (2) a complex of economic institutions, especially industrial production and a market economy; (3) a certain range of political institutions, including the nation-state and mass democracy. Largely as a result of these characteristics, modernity is vastly more dynamic than any previous type of social order. It is a society—more technically, a complex of institutions—which, unlike any preceding culture, lives in the future, rather than the past (Giddens 1998:94).

Discussion Questions

1. What defines an act as terrorism?
2. What are the uniform characteristics common to most definitions of terrorism?
3. How does Black define distance in the social space that makes acts of terrorism more justifiable to those perpetrating such acts?
4. How may globalization and technology impact the incidences of terrorism?

References

Al Qassam website. 2011. "EQB Declares Responsibility for Kfar Sa'ad Operation." Palestine: Ezzedeen AL-Qassam Brigades—Information Office. Retrieved April 14, 2011 (http://www.qassam.ps/news-4391-Al_Qassam_declares_responsibility_for_Kfar_Saad_operation.html).

Barber, Benjamin R. 1996. *Jihad vs. McWorld: How Globalism and Tribalism Are Reshaping the World.* New York: Random House, Inc.

Black, Donald. 2002. "Terrorism as Social Control." Parts I and II. American Sociological Association *Crime, Law, and Deviance Newsletter.* Spring: 3–5 and Summer: 3–5.

Black, Donald. 2004. "The Geometry of Terrorism." *Sociological Theory* 22:14–25.

Cooney, Mark. 1998. *Warriors and Peacemakers: How Third Parties Shape Violence.* New York: New York University Press.

Cooper, H. H. A. 1974. *Evaluating the Terrorist Threat: Principles of Applied Risk Assessment.* Gaithersburg, MD: International Association of Chiefs of Police.

Crenshaw, Martha. 1995. *Terrorism in Context.* University Park, PA: Penn State University Press.

Ganor, Boaz. 2002. "Defining Terrorism: Is One Man's Terrorist Another Man's Freedom Fighter?" *Police Practice and Research: An International Journal* 3:287–304.

Giddens, Anthony. 1998. *Conversations with Anthony Giddens: Making Sense of Modernity.* Stanford, CA: Stanford University Press.

Martin, C. Gus. 2010. *Essentials of Terrorism: Concepts and Controversies*. Thousand Oaks, CA: Sage Pub.

Messner, Steven F. and Richard Rosenfeld. 2004. " 'Institutionalizing' criminological theory." *Advances in Criminological Theory* 13:83–105.

Rosenfeld, Richard. 2002. "Why Criminologists Should Study Terrorism." *The Criminologist* 1:3–4.

Senechal de la Roche, Roberta. 1996. "Collective Violence as Social Control." *Sociological Forum* 11:97–128.

Senechal de la Roche, Roberta. 2001. "Why Is Collective Violence Collective?" *Sociological Theory* 19:126–44.

Senechal de la Roche, Roberta. 2004. "Toward a Scientific Theory Of Terrorism." *Sociological Theory* 22:1

State Department. 2001. Patterns of Global Terrorism. "Preface: Patterns of Global Terrorism, 2001." P. iii. Washington, DC: United States Department of State.

Turk, Austin T. 2002. "Confronting Enemies Foreign and Domestic: An American Dilemma?" *Criminology and Public Policy* 1:345–50.

CONTRIBUTORS

JOSH ADAMS is currently assistant professor of sociology at SUNY Fredonia. His past research has focused on social movements and cultural sociology.

ROBERT AGNEW is the Samuel Candler Dobbs Professor of Sociology at Emory University. His research focuses on the causes of crime and delinquency, particularly his general strain theory of delinquency. Recent works include *Toward a Unified Criminology: Integrating Assumptions about Crime, People, and Society* (NYU Press, 2011) and *Juvenile Delinquency: Causes and Control* (Oxford, 2012). He will serve as president of the American Society of Criminology in 2012/2013.

MIRANDA BAUMANN is a graduate student in the Department of Criminal Justice at Georgia State University.

TIMOTHY BREZINA is associate professor of criminal justice at Georgia State University. His research and teaching interests include criminological theory, juvenile delinquency, and deterrence. Recent publications appear in the journals *Criminology, Justice Quarterly, Journal of Drug Issues,* and *Deviant Behavior.*

JULIE HARMS CANNON is on the sociology faculty at Seattle University, where she teaches courses on social problems, class and inequality, feminist research methods, and feminist theories. She has published articles on amateur stripping, tattooing, caregiving, feminist sociological theory, and multicultural education. She is currently interested in women survivors of global conflict and violence, as well as autoethnographic research methods.

DAVID PATRICK CONNOR is a graduate student in the Department of Justice Administration at the University of Louisville. He holds a BA from Northern Kentucky University. Mr. Connor's research interests include sex offenders and sex offenses, institutional corrections, and collateral consequences associated with criminal convictions.

ADDRAIN CONYERS is an assistant professor in the Department of Criminal Justice at Marist College. His primary research interests are deviance, crime, identity management, and corrections.

DENISE COPELTON is associate professor of sociology at The College at Brockport, State University of New York, and co-editor for the book review section of *Gender & Society.* Her research centers on the social experience of illness, with a special focus on conditions requiring dietary modifications. Her publications have appeared in *Social Science & Medicine, Sociology of Health & Illness,* and *Deviant Behavior.* She is currently writing a book on the social experience of celiac disease and gluten-free eating.

HEITH COPES is an associate professor in the Department of Justice Sciences at the University of Alabama at Birmingham. His primary research explores the criminal decision-making process using qualitative methods. His recent publications appear in *British Journal of Criminology, Justice Quarterly, Criminology & Public Policy,* and *Social Problems.*

MANDEEP K. DHAMI, is a reader in forensic psychology and director of the MSc in forensic psychology at the University of Surrey, UK. Her previous academic appointments include at the University of Cambridge, UK, University of Victoria, Canada, University of Maryland, USA, and the Max Planck Institute for Human Development,

Germany. Dr. Dhami's primary research interests are judgment and decision making in the criminal justice system, and she has studied magistrates, judges, jurors, police officers, forensic experts, offenders, and prisoners. She is lead editor of the book *Judgement and Decision Making as a Skill: Learning, Development, and Evolution* (Cambridge University Press, 2011).

KEITH F. DURKIN is Professor of sociology at Ohio Northern University. He has published dozens of journal articles and book chapters on topics such as sexual predators, Internet crime/deviance, and binge drinking among college students. He also serves as a consultant and trainer for law enforcement, as well as providing expert testimony in high profile sex abuse cases.

ANDREA ELLER is a graduate student in the anthropology department at the University of Oregon. She is interested in comparative primate physiological and osteological phenomenon as related to issues of captivity.

JACKIE ELLER is Professor of sociology and chair of the sociology and anthropology department. Her university experience is extensive serving in leadership positions as director of the MA program in sociology and director of women's studies and with the Chairs Council, the President's Advisory Committee, Graduate Council, Faculty Senate, President's Commission on the Status of Women, and Women's Studies Council. Dr. Eller is a past president of the Mid-South Sociological Association and for three years, she was also co-editor of *Sociological Spectrum*. Dr. Eller's teaching/research interests and publications have been in the areas of social deviance, gender, the sociology of emotions, and qualitative methods. Her most recent research project concerns the presentations of masculinity on Match.com.

JASON A. FORD, is an associate professor in the Department of Sociology at the University of Central Florida. His research interests include substance use among adolescents and young adults and also the factors related to stability and change in crime and deviance over the life course.

KELLY FRAILING is an assistant professor of criminal justice at Texas A&M International University in Laredo, TX. Since getting her PhD from the University of Cambridge, she has published numerous articles and book chapters primarily in two diverse areas: mental health courts and crime and disaster. Kelly has published on other topics as well and her current interest is in the unique operation of the Webb County drug court.

ERICH GOODE is sociology professor emeritus at Stony Brook University. He has taught at a half-dozen universities, including Stony Brook, New York University, the University of North Carolina at Chapel Hill, the University of Maryland, and the Hebrew University of Jerusalem. Goode has published ten books, including *Deviant Behavior* (Prentice Hall, 9th edition, 2011), *Drugs in American Society* (McGraw-Hill, 8th edition, 2012), *Paranormalism* (Prometheus Books, 2nd edition, 2012), and *Moral Panics,* with Nachman Ben-Yehuda (2nd edition, 2009), as well as a hundred articles and a half-dozen anthologies. He is the recipient of a Guggenheim fellowship. Goode lives in New York's Greenwich Village and is at work on a study of exculpation in memoir.

CORIE HAMMERS is an assistant professor in the Women's, Gender, and Sexuality Studies Department at Macalester College. Her research interests are in gender, sexuality, embodiment, and "non-normative" sex practices, and the relationships between and among desire, sex practice, and space. She has published in a variety of journals including

Sexualities, Journal of Contemporary Ethnography, and *Journal of Gender Studies.* Her current work explores women BDSMers and the leatherdyke BDSM communities, with a particular focus on BDSM as a form of "somatic intervention" and queer kinship.

DEE WOOD HARPER is professor emeritus of sociology and criminology and justice at Loyola University New Orleans. His research interest, while varied over his 53-year (and counting) career, is presently concentrated on violence, particularly murder and robbery, and crime within the context of disaster. He is the co-author of three forthcoming books: Violence: Do We Know It When We See It? A Reader (Dec. 2011); *Why Violence? Leading Questions Regarding the Conceptualization and Reality of Violence in Society,* and the 2nd edition of *Crime, Criminal Justice and Disaster* (Spring 2012).

ROBERT JENKOT is an assistant professor at Coastal Carolina University, Department of Sociology. He earned his doctorate in sociology at Southern Illinois University Carbondale. His research leans heavily on the interaction of race, class, and gender as they interact with criminal and deviant behavior and in particular, how these factors influence a person's illicit drug use, sales, and manufacturing.

POCO KERNSMITH is an associate professor of social work at Wayne State University in Detroit, Michigan. Her research examines the role of gender in sexual and intimate partner violence, with a particular focus on female perpetration of violence. Her work with domestic violence and sexual assault service agencies drives her commitment to developing research that will help develop policies to address issues of violence and abuse. More recently, her research has incorporated the role of technology in the perpetration and prevention of interpersonal violence.

ROGER KERNSMITH is an associate professor of sociology, anthropology, and criminology at Eastern Michigan University. His specialties include criminology, juvenile delinquency, and deviance.

PAUL M. KLENOWSKI is an assistant professor and director of criminal justice at Clarion University of Pennsylvania. He earned his PhD in criminology from the Indiana University of Pennsylvania where he received the Outstanding Graduate Research Award for his doctoral dissertation on the motivational differences between male and female federal white-collar offenders. His current research interests include corporate violence, occupational crime, the role of neutralization and strain theories in white-collar deviance, the psychopathology of fraudulent behavior, and evaluation research of community and restorative justice programs. He has recently been published in *Justice Quarterly, Journal of Offender Rehabilitation,* and *Contemporary Justice Review.*

J. DAVID KNOTTNERUS is professor of sociology at Oklahoma State University. He has published extensively in the areas of social theory, social psychology, group processes, social inequality, and ritual dynamics. In recent years he has focused on the development of structural ritualization theory and research which analyzes the role ritual plays in social life. His most recent books are *Ritual as a Missing Link: Sociology, Structural Ritualization Theory and Research* (2011) and, coauthored with Jason S.Ulsperger, *Elder Care Catastrophe: Rituals of Abuse in Nursing Homes – and What You Can Do About It* (2011). He is the co-editor—with Bernard Phillips—of the series *Advancing the Sociological Imagination* (Paradigm Publishers).

MARK KONTY received his PhD from the University of Arizona in 2002. He conducts research and writes on social control from an interactionist perspective. His articles appear in the top criminology and sociology journals.

CHRISTOPHER W. MULLINS, (UMSL—2004) is an associate professor of criminology and criminal justice at Southern Illinois University Carbondale. His research focuses on structural and cultural aspects of crime, especially the intersections of gender, streetlife subculture, and violence. He has authored/coauthored 3 books. He has also published over 30 articles and book chapters on gender and street crime; genocide, war crimes and crimes against humanity; and international criminal law and jurisprudence.

ELIZABETH EHRHARDT MUSTAINE, an associate professor in the Department of Sociology at the University of Central Florida, received her PhD in sociology from the Ohio State University. Dr. Mustaine has written numerous journal articles on child abuse, registered sex offenders, criminal victimization, routine activities theory, violence, violence against women, and stalking. Recently, she completed work on the National Institute of Justice funded project, "Violence Against Homeless Women," which resulted in the co-authored book, *Hard Lives, Mean Streets: Violence in the Lives of Homeless Women*.

SHARON S. OSELIN is an assistant professor of sociology at California State University, Los Angeles. Her research interests include gender, crime and deviance, sex workers, social movements, and culture. Her work appears in a variety of journals, including *American Sociological Review, Sociological Inquiry, Deviant Behavior, Sociological Perspectives,* and *Mobilization*. She is currently at work on a book project that examines the process through which women exit street prostitution.

MELISSA POWELL-WILLIAMS is an assistant professor of sociology at Augusta State University. Her research areas include social psychology, emotions, identity, social movements, and sociology of disabilities. She has published work related to domestic violence advocacy, identity work, and perceptions of same-sex marriages.

JAMES J. ROSS is assistant professor of criminal justice and director of the pre-law program at The College at Brockport. Dr. Ross received both his doctor of philosophy and his doctor of jurisprudence degrees from the University at Buffalo, State University of New York. Dr. Ross has been a practicing attorney and educator for over 10 years, and has been bringing a unique socio-legal perspective to the study of the intersection of law and terrorism.

ZACHARY SANTONI SANCHEZ is a master's candidate in the Department of Sociology and Anthropology at Middle Tennessee State University. Mr. Sanchez's research interests include the intersection between fear and the American horror film, deviance, and sexuality. Mr. Sanchez currently resides in Nashville, Tennessee.

ANSON SHUPE is professor of sociology at the joint campus of Indiana University Purdue University, Fort Wayne campus. He has written and/or edited 30 books and over 100 journal articles and chapter contributions as well as numerous newspaper editorials and magazine articles. His specialties include social psychology, social movements, and clergy malfeasance (as a form of elite deviance). His most recent research interest is in clergy misconduct within the American black church.

RYAN SCHROEDER is an associate professor of sociology at the University of Louisville. His research addresses criminal desistance processes, alcohol and drug use, emotional development, religious transformations, family functioning, and health.

JIMMY D. TAYLOR, is an assistant professor with Ohio University Zanesville. Dr. Taylor has published books and academic articles on topics of masculinities, deviant behavior, cutting and self-mutilation, social problems, and stigma management. He is currently co-author of Alex Thio's *Deviant Behavior* (11th edition) which is scheduled for release in the summer of 2012, and is finishing a monograph on rodeo subcultures.

RICHARD TEWKSBURY is professor of justice administration at the University of Louisville. He has previously served as both editor of *Justice Quarterly* and as research director for the National Prison Rape Elimination Commission. His research focuses on issues of identity construction, experiences of deviants and social control agents, and efficacy of criminal justice agencies and actors.

JASON S. ULSPERGER is an associate professor of sociology and criminal justice at Arkansas Tech University. In 2008, he won the Mid-South Sociological Association's award for publication of the year for an article written with J. David Knottnerus called "The Social Dynamics of Elder Care." He and Knottnerus are also the authors of *Elder Care Catastrophe* (2011), which focuses on deviant behavior in nursing homes. He is currently studying the impact of stress related rituals on mass homicide.

DR. LYNNE VIERAITIS is an associate professor in the School of Economic, Political and Policy Sciences at UT-Dallas in the Criminology Program. Her primary areas of research interest are inequality and homicide, violence against women, and criminal justice policy.

RONALD WEITZER is professor of sociology at George Washington University. His recent research focuses largely on the sex industry in the United States and in Europe. Recent books include *Sex For Sale: Prostitution, Pornography, and the Sex Industry* (Routledge, 2010) and *Legalizing Prostitution: From Illicit Vice to Lawful Business* (NYU Press, 2012). He has also written extensively on the topic of police-minority relations.